Effective Communication
for Colleges
Tenth Edition

Clarice Pennebaker Brantley
President
Innovative Training Team

Michele Goulet Miller
Business and Graphic Arts Division
Milwaukee Area Technical College

THOMSON

SOUTH-WESTERN

Australia · Canada · Mexico · Singapore · Spain · United Kingdom · United States

THOMSON

SOUTH-WESTERN

Effective Communication for Colleges, 10th Edition
By Clarice Pennebaker Brantley and Michele Goulet Miller

Vice President/Editorial Director
Jack Calhoun

Vice President/Editor-in-Chief
George Werthman

Acquisitions Editor
Jennifer Codner

Developmental Editor
Taney Wilkins

Marketing Manager
Larry Qualls

Sr. Production Editor
Tim Bailey

Media Technology Editor
Jim Rice

Editorial Assistant
Janice Hughes

Sr. Design Project Manager
Michelle Kunkler

Cover Designer/Illustrator
Bethaney Casey

Internal Design
Beckmeyer Design
(Cincinnati, OH)

Manufacturing Coordinator
Diane Lohman

Production
Argosy Publishing, Inc.

Printer
CTPS

COPYRIGHT © 2005 by South-Western, a division of Thomson Learning, Inc. Thomson Learning™ is a trademark used herein under license.

Book only ISBN: 0-324-20286-5

Book with CD ISBN: 0-324-27271-5

Library of Congress Control Number: 2003109348

Printed in China by CTPS

2 3 4 5 6 7 09 08 07 06 05

For more information, contact South-Western, 5191 Natorp Boulevard, Mason, OH 45040; or find us on the World Wide Web at www.swlearning.com

THOMSON

SOUTH-WESTERN

Greetings

A text, a workbook, a grammar and format reference—all wrapped into one crisp package!

Written with you in mind, *Effective Communication for Colleges*, 10th edition, presents the Communication-by-Objectives (CBO) approach, a no-nonsense process for preparing effective messages. The CBO approach provides a framework for communicating successfully with diverse audiences whether the message is written or spoken, formal or informal, paper-based or electronic.

The text material keeps pace with current communication requirements and anticipates future requirements. Straightforward communication principles and message strategies are effective and efficient. Case studies emulate workplace situations. Exercises, Internet activities, web site support, and CD material reflect communication trends and offer varied and relevant opportunities to build communication competence.

Opening vignettes prepared by contemporary professionals and input from community leaders, employers, colleagues, and students clearly illustrate the need for skilled communicators. Their insight combined with our ongoing business and classroom contacts result in many new features in the tenth edition. As an adopter of *Effective Communication for Colleges*, 10th edition, you have access to these enhancements:

- Student CD, containing chapter review questions and additional case studies, packaged with the text
- Expanded proposal coverage in Chapter 11, "Reports, Proposals, and Instructions for the Workplace"
- Free subscription to InfoTrac® College Edition, an online library
- Additional e-mail coverage and more Internet search activities
- Refreshed examples, case studies, exercises, and activities

Effective Communication for Colleges, 10th edition, a comprehensive, focused package, demonstrates the value of being a skilled communicator in both your professional and personal life.

Clarice P. Brantley

Clarice Pennebaker Brantley

Michele Goulet Miller

Michele Goulet Miller

Effective Approach
Effective Preparation
Effective Messages

Achieve communication success with the three-step **Communication-by-Objectives (CBO) approach:** *Plan. Draft. Complete.* This convenient, proven approach provides an essential framework for preparing messages *and* enables you to grasp principles of effective messages rapidly and easily.

Section 2: THE COMMUNICATION-BY-OBJECTIVES APPROACH

People create messages to meet specific needs. An effective plan for creating messages is **Communication-by-Objectives (CBO)**, a *whole-into-parts* process. The CBO approach consists of the following steps:

- **Plan a Message.** During the planning step, identify your objective, visualize your audience, gather supporting information, and organize the information.
- **Compose a Draft.** As you compose, choose words, construct sentences, assemble paragraphs, and choose paragraph locations.
- **Complete a Message.** Work from your draft to revise, edit, proofread, and finalize your message.

Following the CBO approach enables you to develop effective, appropriate messages for any communication situation.

Example: You believe that your department needs a color printer. An on-site color printer would allow employees to make in-house proofs, color charts, graphs, and other artwork for design projects. Eliminating the cost of an outside vendor and the time waiting for the vendor to complete the work would save the department money and increase productivity. You prepare your message using the *whole-into-parts* process of the CBO approach.

Culture Frame

When you send a price list to Canadians, specify the currency as United States dollars.

Chapter 1   Partners for Effective Communication   **19**

Effective Communication for Colleges, 10th Edition, incorporates these special features to increase communication competence and to develop critical-thinking skills:

Checklists remind you to "check" your message one more time for all the critical message elements.

Timely Tips offer tidbits of helpful information to direct you toward communication and career success.

Culture Frames and **Culture Views** broaden your communication horizons with meaningful glimpses into international environments. Each chapter "hosts" a different country.

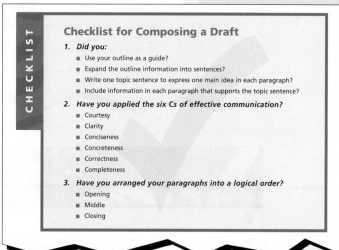

CHECKLIST

Checklist for Composing a Draft

1. **Did you:**
   ■ Use your outline as a guide?
   ■ Expand the outline information into sentences?
   ■ Write one topic sentence to express one main idea in each paragraph?
   ■ Include information in each paragraph that supports the topic sentence?

2. **Have you applied the six Cs of effective communication?**
   ■ Courtesy
   ■ Clarity
   ■ Conciseness
   ■ Concreteness
   ■ Correctness
   ■ Completeness

3. **Have you arranged your paragraphs into a logical order?**
   ■ Opening
   ■ Middle
   ■ Closing

Culture View

Germany
German residents expect punctuality from everyone. Therefore, you should arrive on time for every social and business meeting. In addition to punctuality, you will observe other business rules or patterns, including the following:

■ Agendas are established and strictly followed. To be considered a potential client, you must arrive at a meeting with a fully documented report, including visuals.
■ Last names and appropriate titles are used. Greetings often are more formal than ordinarily would be used in the United States. Usually everyone shakes hands upon arrival and departure. Use Herr (Mr.) or Frau (Mrs. or Miss). Since titles are important, use titles correctly. For example, address Diane Price who has a Ph.D. as Frau Professor Doctor Price.
■ Everyone assumes a "role" in meetings. Never try to switch roles during a meeting. For example, if you are a marketing person, do not try to address engineering issues. Another example may be that a colleague or you are serving as a "customer advocate"; if so, then remain in that role even to the point of sitting on the customer's side of the table.

You will tend to put your German business hosts at ease when you demonstrate a willingness to adopt their meeting patterns and behaviors.

Abundant **examples** correlate with chapter discussion to show you concepts in action.

Exercises

2-1   **Directions:** In the space provided, rewrite the sentences to incorporate the *you* attitude.

1. We need to know the rates for your delivery service.

2. We will show the annual dividend from Plano Investments on your December statement.

TechLinks

Internet
Challenge

4-1 Directions: Go to http://riceinfo.rice.edu/armadillo/acceptable.html for links that relate to acceptable use policies; or use a search engine to search on *acceptable use policies*. Visit two or three sites. On a separate sheet of paper, list the sites (URLs) you visited. For each site, record actions that are not permitted as well as penalties that may be involved as a result of ina_____ _____ternet use.

Case Studies

2-1   **Communication Situation:** You are an assistant manager of the shoe department for a store in the mall. You supervise five salespeople during your shift. The store is open from 9 a.m. to 9 p.m., but you work the afternoon/evening shift from 2 p.m. until 9 p.m. You have been expecting tonight to be a routine evening even though one of your regular employees is out on vacation.

When you begin your shift, you discover that two other salespeople also will be off because of illness. In addition, you find a note from the shoe depart_____ _____ays: *Afterno_____ ___ift is responsible*

Communication Skills Development 4

NAME_____

Part A   Adjective Usage

Directions: Of the words given in parentheses in each of the following sentences, underline the correct adjective.

1. Make environmental issues one of your (principal, principle) concerns.

2. The decision to recycle is a (personal, personnel) choice.

3. Does you_____ ___un sponsor (hazard, he_____ _____te collection da_____

End-of-chapter exercises reinforce chapter content by offering a variety of activities to strengthen your listening, reading, speaking, signaling, and writing skills.

TechLinks help build your Internet search strategies and develop your research skills with Internet assignments and readings from the free online library, **InfoTrac College Edition**.

Case Studies present communication situations likely to be encountered in the workplace. You analyze the situation, use the CBO approach, apply the appropriate message strategy, and incorporate the six *C*s to create an effective message.

Communication Skills Development, at the end of each chapter, reviews and reinforces grammar and spelling.

For your convenience, the handy in-text **Reference Guide** covers essential grammar, word usage, and source format guidelines. The **Format Guide** offers samples of annotated memorandums, letters, and envelopes.

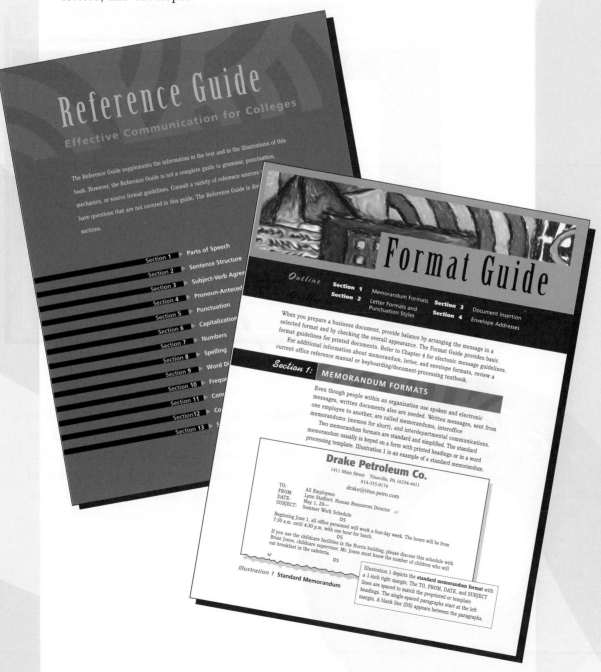

The student link in the **Interactive Study Center** at
http://brantley.swlearning.com contains Ethics in Action cases and
other helpful resources.

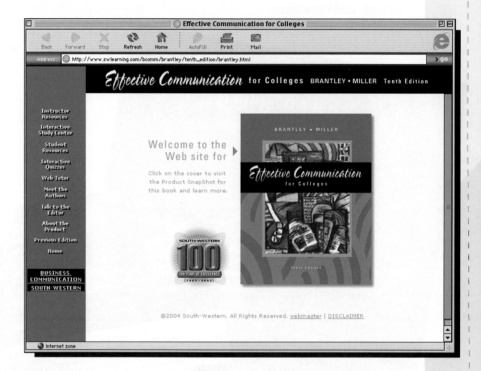

New Student CD, free with new copies of the 10th
edition, contains chapter practice questions, an
additional case study, Reference Guide reinforcement exercises, PowerPoint® previews of
chapter concepts, and Ethics in Action cases.

Table of Contents

1

Principles of Communication

Chapter 1

Partners for Effective Communication

Learning Objectives

1 Name your two partners in originating effective communication.

2 Identify the five elements of the communication cycle.

3 Name potential communication barriers and explain how barriers influence the communication cycle.

4 Name the three major components of the CBO approach.

COMMUNICATION PERSPECTIVES

Effective Communication

Early in my consulting career I witnessed the results of *ineffective communication*. The communication failure between an engineering manager and an assembly line supervisor nearly resulted in a strike.

The problem began with frantic calls to the engineer that a crucial robotic welding line was malfunctioning. The robot had ruined expensive raw materials, and the plant was not going to make the daily quota.

Robots were added amid protests of workers whose jobs the robots had eliminated. Engineers had made the case that robots were "faster, more precise, and more consistent than human workers," and "they never needed a vacation or a lunch break."

When the supervisor entered the engineering office, he was quick to say, "We never had these problems when *people* were running the line. We never should have bought these things in the first place!"

The engineer didn't want to hear *any* of this . . . he had heard it all before. He wanted the problem gone. His *exact* words were, "Get down there, find the problem, and get rid of it!"

The supervisor returned to the line and quickly found the problem. One robot was malfunctioning. Heeding the engineering manager's words, he promptly took the $2 million robot to the trash dock to "get rid of it."

When the engineering manager heard this, he was livid. He wanted the supervisor fired. The supervisor protested that he did "exactly what I was told to do."

The incident escalated. A general strike was called, and plant operations virtually ceased. The company was losing millions, and a vital contract was not being fulfilled.

An arbitrator quickly recognized the underlying problem: A supervisor, angry and resentful of the robots that displaced his workers, and an engineer, whose only motivation was the "bottom line," were not communicating. Neither was willing to "hear" the other. No attempt to communicate and solve the underlying problems was even considered.

The arbitrator assigned blame *equally* on the two employees. He concluded the following:

1. The engineer should have evaluated the situation first-hand and given specific instructions on how to proceed.
2. The supervisor should have questioned the order and received clarification before he acted.
3. Representatives from the robot manufacturer should have been included in the meeting. They were in the same building and were never called.
4. The lack of communication between white-collar and blue-collar employees created an atmosphere of mistrust and resentment that allowed the incident to spin out of control.
5. Every employee needed training in **communication** and **active listening** skills. All training would be conducted with the two groups working together and sharing perspectives.

The arbitrator prevented the strike. The company initiated the mandatory classes and became more efficient, more productive, and more open.

I still consult with them. The "action teams" I work with today include representatives from both engineering and manufacturing. Everyone has an equal voice in the process, and the company has become a leader in the aerospace field.

Mark Snyder, CIO
MSA Consulting Group

Today's communication environment often demands that you, as an originator of messages, make decisions quickly and send messages rapidly. Research has shown that people who prepare and send effective messages are able to:

- Understand the importance of the communication cycle.
- Incorporate the principles of good communication into their original message.
- Develop and maintain an open communication channel.
- Incorporate the principles of effective communication into their responses to other people's messages.

Communication Partners

Your ability to communicate effectively strongly influences your professional advancement and personal success. In the global marketplace of today, many employers believe that the ability to communicate is the most important job-related skill. Regardless of language, country, or education level, effective communicators have two things in common. First, they work within a cyclical communication process. Second, they use identifiable communication techniques.

Effective Communication for Colleges shows you how the communication cycle works and how to use the Communication-by-Objectives (CBO) approach to improve your communication skills. However, the real key to effective communication is your active, knowledgeable participation. Enjoy the benefits of good communication. Build a three-way communication partnership: the communication cycle, the CBO approach, and you!

Elements of the Communication Cycle

Communication is the exchange of information through speaking, signaling, or writing. This exchange involves the following elements:

- **Sender**, the person who originates a message
- **Message**, the information that is exchanged
- **Transmission**, how the message is delivered
- **Receiver**, the person to whom the message is sent
- **Feedback**, the response from the receiver

Your primary goal as a sender is to communicate *effectively*. You succeed when you have accomplished the following:

1. The receiver understands your message.
2. A favorable relationship is established between the receiver and you.
3. The message encourages a desired response from the receiver.

Illustration 1-1, page 5, shows the cyclical nature of the communication process.

Illustration 1-1 **The Communication Cycle**

The Communication Cycle

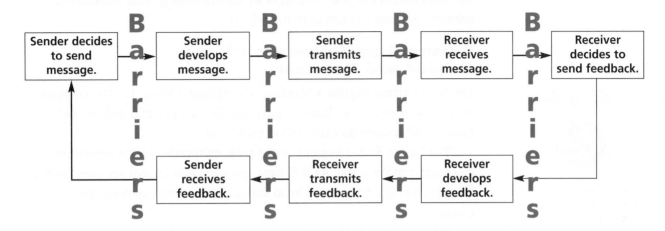

Potential Barriers

- Different Backgrounds
- Signaling
- Communication Situation
- Quality of Message Content

- Writing Skills
- Speaking Skills
- Listening Skills
- Reading Skills

The communication cycle involves two categories of messages: **verbal** (consisting of written or spoken words) and **nonverbal** (made up of visual, audible, or movement clues called **signals**). Generally, messages are verbal with one or more nonverbal influences.

When you act as a sender, first determine the need for a message. Then develop the message by gathering, sorting, and organizing information. While planning and developing a message, consider how well the receiver and you know each other. Analyze the similarities and differences between the receiver and you. Anticipate the receiver's reaction to the message.

After you develop your message, transmit the message to the receiver. In an effective communication process, a receiver becomes a sender and a sender eventually becomes a receiver. As a sender, you want positive receiver **feedback**—correct interpretation of the message and favorable action. However, positive feedback may be negatively influenced at any point in the communication cycle by communication barriers.

Communication Barriers

Communication barriers interfere with sending and receiving messages. Barriers can result in miscommunication with the potentially serious consequences of hurt feelings, wasted time, or missed opportunities.

Obvious communication barriers are distractions, such as sounds and gestures. Other barriers to the sending process include the different backgrounds of sender and receiver, signaling, the communication situation, the quality of message content, writing skills, and speaking skills. Barriers to the receiving process include skill levels in listening and reading. Eliminate or minimize barriers in your messages by understanding what constitutes barriers and how you can overcome them.

Different Backgrounds of Sender and Receiver

Timely Tip

Intercultural communication and *cross-cultural communication* are used interchangeably.

The term **culture** implies a blending of language, values, beliefs, customs, religion, and education. Each country has its own national culture, but cultural differences do exist within each country.

The United States has one of the most culturally diverse populations of any country in the world. As U.S. companies and government agencies conduct business worldwide, multinational staffs are becoming increasingly common.

What happens to the communication process when you participate in **cross-cultural communication** (communication between people who have varying backgrounds, assumptions, and understandings)?

The key to effective communication is research. Find out as much as you can about the people, the city, and the country with which you are doing business. Cultural background can significantly affect message effectiveness. Cultural background includes ethnic and geographic influences. Ethnic influence is reflected by national origin, and geographic influence is reflected by such factors as population, terrain, industrialization, and climate.

Culture View

Canada
Canada, often described as a cultural mosaic, has two predominant languages—French and English. Printed information, from street signs to legal documents, appears in both French and English. When written material appears in English, the British spelling is most widely used. Examples include *cheque* instead of *check* and *colour* instead of *color*.

The division of Canada into ten provinces and two territories represents more than just a geographical division. Since each province has a unique flavor, the residents may tend to focus on their home province as opposed to the country as a whole. For example, in British Columbia, businesses reflect influence from the Pacific Rim; but in Quebec, the French heritage strongly affects business operations. Businesses in Quebec may expect clients and customers to speak French.

Canadians generally reveal a preference for a reserved and formal atmosphere in their business dealings. However, they show a tolerance for and a respect of different cultural values, religions, and lifestyles. Canadians value direct communication. They pride themselves on saying what they mean, and they expect the same from others. Nonetheless, Canadians may take longer to come to a business decision than is usually expected because they prefer to have detailed information to review.

Whether you communicate within or outside an organization, you must exercise an awareness of what is and what is not acceptable within a receiver's culture. Basic knowledge of a receiver's cultural background will help foster positive relationships.

The principles and guidelines in this text help you develop effective messages, and each chapter includes communication tips for a specific country. However, consult specialized international references to ensure appropriate communication for specific receivers.

Signaling

Signaling (nonverbal communication) refers to messages conveyed without words. Signaling includes tone of voice and **body language** (facial expressions, gestures, and other physical movements). The way you walk, stand, and hold your head means something. Even silence communicates a message.

Gestures that are acceptable, understood, and even desirable in the United States may be inappropriate or misunderstood by people from other cultures. For instance, most Canadian gestures are similar to gestures used in the United States. However, regional differences do exist. The "thumbs down" that signals *no* or *bad* in the United States is considered offensive in Quebec.

Written messages also send signals. The appearance of conventional messages—the quality and color of stationery and envelopes, print font, and even ink color—creates a lasting impression. Make choices that create a positive impression.

As shown in the following examples, nonverbal communication may not match spoken or written words.

Culture Frame

Canadians use firm handshakes; women may offer a hand first, or they may nod their heads and not shake hands.

Examples: A listener claimed that he was open to additional discussion, but his crossed arms and rigid posture indicated otherwise.

The words contained in a letter were accurate and concise; but the stationery was wrinkled and stained, giving an impression of carelessness.

Recognizing the importance of nonverbal communication helps you convey effective messages.

Communication Situation

The communication situation influences the most effective way to formulate and transmit (send) any message. For example, mailing a formal announcement printed on heavy card stock, enclosed in both an outer and inner envelope, and addressed with hand calligraphy is inappropriate for a message that reads, "I finally received a promotion!" A short conversation more suitably conveys that kind of simple message to which you want quick feedback. Choosing the most effective message form and transmission mode requires you to analyze the communication situation.

Message Form

The two categories of messages are *verbal* and *nonverbal*. Verbal messages consist of written or spoken words. Nonverbal messages are made up of visual, audible, or movement clues called signals. Both written and spoken messages contain one or more nonverbal signals. Each communication situation has many factors you need to consider. Answering five questions will help you determine whether to develop your message with written words, spoken words, or signals.

Timely Tip

A written format may be desirable for short, uncomplicated messages when documentation is needed.

1. **Do you need a permanent record of the communication?** If the answer is yes, as in the following example, writing is frequently the best choice. If you do not need a permanent record, spoken messages often work well.

   Example: During an employee's performance review, documented evidence is needed.

2. **How difficult will your message be for your audience to understand or accept?** Spoken messages and sign language successfully convey simple messages that are easy to accept. Write your message if the content is complicated and/or contains many details. Business communication often involves complex messages. The following standard formats help reduce misunderstandings:
   - *Memorandums* (memos) for messages within an organization
   - *Letters* for messages between organizations
   - *Reports* for investigation results
   - *Proposals* for suggestions that change how a business operates
       Sometimes emotional reactions may make messages difficult for receivers to accept. In those circumstances, first provide a spoken message; then follow with written information. When emotional reactions may create a strong communication barrier, effective communicators provide added support, such as the following:
   - Written information
   - Comforting signals
   - Follow-up messages

3. **What type of feedback do you want from your audience?** A written message is most effective if you want a formal response. Spoken messages are more effective if you want ongoing, spontaneous audience participation (such as problem solving or brainstorming). People respond to the tone of your voice in the same way they respond to the expression on your face.

Timely Tip

Use sign language in addition to written messages when you want to encourage the active participation of audience members with hearing impairments.

   Example: Before making decisions about vendor proposals, business managers may distribute copies of the proposals to their staffs. Managers also may hold staff meetings to discuss the pros and cons of the proposals.

4. When do you need the feedback from your audience? If you do not need a quick response, writing the message may be the best choice. Otherwise, speaking or signing your message may be more suitable.

Example: To meet report deadlines, employees may call supervisors for information.

5. What are the characteristics and locations of your audience? When your audience is large and scattered, a written form may be the most effective way to communicate your message. However, if your audience is small and local, consider using a spoken message. Sometimes one communication situation involves several closely related messages. Choosing appropriate message forms requires senders to analyze each message separately. Notice that in the next example, effectively communicating all the relevant information calls for more than one message form.

Example: Medical personnel will provide patients with sensitive information, such as distressing medical test results. Medical personnel must meet the immediate emotional and informational needs of the patients and provide written reference material to the patients.

As you analyze the communication situation and determine the message form, consider these factors:

- Permanency Needs: Patients need information for future reference.
- Message Acceptance Difficulty: Message may be long, confidential, complex, detailed, and emotionally difficult to accept.
- Type of Feedback: The senders want to encourage questions and comments from receivers.
- Urgency of Feedback: The senders expect immediate feedback from receivers. The receivers require a quick response from the senders.
- Audience Characteristics: Specific patients of various health care providers will experience this communication situation.

To best meet the needs of this communication situation, the message form would be both a spoken conversation and written instructions.

Use Illustration 1-2, Message Form, to analyze messages and select an appropriate message form.

Transmission Mode

After choosing the appropriate message form, you must decide how to transmit (send) the message to the receiver. Transmission choices for written messages include hand delivery, traditional mail services, e-mail, facsimile (fax), or web sites. Spoken messages may be transmitted face-to-face or by telephone, recordings, broadcasts, or presentations. All transmission modes include opportunities for some type of audible, visual, or movement signals.

Consider these four factors when deciding the most effective transmission mode for your messages: destination, privacy, timeliness, and cost.

Illustration 1-2 **Message Form**

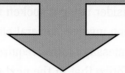

**Combination
Spoken and Written**

1. Partial Permanent Record
2. Complex Content and/or Acceptance Difficult
3. Formal and/or Spontaneous
4. Now and/or Later
5. Small or Large; Scattered or Local

Message

1. Permanency Needs?
2. Message Difficulty?
3. Type of Feedback?
4. Feedback When?
5. Audience Characteristics?

Spoken

1. Temporary Record
2. Simple Content and/or Acceptance Easy
3. Spontaneous
4. Now
5. Small or Large; Scattered or Local

Written

1. Permanent Record
2. Complex Content and/or Acceptance Difficult
3. Formal
4. Later
5. Small or Large; Scattered or Local

1. **Destination:** The expectations of your audience influence appropriate transmission modes. Receivers within a company may be familiar with technical language or specific company issues. General audiences, such as the one discussed in the following example, will not understand technical language or references to in-house issues.

 Example: Readers of an **annual report**, the overview of company operations and fiscal results written for stockholders, appreciate the use of general vocabulary, pictures, and graphs.

The physical location of your audience may also limit your transmission options. Although your message may be emotionally sensitive and best delivered face-to-face, your audience may be spread over a wide geographic area. As shown in the following example, electronic transmission modes protected by special security measures may offer the most appropriate delivery alternatives.

Example: Positive employee attitudes are crucial to long-term success when rival companies merge. Therefore, the merging companies may set up a multilocation videoconference to announce the decision, to inform employees of their career options, and to allow immediate audience feedback and interaction.

2. **Privacy:** When your message contains sensitive or confidential information, as in the following examples, choose a transmission mode that has a high probability of maintaining privacy. These modes include hand deliveries, traditional mail services, and face-to-face conversations.

Examples: Sweepstakes winners receive hand-delivered messages.

Employment dismissal notices are often delivered in face-to-face meetings.

3. **Timeliness:** Determine the speed with which your message must be delivered in order to be effective. Some messages request immediate action from the receiver; others do not.

Examples: Successful stock transactions are dependent on how rapidly messages are sent and received; therefore, computers, telephones, and fax machines are the equipment of choice.

Conversely, sales messages that do not have a short time limit often are in letter format and are distributed through traditional mail services.

Culture Frame

The Canadian postal service, Canada Post, delivers mail Monday through Friday during normal business hours. In some parts of the country, special Saturday or evening delivery is available for an additional cost.

4. **Cost:** Weigh the urgency of your message against the cost of available transmission modes.

Examples: Obtaining signatures on a multimillion dollar international contract clearly justifies the high cost of airline tickets and travel time for a face-to-face transmission.

Office supplies from an out-of-state vendor may be ordered economically and effectively by telephone, e-mail, fax, or overnight delivery service.

Traditional mail service may normally be the most cost-effective way to transmit bill payments across the country. If, however, the payment due date is in two days and the charge for a late payment is substantial, paying for a special delivery service may be cost justified.

The final example on page 9 showed how the answers to five questions helped determine two suitable message forms. The example continues here.

Example: Medical personnel will provide patients with sensitive information, such as distressing medical test results. Medical personnel must meet the immediate emotional and informational needs of the patients and provide written reference material to the patients.

Note how analyzing the four factors of destination, privacy, timeliness and cost helps determine the most appropriate transmission modes for the two message forms selected previously.

- Destination: Specific patients of various health care providers will receive the message content.
- Privacy: The message contains information of high sensitivity and confidentiality.
- Timeliness: The information is urgent and needs to be transmitted quickly. The senders expect immediate feedback from the receivers. The receivers also require an immediate response to their feedback.
- Cost: High urgency and privacy justify a more costly transmission method.
- Message Form: The messages may be confidential, complex, emotionally stressful, and difficult for receivers to accept.

The most appropriate transmission modes are (1) offer patients support in face-to-face conversations, and (2) personally give patients the written instructions.

Use Illustration 1-3, Message Transmission, page 13, to analyze messages and select an appropriate transmission mode.

Quality of Message Content

When the content of a message confuses the receiver, miscommunication results. Effective messages include six qualities to help sender and receiver reach a mutual understanding.

1. **Courtesy:** Write the message to reflect the receiver's point of view and to address the needs of the receiver.
2. **Clarity:** Use appropriate vocabulary and varied sentence structure, length, and placement.
3. **Conciseness:** Eliminate unnecessary words.
4. **Concreteness:** Build mental pictures for the receiver through the use of specific words.
5. **Correctness:** Use references to eliminate some common communication barriers. Verify the accuracy of the message information, grammar, spelling, and punctuation. Make sure the overall appearance of the message gives a positive impression.
6. **Completeness:** Include the information necessary for the receiver to take action in response to the message.

Illustration 1-3 **Message Transmission**

Combination

Live Presentations

1. Varied Audiences
2. None to Low
3. Quick
4. Medium to High

Web Presentations

1. Specialized Audiences
2. None
3. Quick to Delayed
4. Medium to High

Message

1. Destination?
2. Privacy?
3. Timeliness?
4. Cost?

Spoken

Written

Broadcasts

1. Varied Audiences
2. None to Low
3. Quick or Delayed
4. Medium to High

E-Mail

1. Varied Audiences
2. None
3. Quick to Delayed
4. Low

Telephone

1. Specialized Audiences
2. None to Low
3. Quick or Delayed
4. Low to High

Fascimile

1. Specialized Audiences
2. Low
3. Quick to Delayed
4. Low to Medium

In Person

1. Varied Audiences
2. High to None
3. Quick
4. Low to High

Mail Services

1. Varied Audiences
2. High
3. Delayed
4. Low to Medium

Hand Delivery

1. Specialized Audiences
2. High
3. Quick
4. Medium to High

Writing Skills

Many receivers form a lasting impression of you or your employer based on the quality of your written messages. Receivers may pay more attention to errors, inappropriate format, or message appearance than to the message content. Receivers may assume that your organization or you are not competent. As a result, receivers may not respond; and you may never know why. Good writing skills increase the likelihood of positive responses.

Timely Tip

Refer to the Format Guide for the appearance and format of conventional written messages and of e-mail messages.

To prepare effective messages, use good grammar, spelling, and vocabulary. Organize and present your information in an appealing format. *Effective message writing requires practice!* Apply these techniques to develop your writing skills:

1. **Start writing** *today*.
2. **Maintain a positive attitude.** Take time to develop good writing skills.
3. **Practice writing.** Build your confidence and expertise through the experience of making and correcting errors.
4. **Decide why you are writing.** Plan what you want to say before writing.
5. **Write key ideas on paper.** Organize the ideas in an outline, adding or deleting ideas as necessary.
6. **Use your outline.** Write a **draft** (practice copy) of your message by expanding the key ideas. Think from the receiver's viewpoint while developing your message.
7. **Use references to verify correctness.**
8. **Rewrite.** Continue to add and delete information as appropriate. Be critical of your own work. Ensure that your message reflects your intended meaning and encourages the desired response from the reader.
9. **Seek critique.** Ask someone with good writing skills to read and critique your work. Accept constructive criticism.
10. **Rewrite again.** Complete your final message.

Timely Tip

Verify name pronunciation, especially when dealing with French Canadians.

Speaking Skills

Today much of our communication is spoken—over the telephone or in person. The message strategies and qualities in this textbook are appropriate for both spoken and written messages. In fact, if you have a complex or sensitive spoken message to transmit, carefully plan the message content. Then write down the message content and practice saying the message. You will be more secure and effective when you finally speak the message.

To communicate effectively over the telephone, you must become proficient both in speaking and in listening. Often, you must respond immediately. Attentive listening and preparation help you convey your intended message in a limited amount of time.

Another aspect of spoken communication is dictation. **Dictation** involves speaking a message that a person or a machine records. People in various professions dictate messages such as reports, letters, and memos. The machine-recorded messages are **transcribed** (keyed) by someone else who must be able to understand the dictator. As voice recognition capabilities increase, dictation skills will become more imperative. When you dictate messages, you can increase productivity by developing good dictation skills and correctly using dictation equipment.

Word Choice

Our language is constantly changing. Business and medicine, in particular, have generated new words or new definitions for existing words. General audiences may not understand the meanings of specialized words.

Word	Common Definition	Contemporary Definition
burn	destroy with fire	record onto an electronic device such as a CD
surf	wave of the sea	moving around on the Internet
box	container for physical items	euphemism for mental/intellectual restraint
spoilage	the process of decay in food	airline jargon for "empty seats"
window	a glass-covered opening in a wall	any of the areas into which a visual display may be divided on a computer screen

Timely Tip

Think carefully before speaking. Words, once spoken, are difficult to retract.

Creative Combinations Sometimes people use words that are not really words. Avoid creating words that cannot be confirmed in a dictionary or using words that represent nonstandard English.

Examples: Recently, a sailor said, "I will *heist* the flag." (Did the sailor mean *heist* [steal the flag] or *hoist* [raise the flag]?)

After hearing the engineer explain how the equipment worked, I felt *delusioned* by the sales presentation. (Did the speaker mean *deluded* or *disillusioned*?)

A newsletter to investors stated: "*Irregardless* of the economy . . . ." (Did the writer mean *regardless*? *Irregardless* is nonstandard English and should not be used.)

Regional Vocabulary When communicating with people in various parts of a country, you are likely to encounter word meanings that are specific to that region. Be aware of differences in meaning when you prepare messages.

Examples: A large highway is called the *expressway* in Chicago, the *interstate* in Miami, and the *freeway* in Los Angeles.

A Milwaukee resident would drink water from a *bubbler*, but a Jacksonville resident would drink from a *water fountain*.

Culture Frame

Jargon, Slang, and Similes Residents of the United States often use jargon, slang, and similes. Such informal or specialized words may create barriers to effective communication. Keep in mind that the English used in the United States is different from the English learned by English as a Second Language (ESL) speakers. ESL receivers often interpret messages by applying literal (dictionary) definitions to words. Avoid sending messages that contain jargon, slang, or similes unless you know the audience understands the vocabulary.

Canada withdrew paper notes for $1 bills in 1987 and for $2 bills in 1996. Coins for those denominations resulted in two new Canadian slang terms: *loonie* for a $1 coin and *toonie* for a $2 coin. Canadians may ask for "a couple of toonies and a loonie" in exchange for a $5 bill.

Acronyms (a form of jargon) are abbreviations or words formed from the first letters, first few letters, or syllables of other words. Acronyms usually appear in all capital letters with no periods or spaces. Acronyms are pronounced as words.

Examples:	Acronym	Standard Meaning
	NAFTA	North American Free Trade Agreement
	NATO	North Atlantic Treaty Organization
	OSHA	Occupational Safety and Health Administration
	radar	Radio Detecting and Ranging

Slang is nonstandard vocabulary that attaches different meanings to established terms.

Examples:

Term	Standard Meaning	Slang Meaning
shine	reflect or transmit light	make an outstanding achievement
bottom line	last of a series of lines	end result
cool	chilly	trendy or admirable

Similes are figures of speech that use *as* or *like* to compare dissimilar things, such as *slippery as an eel* and *round like a basketball*.

Pronunciation

You will create a positive impression and enhance receiver (listener) understanding by pronouncing words correctly and clearly.

Examples: *Hyperbole*, an exaggeration for effect, is pronounced hī-pûr′-bə-lē (with emphasis on the second syllable). A distracting mispronunciation such as hī′per-bōl (with an accent on the first syllable) may cause the listener to miss important message content.

Octagon is a common word (pronounced ŏk′-tə-gŏn′ with emphasis on the first and last syllables). Listeners may become distracted by a mispronunciation, such as ok te′ gon with emphasis on the middle syllable.

Word emphasis, volume control, pitch, and voice intensity also have an impact on receiver interpretation of your spoken message.

Listening Skills

Listening is one of the most important but least practiced workplace skills. Poor listening skills interrupt the communication process by preventing the receiver from correctly understanding the content of the sender's message. Listening and hearing are different activities. **Hearing** is the physiological process through which your ears receive sound. **Listening** is the mental activity that involves processing the sounds you have heard.

Selective Listening

Because you are asked to absorb so much information in a single day, you learned early in life to become a selective listener. **Selective listening** means filtering out sounds that you believe are impairing your listening ability or information that you believe is of no interest or concern to you. Occasionally, you may inadvertently filter valuable information, such as the following:

- The date, time, or location of an important appointment
- Important instructional details from your manager
- Clues from customers about how to influence their buying decisions
- Instructions for an assignment

Active Listening

As a listener, you share the responsibility of making a communication attempt successful. **Active listening** requires you to concentrate, to relate what you hear with what you already know, and to analyze the speaker's signals for a deeper understanding of the message. Improve your active listening skills by using seven techniques.

1. **Begin with an open mind.** Carefully analyze your biases, and set them aside (at least temporarily) so that you can listen more objectively.
2. **Determine the speaker's approach to the material.** Some speakers present the main idea quickly and follow with the explanation. Others present the explanation and follow with the main idea. Understanding how information is organized helps you to understand the message.
3. **Jot down key words when appropriate.** If you are in a position to respond to the speaker, wait your turn; do not interrupt. Making note of key words will help you remember your questions.
4. **Concentrate.** Listening is an intense mental process. Concentrate to keep your attention from wandering.
5. **Maintain eye contact with the speaker.** You are likely to listen to what is being said if you look at the speaker. Provide some positive nonverbal feedback, such as a nod, to let the speaker know that you are attentive.
6. **Withhold judgment until you have heard the entire message.** Otherwise, your mental editing may sidetrack you.
7. **Analyze the message.** Has the speaker offered enough information to support his or her position? Do you have enough information to make a sound decision? Where can you find additional information?

Timely Tip

The expected amount of eye contact varies among cultures.

Reading Skills

In today's world, you depend on written information to make many daily decisions. Road signs help you to drive safely and find your way to your destination. Menus spell out your meal choices at restaurants. Newspapers keep you up-to-date about your community. Reading skills are also vital at work. Every job requires employees to read and follow instructions.

Most jobs also demand the ability to read, understand, and evaluate memorandums, letters, forms, and reports. Reading for **comprehension** (understanding) is the process of determining the meaning of a message. What you comprehend depends on your knowledge of word definitions and sentence structures. Reading for full comprehension takes longer than reading for an overview of a topic.

Reading for **verification** (proofreading) is another on-the-job skill you will need. *Verifying* is the process of determining the correctness of written information. Proofreaders often use a reference to verify correctness. When you read a reference, **scan** (read rapidly for key words) to locate the necessary information. Once you locate the information, read slowly for full comprehension.

Example: You are looking for popular places to visit in Canada. First, scan page headings in the encyclopedia to locate information about Canada. Then scan the material for titles or key words that direct your attention to favorite tourist sites. Finally, gather specific information by reading for comprehension.

Poor reading skills interrupt the communication process by preventing the receiver from correctly understanding the content of the message. Insufficient reading skills may cause the receiver to have trouble decoding the vocabulary or sentence structure used in the message. As a result, the receiver may misinterpret the sender's intention or misunderstand the message content.

Use the following techniques to increase your understanding and retention of written messages:

1. **Scan the material.** Determine the writer's approach to the information.
2. **Concentrate.** Identify the main ideas. Notice how the writer builds the ideas to conclusion. Determine whether the writer presents ideas logically. Think about how what you are reading relates to what you already know.
3. **Take notes.** Jot down key words of main and supporting ideas.
4. **Review.** Confirm your understanding of the material.
5. **Withhold judgment until you have read all the material.** Do not be sidetracked by your mental editing.
6. **Analyze the material.** Has the writer offered enough information to support his or her position? Where can you find additional information?

Keep the following Checklist for Reading Productively readily available. Refer to the checklist as you read for comprehension or verification.

Checklist for Reading Productively

Did you:

1. Scan the material?
2. Concentrate?
3. Take notes?
4. Review the material to make sure you understand?
5. Withhold judgment until you had read all the material?
6. Analyze the material?

Section 2: THE COMMUNICATION-BY-OBJECTIVES APPROACH

People create messages to meet specific needs. An effective plan for creating messages is **Communication-by-Objectives (CBO)**, a *whole-into-parts* process. The CBO approach consists of the following steps:

- **Plan a Message.** During the planning step, identify your objective, visualize your audience, gather supporting information, and organize the information.
- **Compose a Draft.** As you compose, choose words, construct sentences, assemble paragraphs, and choose paragraph locations.
- **Complete a Message.** Work from your draft to revise, edit, proofread, and finalize your message.

Following the CBO approach enables you to develop effective, appropriate messages for any communication situation.

Example: You believe that your department needs a color printer. An on-site color printer would allow employees to make in-house proofs, color charts, graphs, and other artwork for design projects. Eliminating the cost of an outside vendor and the time waiting for the vendor to complete the work would save the department money and increase productivity. You prepare your message using the *whole-into-parts* process of the CBO approach.

Culture Frame

When you send a price list to Canadians, specify the currency as United States dollars.

- **The Whole:** Convince the department supervisor to purchase a printer.
- **Part One:** Cost savings is one justification for your request.
- **Part Two:** Increased productivity is another justification.
- **The Whole-into-Parts:** You organize your message to persuade the supervisor to buy the printer based on projected savings and increased productivity.

Summary

Communication is a cyclical process: A sender originates and transmits a message to a receiver. The receiver interprets the message and transmits feedback to the sender. The sender's objective is to communicate effectively by conveying the intended message and by encouraging the receiver to respond with positive feedback.

Effective Communication for Colleges shows you how to make the communication cycle and the Communication-by-Objectives approach your communication partners. Elements of the communication cycle include the sender, message, transmission, receiver, and feedback.

Communication barriers may negatively influence communication. Barriers to the sending process include different backgrounds, signals, the communication situation, the quality of message content, writing skills, and speaking skills. Barriers to the receiving process include listening skills and reading skills.

The CBO approach is a whole-into-parts process for creating messages. Apply good writing, speaking, signaling, listening, and reading skills to develop effective messages.

Improve your professional advancement and personal relationships through better communication skills. Enjoy the benefits of good communication skills by building an effective three-way communication partnership: the communication cycle, the CBO approach, and you!

Complete Communication Skills Development 1, pages 27–28. For additional noun review, see the Reference Guide, pages 410–412.

Ethics in Action

Access http://brantley.swlearning.com. Analyze the Ethics in Action for Chapter 1.

Exercises

1 - 1 **Directions:** Collect ten employment advertisements representing a variety of careers. Underline words that identify communication skills that employers value. Be prepared to discuss your findings.

1 - 2 **Directions:** Watch a television newscast. Take notes on the newscaster's presentation. Specifically observe these signals:
- Facial expressions, gestures, and appearance
- Tone of voice and pitch of voice

Explain how the newscaster's signaling affects the audience. In addition, explain your perceptions of the newscaster's ability and personality based on your observations.

1 - 3 **Directions:** Locate samples of printed messages. Observe the signaling effects such as paper quality, layout, and print size. Discuss your observations with class members.

1 - 4 ## PART A

Directions: Using a current dictionary, write the definition of each of the following words in the space provided.

1. format (n.)

2. barrier

3. transmit

Exercises

PART B

Directions: Using a thesaurus, list at least three synonyms for each of the following words.

1. exacerbate

2. jeer (v.)

3. ubiquitous

1 - 5 **Directions:** Read the following sentences aloud. Each time you say a sentence, emphasize the bold-faced word. Be prepared to discuss how emphasis changes the meaning of the message and how those changes may influence audience interpretation.

1. He told me when they could go.

2. He **told** me when they could go.

3. He told **me** when they could go.

4. He told me **when** they could go.

5. He told me when **they** could go.

1 - 6 **Directions:** Those who do not speak English as their primary language may apply literal definitions to the words and phrases they hear in the United States. This exercise will help you understand the miscommunication that may result when slang, jargon, or similes are used.

Exercises

Part A

Directions: In the space provided, write five sentences that use common slang words or similes, such as *stuff*, *posse*, *what's up*, and *eyes like sparkling diamonds*.

Part B

Directions: Rewrite your sentences, and apply the literal meanings to your choices.

Part C

Directions: Discuss how literal translations applied to jargon may result in misunderstanding and confusion.

1 - 7

Directions: Attend a lecture or meeting (preferably of a career-related organization). Apply the techniques presented in Active Listening on page 17. Listen to the speaker and take notes. Be prepared to discuss your interpretation of the speaker's message.

Internet
Challenge

1-1 Directions: Search for Canadian holidays that could affect message transmission or delivery options for senders in the United States and receivers in Canada. On a separate sheet of paper, identify the holidays.

1-2 Directions: Do an online search for the keywords *reading efficiently* and *efficient reading.* On a separate sheet of paper, write a summary of your findings.

InfoTrac

Directions: Using the InfoTrac subject search, locate two articles with suggestions for improving listening skills. After reviewing these articles, use a separate sheet of paper and create two paragraphs explaining why each article is helpful. Identify each article by including the author's name, the name of the article in quotation marks, the publication's title (underlined or italicized), the date of the publication, and the page number of the article. Section 13 of the Reference Guide shows correct notation formats.

WebTUTOR
Advantage

Directions: Access your WebTutor Advantage product. Complete the short-answer portion for Chapter 1 and send the answers to your instructor.

Case Studies

1 - 1 **Communication Situation:** Over 100 health care providers in your area have decided to provide general health care information to their patients. Patients will frequently refer to the information as they learn to manage their particular health needs.

Task A: Use the example on page 9 as a guide. Decide which *message form* best suits the communication situation. In the space provided, write the results of each step of your analysis.

Task B: Now that you have decided on the appropriate message form, determine the most effective *transmission mode*. Use the example on page 12 as a guide. In the space provided, write the results of each step of your analysis.

Case Studies

1 - 2

Communication Situation: You are the chief executive officer of a new computer software company. The company has grown quickly. Wall Street analysts have been watching the company's stock, earnings performance, and management structure. The board of directors created a new position of chief operating officer. You and several board members interviewed two of your best managers and made a selection. This appointment is very important to your stockholders, your employees, and the two candidates.

Task A: Use the example on page 9 as a guide. Decide which *message forms* best suit the communication situation. In the space provided, write the results of each step of your analysis.

Task B: Now that you have decided on the appropriate message form, determine the most effective *transmission mode*. Use the example on page 12 as a guide. In the space provided, write the results of each step of your analysis.

Part A   Noun Usage

Directions: Underline the noun(s) in each of the following sentences.

1. You should learn which gestures are inappropriate in Canada.

2. Verbal and nonverbal are two categories of messages.

3. When you want a formal response from your audience, a written reply is preferable.

4. Miscommunication results when the receiver does not understand the message.

5. Listening, reading, speaking, and writing are important skills.

6. Good listening skills promote understanding and cooperation.

7. Can you describe the types of terrain in your country?

8. Develop a broad vocabulary that includes both specialized and general terms.

9. Consider receiver expectations and needs when you select how to transmit a document.

10. Although foreign visitors may speak fluent English, they are not likely to be familiar with regional slang.

11. How do education and religious beliefs affect communication?

12. The transmission of a message can create barriers.

13. Cultural factors play a part in effective communication.

14. Stationery can create a positive impression.

15. Pronounce your words clearly and distinctly.

16. Coworkers and customers appreciate good language skills.

17. Use references to verify correctness.

18. Slang, jargon, and similes may create communication barriers.

19. Which expressions would be considered rude in your culture?

20. Poor grammar may result in miscommunication.

Part B — Skills Application

Directions: In the following memo, underline each error in spelling and noun usage. Write the correction above the error. (Ordinarily, memos are single-spaced. In this memo, extra space has been added for you to insert corrections.)

Jefferson Life Insurance Company

INTEROFFICE MEMORANDUM

TO: Sales Associates

FROM: Marlina cruz

DATE: november 2, 20—

SUBJECT: Sales Stradegies

The following suggestions will help you increase your sales abilityes:

1. Remember your positives, and forget your failures. See yourself as a winner. Visualizing success leads to confidence, assertiveness, and positive self esteem.

2. Continue to learn. Talk to peoples you meet. Read books, journals, and Internet articles.

3. Be accountable. Assume responsibility for your actions. Do not blame your boss, the Economy, or your products for lack of success.

4. Place yourself in your customers shoes. Attempt to understand the concerns and fears that others feel. Develop a sense of caring about what others want to accomplish.

5. Keep your customers happy. Always provide added value when you meet, see, and talk to people. Give them an idea, an improvment, or a new approach to problems.

6. Focus on your uniqueness. Determine what you do best.

7. Deliver more than you promise. Follow this concept to keep customers' satisfied.

Chapter 2

The Six Cs of Effective Messages

Learning Objectives

1 Revise messages to reflect courtesy.

2 Revise messages to enhance clarity.

3 Apply techniques that ensure concise messages.

4 Make messages concrete by providing specific information.

5 Review messages for correct content, mechanics, and appearance.

6 Determine whether a message meets the completeness criteria of *who, what, when, where, why,* and *how.*

COMMUNICATION PERSPECTIVES

Correct Word Choice

As the polling editor for USA TODAY for the past 15 years, my fundamental task has been to meld two professions—public opinion research and daily journalism—that exist to communicate.

For me, the communication process consists of two steps:

- First, I help create polls. Each poll is, in effect, listening to what Americans think about the issues of the day.
- Second, I help the newspaper publish articles about the poll results. The paper speaks to Americans about their attitudes on the issues of the day.

Anyone who works as a newspaper reporter for very long winds up in the embarrassing position of having to run a correction to a story. I have been involved in my share. Printing corrections certainly drives home the point of how difficult communicating clearly and correctly can be.

The most concrete lessons I've learned about how easily communication can "jump the tracks" have come from the polling side of my job. The lessons are concrete and measurable.

One example occurred in July 1999. The USA TODAY/CNN/Gallup polling team wanted to know how Americans thought the federal budget surplus should be used. We asked half the people in our poll, "Would you prefer to see the budget surplus used to increase spending on other government programs or to cut taxes?" We realized, however, that the phrase "spending on government programs" had powerful negative connotations for many respondents. For the other half of the people being polled, we spelled out some of the ways the money might be spent: "Would you prefer to see the budget surplus used to increase spending on education, defense, Medicare, and other programs or to cut taxes?" The addition of those few words caused support for spending to jump from 28 percent to 61 percent.

Time and time again I have seen such seemingly minor question tweaking lead to major shifts in responses. Each time it happens, I am reminded once again how powerful words are and how elusive the goal of effective communication can be.

Even though no one can ever achieve total mastery of the art of communication, lessons are to be learned that can improve one's efforts. The rewards for such improvements are well worth the effort.

James Norman, Polling Editor
USA TODAY

Section 1: COURTESY

Courtesy helps you maintain goodwill by showing concern for the reader. **Goodwill** is a feeling of confidence based on honesty and reliable service.

You can also describe courtesy as diplomacy. For example, when government officials from different countries meet, they employ some of the same strategies you use in showing concern for the reader of your messages. Both parties prepare by researching the other's culture and language (developing the *you* attitude). If a disagreement arises, the representatives try to be objective and polite (using positive words) rather than insulting. The officials use appropriate gender references during their dialogue (selecting gender-free terms). After the meeting, further negotiations and relations between the two countries are aided by meeting communication deadlines (responding to messages promptly).

All communicators should demonstrate courtesy by following these methods:

- Develop the *you* attitude.
- Use positive words.
- Select gender-free terms.
- Respond to messages promptly.

Develop the *You* Attitude

To develop the *you* attitude in communication, a writer or speaker must project empathy into business messages, replace *I* or *we* with *you* or *your*, and address the receiver by name.

Empathy means imagining yourself in the receiver's position. In written communication, apply the same tact that you would use if you were talking directly to the receiver. When you talk with a person, body language helps project your meaning. When you write, you have only words to convey the meaning. The reader must understand exactly what you intend because many business decisions depend entirely on the written word. A misused or misunderstood word can confuse the reader and cost a business money. Thus, when you write or speak, avoid colloquialisms, jargon, and any words or phrases that might be offensive.

Replace *I* or *we* with *you* or *your* to establish your friendly intent as a writer. In your message, emphasize the benefits to the reader. Consider the following examples:

Examples:	I/We Attitude	You/Your Attitude
	I will issue a $25.82 credit to you on your December invoice.	You will receive a $25.82 credit on your December invoice.
	We will provide free event shirts for volunteers to wear at the race.	All volunteers may wear free event shirts at the race.

Even requests for action and unfavorable responses may create goodwill when the emphasis is on the reader's benefits. The following examples illustrate how an unpleasant message can be courteous and incorporate the *you* attitude.

Examples:	I/We Attitude	You/Your Attitude
	After September 15, I will drop all students who have not signed and returned their Acceptable Use Form.	Please protect your enrollment. Sign and return your Acceptable Use Form by September 15.
	We require a $300 minimum balance in order for customers to receive free checks.	When you maintain a $300 minimum balance, you receive free checks.

Timely Tip

Jargon includes technical or specialized language used in a profession, trade, or group.

Use the reader's name in the message to emphasize the person's importance. When you respond to a written message, obtain the correct spelling of the name from the sender's message. If you originate the message and you are unsure of the correct spelling, call the business and ask for the correct spelling of the individual's name and title. Illustration 2-1 on page 33 shows how a person's name can be used effectively in a message.

Use Positive Words

Courteous messages use positive words. Positive words show respect for the reader and reflect the *you* attitude. People are more open to the content of positive messages than of negative ones. Refer to Table 2-1 for a list of negative words that undermine positive messages.

Table 2-1 Negative Words

Negative Words			
blame	damaged	fear	no
complaint	doubt	lazy	not
criticize	failed	never	sorry

Both word choice and sentence structure can change a negative tone into a positive tone. Structure your sentences to state what can be done rather than what cannot be done. The next examples show how word choice can change a negative tone into a positive tone.

Examples:

Negative Tone	**Positive Tone**
Never allow customers to shop without first greeting them.	Always greet customers as soon as they arrive.
We do not make exchanges for purchases without receipts.	With your receipt, you may exchange any purchase.

Select Gender-Free Terms

Some nouns, especially job titles, refer to either men or women. **Gender-free** terms grant both sexes equal status and respect. Terminology that stereotypes or indicates bias against either men or women is called **sexist** language. Stereotypes may imply that racial and ethnic groups, women, men, or individuals with disabilities are superior or inferior to others. Thus, words that stereotype people may offend readers and lessen opportunities to create goodwill. Alternatives to sexist terms are listed in the following examples.

Examples:

Sexist	**Gender-Free**
policeman	police officer
bellman	customer service assistant
craftsman	craft worker
fireman	firefighter
foreman	supervisor or manager
mailman	mail carrier
waitress	server

Branson

CONVENTION AND TOURISM COMMISSION

101 Main Street • Branson, Missouri 65616-2730
http://www.tourism_branson.com
Telephone: 417.555.1000 • Fax: 417.555.1100

March 10, 20—

Mr. Hayato Matsumi
International Publishing Co. Ltd.
2338, Shiokawa
Maruko-machi
Chiisagara-gun
NAGANO-KEN 386-04

Dear Mr. Matsumi:

Thank you for stopping at the Tourist Information Center during your recent
visit to Branson, Missouri. While you were in the Center, you were kind
enough to sign the Visitor Register.

Please complete and return the enclosed visitor profile survey. The information
that you provide will allow us to better serve the needs of our future visitors.
When your completed survey is received, a $100 Bass Pro Shops Outdoor
World Gift Certificate will be mailed to you. The certificate is redeemable in the
online store at http://www.basspro.com.

Mr. Matsumi, please plan a return visit to Branson in the near future.

Sincerely,

Marsha Dickerson

Marsha Dickerson
Awards Manager

jb

Enclosure

Illustration 2-1 **Personalized Message**

When you refer to a category of people that may include both men and women, one option, shown in the next examples, is to make the noun plural and use a plural (gender-free) pronoun.

Examples:	**Sexist**	**Gender-Free**
	The doctor should listen to his patients.	Doctors should listen to their patients.
	Treat the customer courteously so she will continue to shop in our store.	Treat customers courteously so they will continue to shop in our store.

Respond to Messages Promptly

Timeliness is the watchword for diplomatic communication. Therefore, prompt responses enhance the effectiveness of written communication. A favorable business reputation is built on orders that are shipped early. In addition, a timely response may turn a complaint into a business opportunity.

Business etiquette dictates that you send congratulations within two days of an event and that you answer requests within five working days of receipt. Practice courteous communication.

Message clarity, a *C* quality that enhances courtesy, is discussed in Section 2.

Culture View

Japan

In Japan, courtesy requires indirect communication: *yes* may mean "no" or "maybe." In contrast, business courtesy in the United States calls for direct communication: asking direct questions, requesting action plans, and stating specific concerns.

Since the Japanese value the outward appearance of harmony, they will never say no during a negotiation. Instead, the Japanese will listen respectfully—even to unacceptable ideas. Etiquette requires them to demonstrate attentiveness by nodding their heads or saying yes at short intervals. Understand that positive words and body language are the Japanese way of saying, "Yes, we hear you."

In the Japanese view, you, the listener, have the responsibility to listen for the true meaning by understanding implied information. Therefore, listen carefully to the full replies of Japanese colleagues to determine what they mean.

Clarity means writing easy-to-read and easy-to-understand messages. A clear message keeps the intended receiver in mind. The message should focus on expressing a thought, not on impressing the reader.

In the following, the unclear examples on the left are written to impress the reader; the clear examples on the right are written to express the thought.

The Six Cs
Courtesy
Clarity
Conciseness
Concreteness
Correctness
Completeness

Examples:

To Impress	*To Express*
The English language device known as capitalization, using in printed matter designated letters of larger size, not only is a punctuation tool of considerable importance but also is a tool whose function varies in accordance with differing, prescriptive language rules.	Capitalization, a punctuation tool, varies based on different language rules.
The self-explanatory purpose of the letter address is both to designate the person to whom the mailed correspondence is to be received and to stipulate the location to which the said mailed article of correspondence is to be delivered.	The letter address names the message receiver and specifies the delivery location.

At first, you may hesitate to make changes in messages that you create. Strive, however, to form the habit of rewriting to improve clarity. Use these points to check messages for clarity:

- Select appropriate words.
- Place words in an orderly sequence.
- Limit use of *it* and *there*.
- Position phrases correctly.
- Position clauses correctly.
- Keep sentences short.

Select Appropriate Words

Appropriate word choice improves understanding between writer and reader. Words that look alike or sound alike frequently cause confusion. Verify word meanings in a dictionary to avoid offending or misleading a reader. When preparing spoken messages, use a dictionary to verify pronunciations. Study the examples of frequently confused words listed in Table 2-2, page 36, and in the Reference Guide.

Table 2-2 Frequently Confused Words

Word	Meaning	Example
a lot	many; much	Connie had a lot of anxiety.
alot	*not acceptable usage*	
accept	to take or receive	Midori agreed to accept the trophy.
except	to leave out; other than	Read all the notes except those on page 22.
affect	to influence or change	Changing chairs did affect his posture.
effect	a result	We cannot see any effect of Carolla's new diet.
all right	without error; correct	Zeke's answers were all right.
alright	*not acceptable usage*	
its	belonging to it	The dog had its nails clipped.
it's	contraction of *it is*	The driver said, "It's time to go."
lay	to put or place in position	You may lay the book on the desk.
lie	to recline; to be found in a particular place or position	Lie on the sofa and rest for a few minutes.
to	in the direction of; toward	Move your printer to the right.
too	besides; also; very	The holiday ended too quickly.
two	more than one	We do not have chairs for two desks.
your	belonging to you	Your keyboarding skill is excellent.
you're	contraction of *you are*	You're correct about the answer.

Place Words in an Orderly Sequence

Reading messages aloud helps reveal unclear word placement. If the word order makes you hesitate or reread the statement, try a different word arrangement. The pattern of subject before verb usually provides the clearest sequence.

The remarks "Baked is the bread" and "Scrambled are your eggs" sound awkward. Both statements place the verb before the subject, and the order appears illogical. In the next examples, notice how placing the subject before the verb makes the sentences easier to read and understand.

Examples:

Unclear Word Order	**Clear Word Order**
Enclosed is your check.	Your check is enclosed.
Burned was the toast.	The toast was burned.

When using a pronoun, be sure that the pronoun restates the intended reference, the **antecedent**. Change the word order or word choice when any confusion exists between a pronoun and an antecedent. Sentences containing expressions such as *his or hers, he and she,* or *him or her* are confusing to readers. Try rewriting the sentence with a plural antecedent and plural pronouns. The following examples illustrate how to correct unclear pronoun references:

Examples:	Unclear Antecedent	Clear Antecedent
	Felix called his agent while he was reading the script. (Does *he* refer to Felix or to Felix's agent?)	While Felix was reading the script, he called his agent. *or* Felix called his agent, who was reading the script.
	Pronouns should not be used in definitions because they have unclear meanings. (*They* could refer to pronouns or to definitions.)	Definitions containing pronouns may have unclear meanings. *or* Pronouns used in definitions may have unclear meanings.

Limit Use of *It* and *There*

It, an indefinite reference, often causes the reader to search for a correct meaning or relationship. With a minimum of effort, you can state exactly what you mean and limit the use of *it*. By being specific, you may also shorten your message. Compare the following sentences:

Examples:	Indefinite **It**	Improved Clarity
	It is recommended that you label your clothes with a waterproof marker.	Please label your clothes with a waterproof marker.
	After the program ends, *it* is time for you to leave.	After the program ends, you may leave.

Just as removing *it* from sentences often improves clarity, so does reducing the use of *there*. When used correctly, the word *there* refers to a specific place. Note how both clarity and brevity improve when *there* is eliminated in the following examples:

Examples:	Indefinite **There**	Improved Clarity
	There are six steps you can use to ensure message clarity.	You can use six steps to ensure message clarity.
	There is no other membership requirement except age.	Age is the only membership requirement.

Position Phrases Correctly

Humor can be an asset in messages. However, you want the reader to laugh with you, not at you. Incorrectly placed phrases can create unintended humor, cause misunderstanding, and reduce your credibility. Correctly positioned phrases reduce the chance of unintended humor, as shown in these examples:

Examples:	Incorrect Positioning	Correct Positioning
	Victor ordered rugs for the new apartment of various colors.	Victor ordered rugs of various colors for the new apartment.

Incorrect Positioning	**Correct Positioning**
Dr. Zayas wrote the letter while flying from Washington to Los Angeles on the back of an envelope.	While flying from Washington to Los Angeles, Dr. Zayas wrote the letter on the back of an envelope.

Position Clauses Correctly

The words *which* and *that* frequently introduce a clause. If the sentence is clear and correct without the clause, the clause is *nonrestrictive* and should be set off with commas. When the clause is needed for clarity or correctness, the clause is *restrictive* and commas should not be inserted. *Which* generally introduces a nonrestrictive clause, and *that* generally introduces a restrictive clause. Correctly placed clauses make the meaning clearer. Incorrectly placed clauses can create confusion, as shown in the following examples:

Examples:

Incorrect Positioning	**Correct Positioning**
Julia returned the support cast for her injured leg that she bought.	Julia returned the support cast that she bought for her injured leg.
Please place your donation in the jar, which is appreciated.	Please place your donation, which is appreciated, in the jar.

Keep Sentences Short

State your message in as few words as possible. Lengthy sentences often cause readers to lose the intended meaning. Most sentences range from 13 to 20 words; the average sentence contains 16 words. Short sentences are forceful and emphatic. However, short sentences can become choppy unless you write thoughtfully.

Combine words into sentences that show concern for the reader and that are easy to understand. Thus, you can maintain courtesy and clarity with brief sentences. Section 3 contains techniques for writing concise messages.

Timely Tip

Use transitional phrases or words such as *however*, *next*, and *therefore* to connect thoughts.

Section 3: CONCISENESS

Keep in mind the exact message that you want to convey to the reader. **Conciseness** means saying what needs to be said in as few words as possible. When you write with brevity, not abruptness, your messages remain both concise and courteous. Remember that courtesy helps you build and maintain goodwill. Critique your writing, and make every word meaningful. As you edit and revise your writing, use the following methods to develop concise messages that are courteous and clear:

- Eliminate unnecessary words.
- Select action verbs and efficient words.

- Use necessary modifiers.
- Write in the active voice.

Eliminate Unnecessary Words

Write naturally! Keep that two-word command in mind as you write messages. Use a conversational tone that is easy to read. Enhance clarity and conciseness by using only the necessary words. After you compose a draft, edit your message to eliminate unnecessary words.

Note the difference in this example:

Example:

Wordy

You will quickly come to the conclusion that unless you communicate in a consistent manner, you will jeopardize your relationships with your coworkers.

Concise

Communication consistency builds trust with coworkers.

The wordy version contains 23 words. The concise version eliminated unnecessary words and reduced the word count to six words.

Select Action Verbs and Efficient Words

Some writers use wordy phrases even though action verbs make clearer, shorter, more concise statements. Compare the wordy phrases with the action verb messages in the next examples.

Examples:

Wordy Phrases

Please make an agreement to purchase the Marco system.

Dr. Parker made a contribution of $500 to St. Jude's Hospital for Children.

Action Verbs

Please agree to purchase the Marco system.

Dr. Parker contributed $500 to St. Jude's Hospital for Children.

Timely Tip

Write clear sentences that readers can read once and understand.

After you choose action verbs, check for efficient, concise words. In the following examples, note how concise expressions reduce the word count:

Examples:

Wordy Phrases

Every one of the students entered the contest.

Please move the box *off of* the desk.

Concise Words

Every student entered the contest.

Please move the box *off* the desk.

Review Table 2-3 for concise expressions that you can use to replace inefficient words and phrases. You may review additional examples of concise expressions in the Reference Guide.

Table 2-3 Concise Expressions

Avoid Inefficient Words and Phrases	Use Efficient Words and Phrases
acknowledge receipt of	thank you for
as a matter of fact	in fact; indeed
at an early date	*Give a specific date.*
at that point in time	then
at this time; at this point in time	now
because of the fact that	because
during the month of May	during May
each and every	each
enclosed herewith	enclosed
for an extended period of time	*Give an exact time.*
for the amount of $320	for $320
I would appreciate it if	please
in accordance with your suggestion	as you suggested
in spite of the fact that	although
in the city of Cincinnati	in Cincinnati
in the last analysis	*Do not use this phrase.*
off of	off
please do not hesitate to contact us	please contact us
please find enclosed	*State what is enclosed.*
thank you in advance	*Do not use this phrase.*
until such time as	until

Use Necessary Modifiers

Select a word or phrase only when the word or phrase serves a purpose. Avoid unnecessary modifiers and **doublet phrases**—phrases that say the same thing twice, such as *the honest truth*. Compare the following sentences:

Examples:

Unnecessary Modifiers	**Revisions**
Follow the *road west in direction* until you see our facility on the right.	Follow the road *west* until you see our facility on the right.
The team leader suggested a *very unique* solution.	The team leader suggested a *unique* solution.

Review the unnecessary modifiers and doublets listed in Table 2-4.

Table 2-4 Necessary Modifiers

Avoid Doublets and Unnecessary Modifiers	Use Necessary Modifiers
actual truth	truth
basic fundamentals	fundamentals
consensus of opinion	consensus
each and every	each *or* every
entirely complete	complete
exactly identical	identical
first and foremost	first *or* foremost
honest truth	truth
important essentials	essentials
in the year of 2010	in 2010
long in length	long
maximum possible	maximum
merge together	merge
orange in color	orange
repeat again	repeat
return back to	return
round in shape	round
rules and regulations	rules *or* regulations
small in size	small
three in number	three
very unique	unique
west in direction	west

Write in the Active Voice

In the **active voice**, the subject of the sentence performs some action. The **passive voice** shows the subject receiving the action. Passive constructions add unnecessary words, usually in the form of prepositional phrases. Changing from the passive to the active voice makes the messages more succinct.

Examples:

Passive Voice	*Active Voice*
The old car *was painted* by the technicians.	The technicians *painted* the old car.
The overgrown trees *were trimmed* by the power company.	The power company *trimmed* the overgrown trees.

Select the passive voice when you want to avoid placing specific blame on someone. In a negative situation, the passive voice sounds more diplomatic and tactful than the active voice. Note how the active voice examples have accusatory tones:

Examples:

Active Voice	Passive Voice
Dora *placed* the books in the incorrect positions.	The books *were placed* in the incorrect positions by Dora.
Alex *cut* the pattern too small.	The pattern *was cut* too small by Alex.

Unless you choose the passive voice to ensure diplomacy, use the active voice to achieve both conciseness and clarity. You can further refine conciseness and clarity by checking your messages for *concreteness,* as discussed in Section 4.

Section 4: CONCRETENESS

The Six Cs
Courtesy
Clarity
Conciseness
Concreteness
Correctness
Completeness

Concreteness means conveying a message with precise terms. As a message sender, you build mental pictures for your readers through your use of words. The readers' backgrounds influence their perceptions of your words. Thus, words have different meanings for different people. If you said, "Charles has a hit," a baseball coach might think that Charles will help win the game. A music producer might think that Charles has composed a song that soon will be at the top of the sales charts. Use words or phrases that have definite meanings to convey a concrete message.

These steps will help you write concrete messages.

- Establish contact with the reader.
- Use precise modifiers.
- Avoid opinions or generalizations.
- Provide specific details.

Establish Contact with the Reader

Concreteness in written messages compares with exactness in spoken messages. When a young boy catches a fish and tells his friends about the event, he uses his hands, posture, and words to describe the size of the fish. Even more hand gestures illustrate the struggle he had in pulling the fish into the boat.

When the boy writes to a relative, he may include with the fishing story recollections of other family incidents. These recollections help the reader visualize the fishing adventure. You can use the same approach to establish contact with readers. When you write a message, build on shared personal or business backgrounds.

Business communication often involves mutual experiences, such as the following:

- Sending and receiving documents
- Shipping and possibly returning orders
- Applying for credit and being either accepted or rejected
- Asking for or writing recommendations

If you do not have an experience in common with the receiver, establish contact and build a concrete message through these techniques:

- Mentally picture the person.
- Collect as much background information as possible.
- Consider the person's culture and occupation.
- Use concrete words that have well-understood meanings.

Use Precise Modifiers

Dynamic verbs show action and motion, whereas static nouns name objects and ideas. Modifiers (adjectives and adverbs) add meaning and intensity to other words. When you use adjectives and adverbs, you add strength and color to nouns and verbs.

Select precise modifiers because research reveals the following facts:

- Readers remember precise (concrete) words longer than general words.
- Specific terms translate more easily than do broad, general words.

You probably would receive three different answers if you asked three people the question, "What is a good price for a printer?" Each person would have a different interpretation for *good,* and you did not give adequate information about the type or speed of the printer or about how much you were willing to pay. The next examples illustrate how precise modifiers or details provide more concreteness than vague modifiers.

Examples:	**Vague Modifiers**	**Precise Expressions**
	Our storage facility offers *large* climate-controlled units. (Will readers agree on what *large* means?)	Our storage facility offers *15-by 20-foot* climate-controlled units.
	Our new product will arrive *soon.* (Will all customers have the same concept of *soon*? Indicate an exact date.)	Our new product arrives *October 1.*

Business writing uses Standard English rather than formal English. Formal prose is usually reserved for academic and literary writing. Overuse of formal vocabulary makes a business writer sound pretentious.

Also, overusing modifiers may make messages sound insincere and may create a sense of distrust. Replace vague terms with precise modifiers. Develop and maintain credibility by writing clearly and precisely.

	Examples:	**Overused Modifiers**	**Precise Expressions**

Examples:

Overused Modifiers

Take advantage of the *very lowest* prices you'll *ever* find *anywhere*!
(The typical customer does not believe superlatives.)

Customers who use Expo Marketing products build a *more positive* image.
(Will everyone agree on how to measure a positive image?)

Precise Expressions

Take advantage of the 50 percent discount off our regular prices.

Customers who have used Expo Marketing products have shown a *10 percent gain* on the Baker Image Scale.

Review Table 2-5 for suggestions on how to change vague modifiers to precise modifiers.

Table 2-5 Precise Expressions

Vague Modifiers	How to Avoid Vague Modifiers	Use Precise Expressions
as soon as possible	State an exact date or time.	Please return the form by Monday, June 12.
better	Provide specific information.	The 250-LK scans six pages per minute, which is two pages faster than the 150-LK model.
big	State the size or measurement.	You will need $8\frac{1}{2}$-inch by 14-inch paper for the form.
fast	State the exact rate of speed.	Rafael inputs text at the rate of 65 words per minute.
few	State a number.	Carmen bought three reams of paper.
good	Describe fully.	Yoriko used 20-pound bond paper with 25 percent rag content.
high	State the exact height.	The windows begin 10 inches above the floor and measure $4\frac{1}{2}$ feet wide by 9 feet high.
little	Describe the size.	Aluminum foil measures 660 microns thick, but plastic wrap measures only 25 microns thick.
long	State the distance or measurement.	Bonito commutes 42 miles to work each morning.
many	State a number.	Alex requested 30 new printers.
more	State the difference in numbers.	Jennifer completed five mailable letters; Melissa produced three draft copies.
most	Quote an exact number or percentage.	Sang completed 97 percent of the problems within the time limit.
several	State a number.	Savita purchased seven printer cartridges.
slow	State the exact rate of speed.	The 125-IT printer produces 15 pages per minute.

Table 2-5 Precise Expressions (continued)

Vague Modifiers	How to Avoid Vague Modifiers	Use Precise Expressions
some	Quote an exact number or percentage.	Manuel sold six ads for the newspaper.
soon	State an exact date or time.	Wendy, please fax the message by 2 p.m. today.
too much	State exactly how much variance occurred.	Curt's score on the math test was three points below the acceptable limit.
worthwhile	Explain the benefit.	Donors receive a ticket to the awards banquet and a tax deduction.

Avoid Opinions and Generalizations

When people ask for your opinion, think about what information they need before you respond. If you have a negative opinion or if you do not agree with their position, exercise caution. When you are not sure what information they really want, ask for clarification. The following examples demonstrate the differences between opinions and requests.

Examples:

Opinions	**Courteous Requests**
You should join our focus group.	Please join our focus group.
I think the data would look better in table format.	Please consider displaying the data in table format.

Generalizations, vague or sweeping statements, often appear in written messages when the writer is attempting to persuade readers. Advertisers sometimes make broad, inclusive claims. Experienced advertisers exercise caution with generalizations because many consumers do comparison shopping. Note how these examples change generalizations into specific descriptions:

Examples:

Generalization	**Specific Information**
Our kit offers the *ideal* solution for accessing the Internet. (Will everyone have the same concept of *ideal*?)	Our ZoomPorte, a complete Internet kit, includes the V.34 external data fax modem and $400 worth of software on one CD.
Our holiday jewelry sale offers *extraordinary* values on gold pendants. (Will all customers define *extraordinary* in the same way?)	Our 14kt gold pendants are $70.50, a savings of 30 percent during the holiday sale.

Timely Tip

Effective communication serves as a bridge between cultures, allowing people to interact and enrich their understanding of how other people live.

Provide Specific Details

Effective messages contain specific details that are clear to both the sender and the receiver. Show concern for the receivers by providing specific details, such as sources of information your readers may need or want.

Suppose prospective clients called a vendor and asked that someone meet them at the airport. The vendor, eager to make a sale, agreed to meet the clients at the baggage claim area at 7:30. Unfortunately, the agreement lacked specific details, such as the name of the airline carrier and whether the arrival time was a.m. or p.m.

Imagine the vendor's concern when the clients could not be located at the luggage carousel for any 7:30 a.m. incoming flight. In a large airport, checking all carriers and incoming flights could take hours. The clients had not indicated the name of the carrier and the 7:30 p.m. arrival time. Also, the vendor should have asked for vital information. Complete details would have saved time and concern for all parties.

A concrete message is exact. As you develop concrete messages, you also verify correctness. *Correctness*, the next quality of effective messages, is discussed in Section 5.

Section 5: CORRECTNESS

The Six Cs
Courtesy
Clarity
Conciseness
Concreteness
Correctness
Completeness

Correctness means that the details of a message are accurate. Details involve not only the message content but also the message appearance. The correctness of your messages depends on your proofreading skills. Good proofreaders use reference tools to check message content and evaluate message appearance. The following four reference tools will help you produce correct messages:

1. A dictionary
2. A thesaurus (either printed or electronic version)
3. A word division manual
4. A format guide

Use a dictionary as a general reference to check spelling and word meaning. Consult a thesaurus for acceptable word choices. Verify preferable word division points in a word division manual. Refer to the Format Guide for acceptable message layouts.

Sending correct messages builds your credibility. In the workplace, a reputation for accuracy enhances your competence and helps you build a successful career. After you have written a draft of your message, complete the following tasks to ensure message correctness:

- Verify spelling.
- Select correct words or phrases.
- Insert appropriate punctuation.

- Check names, places, dates, times, and amounts.
- Evaluate message appearance.

Verify Spelling

Misspellings of frequently used words may be difficult to locate if you just give your message a quick once-over. However, a misspelled word may change the meaning of a sentence or may create a negative impression about you and your organization. Be absolutely sure every word is correct before you transmit your message.

In addition to a standard dictionary, you may need a trade or professional dictionary to check the spelling of technical or specialized terms. When you key a document in a word processing program, use the spell checker. However, do not rely on an electronic spell checker to detect errors in word usage. Spell checkers cannot determine whether you have used a word properly in the context of your message. Recheck spelling when you add new text or change word endings during the writing process.

Select Correct Words and Phrases

Selecting the word or phrase that correctly communicates your meaning can be challenging. The English language has borrowed words and expressions from many languages. As a result, English contains many **homonyms** (words that are spelled and pronounced alike but have different meanings) and **homophones** (words that sound alike but have different spellings and meanings). Select correct words and phrases for accurate messages. Be especially alert for words and phrases that sound alike but have different spellings and meanings. These examples illustrate how word choice affects meaning:

Examples:	*Word Choice*	*Discussion*
	Answering e-mail messages is an *everyday* activity for me.	*Everyday* as one word means "usual" or "routine."
	Every day provides you with opportunities to develop new skills.	*Every day* indicates each new day.
	Nobody answered the phone.	*Nobody* as one word indicates a person.
	No body of county officials has permission to appoint a city mayor.	*No body* represents a group composed of people.

Table 2-6, on page 48, lists selected words and phrases with proper meanings and examples.

Selecting correct words and phrases also involves checking your messages for subject and verb agreement and for parallel structure. **Parallel structure** means using the same grammatical form throughout a list or within a sentence. These examples illustrate nonparallel structures and show how to make the statements parallel:

Examples:

Nonparallel Structure

Minimum maintenance should include the following:
1. Check oil and water levels
2. Balancing tires
3. Check air pressure

The computer operator's duties are completing the log, starting and stopping all runs, and to make minor repairs.

Parallel Structure

Minimum maintenance should include the following:
1. Checking oil and water levels
2. Balancing tires
3. Checking air pressure

The computer operator's duties are to complete the log, start and stop all runs, and make minor repairs.

Table 2-6 Correct Word Choice

Word or Phrase	Proper Meaning	Example
altogether	completely; wholly	Your suggestions are altogether correct.
all together	in one group	The business teachers were all together at the conference.
always	forever; consistently	Always proofread your messages.
all ways	every possible choice	Please consider all ways of transmitting your messages.
among	implies division with three or more elements	The manager divided the tasks among four employees.
between	implies division with two elements	Timothy divided the cake between Elizabeth and me.
can	shows ability	She can play a violin.
may	implies permission; indicates possibility	You may go to Europe. We may complete the project by Monday.
different from	unlike	How is their accounting method different from ours?
different than	*not acceptable usage*	
few	amounting to a small number (countable)	Galen sold a few oranges.
less	not so much; not so well; (uncountable)	The architect allocated less space for attic storage.
good	pleasant; attractive; appealing (adjective)	They toured a good museum in Ohio.
well	in a satisfactory manner (adverb), fortunate; healthy (adjective)	Sergio works well in the computer lab. I feel well today.
regardless	having or taking no concern	Regardless of the time, she works until she completes the task.
irregardless	*not acceptable usage*	
who	takes the place of a person as the subject of a verb	Who answered the question?
whom	takes the place of a person as the object of a verb, a preposition, or an infinitive	You will go to the meeting with whom?

Insert Appropriate Punctuation

Punctuation marks serve as traffic signs for readers. Commas indicate caution—slow down or pause to comprehend the meaning. Semicolons tell readers to yield for the next thought. Periods and question marks mean readers should come to a complete stop before they proceed to the next sentence. Punctuate messages according to punctuation rules. When you insert appropriate punctuation in the correct locations, you maintain clarity for readers.

Punctuation can change the meaning of a sentence. Compare the following two examples:

Examples:

Punctuation Effect	Discussion
"Sprouted grain bread," said the nutritionist, "can be traced to ancient times."	The first example indicates that a certain type of bread can be traced to ancient times.
Sprouted grain bread said the nutritionist can be traced to ancient times.	The second example implies not only that bread is speaking but also that a certain nutritionist can be traced to ancient times.
For her research, Celia consulted with the architect, Corrine, Mr. Jeffries, the builder, and Stacy, the interior designer.	The third example lists five people.
For her research, Celia consulted with the architect; Corrine; Mr. Jeffries, the builder: and Stacy, the interior designer.	The fourth example lists four people.
For her research, Celia consulted with the architect, Corrine; Mr. Jeffries, the builder; and Stacy, the interior designer.	The fifth example lists three people.

Proofread aloud to be sure you insert the correct punctuation. If the message sounds awkward or causes you to hesitate, check the punctuation.

Check Names, Places, Dates, Times, and Amounts

Effective messages contain complete and correct names, places, dates, times, and amounts. Avoid confusion, lost time, effort, and money for your receivers. Check names, places, dates, times, and amounts twice for accuracy.

Evaluate Message Appearance

After verifying content correctness, evaluate the message for correct appearance. Correct appearance includes the style and placement of the message.

Most business messages follow standard company guidelines and practices. The Format Guide illustrates business and personal message formats. The message placement on a page, form, screen, or letterhead produces an image in the reader's mind. To make a good impression, the message should be formatted correctly and attractively, as well as be free of keying errors.

Section 6: **COMPLETENESS**

The Six Cs
Courtesy
Clarity
Conciseness
Concreteness
Correctness
Completeness

Individual words express parts of a whole thought. Several words work together to express an entire thought in a sentence. Sentences become building blocks for messages. A **complete message** uses sentences to answer the questions *who, what, when, where, why,* and *how.* A complete message also promotes goodwill.

Answer *Who, What, When, Where, Why,* and *How*

When you are developing a message, you do not need to answer the questions *who, what, when, where, why,* and *how* in a prescribed order. You must include all the appropriate answers, however, to have a complete message. After writing a draft of your message, use the criteria in Table 2-7 to evaluate your message for completeness.

Table 2-7 Completeness Criteria

Who?	Who is the intended receiver? Is the content appropriate for the intended receiver?
What?	What is your objective? Will the reader know what to do?
When?	When should the reader respond? Have you included complete, accurate details?
Where?	Where should the reader respond? Have you identified names, postal and electronic addresses, telephone and fax numbers?
Why?	Why should the reader respond? Have you stated a benefit for the reader?
How?	Have you encouraged a positive response? Does your message promote goodwill?

Illustration 2-2 shows a complete, clear message.

THOMPSON COUNTY CHAMBER OF COMMERCE

Suite 1-B • 3110 West Palafox Street • Orlando, FL 32968-0110
http://www.thompsonchamber.org
Telephone: 619.555.1890 • Fax: 619.555.1820

April 16, 20—

Mrs. Betty Williams
The Williams Agency
4211 Palm Way
Tampa, FL 33946-4211

Who

Dear Mrs. Williams

When

Thank you for agreeing to speak at the Third Annual Thompson County Business Development Conference from 9 a.m. until 11 a.m. on Thursday, June 12. The conference committee appreciates your willingness to focus your presentation on the tools needed for successful grant writing.

What

Where
Why
How

Twelve chamber members, as well as 24 local business leaders, will join you in the Great Oaks Convention Center, 1190 West Cervantes Street, for your two-hour presentation. Since the committee must submit grant proposals by July 1, please specifically address the following issues:

- Grant-writing principles
- Potential state and federal funding sources
- Pitfalls to avoid when writing and submitting grant proposals

Closing builds goodwill.

A copy of the conference brochure is attached. Please be our guest at any session convenient for you.

Sincerely

Alice Butler

Alice Butler
Executive Director

kw

Attachment

Illustration 2-2 **Complete Message**

Notice how the following example does not satisfactorily answer the questions *who, what, when, where, why,* and *how:*

Example: Please attend our in-service meeting on Thursday at 5 p.m. The meeting will end by 6:30 p.m.

Who? Your name was included on the distribution list, but you do not know who is sponsoring the meeting.

What? An in-service meeting is being held, but you do not know what kind of a program is planned.

When? The meeting begins at 5 p.m. and ends by 6:30 p.m., but you do not know which Thursday to attend.

Where? You do not know the location of the meeting.

Why? The reason for this particular meeting is unknown.

How? You do not know how the meeting will benefit you.

Maintain Goodwill

Develop clear, complete messages so readers will understand you. Your complete message will more effectively promote goodwill when readers know exactly what you are asking for or what you are offering to do.

Summary

Make sure your messages incorporate the six *C*s of effective messages.

Quality	Purpose
Courtesy	Show concern for the intended receiver.
Clarity	Compose messages that are simple and easy to understand.
Conciseness	State what needs to be said in as few words as possible.
Concreteness	Convey a message with precise terms.
Correctness	Provide accurate details in an acceptable format.
Completeness	Include all pertinent information.

All six *C*s are necessary for effective communication. Use effective communication to promote goodwill and to obtain positive responses from your readers.

Complete Communication Skills Development 2, pages 67–68. For additional pronoun review, see the Reference Guide, pages 412–415.

Exercises

2 - 1

Directions: In the space provided, rewrite the sentences to incorporate the *you* attitude.

1. We need to know the rates for your delivery service.

2. We will show the annual dividend from Plano Investments on your December statement.

3. I have added your name to our preferred customer list.

4. We've made your new statement easier to read.

5. We're delighted you chose an Orion scanner.

6. I think your report was interesting, well researched, and well written.

7. I am giving you a bonus for your energy-saving suggestion.

8. We need to receive up-to-date sales figures from you each day.

9. We offer three billing options from which you may choose.

10. I will deliver your products on Tuesday.

11. We appreciate your buying our products.

12. We accept credit cards.

13. We think your quarterly report will become a useful document as you plan your investments.

14. Allie, we want to thank you for completing the survey.

15. I want you to change the sexist terms to gender-free terms.

Exercises

2-2

Directions: Change the negative statements to positive statements.

1. Do not use negative words in your messages.

2. Do not hesitate to call us when you need additional information.

3. You should not react negatively to constructive criticism.

4. Avoid separating the icons from the margin notes.

5. Never fail to clean your work area before you leave each day.

6. Do not use the express lane if you have more than ten items in your shopping cart.

7. Refrain from opening sentences with the word *there*.

8. You should not misspell names in a message.

9. You may not use the drive-through banking service before 9 a.m.

10. Do not forget to lock the door when you leave.

Exercises

2 - 3   **Directions:** Change the sexist terms below to gender-free terms.

1. A personal trainer must have her current CPR card.

2. The realty company is seeking a new salesman.

3. Maxum Productions needs two cameramen to film the performance.

4. A student who plans to become a computer engineer must include higher-level math courses in his degree plan.

5. Three firemen were injured while they brought the fire under control.

6. The mailman used proper lifting techniques to move the heavy bag.

7. A lawyer should do her best to defend her clients.

8. Does the league need a soccer linesman?

9. The labor force needs skilled workmen.

10. Ask the waitress to bring our check.

Exercises

2 - 4

Directions: Underline the word that makes the statement complete and correct.

1. When the area code changes, please order new (stationery, stationary).

2. (Your, You're) analysis covers all sides of the issue.

3. The (cite, site) for the new clinic is 1107 Jackson Street.

4. Because the temperature was (to, too) cold, the ceremony was rescheduled.

5. We (complimented, complemented) the caterer who prepared the dessert.

6. Dr. Hallock asked the (personnel, personal) to please be quiet.

7. He has the (rite, right) to expect their cooperation.

8. Mrs. Kruger asked Dr. Hallock for permission to (lay, lie) down for five minutes.

9. The clinic administrator asked Dr. Hallock to serve on the local medical (council, counsel).

10. Dr. Fitzpatrick (preceded, proceeded) Dr. Hallock as the clinic representative.

11. Dr. Hallock will travel (farther, further) than other medical representatives.

12. The clinic is located two blocks (past, passed) the Wingate Store.

13. The administrator gave two directions; the nurse followed the (latest, latter) one.

14. Dr. Smythe and Dr. Lambert earned (their, there) degrees from the same university.

15. (To, Too) many graphs and charts can be confusing for the reader.

16. The office manager purchased (loose, lose) pages to refill the training manuals.

17. Our staff members appeared (quiet, quite) pleased with the manuals.

18. The members asked (weather, whether) they could keep the manuals on their desks.

19. The office manager encouraged everyone to make a (conscience, conscious) effort to review the manuals.

20. Since the (fiscal, physical) year ends on June 30, please send your reports to Dr. Lambert by July 10.

Exercises

2 - 5

Directions: In the space provided, rewrite the sentences to eliminate the words *it* and *there*.

1. There are hundreds of claims that have been filed.

2. It is a good idea to arrive early for an interview.

3. It is a requirement for you to attend every meeting.

4. It is important to maintain a balanced diet.

5. Can you see if there is anyone outside the building?

6. There were eight times when we had to reschedule patients.

7. It was stated by Heather that an hour of dancing can burn between 200 and 400 calories.

8. There is a Mr. Stuart from Omni Associates here to talk with you.

9. It will be February 10 before you will receive your materials.

10. There are numerous learning projects available on the Internet.

11. This letter isn't dated, is it?

12. We expect a demand for this printer, and we may not have enough stock to meet it.

13. It was recommended by Eric Templeton that you form the habit of rewriting to improve message clarity.

14. There is no other entrance requirement except a 90 percent test score.

15. It is necessary to balance the budget by next year.

Exercises

2 - 6

Directions: In the space provided, rewrite the following sentences; use action verbs and efficient words and phrases.

1. The new mouse pads are exactly identical to the old ones.

2. The coach stressed the basic fundamentals in basketball.

3. The watch was mailed under separate cover.

4. In the majority of instances, credit isn't free.

5. You may preview the tapes for an extended period of time.

6. Rosa said, "The mayor's speech was long in length."

7. Please find enclosed your dividend check.

8. Did you know that the first major league night baseball game was played in the city of Cincinnati in the year of 1935?

9. James has made a decision to give each and every employee a two-week holiday in the month of December.

10. Every one of the employees accepted his offer.

11. I would appreciate it if you would send me a catalog.

12. Ralph made a contribution of $5,000.

13. The chest was made out of walnut.

14. Victor signed a contract in the amount of $125,000.

15. Chris and Elizabeth provided a solution for the traffic problem.

Exercises

2 - 7

Directions: In the space provided, rewrite the following e-mail message to improve conciseness and clarity.

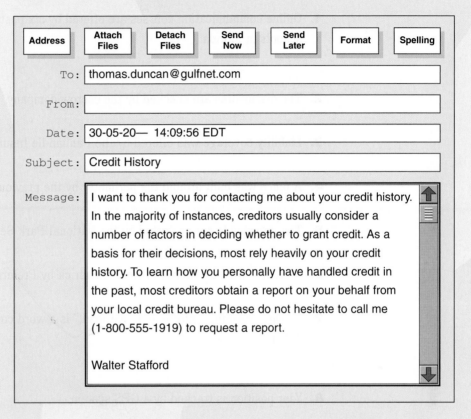

Address	Attach Files	Detach Files	Send Now	Send Later	Format	Spelling

To: thomas.duncan@gulfnet.com

From:

Date: 30-05-20— 14:09:56 EDT

Subject: Credit History

Message: I want to thank you for contacting me about your credit history. In the majority of instances, creditors usually consider a number of factors in deciding whether to grant credit. As a basis for their decisions, most rely heavily on your credit history. To learn how you personally have handled credit in the past, most creditors obtain a report on your behalf from your local credit bureau. Please do not hesitate to call me (1-800-555-1919) to request a report.

Walter Stafford

Exercises

2-8

Directions: In the space provided, rewrite the sentences. Change the passive voice to the active voice.

1. Online communication courses are offered by six postsecondary schools in Florida.

2. The disclosures are checked by the escrow company.

3. Liability coverage was offered by the Panhandle Insurance Company.

4. A fence was built around the perimeter by the previous owner.

5. The grasslands are protected by the National Park Service.

6. A credit card was offered to Heidi Kendrick by Preferred Credit.

7. *Infobog*, meaning "information overload," is a word coined by Charles Arlen.

8. Your position is tracked by a GPS system.

9. The telephone was answered by Mr. Johnson.

10. The application was given to Mr. Lopez.

11. A new software program was designed by the drafting department.

12. The documentation is read by the programmer and the systems analyst.

13. Modifications were made to the flowchart by the systems analyst.

14. A spreadsheet program was submitted to the accountant.

15. Two railways have been converted into bike trails by state officials.

Exercises

2-9

Directions: Underline ten vague modifiers in the following e-mail message. Discuss your suggested changes.

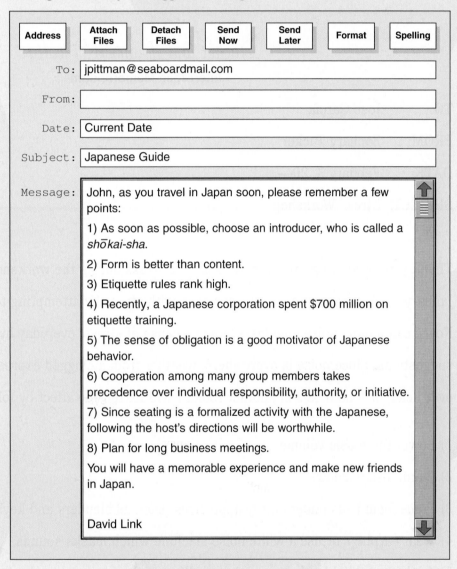

| Address | Attach Files | Detach Files | Send Now | Send Later | Format | Spelling |

To: jpittman@seaboardmail.com

From:

Date: Current Date

Subject: Japanese Guide

Message:

John, as you travel in Japan soon, please remember a few points:

1) As soon as possible, choose an introducer, who is called a *shōkai-sha*.

2) Form is better than content.

3) Etiquette rules rank high.

4) Recently, a Japanese corporation spent $700 million on etiquette training.

5) The sense of obligation is a good motivator of Japanese behavior.

6) Cooperation among many group members takes precedence over individual responsibility, authority, or initiative.

7) Since seating is a formalized activity with the Japanese, following the host's directions will be worthwhile.

8) Plan for long business meetings.

You will have a memorable experience and make new friends in Japan.

David Link

Exercises

2-10   **Directions:** Underline each word, phrase, spelling, and punctuation error in the memo. Write the correction above the error.

Tucker and Lambert Realty
Interoffice Memorandum

TO: Jose Garcia

FROM: Zachary Tucker

DATE: Febuary 3, 20—

SUBJECT: Stress Workshop

Thank you for sharing tips on how to handle stress during the workshop on Wednesday January 32. You were rite—I all ways cope with stress by attempting to ignore the sources. Now I can handle noise, one lesser known cause of stress, everyday by following your suggestions. Since noise is everywhere, weather from a clogged expressway, an airplane over head, or loud music in another room, I will lessen the affect by following these methods;

1) Lower the music volume.

2) Caulk lose windows.

3) Place foam pads under noisey appliances, such as blenders and keyboards.

4) Wear earplugs or use a white-noise machine which masks sounds.

5) Advise potential home buyers, irregardless of the location, to check airplane flight paths.

Exercises

2-11   **Directions:** Determine whether the following message meets completeness criteria. In the left margin, indicate where the message meets each criterion (*who, what, when, where, why, how*).

THOMPSON COUNTY CHAMBER OF COMMERCE

Suite 1-B • 3110 West Palafox Street • Orlando, FL 32968-0110
http://www.thompsonchamber.org
Telephone: 619.555.1890 • Fax: 619.555.1820

May 13, 20—

Mr. Juan DeSantos
DeSantos Enterprises
2104 West Eva Street
Leonard, FL 32972-0104

Dear Mr. DeSantos

Please participate in the Third Annual Thompson County Business Development Conference. Dr. Williams Stevens from the University of East Florida will discuss urban redevelopment. The discussion is on Thursday, May 30, from 1:00 p.m. until 2:30 p.m. in the Great Oaks Convention Center, 1190 West Cervantes Street.

Dr. Stevens, a nationally recognized consultant, will provide a detailed overview of the pros and cons of urban redevelopment in Thompson County. His comments should initiate a positive action plan for our area.

Please call 619-555-1890, Ext. 59, by Friday, May 24, to confirm your attendance. Your call will reserve a seat for you during the session.

Sincerely

Alice Butler

Alice Butler
Executive Director

kw

Internet Challenge

2-1 Directions: Locate online sites that contain information and resources related to gender equity. On a separate sheet of paper, summarize your findings and give reference citations. Use one of the citation styles shown in the Reference Guide.

2-2 Directions: Search online sites for information helpful to doing business in Japan. On a separate sheet of paper, write a short article summarizing three concepts businesspeople should know if they plan to work in Japan. Try the following key phrases in your search:

- Japanese business etiquette
- Business in Japan
- Working in Japan

InfoTrac

Using the InfoTrac search, locate an article that discusses reader-friendly writing. After reviewing the article, use a separate sheet of paper and create two paragraphs explaining how you can incorporate the suggestions into writing effective messages. Give reference citations. Use one of the citation styles shown in the Reference Guide.

WebTUTOR Advantage

Directions: Access your WebTutor Advantage product. Complete the short-answer portion for Chapter 2 and send the answers to your instructor.

Case Studies

2 - 1

Communication Situation: You are an assistant manager of the shoe department for a store in the mall. You supervise five salespeople during your shift. The store is open from 9 a.m. to 9 p.m., but you work the afternoon/evening shift from 2 p.m. until 9 p.m. You have been expecting tonight to be a routine evening even though one of your regular employees is out on vacation.

When you begin your shift, you discover that two other salespeople also will be off because of illness. In addition, you find a note from the shoe department manager that says: *Afternoon/night shift is responsible for taking inventory of all shoes displayed on the floor as well as the new shipment received yesterday.*

Taking inventory of the display shoes usually requires the full-time attention of one salesperson. The inventory of the last shipment received also requires the full-time attention of one salesperson. In addition, you quickly count 27 elderly shoppers who are circulating in the department. The elderly shoppers' name badges indicate that they are registered for the Southeastern Senior Spirit Conference, which meets in the hotel adjacent to the mall.

You and your reduced sales staff are expected to meet the increased number of customer assistance requests as well as complete both inventories. Needless to say, the inventories were not completed.

Task: In the space provided, compose a note to the shoe department manager explaining why the inventories were not completed. Make sure your message reflects courtesy, clarity, conciseness, concreteness, correctness, and completeness.

Case Studies

2-2

Communication Situation: You work as a customer service representative for a local cable company. Your job is to take incoming calls from customers who have problems with their service. You begin working your normal shift on Super Bowl Sunday when the main satellite dish for your company is struck by lightning. The volume of calls rapidly increases as customers call to ask why they have no service. As you ask one customer to hold, he states in an agitated voice, "What do I have to do to get someone to talk with me about my not having cable service?"

Task: In the space provided, write your response to the customer. Use a positive approach that emphasizes how he is a valued customer.

Communication Skills Development 2

Part A   Pronoun Usage

Directions: In the following sentences, underline the correct pronoun of the words given in parentheses.

1. The newest member of the team was (her, she).

2. Other speakers, along with Professor Lipscomb, stressed positive statements in (his, their) presentations.

3. Eliminating *it* and *there* in messages was (my, mine's) suggestion.

4. Dr. Farrow, as well as his assistants, presented (his, their) suggestions for writing clear directions.

5. Patient education sessions will be divided among Lisa, Joyce, and (I, me).

6. Dr. Farrow (hisself, himself) explained how to write concise reports.

7. Our patients find (themselves, theirselves) able to follow Dr. Farrow's instructions.

8. With (who, whom) should patients discuss (his, their) treatment?

9. (We, Us) assistants coordinate 11 doctors' schedules.

10. Dr. Farrow asked the coordinators to report any problems to Margaret and (him, he).

11. (Whose, Who's) willing to tell the staff how to write in the active rather than the passive voice?

12. Has (somebody, some body) benefited from (me, my) advising the patients?

13. Dr. Farrow explained to the patients that (were, we're) here to develop treatment plans that will satisfy (their, them) needs.

14. The plans contain specific details that (anyone, any one) of you can follow.

15. If you have any medications, please bring (they, them) for (we, us) to check the expiration dates.

16. Sometimes patients forget to bring (there, their) medical records.

17. (Your, You're) going to need some time to collect the needed information.

18. Your payment record is confidential; only you and (I, me) will have access to the payment codes.

19. (Our, Ours) billing staff will work with you on a payment schedule.

20. The medical-research grant winner was (he, him).

Part B   Skills Application

Directions: Underline errors in noun and pronoun usage and spelling in the second paragraph of the following e-mail message. Rewrite or key a corrected version of the paragraph.

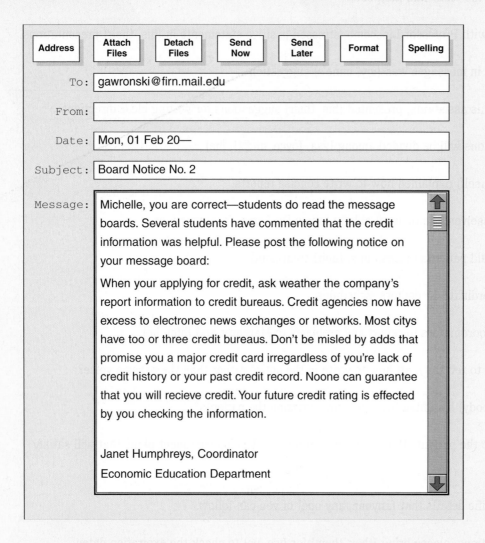

| Address | Attach Files | Detach Files | Send Now | Send Later | Format | Spelling |

To: gawronski@firn.mail.edu

From:

Date: Mon, 01 Feb 20—

Subject: Board Notice No. 2

Message:

Michelle, you are correct—students do read the message boards. Several students have commented that the credit information was helpful. Please post the following notice on your message board:

When your applying for credit, ask weather the company's report information to credit bureaus. Credit agencies now have excess to electronec news exchanges or networks. Most citys have too or three credit bureaus. Don't be misled by adds that promise you a major credit card irregardless of you're lack of credit history or your past credit record. Noone can guarantee that you will recieve credit. Your future credit rating is effected by you checking the information.

Janet Humphreys, Coordinator
Economic Education Department

Visit the Interactive Study Center at **http://brantley.swlearning.com**

Chapter 3

The Communication-by-Objectives Approach

Learning Objectives

1 Plan a message using the Communication-by-Objectives approach.

2 Compose a message draft following the Communication-by-Objectives approach and incorporating the six Cs of effective messages.

3 Identify the activities involved in Complete a Message, the third step of the Communication-by-Objectives approach.

COMMUNICATION PERSPECTIVES

Determine Your Objective

As a financial advisor, my objective is to communicate with our clients effectively so they feel the excitement and positive effects of implementing their wealth management plan. No matter how much good advice I have about investments, unless I can impact clients' knowledge in such a way that they understand and will be persuaded to take action, I have failed.

I listen and question, listen and question, listen and question to make sure I have a clear understanding of my client's needs. This profile will enable me to create a tailor-made, realistic, wealth management plan that accurately reflects time goals, money needs, special expenses such as college, vacations, vacation homes, and elderly parents' health care. I must start with the end in mind—the ultimate end being, "not to outlive your money."

One question and answer session is not enough. The first session is to get general ideas. The second is to get more specific on investment psyche, and the third is to finalize the tailor-made wealth management in writing for the investor.

69

"The only constant in life is change." Markets change, economic conditions change, people change, and objectives change. "Communication is a journey, not a destination!" Therefore, quarterly or semiannual communication is necessary to update wealth management plans. Investors invest when they believe their ongoing needs are heard and understood.

Lack of clear communication could lead to the following situation: Two men had no wealth management plan. One said, "I'm sick and tired of being broke all the time." To which his friend replied, "Don't worry, friend, we'll have plenty of money when we get old; least I'm hoping that's why they're called the 'golden years.'"

Patricia Windham-Harvey
Senior Vice President—Investments
Prudential Financial, Inc.

Section 1: PLAN A MESSAGE

Plan a Message
- Identify the Objective
- Visualize the Audience
- Gather Supporting Information
- Organize the Information

Compose a Draft

Complete a Message

The **Communication-by-Objectives (CBO) approach** is a step-by-step, whole-into-parts method. CBO provides a framework for developing effective messages. An effective message conveys your intended meaning to the receiver and creates a positive image for you and your organization. The CBO approach includes planning a message, composing a draft, and completing a message. When your message demonstrates courtesy, clarity, conciseness, concreteness, correctness, and completeness, you increase your chance of achieving your objective. You also promote trust and goodwill between your receiver and you.

Planning provides the foundation of effective communication, whether a message will be spoken or written. Planning helps you achieve your communication objective. The four activities in the planning process are listed here:

1. Identify the objective.
2. Visualize the audience.
3. Gather supporting information.
4. Organize the information.

Identify the Objective

The first activity of the planning process is to identify the message objective. The objective is why you are creating the message. Are you trying to persuade readers? Do you want to tell a reader yes or no? Are you reporting information, or are you responding to an inquiry for information? Basically, your objective will be to persuade, to inform, or to inquire.

State the objective of your message simply, clearly, and concisely. The following example summarizes the objective of the City Department Store (CDS) in one short sentence:

Example: Persuade people to shop at City Department Store.

Visualize the Audience

Once you determine the message objective, the second activity is to visualize the receiver of the message. In other words, create a mental picture of your audience. Knowing as much as possible about the receiver will help you develop a message that is more likely to achieve a favorable response.

When you know your receiver or when you respond to an inquiry, you have some knowledge about the receiver's interests or concerns. In some communication situations, however, you may not have this knowledge. To help visualize your audience, answer these six questions:

1. Who is my target audience (receiver)? One person or more than one person?
2. What characteristics do I know or what can I learn about my target audience that will help me prepare the message?
3. When will the audience receive the message?
4. Where will the audience members be when they receive the message?
5. Why will the audience be interested in the message?
6. How can I learn more about my target audience?

The answers to the six questions will help you decide what information to include in your message, how to organize that information, and how to transmit your message to your receiver. In the next example, the CDS marketing manager is visualizing the audience for an advertisement in the local paper.

Example: **Visualizing the Target Market for CDS**
1. Consumers are the target audience.
2. Consumers need access to shopping at various hours, have an average household income of $50,000, have an average of two school-age children, use a motor vehicle for transportation, and shop within a five-mile radius of home.
3. The audience will receive the message in the Sunday paper.
4. The audience members will probably be at home when they receive the message.
5. The audience will be interested in the message because (a) they want to see the newly remodeled store and (b) they will want to save money with the grand-opening specials.
6. More information about the target audience may come from census reports, labor reports, and chamber of commerce reports.

Gather Supporting Information

In the third activity, you gather supporting information. You generate and choose ideas that relate to the message objective. Check sources such as organizational documents, people, libraries, and the Internet. As you begin gathering information, the ideas that you generate and the information that you collect do not have to be in any particular order.

Generate Ideas

When you generate ideas, your goal is to stimulate your thinking. Two key actions will help you successfully generate ideas:

- Turn off the analytical function of your brain.
- Encourage the creative function of your brain.

The analytical function supplies clarity, correctness, and completeness through logic, format, grammar, and punctuation. The creative function contributes courtesy, conciseness, and concreteness through empathy, originality, insight, and rhythm. Both functions are necessary to effective communication. However, research has shown that human brains cannot simultaneously analyze and create. One function inhibits the other.

Brainstorming, nonstop writing, and **bubble writing** are techniques that encourage the flow of ideas. Keep the ideas flowing by following this rule: No judgments allowed during idea-generating activities!

Brainstorming

Record *all* ideas whether or not they seem appropriate. When the flow of ideas ends, select the ones most relevant to your objective. Brainstorming helps you avoid **writer's block** (not having any ideas) and leads you to useful ideas. If you encounter writer's block, get up and move around or do some form of physical exercise. These activities may give you a fresh start. Illustration 3-1, page 73, depicts the results of a brainstorming session at City Department Store.

Nonstop Writing

Write something, anything, to maintain a flow of ideas when using nonstop writing. Nonstop writing is also referred to as freewriting. If you experience writer's block again, write *I can't think of anything to write* over and over until an idea comes to you. At the end of a set period of time (ten minutes, for example) of nonstop writing, underline anything in your notes that you think may be useful. Repeat the process several times. Then study the underlined notes to determine their relevance.

Bubble Writing

Write your objective inside a large bubble (circle) at the center of a page. Write main ideas that relate to the objective in smaller connected bubbles. In smaller bubbles, write spin-off ideas. Illustration 3-2, page 74, shows bubble writing.

Select Ideas

Carefully evaluate and select the pertinent ideas from among those you generated. Some ideas are more relevant than others. The most important idea becomes the main point of the message.

Sometimes your audience may consist of distinctly separate groups. Your message interests each group for different reasons. Decide which is most desirable: sending a different message to each group, sending a

Illustration 3-1 **Brainstorming**

GRAND-OPENING HOOPLA

EXTRA LONG HOURS

FREE SNACKS

LIVE BANDS

FRIENDLY STAFF

CELEBRITY VISIT

FREE PARKING

GIFT WRAPPING

EXTRA 20% DISCOUNT

CDS CHARGE CARD

25% DISCOUNT COUPONS

NEW DEPARTMENTS

CDS KEY CHAINS

SNAZZY COLORS

MALLWIDE 10% DISCOUNT

EXTRA STAFF

message targeted to only one group, or sending a message that appeals to all groups. The emphasis of your message may change according to your audience. Again, consider the City Department Store case.

Example: The objective of the message is to persuade receivers to shop at CDS. The main idea is the grand opening. Supportive points include special discounts on purchases and customer incentives, such as free snacks and gifts. New departments and a friendly staff are important services that encourage customers to return. These ideas support the message objective.

Illustration 3-2 **Bubble Writing**

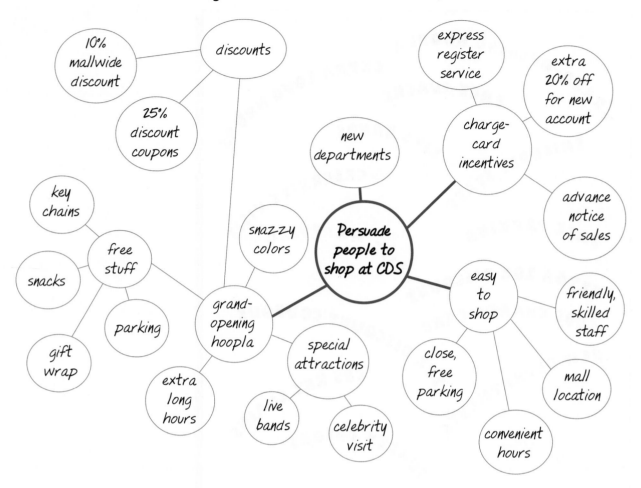

Organize the Information

After gathering, evaluating, and choosing information to support your ideas, you begin the fourth activity: Select an organizational pattern. The organizational pattern provides a logical framework for your ideas. A logical framework helps receivers understand and remember your message. Once you decide on an effective organizational pattern, develop an outline of your message.

Direct and Indirect Patterns of Organization

The direct and indirect patterns are two basic patterns of organization. The pattern you choose depends, in part, on how you expect your reader to react to the message content.

The **direct pattern** of organization is appropriate for messages containing good, neutral, or routine news. Two types of messages often use the direct pattern:

- Messages that say yes to a receiver's request
- Messages that inquire about products or services

The direct pattern of organization opens with the main idea. Supporting information that explains or clarifies the main idea comes next. Finally, as shown in the following example, the message closes on a positive note.

Example: Your valuable new City Department Store charge card is enclosed. For your protection, you must call our credit security line at 800-555-0196 to activate your new card. Once you have activated your card, you may make purchases in any department. You will receive a bonus discount of 5 percent on your very first purchase.

The **indirect pattern** of organization is appropriate when a message contains unfavorable news, such as a denial of a receiver's request. The indirect pattern of organization opens with a pleasant or neutral statement called a **buffer.** The buffer should attract the receiver's attention. Supporting (explanatory) information follows the buffer and prepares the receiver for unfavorable news (the main idea). Then comes the unfavorable news. When possible, follow the unfavorable news with additional supporting information. Supporting information should neutralize or soften the impact of the unfavorable news. The message closes on a positive note as shown in the next example.

Example: Thank you for shopping at City Department Store. Your special orders are always welcome. However, the HIGH ELEGANCE style you ordered has been discontinued by the manufacturer. After checking with the outlet broker for the region, we were unable to obtain the dress. You may be interested in a similar style (by GLITZY) that we can order for your consideration. Please call Brenda at 555-0105 to place an order for overnight delivery.

A variation of the indirect pattern is used for persuasive messages. Persuasive messages open with a statement that attracts the receiver's attention. Next comes supporting information, designed to convince the receiver. Finally, the message asks the receiver to take action.

Action statements invite the receiver to perform such tasks as purchasing a product or making a donation. Note the supporting information and action statements in the following example:

Example: Contribute money to your community schools without spending an extra dime! At your request, City Department Store will donate to the local school district 3 percent of every charge-card purchase you make in December. Just apply the enclosed sticker to the front of your CDS charge card, and use your CDS charge card as you normally would.

Traditional and Indented Outline Formats

An **outline** lists key terms that represent the ideas for your message. Use key terms, not complete sentences, in an outline to represent your ideas. The outline helps you decide where to put what. Revise an outline as many

Timely Tip

In the indirect plan, providing supporting information generally is appropriate both before *and* after the main idea is stated.

times as necessary to ensure that your message is complete. The length and detail of each outline are determined by the complexity of the message—the more complex the message, the longer the outline.

The **traditional outline format** uses indented numbers, letters, and spacing to identify message parts. A traditional outline moves from general ideas to specific ideas. Each progressive indention represents information that is more specific than the previous information.

Illustration 3-3 shows a traditional outline format. The information is organized in the direct pattern to present good, neutral, or routine news.

Illustration 3-3 Traditional Outline Format—Direct Pattern

Organization of Message Content	Message Parts
I. Good, Neutral, or Routine News	Opening: main idea
II. General Information Supporting I	Middle:
A. Specific Information Supporting II	supporting information
1. Details supporting IIA	supporting information
2. Details supporting IIA	supporting information
B. Specific Information Supporting II	supporting information
III. Friendly Ending	Closing

The **indented outline format,** an informal presentation, shows the progression from general to specific through indentions and spacing. The indented outline format does not use numbers and letters to organize ideas. Illustration 3-4 shows the indented outline format. In this illustration, unfavorable news is organized in the indirect pattern.

Illustration 3-4 Indented Outline Format—Indirect Pattern

Organization of Message Content	Message Parts
Neutral Statement	Opening: buffer
General Information Leading to Unfavorable News	Middle Part 1:
Specific Supporting Information	supporting information
Details supporting specific information	supporting information
Details supporting specific information	supporting information
Unfavorable News	Middle Part 2: main idea
General Information to Neutralize	Middle Part 3:
Unfavorable News	supporting information
Friendly Ending	Closing

Germany

German residents expect punctuality from everyone. Therefore, you should arrive on time for every social and business meeting. In addition to punctuality, you will observe other business rules or patterns, including the following:

- Agendas are established and strictly followed. To be considered a potential client, you must arrive at a meeting with a fully documented report, including visuals.
- Last names and appropriate titles are used. Greetings often are more formal than ordinarily would be used in the United States. Usually everyone shakes hands upon arrival and departure. Use Herr (Mr.) or Frau (Mrs. or Miss). Since titles are important, use titles correctly. For example, address Diane Price who has a Ph.D. as Frau Professor Doctor Price.
- Everyone assumes a "role" in meetings. Never try to switch roles during a meeting. For example, if you are a marketing person, do not try to address engineering issues. Another example may be that a colleague or you are serving as a "customer advocate"; if so, then remain in that role even to the point of sitting on the customer's side of the table.

You will tend to put your German business hosts at ease when you demonstrate a willingness to adopt their meeting patterns and behaviors.

Section 2: COMPOSE A DRAFT

After planning your message, you are ready to begin the second major CBO step, *Compose a Draft*. The secret of writing a draft is to start with your outline and to expand on your ideas. Now is the time to consider the following:

- Vocabulary
- Sentence construction
- Paragraph assembly
- Paragraph location

Choose Words

The first activity in composing a draft is selecting words that reflect the six *C*s of effective messages. Concrete words promote understanding. Words that invoke sight, sound, taste, smell, and touch create interest and help the receiver form a mental picture. Positive words are especially important when the news is negative. Select words that support the message objective and are appropriate for the audience.

Construct Sentences

The second activity in composing a draft is constructing sentences. A **sentence** is a group of related words that contains a subject

Plan a Message
Compose a Draft
- Choose Words
- Construct Sentences
- Assemble Paragraphs
- Choose Paragraph
- Locations
Complete a Message

Culture Frame

Be careful to speak in complete sentences because the end of a sentence (often the final word) is especially important in German.

and a verb and expresses a complete thought. A sentence is a grammatically independent unit. A **topic sentence** expresses the main idea.

Notice how the topic sentence in the next example captures the receiver's attention and states the main idea.

Example: If you enjoy people, if you thrive on challenges, if you want a long-term career, then CDS may be the employer for you.

Supporting sentences provide detail to explain or reinforce the topic sentence. The following sentences expand on the main idea of the topic sentence from the previous example.

Example: Current openings include positions for sales associates, credit analysts, and display designers. Bring your résumé to Herman Sanchez, Personnel Specialist, on the third floor of City Department Store at Blackhawk Mall.

A **concluding sentence**, such as the following one, summarizes the main idea.

Example: Build your career at City Department Store.

Understanding how to arrange sentences for coherence and emphasis will help you compose a draft of your message.

Transitionals are words and phrases that help readers move smoothly from one thought to the next. Use transitionals in the following ways:

- To clarify sequencing
- To emphasize a comparison
- To introduce a contrast
- To present a result
- To add more information

Table 3-1 shows common transitional words and their relationship categories.

Table 3-1 Transitionals and Their Relationships

Addition	Contrast	Example	Sequence	Comparison	Result or Consequence
additionally	however	for example	first	likewise	accordingly
also	nevertheless	for instance	second	similarly	as a result
besides	nonetheless	in fact	third		consequently
furthermore	otherwise		next		therefore
in addition	yet		then		thus
moreover			finally		

Voice

Evaluate the communication situation before deciding whether to use the active voice or the passive voice in your message. The active voice generally attracts more attention and provides greater clarity and conciseness than the passive voice. However, the passive voice may be more **diplomatic** (tactful) in some instances. Compare the clarity of the following examples:

Examples:

Passive Voice	***Active Voice***
Today the City Department Store charge card was applied for by 100 customers.	Today 100 customers applied for the City Department Store charge card.

Length

Generally, short sentences are emphatic and attention-getting. However, paragraphs consisting only of short sentences are choppy and hard to read. Long sentences may be difficult to remember or to understand. Average sentences contain 13 to 20 words. Vary the length of your sentences within the paragraph to maintain the receiver's interest.

Assemble Paragraphs

The third activity in composing a draft is assembling paragraphs. A standard **paragraph** consists of a topic sentence, supporting sentences, and a concluding sentence that relate to one main idea. One topic sentence per paragraph stresses the main idea. The supporting and concluding sentences add interest and maintain coherence. To keep a receiver's attention, limit paragraphs to four to six lines. To emphasize a point, an occasional paragraph may consist of a single sentence.

Culture Frame

On German letterhead, a small telephone symbol ☎ often appears instead of the word *Telefon*.

Placement

Receivers notice and remember information placed at the start or the end of a message. A topic sentence at the beginning of a paragraph orients the reader to the content of the paragraph. Thus, the beginning of a paragraph is the typical position for a topic sentence. In the following example, the sentences that follow the topic sentence provide explanatory information.

Example: *You have won $500!* Yes, your name was drawn as the lucky winner during our Blackhawk Mall summer celebration. Simply visit the information booth located at the north entrance to obtain your $500 mall certificate.

Sometimes presenting supporting information before the topic sentence is more effective. When the supporting information is presented first, the supporting sentences lead to the topic sentence. In the next example, note how the topic sentence serves as a summary of the preceding information.

Example: If you have a special occasion or need to replenish your wardrobe but don't have the time to shop, we can help. If you have a closet full of clothes but nothing seems to match, we can help. If you need special sizes or specialty clothes, we can help. Call CDS now to make an appointment with your personal wardrobe consultant.

Sequence

Sequence sentences within a paragraph to help the receiver understand the order of the information. Typical sequencing arrangements include time, logic, cause and effect, and comparison and contrast.

Time

Time refers to order of occurrence. For **chronological order,** arrange events from the least recent to the most recent (oldest to newest). For **reverse chronological order,** arrange events from the most recent to the least recent (newest to oldest). Time sequencing is the most effective arrangement for historical events and progress reports. The following example is from a progress report presented in chronological order.

Example: By September 1, the CEO and the department heads had placed each department on the organizational chart. By September 30, the CEO and the department heads had developed and confirmed departmental objectives. The CEO notified department heads on October 18 to prepare their staffing recommendations.

Logic

When organizing ideas rather than specific actions or events, use a logic pattern. Logic organizes information in reasoned, ordered patterns. The following patterns are ways to arrange ideas by logic:

- Familiar to less familiar points
- Simple to more complex points
- Less important to more important points
- General to specific points
- Specific to general points

The next example follows a general-to-specific logic pattern.

Example: Teenagers need jobs! The Mayor's Council on Teen Employment has released the latest report. Sixty-five percent of the teens in our city who want jobs are unemployed. City Department Store and the Blackhawk Mall will organize and sponsor a Teen Job Fair from April 20 to 23. Call 555-0106 for more information.

Cause and Effect

The cause-and-effect arrangement first explains why something happened (the cause) and then describes the result of the occurrence (the effect). Research reports and proposals, such as the following example, are often organized in cause-and-effect arrangements.

Example: Road construction has blocked the main entrance of Blackhawk Mall for the past three weeks. Therefore, customers cannot conveniently enter the mall. As a result, the number of mall visitors is down 40 percent over this same period last year.

Timely Tip

The *effect-and-cause* arrangement uses opposite logic to the *cause-and-effect* pattern. The *effect-and-cause* arrangement begins with the effect and leads to the cause.

Comparison and Contrast

A comparison arrangement shows the *similarities* between objects, ideas, or situations. A contrast arrangement shows the *differences* between objects, ideas, or situations. Two situations appropriate for comparison-and-contrast arrangements are sales messages and purchase justifications. Notice how the next example persuades through the compare-and-contrast method.

Example: Our version costs $99.95; their version costs $159.95. Our store provides 24-hour catalog service; their store does not.

Choose Paragraph Locations

The fourth activity in composing a draft is choosing paragraph locations. Messages have three basic parts: the opening, the middle, and the closing. Openings and closings are the places of emphasis. The middle of the message may contain several paragraphs of supporting or explanatory information. Review the objective of your message; then position sentences within paragraphs and paragraphs within messages to meet your communication goals.

The Opening

The opening and the closing are the most important parts of a message. At the **opening,** the receiver decides whether to continue reading or listening. The purpose of the opening is to capture the receiver's attention. A long opening does not invite further reading or listening. Occasionally, a one-sentence opening paragraph is a good way to attract the receiver's attention.

Example: You, the preferred customer of City Department Store, now have the opportunity to set your own prices.

Focus on the receiver by using the *you* attitude. A *you* opening immediately draws the receiver into the message and demonstrates your interest in the receiver.

When the objective of the message is to relay favorable news, use the direct pattern and give the good news immediately.

Example: Congratulations! You won the City Department Store $5,000 scholarship in retail studies.

Use the indirect pattern to relay unfavorable news. Open with a positive or neutral buffer. A buffer opening allows you to explain before you present the unfavorable news. The following example shows the opening of a letter that will ultimately refuse a charge-card application.

Example: Thank you for applying for a City Department Store charge card.

When you want to persuade someone to do something, open with an attention-getting statement. The next example announces the opening of a new discount department at CDS.

Example: Run up some savings at CDS!

The Middle

The information in the **middle** of the message contains the explanation that supports the message objective and promotes the main idea. The middle generally consists of one or more paragraphs. The number of paragraphs depends on how much information is necessary to achieve the objective. To maintain receiver interest, limit each of the middle paragraphs to four to six lines.

In the direct pattern, used in the next example, the supporting information follows and clarifies the main idea.

Example: Take advantage of the great values in the new discount department at City Department Store. Overstocks of top-quality merchandise from every department are available at substantial discounts. Save 10 to 50 percent off our normal low prices.

In the indirect pattern, supporting information precedes as well as follows the main idea. The indirect pattern downplays unfavorable news by offering supporting information to soften the impact. In the following example, note how favorable news on a separate but related topic is included. The related supporting information directs the receiver's attention away from the unfavorable news.

Example: Your plan for improving customer satisfaction in the CDS shoe department has been evaluated by the marketing staff. Currently, customer survey results do not support the suggested approach. However, Horace Green, the marketing manager, is impressed by your idea of a Sock-Club Card; he will research the practicalities of implementation.

The Closing

The **closing** of a message is as important as the opening. Keep your closing paragraph short. Maintain a courteous, positive tone to reflect sincerity and promote goodwill.

Examples: Please use the enclosed customer-appreciation coupon on your next purchase. The 25 percent discount applies to all in-store merchandise—even sale items. Thank you for shopping at CDS.

Your community's support of fundraisers during the last semester raised 50 percent of the School Library Technology Drive. By using your CDS Value Card this holiday season, you and City Department Store can finish the job.

Expanding on the ideas in your outline is the key to composing message drafts. However, suitable vocabulary, correct sentence construction, logically assembled paragraphs, and appropriate paragraph locations are what make the difference between an adequate draft and an effective draft. Refer to Illustration 3-5, page 83, for an example of a paragraph draft.

1. Assume you will find errors; this assumption will help you find the errors.
2. Start proofreading with the first line on the page. Place a ruler or straightedge under one line at a time so that you can see and concentrate only on those words.
3. Read the material aloud word for word.
4. Check numerical information, such as dates, dollar amounts, and order numbers. Proofread each digit; carefully look for **transposed** (reversed order) numbers as well as incorrect numbers. Recheck all calculations.
5. Use a dictionary to confirm spelling and meaning if you hesitate on a word as you proofread. Hesitation often signals a misspelling or an inappropriate word choice.
6. Put the document away. For a good news message, wait at least 30 minutes before reading the message again. For a bad news message, wait at least 60 minutes before reading the message again. Sometimes errors that were not obvious in the first reading will be apparent during later readings.
7. Ask for proofreading assistance from someone with good writing skills.

Use Proofreader Marks

Indicate changes directly on the draft by using proofreader marks. These standard marks, shown in Illustration 3-6, page 86, make editing more efficient. Standardized proofreader marks also enable someone other than the document originator to key material from an edited copy.

Edit

Editing, the second activity in composing a message, involves reading your message draft carefully and using proofreader marks to indicate needed changes. Analyze your draft from the receiver's point of view. Make sure you have clearly stated how the reader will benefit. Refer to the Format Guide for appropriate document formats. Ensure that your message reflects the six *C*s of effective messages.

1. **Incorporate courtesy.** Does the message reflect the *you* attitude? Have the receiver's needs been addressed?
2. **Check for clarity.** Is the vocabulary easily understood? Do the words clearly express your intended meaning? Do sentence structure, length, and placement maintain receiver interest? Does the message support your objective?
3. **Rephrase for conciseness.** Are unnecessary words eliminated? Is the active voice used in most instances? Is passive voice used appropriately?
4. **Choose concrete words.** Are specific words used to build mental pictures for the receiver? Are any technical terms suitable for the audience?
5. **Check for correct content and mechanics.** Is the information accurate? Are the grammar, spelling, and punctuation correct? Does the overall appearance give a positive impression?

PROOFREADER MARKS

Meaning	Example
align	‖ 1. Milwaukee Bucks ‖ 2. Detroit Pistons
begin new paragraph	¶Call a CDs personal shopper at 555-0105.
capitalize	mr. ewald
change copy as indicated	~~compare~~ contrast
close up	p. m.
delete and close up	conveniient
double-space copy	Enclosure DS c Roger Tai
insert	accomodate (m)
insert apostrophe	Laura's message
insert comma	edit revise and proofread
insert period	Dr Geisler
insert space	hisfile
let the original material stand	~~standard~~ form *or* stet ~~standard~~ form
make bold	bf final copy
move copy as indicated	I do agree (certainly)
move left	File the petition.
move right	File the petition.
single-space copy	Markham Goodwin SS Vice President
spell out	(5) sp
transpose letters or words	recieve
use italics	ital Effective Communication for Colleges
use lowercase	Psychology Class

Illustration 3-6 **Proofreader Marks**

6. **Review for completeness.** Does the message provide the information necessary for the receiver to take action? Does the message answer *who*, *what*, *when*, *where*, *why*, and *how*? Does the message promote goodwill?

Review Illustration 3-7, the edited version of Illustration 3-5.

Illustration 3-7 Edited Version of Draft in Illustration 3-5

Revise

Revising, the third activity in composing a message, involves making the changes that you marked during the editing process. Once the changes are complete, reedit the draft to ensure appropriate communication of your message. Repeat the editing and revising activities as often as necessary. *Good communicators often complete the proofreading, editing, and revising activities three or more times.*

Finalize

The fourth and last activity of completing your message is to finalize the message. The final message represents you and your organization. Not only the content but also the appearance of the final message creates a lasting impression. Make sure that the impression is positive.

Select Acceptable Format

Prepare the final message in an acceptable format. (Format is discussed in the Format Guide.) Continue to proofread to ensure that the final message is perfect. Your signature on a document signifies that you have approved the content and appearance of the document.

Timely Tip

There are days when the result is so bad that no fewer than five revisions are required. In contrast, when I'm greatly inspired, only four revisions are needed.

—John Kenneth Galbraith
Harpers Magazine
November 1975

Proofread Final Copy

Proofread the final copy one last time. If you have been working steadily on a message (to meet a deadline, for example), ask a knowledgeable coworker to proofread the final message. A "fresh" reading before you transmit the message may save you later embarrassment. See Illustration 3-8, the final paragraph from Illustration 3-7.

Illustration 3-8 **Final Copy of Edited Draft in Illustration 3-7**

Add savings and convenience to your shopping experience! City Department Store invites you, our preferred customer, to apply for the CDS Value Card. As a CDS Value-Card holder, you will receive the following:

- Special discounts

- Express service at registers

- Advance notice of sales

Begin saving immediately. Apply today!

Summary

The Communication-by-Objectives approach is a whole-into-parts method that breaks the message development process into three major steps. Each CBO step includes four specific activities.

Plan a Message
- Identify the Objective
- Visualize the Audience
- Gather Supporting Information
- Organize the Information

Compose a Draft
- Choose Words
- Construct Sentences
- Assemble Paragraphs
- Choose Paragraph Locations

Complete a Message
- Proofread
- Edit
- Revise
- Finalize

Complete Communication Skills Development 3, pages 99–100. For additional verb review, see the Reference Guide, pages 415–419.

Exercises

3-1

Communication Situation: As the president of the Student Marketing Association, you will prepare a message to persuade other members to serve as volunteer courtesy clerks during the Celebrity Volunteer Day at the City Department Store. CDS will donate to your association 2 percent of the sales made between 9 a.m. and 1 p.m. on Saturday, April 3. The association will use the donation to help pay the cost of sending members to the state competitive events.

Part A

Directions: In the space provided, write the message objective.

Part B

Directions: Using the CBO approach, visualize your intended audience. In the space provided, list a minimum of three characteristics that are reasonable to assume about your intended receivers.

Part C

Directions: In the space provided, use brainstorming, bubble writing, or nonstop writing to generate ideas for this persuasive message.

Part D

Directions: After you have generated ideas, put a square around those ideas that best support your objective.

3 - 2

Communication Situation: Inform students that the newly remodeled workout facility is now open. Supporting information includes:

- 10,000-square-foot facility
- Open 6 a.m. to 10 p.m. Monday through Friday; 8 a.m. to 8 p.m.
- Saturday and Sunday
- Olympic-sized lap pool
- State-of-the-art equipment and machines
- Jacuzzi and sauna
- Personal trainers available for consultation
- Nutritionist on site
- Free aerobics, yoga, tai-chi, and spinning classes
- Nutritional shakes, drinks, and snacks available in snack room

Part A

Directions: In the space provided, write the message objective.

Part B

Directions: Visualize your audience. Identify characteristics of the audience.

Part C

Directions: In the space provided, use the direct pattern and the traditional outline format to organize your information.

Exercises

3-3

Part A

Directions: Put brackets around the topic sentence in each paragraph. Write an appropriate transitional word or phrase wherever a blank is provided.

Direct Line provides you with instant access to financial information and

services. _____, dial 1-800-555-0001 on your

touch-tone telephone. _____, enter your personal code

to access the information directory.

Follow the verbal prompts to access desired account information.

You can, _____, request your account balance

or current interest rate. _____, you can change investment

contributions or options.

Part B

Directions: Put brackets around the topic sentence. Write an appropriate transitional word or phrase wherever a blank is provided.

_____ the active voice helps create clear and concise

sentences, sometimes you may choose the passive voice. Passive voice,

_____, reduces the likelihood of your message

expressing a direct accusation. _____, the passive

voice is appropriate when you want to express sympathy. When you select the

passive voice, _____ make the subject receive the

action expressed in the verb. _____, use a form of

the *be* verb. _____, you may elect to add a *by phrase*.

Exercises

3 - 4

Part A

Directions: Arrange the sentences in the order that will make the most sense to the receiver. In the space provided, indicate which sentence should come first, which sentence second, and so on. For example, if you think that sentence 3 should be first, write "1" in the space to the right of sentence 3.

Sentences   **New Order of Arrangement**

1. Do not make business appointments or send priority mail during July, August, and December; most German residents take long vacations during those months.   _____

2. German businesspeople take business meetings seriously and expect punctuality from everyone.   _____

3. Most business appointments are scheduled between 11 a.m. and 1 p.m. or between 3 p.m. and 5 p.m.   _____

4. Therefore, make appointments well in advance and arrive on time.   _____

Part B

Directions: Arrange the sentences in the order that will make the most sense to the receiver. In the space provided, indicate which sentence should come first, which sentence second, and so on. For example, if you think that sentence 3 should be first, write "1" in the space to the right of sentence 3.

Sentences   **New Order of Arrangement**

1. When coming from the airport, train station, or autobahn, you observe a modern city that is clean and tidy.   _____

2. After you complete your Dusseldorf visit, share your impressions with others.   _____

3. Start planning a trip to Dusseldorf today, where you can experience an attractive city filled with cheerful, enthusiastic citizens.   _____

Exercises

4. On closer inspection, you will discover the harmony of old and new. _____

5. Museums, banks, theaters, and large department stores are showplaces in the modern city; old alleys filled with quaint art galleries, boutiques, and taverns are visible in the older sections. _____

3 - 5 Part A

Directions: Write the letter of the sentence from each pair that best represents a direct pattern opening and that reflects the six *C*s of effective messages.

1. **a.** When you speak with a German resident, never use titles incorrectly.

   b. When you speak with a German resident, always use titles correctly.

2. **a.** We would appreciate it if you would send us the blueprints soon.

   b. Please send the blueprints by next week.

3. **a.** Culbertson & Davidson plans to offer a two-day workshop, "Developing Your Communication Skills."

   b. Please attend Culbertson & Davidson's two-day workshop, "Developing Your Communication Skills."

4. **a.** I would appreciate it if you would copy these reports.

   b. Please copy these reports.

5. **a.** Thank you for your order.

   b. We acknowledge receipt of your order.

Part B

Directions: Write the letter of the sentence from each pair that best represents an indirect pattern opening and that reflects the six *C*s of effective messages.

1. **a.** You should have called us when you had a problem with the alarm system.

   b. The Marco Alarm System guarantees a response within five minutes.

2. **a.** Your application has been evaluated carefully by our personnel director.

   b. Your application looks good, but someone else was better qualified for the job.

Exercises

3. a. The tourism board always provides a complete promotional package.

  b. The tourism board never fails to provide a complete promotional package.

4. a. We have not received your payment from last month's invoice.

  b. You have a long-standing reputation for prompt payment.

5. a. Thank you for considering Kugel and Associates in your employment search.

  b. The position for which you applied has been filled.

3-6 **Directions:** Collect two business letters; provide the following information for each letter. Prepare to discuss your findings in class.

  a. Identify the message objective (to persuade, to inform, or to obtain information).

  b. Identify the message pattern (direct or indirect).

  c. Label the opening, explanation, and closing.

  d. Underline the topic sentence in each paragraph.

  e. Circle words that appear to be barriers to effective communication.

3-7 **Directions:** Use proofreader marks to edit the following paragraph. (Refer to Illustration 3-6, page 86, for a listing of proofreader marks.) Then use the space provided to rewrite the paragraph.

Knowing message qualities and organizational patterns enhanse a commuincators proofreading, edit, revising, abilities a communicator prepares a final message buy proofreading editing revising, & proofreading the draft. Then the communicator evaluates the message too determine content accruacy and lay out attractiveness using standard marks marks to indicate any changes necessary. Efective communicators proofread one last time before transmitting the final message.

Internet *Challenge*

3-1 Directions: Search online sites for information helpful to doing business in Germany. On a separate sheet of paper, write a short article summarizing what you should know about gifts, gestures, and dress code when you plan to work in Germany. Try the following key phrases in your search:

- German protocol
- Business entertaining in Germany
- Working in Germany

3-2 Directions: Use the key phrase **Venn diagrams overview** and locate at least three online sources that discuss these questions: What is a Venn diagram? How is a Venn diagram used?

On a separate sheet of paper, summarize your findings and give reference citations. Use one of the citation styles shown in the Reference Guide.

InfoTrac

Directions: Using the InfoTrac search, locate an article that discusses **overcoming writer's block.** On a separate sheet of paper, summarize the article and give a reference citation. Use one of the citation styles shown in the Reference Guide.

WebTUTOR Advantage

Directions: Access your WebTutor Advantage product. Complete the short-answer portion for Chapter 3 and send the answers to your instructor.

Case Studies

3 - 1

Communication Situation: You are an intern with the public relations director at a new resort (70000 Gulf Boulevard, Navarre, Florida 32566). In addition to being located on the white, sandy beaches of the Gulf of Mexico, the resort features an outstanding 18-hole golf course. The resort also offers guided recreational tours, including Landrum Deep Sea Fishing, Birding Tours, Island Walks, and Gulf Zoo Excursions. Guests are encouraged to stroll the beaches and to explore the island by bicycle.

You recently conducted a "Name-the-Resort-Contest," and Miss Elizabeth Scott (813 Jodi Avenue, Hammond, Louisiana 70403-8130) won the three-day visit. You need to notify Miss Scott that she is the winner; she must claim the reward between March 31 and May 1. To confirm her reservation, Miss Scott must call 1-800-555-0100.

Task A: Provide the following information:
  a. The objective of the message:

  b. The audience for the message:

  c. Supporting information:

Task B: Use the direct pattern and the traditional outline format to organize your information.

Case Studies

3 - 2

Communication Situation: You work Tuesday through Saturday, 1 p.m. to 9 p.m., in the Collections Department of the City Department Store. Your supervisor has asked you to write a message to CDS customers who are 30 days late in making a charge-card payment. In the letter, you must ask for a payment, remind the customer of the $30 fee for late payments, and offer to discuss the situation with the customer.

Your supervisor reminds you that these customers are important to CDS and would not have been issued a charge card if they had a poor credit rating. Your supervisor has also given you a brochure that summarizes the benefits of a CDS charge card: convenience of cash-free shopping, advance notification of sales, additional discounts on sale prices, and no interest charges when the customer pays the account in full each month.

Task A: Plan a message. Using key terms and phrases, complete the following activities:

a. Identify the objective of the message.

b. Visualize the audience. Name three characteristics of the audience.

c. List the supporting information you have.

d. Choose a pattern of organization (direct or indirect). Explain why that pattern is most appropriate.

Task B: In the space provided, organize the information in the indented outline format.

Communication Skills Development 3

NAME_____

Part A   Verb Usage

Directions: Underline the verb(s) in the independent clause(s) in each sentence. When a verb form is incorrect, write the correct verb form in the space that follows each statement.

1. What kind of message best serve an audience of business executives?

2. As you edit the message draft, you applied the six *C*s of effective messages.

3. The most important idea becomes the focus of the message.

4. Do not sacrifices completeness for conciseness in your messages.

5. After brainstorming, keep the good ideas and threw away the bad ideas.

6. Inquiries often follows the direct pattern of communication.

7. Knowing as much as possible about receivers are helpful.

8. For arranging sentences in a paragraph, chronological order are effective for historical events.

9. Each new topic appear in a new paragraph.

10. Tips includes using short sentences, active voice, and proper sequence.

11. The use of standard proofreader marks promote more efficient editing.

12. The indented outline format or the traditional outline format are appropriate for organizing ideas.

13. Transitional words and phrases promotes a smooth flow from one idea to the next.

14. When proofreading, content, mechanics, format, and meaning is important points to keep in mind.

15. The communication situation determines whether you use the active voice or the passive voice.

16. Progress reports, for example, are most effectively arranged by time.

17. An attention-getting statement attract a receiver's attention.

18. When information is organized in the indirect pattern, you provide an explanation first; then you present the main idea.

19. In the closing of your message, express sincerity and goodwill.

20. When you arrange information by time, you generally sequenced ideas in chronological order or in reverse chronological order.

Part B Skills Application

Directions: Underline each noun, pronoun, and verb usage error and each spelling error in the following memorandum. Write the correction above each error in the space provided. (Ordinarily, memos are single spaced. In this memo, extra space has been added for you to write corrections.)

TO: Travel Plus Staff
FROM: Maritza Santiago, Regional Manager
DATE: December 11, 20—
SUBJECT: Accuracy Guarantee

The accuracy guarantee that was implement in August has dramatically increased are business. Client's have frequently express there appreciation for our services buy recommending others too Travel Plus.

For all staff members to benefit from increased revenue, we must keep costs down—especially costs that can be controled by proofreading. As your process client documents, please remember that Travel Plus reimburses clients for inconveninces that the clients experience as a result of our errors. These kinds of errors cause a lose of money and goodwill. Therefore, accuracy is critical.

Verifying all numberical information with the original invoice and carefully filing all documents in the appropriate client folder not only reduces errors but also improves efficiency.

Do you has other ideas to improve client service without significantly increasing expenses? If you do, lets discuss them.

Chapter 4

Technology and Electronic Communication

Learning Objectives

1 Conduct efficient, productive Internet searches.

2 Explain the appropriate use of various transmission modes to communicate the written and spoken word effectively.

3 Practice netiquette.

COMMUNICATION PERSPECTIVES

Technology and Responsibility

Technology has always brought difficult changes to the way the world communicates. From the invention of cast metal movable type by Johannes Gutenberg in 1440, to the introduction of the typewriter, telegraph, telephone, and copier, we have had to adjust to new ways of doing things while making sure that the changes in methods and procedures would not impair or compromise what we wanted to say.

The introduction of modern word processing, which began in the early 1970s, the fax machine in the 1980s, and Internet e-mail in the 1990s have exposed many communications to a particular vulnerability that can lead to disaster. These technologies, which have yielded huge savings in time and effort, also make it all too easy to communicate the wrong information to the wrong people. Let's consider a few examples.

In 1986, a word processing operator in a large New York City law firm typed the amount in a draft of an amendment to a ship mortgage as $92,885.00. The correct amount was $92,885,000.00, a difference of $92,792,115.00. The draft was later used to prepare templates for a

101

number of similar amendments and other documents, and the error was propagated. This was a large, complicated transaction, and the time pressure was intense. Unbelievable as it may seem, no one among the many lawyers, lenders, and ship owners involved, or any of their support staffs, noticed the error until several years later when it became necessary to enforce the mortgages. A simple word processing typo that could have been corrected with a few keystrokes caused much embarrassment and a loss of many millions of dollars in litigation and settlement costs before the dispute was finally settled.

In 1997, the Phoenix office of the FBI intended to send a highly confidential memo to the U.S. Attorney's office. But the sender pressed the wrong speed dial button on the fax machine, and the memo was sent to every newspaper and television and radio station in the state.

Though modern technology makes it very easy to prepare and send communications, this ease of use imposes a heavy responsibility on everyone involved—from senior management to the person operating the word processor or sending the fax or e-mail—to be very careful.

- Ease of use is not a license to be careless.
- Small, simple mistakes can communicate a message you never intended to send.

Thomas J. Hawley, Attorney
Burke & Parsons

Section 1: THE INTERNET

Timely Tip

Many internet systems exist. When referencing a system that is not linked to *the* Internet, such as a local area network (LAN), write *internet* with a lowercase *i*.

The Internet was originally designed by the United States Department of Defense to maintain data communication among computer systems in case of nuclear war. The **Internet** is a global system that facilitates data transfer and communication services among interconnected computers called networks. A **network** is two or more computers and their related devices that are connected to share resources. The Internet is sometimes called a *network of networks* because the Internet is a collection of computer networks, each of which is composed of smaller computer networks. The Internet expands the reach of the smaller networks; and today, millions of people all over the world use the Internet to exchange, store, and retrieve information.

World Wide Web

In the late 1980s, the World Wide Web (WWW or the Web) was created at a research institute in Switzerland to organize the vast resources of the Internet. The **World Wide Web** is a collection of web sites that uses *servers* (computers) to provide graphics and text pages. **Web sites** provide documents formatted in a special script called Hypertext Markup Language (HTML); the sites typically incorporate colorful images, dynamic materials such as audio and video, and **hypertext** (highlighted words that link or connect related sites when activated). These characteristics enable Internet users to enter the world of multimedia at the click of a button.

Computer software programs called **browsers** provide easy access to the World Wide Web. Common browsers are Mosaic, Netscape Navigator, and Microsoft Internet Explorer.

One way to access the Internet from your computer is by a modem and an Internet service provider (ISP). A **modem** is a device that connects a computer to a telephone line in order to send and receive data, and an **ISP** is an organization that offers Internet access for a fee. Some ISPs are America Online (AOL), Microsoft Network (MSN), and EarthLink. A *cable modem* provides faster access to the Internet than does a dial-up modem because a cable modem plugs into a cable network and receives data over the same type of cable used for cable television. High-speed connections to the Internet are also available through a digital subscriber line (DSL). **DSL** is a permanent connection using special hardware and the copper wiring found in most homes and offices.

The location of each web site is indicated by its Uniform Resource Locator (URL). The **URL** specifies the **domain name**, the address of the site on the Web where resources such as documents and pictures are found. A domain name reflects a hierarchy of responsibility within the address, with each subgroup separated by periods. As you read a URL from left to right, you go up in the hierarchy to the top-level domain, the part that appears farthest to the right.

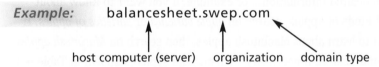

Example: balancesheet.swep.com

host computer (server)   organization   domain type

Timely Tip

Web page or **homepage** is the opening page(s) to a web site. *Homepage* is written as one word; *web site* and *web page* are two words.

Domains are determined according to some similarity (government agency, nonprofit institution, etc.) or by geographical location (country, territory, etc.) as shown in Table 4-1.

Table 4-1 Top-Level Internet Domains and Country Codes

Name	Description
.com	commercial entities
.edu	educational institutions
.gov	nonmilitary U.S. government agencies
.info	information-based services
.net	network providers
.org	nonprofit entities
.mil	U.S. military institutions
.ar	Argentina
.bw	Botswana
.cz	Czech Republic
.us	United States

Internet Searches

Timely Tip

When a URL doesn't seem to work, try deleting parts of the address starting at the right end of the address and stopping at every /. Activate the address. If you still cannot access the web site, try deleting up to the next /.

The Internet contains a wealth of information, but finding the information you want may be challenging. **Search engines** are user-friendly tools that locate resources on the Web based on **keywords** (words or phrases representative of a topic) supplied by the user. Unless you know something about search engines and searches, your efforts may result in considerable irrelevant information. Here are six popular search engine addresses.

http://www.google.com	http://search.msn.com
http://www.alltheweb.com	http://www.yahoo.com
http://www.askjeeves.com	http://www.webcrawler.com

Before you visit search engine sites, review these basic search strategies to optimize your search results:

1. Define your topic, and list words that are associated with the topic.
2. Investigate different search engines to determine which will meet your needs.
3. Choose a search engine based on your investigation of its features and capabilities. Once you activate the site, check the *help page* and the *advanced search page* to learn about features specific to that search engine.
4. Apply the tips from the site to conduct your search.
5. Use specific keywords to conduct the search. The more specific the keyword(s), the narrower the search. Keyword *phrases* are more likely to return desired information. For example, if you want to know about different kinds of apples, search on *apple varieties* or *varieties of apples*. If you want to learn about Macintosh apples, then search on *Macintosh apples*.
6. Refine your search, if necessary, by using the symbols shown in Table 4-2, page 105. These symbols work for most search engines and often improve your results.

Different search engines frequently produce different results. Use more than one search engine to gather information.

Acceptable Use Policies

Internet usage has grown rapidly with little or no supervision. Thus, files and sites may contain items that are illegal, defamatory, or potentially offensive to some people. Schools, libraries, and businesses that make the Internet available are requiring users to agree to specific conditions of Internet usage. These conditions, referred to as **acceptable use policies (AUPs)**, range from a basic set of rules to a comprehensive set of rules. Violating acceptable use policies may result in loss of access as well as other disciplinary or legal action. AUP coverage generally focuses on actions that are *not* permitted, such as the following:

- Sending or displaying offensive messages or pictures
- Using obscene language
- Harassing, insulting, or verbally attacking others

Table 4-2 Search Symbols and Their Functions

Symbol	Function
	Note: When using the following symbols in a search, insert a space *before* the symbol but not after the symbol.
+	The plus symbol (+) *adds* and finds pages with occurrences of *all* the words entered. *Example*: You want site references that mention both Elvis and Priscilla Presley. **Search entry:** +Elvis +Priscilla *Example*: You want site references that mention Elvis, Priscilla, and Graceland. **Search entry:** +Elvis +Priscilla +Graceland
−	The minus (−) symbol *subtracts* and finds pages with occurrences of one word but not the other. *Example*: You want site references that mention Elvis but not Priscilla. **Search entry:** +Elvis −Priscilla
+ −	The combination of the plus and minus symbols further targets desired information. *Example*: You want site references that mention Elvis and Priscilla but not Graceland. **Search entry:** +Elvis +Priscilla −Graceland
"	Enclosing phrases in quotation marks finds pages with the terms appearing exactly as entered. *Example*: You want site references that specifically refer to Elvis's greatest hits. **Search entry:** "Elvis's greatest hits"

- Damaging computers, computer systems, or computer networks
- Violating copyright laws
- Using another person's password
- Accessing another person's folders, work, or files without permission
- Revealing personal addresses or phone numbers without permission

Authoritative Research

The flexibility of the Web allows the publication of specialized or time-sensitive material more quickly, efficiently, and cost effectively than any other publication method. However, the Internet contains vast amounts of information. Anyone can post information on the Web, but no one validates the accuracy of the information or enforces the quality of the sites. In addition, web sites can be modified at any time; so you may quote from a web site only to return to the site and find that the passage you quoted has been deleted or revised. Thus, web site resources may be considered less authoritative than traditional print sources.

As a Web user, you need not only to find relevant information but also to determine its authority and accuracy. Sifting through vast amounts of information on the Web is not easy because search tools locate both authoritative (documented) research and research that is *not* documented but is presented as fact.

The ability to evaluate Internet resources is a valuable skill. The best way to develop your evaluating skill is to develop a familiarity with your topic. Examine a variety of sources, such as traditional print journals, books, and articles before you begin your Web investigation. This will help you detect erroneous or questionable information as you compare and select sources. You can relate how new information compares with what you already know.

When evaluating a site, print the information from the site. Then compare the printed Web material with traditional print sources. Use the evaluation criteria provided in Table 4-3, page 107, as you sort substandard information from valuable information.

Culture View

People's Republic of China

The Chinese writing system is a system based on characters not on an alphabet. A character is made up of strokes that are written in the same direction in a set order. Each character, regardless of the number of strokes, is given the same amount of space and is written with no space between characters. Typically, a Chinese character has two components: one that approximately classifies the meaning (the *radical*) and one that represents the sound. Although each character has a meaning, most individual characters do not represent a word. Most Chinese words are composed of at least two characters.

When a foreign word is introduced into the language, the Chinese almost always create a new Chinese word by "translating" the concept into characters rather than directly importing the word.

Learning to read and write Chinese can be a challenge—even to the Chinese. The process of simplifying characters to make them easier to read and write continues. Today, people who learn Chinese begin by learning *pinyin*. *Pinyin* is a phonetic system introduced by the Chinese government in the late 1950s to aid in pronunciation and understanding.

Section 2: COMMUNICATING THE WRITTEN WORD

E-mail, instant messaging, and facsimile transfer are routinely used to communicate the written word. **E-mail** (electronic mail) is a message that is transmitted within seconds by a computer to one or more receivers anywhere in the world. E-mail is **asynchronous**, which means that a sender can transmit a message at any time; and a receiver can read and respond at his or her convenience. **Instant messaging**, a by-product of e-mail, enables users to identify people online and to exchange messages with them in **real time** (right now). **Facsimile** transfer (fax) is the transmission of digitized text and images to be received as hardcopy in its original image. The written word also may be transmitted by **personal digital assistants** (PDAs) and web sites.

Table 4-3 Web Site Evaluation Criteria

Evaluation Criteria	Evaluation Discussion
• **Purpose** Who is the audience? What is the primary purpose of the site? What biases are evident?	Web sites typically fall into these categories: informational (presents factual information); advocacy (influences public opinion); business (promotes products); news (provides current newsworthy information); or personal (presents individual information).
• **Authorship/Sponsorship** Who is the author? Are the author's qualifications satisfactory? Is the author associated with a reputable institution or organization? Who is responsible for content? Does a link indicate who is hosting or sponsoring the web site? Does the host or sponsor promote special interests that influence objectivity? Can the author/sponsor be contacted?	The author's credentials, including relevant institutional affiliations and previous publications and experiences, should be easily identifiable. Sponsor or host information should be evident. The site should contain or link to contact information, such as e-mail addresses, postal addresses, and/or phone numbers.
• **Currency** When was the web site created? How often has the site been revised? Does the site have an update/change page that lists all modifications? Is the material current for the topic?	Topic areas of rapid development require current information, so frequent updates may be desirable to reflect changes. Other topic areas may not require frequent updates, especially when the information is historical. Revision dates and dates indicating the collection of statistical data should be listed.
• **Content** Is the content organized logically? Are the main points presented clearly? Have the basic rules of grammar, spelling, and composition been applied? Is the writing style appropriate for the topic and audience? Does the article present a new perspective or summarize other sources? Is the information fact, opinion, or advertising? Are the ideas presented in line with other similar works?	Credibility is enhanced when the information is presented in standard language with correct grammar and spelling and clear, coherent organization. Separating fact (verifiable information) from opinion is important. Information that radically departs from similar sources requires investigation.
• **Reliability** Is the document well researched and supported by evidence? Can the sources for factual information (works cited) be authenticated? Has the site been reviewed or ranked by a reviewing agency? Does the site contain working, up-to-date, relevant links?	References to peer or agency reviews, citations of legitimate works, and operational links to other timely resources are important to verify the reliability of the site.

Electronic Mail (E-mail)

E-mail, which began as a personal, sometimes cryptic form of correspondence, has evolved into a primary form of business communication because of these desirable characteristics: *convenience*, *efficient delivery*, and *cost savings*.

E-mail systems are convenient and easy to use. In addition, messages can be delivered within seconds to e-mail destinations around the world; and a recipient does not have to be available "to take" a message. E-mail messages can be delivered to one person or to a large audience (e-mail lists) quickly and efficiently. Finally, delivery by e-mail costs considerably less than delivery by traditional mail or by telephone.

E-mail is business correspondence. The image your e-mail message conveys is important because the message represents *your organization* as well as *you*. In fact, e-mail may be the only contact you have with a receiver; so you want your e-mail messages to be opened, read, and acted upon. Understanding when and how to use e-mail in a professional environment will help you to achieve your goals.

E-mail is good choice when delivery time is important, the content is brief and routine, and privacy is not an issue.

Timely Tip

External e-mail systems enable users to communicate both inside and outside an organization; internal e-mail systems allow users to communicate only inside an organization.

E-mail Addresses

To send e-mail messages over the Internet, you need to establish an e-mail account and determine an e-mail address, also known as a *screen name*. An e-mail address has these parts: **user i.d.** or **account name** (user's name), @ symbol, and **domain** of the host on which the user has an account. The user i.d. is placed to the left of the @ symbol. The domain appears to the right of the @ symbol and has more than one part, with each part separated by a period. The first of the following example addresses is read as *c m brantmil at p cola dot gulf dot net*.

Examples: user i.d.   domain   user i.d.   domain

cmbrantmil@pcola.gulf.net *or* **millerassociates@pcola.gulf.net**

Before deciding on an e-mail address, think carefully about the image you want to project. Your e-mail address for business purposes should project a positive, professional image and include your name, as shown in the preceding examples. A personal address may be a "fun" name, a nickname, or a name that reflects your personal interests, such as wiseone@pcola.gulf.net.

Timely Tip

You are likely to use e-mail for business, personal, and educational purposes. Using different screen names for different purposes is a good idea.

E-mail Appropriateness

Consider the topic and how the receiver will perceive the information as an e-mail message. Is e-mail the best choice to confirm a meeting with team members? notify employees of a layoff? send a note of congratulations? persuade coworkers to contribute to a company-sponsored charity?

Evaluate the circumstance before choosing e-mail by asking yourself: *In this circumstance, how would I feel if I received this information as an e-mail?* The following messages *are not* suitable as e-mail messages and may be handled better as a phone call, a face-to-face conversation, or a paper-based document.

- **Negative or emotionally significant messages.** Messages that contain negative or emotionally significant information, such as job actions, employee reprimands, condolences, and other bad news, should not be handled as an e-mail.

- **Time-sensitive messages.** Not everyone reads e-mail frequently during the day, so a quick delivery doesn't guarantee a quick response. Messages that require immediate acknowledgment, such as short-notice meeting cancellations and appointment changes, are better delivered by telephone.

- **Long and/or complicated documents.** When a long, complicated document is sent through electronic mail, the document should be prepared as an attachment. An **attachment** is a separate file that accompanies the e-mail message. The actual e-mail message is brief and refers to the attached document and its purpose. The receiver downloads the file to read the message offline. Seek permission from a receiver *before* sending an attachment.

- **Confidential messages.** E-mail can be intercepted by an unintended receiver, and e-mail messages can be retrieved even when they have been "deleted." Messages can be easily forwarded, printed, and distributed without the sender's knowledge. In addition, employers can legally monitor company e-mail; and many organizations store e-mail that can be accessed years later. *E-mail is not private.*

- **Messages that may be misinterpreted.** Body language, tone of voice, and other verbal clues that can clarify the intent of a message, are absent in e-mail. Messages that need nonverbal cues for clarification should not be sent as e-mail.

Timely Tip

When you receive an attachment, *do not* open the file until you have run a virus scan to ensure the attachment is clean.

Effective E-mail Messages

E-mail not only enables users to exchange business information but also contributes to greater opportunities for cultural awareness and understanding. When you have determined that an e-mail is appropriate for the situation, prepare the content. Address communication barriers, apply netiquette, and format your message to increase effectiveness.

Communication Barriers

When e-mail is used in business, the message requires a certain degree of formality. Otherwise, communication barriers may arise; specifically, barriers resulting from poor language skills, e-mail abuse, and casual style. (Review Communication Barriers in Chapter 1, pages 5–9.)

Timely Tip

Do not open messages perceived as spam. Opening such messages validates to the spammer that a live person is at the other end of the e-mail address and encourages more spam.

- **Apply the rules of grammar, spelling, and punctuation.** E-mail began as an informal means of exchanging information, and users often neglected standard language usage. When the rules of grammar are ignored, including punctuation and spelling, a message appears sloppy. A sloppy message distracts the reader, diminishes the clarity and importance of the message, and ultimately reflects badly on the sender. Precise language and standard language mechanics help everyone understand the intent of your message.

- **Send relevant messages.** The characteristics that have made e-mail so popular in both professional and personal environments—convenience, efficient distribution, and cost savings—have also led to e-mail abuse. E-mail mailboxes are often filled with unsolicited and irrelevant messages. Some of those messages are referred to as **spam**, which is e-mail sent to many people without their consent. Product and service advertisements and chain letters are examples of spam. Receivers have to sort the important messages from the unimportant messages; and sorting through a glut of unnecessary messages is time-consuming and creates ill will.

- **Avoid e-mail jargon.** From inception, e-mail encouraged a casual, personal writing style; so users quickly developed their own language, e-mail jargon. E-mail **jargon** consists of emoticons (symbols that represent emotions) and abbreviations. Jargon *is not* suggested for business e-mail. Emoticons and abbreviations are not universally understood, so miscommunication is likely to occur. Also, messages that use e-mail jargon may be perceived as too casual, especially outside an organization.

  Emoticons and abbreviations are not substitutes for clear, concise writing. If jargon is acceptable within a specific environment (for example, among department personnel who communicate often), a reference list of common emoticons, abbreviations, and their definitions will help avoid misunderstandings. Examples of emoticons are shown below in Table 4-4; and examples of typical abbreviations are shown in Table 4-5, page 111.

Netiquette

E-mail has an impersonal side, which sometimes causes senders to forget that a human is on the receiving end. In fact, users tend to say things they

Table 4-4 Emoticons

;)	winking	:-D	laughing
:-)	smiling	"-!	foot in mouth
:-(	frowning	:-<	upset
:-s	confused	:`-(	crying
:")	embarrassed	: 0	hungry
Note: To read, tilt head to the left.			

Table 4-5 E-mail Abbreviations

2L8	too late	CYL	see you later
AKA	also known as	EOM	end of message
BFN	bye for now	GAL	get a life
BRB	be right back	IMO	in my opinion
CSL	can't stop laughing	WDUT	what do you think

would not ordinarily say in person. Therefore, the CBO approach, the six *C*s of effective messages, and common sense are essential for e-mail messages. **Netiquette**, an unofficial code of conduct and rules for online interaction and behavior as shown below, essential for e-mail messages, instant messaging, voice mail, and newsgroup postings.

- **Develop a single-topic, concise message that can be covered in three or fewer key points.** Typically, each topic warrants a separate message so that each topic receives adequate attention. Messages can be filed and retrieved by topic, if desired.
- **Write a concise, descriptive subject line to encourage reading.** Receivers often decide whether to open a message based on the subject line. A meaningful subject line not only identifies the purpose of the e-mail but also enables users to file and retrieve by subject. An e-mail with a vague subject line or no subject line is likely to be deleted.

Examples:

Vague Subject Line	Concise, Informative Subject Line
Meeting	June 12 Finance Committee Meeting
Information	Airline tickets to Phoenix

- **Do not arbitrarily designate a message as *urgent* or *priority*.** Time-critical words are appropriate *only* when the situation requires immediate attention. Using these kinds of words to attract attention eventually will have the opposite effect.
- **Get to the main idea quickly; stay on topic.** The most important statements should appear in the first paragraph. Irrelevant information causes receivers to lose interest or ignore much of the message while scanning for the main idea.
- **Send copies only to those who need to receive the message.** Not everyone needs to know everything; receivers become irritated when they receive messages that are not relevant to them.
- **Determine an appropriate greeting.** A person's professional or courtesy title and last name, with or without a salutation, is usually safe when you do not know the recipient.

Examples: Dear Professor Wulf or Ms. Wulf

Timely Tip

Before you hit the "send" button, ask: *Would I say this to someone face-to-face?*

When you know the recipient, you will reference that person like you normally would, with or without a salutation.

Examples: Dear Max **or** Max **or** Dear Professor Drumm

When replying to a message, you can be guided by the person's signature.

Greetings across cultures may present special challenges. Many cultures outside the United States, for example, expect deference (a respectful attitude) toward people in positions of authority or people of mature years. Also, name structure may be different, i.e., last name first or maiden name versus spousal name. Many specialty references are available; so to avoid negative impressions, investigate correct forms of address before preparing a message.

- **Use irony and humor with care.** Humor is a matter of interpretation, and people do not always interpret humor the same way. The risk for misinterpretation is even greater when the receiver speaks English as a Second Language.
- **Do not flame. Flaming** refers to using threatening or angry language.
- **Do not key your message in all capital letters.** A message keyed in all uppercase is perceived as shouting at the receiver.
- **Review your message before hitting the Send button to make sure that what you say is what you intend.** Responding to an e-mail that is emotionally provoking deserves additional consideration. An immediate response in these situations usually is terse and may be perceived as *flaming*.
- **Identify yourself.** Receivers need to know who you are, and sometimes your screen name does not adequately identify you or your business affiliation.
- **Do not automatically send attachments or forward someone else's e-mail.** Viruses are introduced into systems by attachments, and forwarding someone else's correspondence may be viewed as a violation of privacy. You need to seek confirmation from the people involved before carrying out either of these actions.
- **Confirm the recipient.** Are you responding to one or many? You will be embarrassed if a personal message ends up on a mailing list.
- **Check your e-mail regularly; in most cases, respond promptly.** Emptying your mailbox a few times a day helps keep mail and responses under control.

Format

The format of an e-mail message is similar to that of a memorandum. (Memo formats are discussed in the Format Guide.) The header of an e-mail

Timely Tip

For international exchanges, address receivers formally unless you are invited to do otherwise.

typically includes sender and receiver e-mail address lines, a dateline, a copy notation line, and a subject line. Illustration 4-1, page 114, shows a completed e-mail.

Incorporate these format guidelines to enhance your professional image as you key your e-mail message.

- **Check the accuracy of the recipient's address to ensure that the e-mail is directed to the *intended* receiver(s).** A "slip" of the key can send the message to an unintended receiver or back to you, undelivered.
- **Present information in lists when appropriate.** Reading is easier when key points are presented in a list.
- **Use a professional e-mail address.** A professional e-mail address projects a professional image. Also, some systems allow the sender's name to appear with the e-mail address as part of the header information. This format clearly identifies the sender.

Example: cmbrantmill@pcola.gulf.net [Clarice M. Brantley-Miller]

- **Key messages in traditional upper- and lowercase combinations.** All uppercase or all lowercase letters not only make the message difficult to read but also carries a nonverbal message. All uppercase letters signifiy shouting, which is rude; and all lowercase letters appear unprofessional.
- **Use easy-to-read fonts, sizes, and colors; and avoid graphics.** A recipient's e-mail program may not support the same elements that your system supports. Overlapping fonts and pastel colors often are difficult to read, and graphics do not always transmit clearly or accurately.
- **Keep messages short, and separate paragraphs with a blank line.** Short messages are easier to read onscreen (some people encourage a 25-line maximum). Short sentences, two or three paragraphs of three or four lines, and white space between paragraphs improve readability. *Do not* sacrifice completeness for brevity; if necessary, use a different message form or transmission mode to ensure completeness. Long messages may require an attachment (see an explanation of *attachment* on page 109).
- **Include a signature, but eliminate a complimentary close.** A signature is important, and most e-mail programs allow users to create an identifying block of text (four or fewer lines) that can be automatically inserted at the end of a message. Create separate signature files for personal and business use. A business signature should include your name, title, company name, and alternate way to contact you. Do not duplicate information that you have in your header.

Timely Tip

Send a "test" message to yourself and to some of your friends. Ask for their opinions about the appearance of your message.

Therese L. Kresjke, Project Manager
South-Western/Thomson Learning
513.555.0197

- **Include relevant parts of an original message when responding.**
  When you reply to an e-mail, include (copy) small amounts of the original message in your response to help the recipient place your reply in context. Identify text from the original message by surrounding the quoted text with symbols like these: <quoted material>.

Instant Messaging

Instant messaging (IM) is the informal side of e-mail—faster, more spontaneous, and *live*. Instant messaging options vary but enable users to identify people who are online and to exchange messages with them. Several people can participate in instant messaging at the same time. To communicate by instant messaging, the sender and receiver must be using the same communication software; and each person's name must be on a **buddy list.** You can send messages to and receive messages from anyone on your list as long as that person is online. A typical instant messaging

Illustration 4-1 **E-Mail Message to Send**

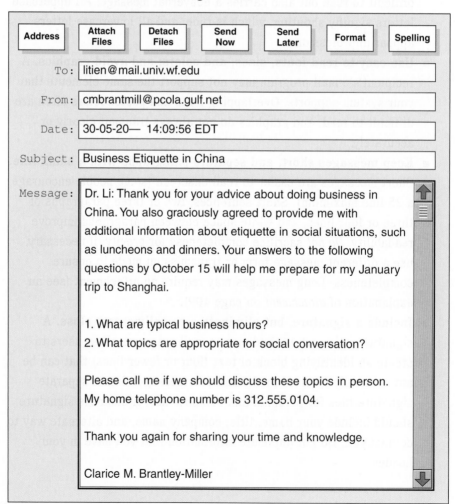

| Address | Attach Files | Detach Files | Send Now | Send Later | Format | Spelling |

To: litien@mail.univ.wf.edu

From: cmbrantmill@pcola.gulf.net

Date: 30-05-20— 14:09:56 EDT

Subject: Business Etiquette in China

Message: Dr. Li: Thank you for your advice about doing business in China. You also graciously agreed to provide me with additional information about etiquette in social situations, such as luncheons and dinners. Your answers to the following questions by October 15 will help me prepare for my January trip to Shanghai.

1. What are typical business hours?
2. What topics are appropriate for social conversation?

Please call me if we should discuss these topics in person. My home telephone number is 312.555.0104.

Thank you again for sharing your time and knowledge.

Clarice M. Brantley-Miller

system alerts the user when a buddy is online; and instant messaging begins when someone sends a message. Sending a message opens a small window in which a text message is keyed.

Although instant messaging has some similarities to e-mail, IM has some significantly different characteristics. The most significant characteristic is that instant messaging takes place in *real time*. For example, a message arrives instantly and requires an instant response if a conversation is to take place. An awkward situation may result if the receiver doesn't want to "talk" right then. Another significant characteristic is the lack of privacy. Anyone who knows your user name and who has the same communication software will know when you are online. Also, conversations are visible to all the participants; and conversations can be printed or saved to a file.

Instant messaging is productive and efficient for virtual conferences, project collaboration, and other work-related messages among colleagues.

Instant messaging is best used for brief exchanges—a thought or two at a time—that do not require privacy.

Whether your instant message is personal or business, instant messaging manners apply.

- **Ask before you enter.** Sometimes a receiver is not able or willing to chat. Be polite, and ask first if you are intruding before you begin an instant message session.

Examples: "Are you available?" or "Can you talk?"

   The inquiry gives the receiver the opportunity to decline if the time for a chat isn't good. If the receiver doesn't respond to the inquiry, take the hint and e-mail your message.

- **Use "busy" or "away" alerts.** A message alert tells your buddies that you cannot participate in an online chat. Respect the same kind of alert from your IM buddies.

- **Respect time schedules.** Just because a buddy is online late at night does not mean he or she will welcome a business-related message. Other than for an emergency, would you normally telephone someone at 2 a.m.? Use common sense.

- **Keep messages brief.** IM systems limit the number of characters you can enter in each message. If your messages frequently hit the word limit, deliver them another way, such as by e-mail or telephone. Get to the point and stay focused.

- **Be professional.** People don't expect perfect instant messages. Instant messaging is meant to be casual, short, and quick but *not* sloppy or careless. The quality of your message reflects your professionalism. Reread what you write before sending.

- **Avoid multitasking.** Not everyone can handle a conversation with more than one person at a time. Don't let your communication skills suffer because you are trying to handle too many conversations. Pay attention to the participants as you key your comments.

Discussion Groups

A **discussion group** is a general term that is used to describe an online exchange of information about topics of common interest. Users enter (post) messages in a designated area, read the messages of others, and respond to messages. Discussion groups take on different forms, such as e-mail lists and online forums. Many web sites offer discussion opportunities so that users can share information and opinions.

Newsgroups are similar to discussion groups, except that users must subscribe in order to participate. Thousands of discussion groups and newsgroups exist. They are typically "self-governing," which means that participants regulate message postings by letting each other know what is acceptable and what is not. Practicing *netiquette* and reading the FAQ (frequently asked questions) at the site provide helpful participation guidelines.

Timely Tip

Follow this rule when you participate in a discussion group: *Do unto others as you would have them do unto you.*

Facsimile (Fax) Transfer

A **facsimile** is considered an exact reproduction of the original design of a document. Therefore, both written material and pictorial material are received in the same form they were sent. Faxes can be sent from a stand-alone fax machine, a computer with fax capabilities, or over the Internet.

When a standalone fax machine is used, the user feeds an original document into the unit for transmission. The receiver's fax number is activated, and transmission begins immediately or at a later designated date. Since fax transmission is activated by the push of a button, you must be careful that the receiver's fax number is accurate and that you are transmitting to the intended receiver.

Faxing remains a popular transmission choice because of its convenience and delivery options. Pictures, letters, and other documents can be sent and received to fax equipment anywhere in the world. Fax equipment and software can be programmed to activate receiver numbers automatically and transmit at designated times. In addition, messages may be sent to one person or may be broadcast, which means that a mailing list is entered and delivery is to everyone on the list.

Facsimile transfer is used when original document appearance and speed of delivery are important.

Culture Frame

The fax machine is an important communication device in China because a message written in Chinese characters is easily transmitted.

Facsimile Identifiers

A fax message must be accompanied by a document identifier, such as an adhesive label or a separate cover sheet. An adhesive label, adhered to the document to be transmitted, is commonly used when a one-page document is transmitted. A label provides minimal space for essential information as shown in Illustration 4-2.

Illustration 4-2 **Post-it® Fax Note 7671**

Post-it® Fax Note 7671	Date	# of pages ▶
To	**From**	
Co./Dept.	Co.	
Phone #	Phone #	
Fax #	Fax #	

Courtesy of 3M Company.

A separate cover sheet should accompany a document of more than one page or a document sent outside the organization. A sample cover sheet is shown in Illustration 4-3, page 118. The cover sheet is transmitted first, followed by the document. Sometimes the cover sheet alone contains the message. Information on a fax cover sheet varies based on organizational circumstances (multiple users, multiple machines, and so on) and sender preferences. Minimally, a fax cover sheet provides space for this information:

- Transmission date
- Number of pages to be transmitted
- Receiver name, organization name, and fax number
- Sender name, organization name, fax number, and telephone number
- A telephone number to call if transmission is not successful
- Confidentiality statement
- Space for a brief accompanying message

The heading on a fax cover sheet may vary depending on the destination. For faxes sent externally, heading material usually includes complete contact information: company name, address, telephone number, fax number, and e-mail address. Sometimes company mottos or logos are included. Heading material for faxes sent internally may include only basic departmental contact information, such as department name and fax number.

Fax Messages

Follow the CBO approach, and incorporate the six *C*s when you develop a message for faxing. In addition, use the following guidelines to communicate by fax effectively.

- **Consider the topic.** How will your receiver perceive the information as a fax message? Is the information confidential or sensitive? When you fax confidential or sensitive information, (1) confirm that the receiving end is a confidential site; and (2) follow up immediately with a telephone call to confirm receipt of the document.
- **Determine the conversion quality of images and text before faxing.** Handwriting, small print, newspaper articles, detailed images, certain colors, and documents of poor quality do not fax clearly.
- **Consider cost**. Telephone long-distance charges may apply.
- **Prepare the cover sheet and any messages in an easily readable font size and style.** A 10- to 12-point font size and a font style with

Timely Tip

Complicated designs slow transmission or may not transmit clearly.

letters that are clearly distinguishable and do not overlap are the best choices for facsimile transfer. (Depending on the font style, 10-point size may be too small.) Avoid script fonts and big, bold block letters. Keep the cover sheet clutter-free and graphics to a minimum.

- **Check the information on the cover sheet.** Proofreading the cover sheet confirms that both the sender information and the receiver information are correct. If a fax is misdirected, the "mistaken" receiver will be able to contact the sender. To prevent dialing the wrong fax number, write the number on a separate paper to read while you are dialing.

Personal Digital Assistant (PDA)

A **personal digital assistant (PDA)**, also called handheld computer or pocket computer, is a handheld device that was developed mainly as a personal organizer. Today, PDAs can run computer programs (including word processing, spreadsheets, and presentation programs), access the

Illustration 4-3 **Sample Facsimile Cover Sheet**

Fax: 270.555.0194
Phone: 270.555.0195

E-mail: rja@mail.com

R J A & Associates

12559 West Goldfinch Road
Leitchfield, KY 42754

F A C S I M I L E T R A N S F E R

To: From:

Fax: Pages (including cover):

                             Date:

Re:

**If transmission is incomplete or if you receive this fax in error,
please call 270.555.0195 immediately.**

Message:

Internet, and function as a cell phone or fax sender. Some have voice recognition capabilities, and many models incorporate wireless network cards, which enable the PDA to access a network to load or save data files. Coffeehouses, airports, and many hotels provide free wireless access to the Internet for PDA users.

Surveys show that owners routinely store work and personal passwords, personal identification numbers (PIN), and credit card numbers on their PDAs. Surveys also show that owners *do not* apply appropriate security measures to protect this highly confidential information. If the PDA is lost or stolen, the owner may be subject to identity theft, liable for charges to charge cards, and responsible for unauthorized access to company information. Stored information must be protected.

As the communication capabilities of PDAs advance, users need adequate language skills to compose and send brief, complete messages quickly.

Web Sites

Today's web sites may incorporate graphics, audio, video, and animation as well as text. Depending on the intent of the originating site, users may interact with web sites, e-mail by way of the site, and exchange information in chat rooms. Language skills and acceptable behavior are critical for the development and distribution of effective messages using today's communication technologies.

References

Learning where to locate information is essential to workplace success. Both print and electronic references are available to help you prepare accurate and effective messages.

Print References

Commonly used print references include dictionaries, thesauruses, and office reference handbooks. A typical dictionary provides the spelling, definition(s), grammatical form(s), and pronunciation of words. Depending on size, some dictionaries may include common abbreviations, punctuation rules, forms of address, and geographic and bibliographic information. A thesaurus provides **synonyms** (words with similar meanings) and sometimes **antonyms** (words with opposite meanings), other related words, and definitions. Office reference handbooks provide information about office procedures, writing style, grammar, punctuation, and message format.

Electronic References

Most word processing software programs include a spell checker, thesaurus, and grammar checker, which are also available as separate software packages. Dictionaries and thesauruses are also available as handheld devices. Some e-mail systems have spell checkers and grammar checkers with limited capabilities. Instant messages are not spell checked.

Timely Tip

Print and electronic specialized references are available for various languages and professions.

A **spell checker** searches a document for words that do not match those in the spell checker dictionary. Once those words are identified, the spell checker may offer alternatives but does not indicate which alternative is appropriate. A spell checker does not include many proper nouns, such as the names of people, cities, or streets. A spell checker does not distinguish between words that are spelled correctly but used incorrectly, such as *which* and *witch*, and does not catch number errors. An **electronic thesaurus** provides synonyms for a given word but does not indicate which word best fits the intent of the sender. A **grammar checker** reviews the content of a message for grammar, style, and punctuation violations. A grammar checker highlights areas to review and presents alternatives, but a grammar checker cannot evaluate the intent of a message. Sometimes, suggested corrections are not appropriate. For example, the grammar checker may suggest the use of the active voice even though the passive voice is desirable for some message situations, such as bad news.

Electronic tools are helpful, and you should use them when they are available; but they *are not* substitutes for language skills and the application of the Communication-by-Objectives approach.

Section 3: COMMUNICATING THE SPOKEN WORD

The telephone (landline and cell) is the most popular tool for transmitting the spoken word. Voice mail and voice recognition are additional transmission modes for the spoken word.

Culture Frame

The Chinese use different tones for the same sound to express different ideas. One sound pronounced in various tones has many different meanings. High tone, low tone, rising tone, falling tone—tone can change meaning or make words incomprehensible. Foreigners will create favorable impressions, however, if they practice and express simple, courteous phrases in Chinese.

Telephone

The telephone is a valuable tool that can increase productivity, provide opportunities for positive interaction, and promote goodwill. In fact, telephones enable people who have never seen each other to develop powerful business relationships. Phone users typically are dependent on what each hears; so listening skills as well as speaking skills are key elements to successful phone communication. (Review Speaking Skills and Listening Skills, pages 14–17, in Chapter 1.)

Telephone delivery is best when speed is important, the message is not complicated, and body language is unimportant.

Telephone Conversations

Sometimes you have time to prepare for a phone conversation. Many times, though, exchanges are spontaneous; and you have little time to think about your words. If you determine that a message is appropriate for telephone delivery, your goal (as with any other message) is to convey your meaning accurately. Train yourself to use the CBO approach and the six Cs whether your conversations are planned or spontaneous. Follow these guidelines when participating in a telephone conversation.

- **Keep the message short.** Prior to the call, note the points you want to make. Avoid multiple topics, and stay focused. Long or complicated messages are not appropriate for phone delivery. Listeners may lose track of important points or lose interest while waiting for the main idea.
- **Recognize that body language is not available.** Avoid using the telephone to deliver a message when body language may be a critical component to receiver understanding.
- **Open with a firm, welcoming greeting—similar to a firm handshake.** Identify yourself, and give a brief reason for your call.
- **Use the listener's name correctly.** If necessary, write the phonetic pronunciation, so you can say the name correctly. Ask for (and write down) the correct spelling for future reference. Address the listener the same way the receiver identifies himself or herself, and personalize your conversation by using the caller's name.
- **Take notes during the conversation.** For quick reference, keep a notepad, company directory, and list of frequently called numbers within easy reach. Repeat important information (telephone numbers, names, and so on) to ensure correctness.
- **Listen actively.** Respond with remarks, such as "yes" and "I understand." Do not do other tasks while you are on the phone.

Telephone Image

Project a positive image through your voice qualities: tone, audibility, and articulation. Cell phones are more sound-sensitive than landline phones, so you usually can speak in a lower-than-normal voice and still be heard.

Tone. The tone of your voice conveys your emotions. Convey friendliness, courtesy, and an upbeat attitude. Some organizations keep mirrors on each service representative's desk to remind the representative to smile when talking to a customer, so the customer "hears" the smile.

Audibility. The volume (loud to soft) and pitch (squeaky to deep) of your voice as well as the rate at which you speak determine how a receiver hears you. For most receivers, a moderate volume and speed and a mid- to low-range pitch best ensures understanding.

Articulation. The way you articulate or say words affects clarity. Common speech faults include chopping off word endings (especially *ing*) and running words together. Slow down, and say all parts of the word.

Examples: Have you been waitin long? (waiting)
     Whereya goin? (Where are you going?)

Cell Phone Etiquette

Cell phone use has increased dramatically in the last few years. Their portability provides many personal and business benefits for users, but cell phone use requires additional attention because they are easily misused. Practicing cell phone etiquette is essential to maintaining a harmonious communication environment. Even the cell phone industry is encouraging users to use their phones responsibly. Apply common sense and these etiquette tips for cell phone use:

- **Remember that people take priority over a phone call.** Avoid phone conversations when you are with someone else (most social situations). Otherwise, you risk being viewed as rude. If you are expecting a call that you must answer, inform the other person(s) that you are expecting a call and get permission to answer the call.

- **Respect the rules.** Refrain from using your phone when asked. *Turn off* the phone in meetings, movies, theaters, classes, worship services, and other places where your call will be disruptive.

- **Use the features of your phone to avoid disruption.** Tone down the ringer by choosing a simple, low-key sound. Use the vibrate feature when you need to take a call but do not want to disturb others with the ringing. Check the caller ID to confirm that an incoming call needs answering. Otherwise, let incoming messages go to voice mail.

- **Save private conversations for a private place.** When you must make or answer calls, conduct the calls away from a public area. In fact, consider using a landline phone or personal meeting for serious issues to avoid "dropped connection" frustration and eavesdroppers, including electronic eavesdroppers. Avoid talking at a restaurant table. If you must take a call, set the vibrate feature, excuse yourself from the table, and move to a private place.

- **Focus on safety.** Do not use cell phones when they interfere with your ability to drive or walk.

Timely Tip

Use the cell phone to enhance communication rather than to interfere with communication.

Voice Mail

Voice mail, also called **voice messaging**, is similar to e-mail except that the message is spoken. Voice mail is popular for transmitting the spoken word because information can be sent or requested without people engaging in a two-way conversation. Users can organize thoughts ahead; and messages can be created, stored, and distributed simultaneously to one or more receivers (using a voice mail list) at any time from any location. Other features include date and time stamps, message scan, and integration with computers and other electronic devices.

Voice Mail Messages

Consider the topic and how the receiver will perceive the information as a voice mail message. Messages that convey bad news or messages that require written documentation *are not* suitable as voice mail messages. Other message forms or transmission modes are better choices in those situations.

Also, consider potential communication barriers. For example, time limitations for recorded messages may cause users to send incomplete messages. Poor grammar and articulation make listening and understanding difficult and result in dissatisfaction and negative impressions.

Voice mail is an appropriate choice when speed of delivery is important and the message is brief, uncomplicated, and not controversial.

When voice mail is appropriate for your message, use the CBO approach, the six Cs, and the following guidelines to convey the intended message. Notice that many of the guidelines for leaving a voice mail message are similar to guidelines for telephone conversations.

- **Develop a single-topic, concise message.** Plan ahead, jot down key words, and limit the points to cover. Get to the point, and stay focused.
- **Be brief.** Try to keep a voice mail message to one minute or less. Consider the recording time when developing a message so that you can deliver a *complete* message within the time allotted.
- **Identify yourself and the intended receiver.** Open with identifying information, such as *This message is for Jeff Stone from Anita Alvarez.*
- **Provide adequate information.** Be specific about your reason for calling, and state what response is expected. Suggest a callback time to prevent frustration. Also, state the time and date of your call in case the system does not record that information.
- **Close the message by giving your contact information.** Give your contact information at the end of the message, so the receiver has time to write down the necessary details.
- **Project a positive image through your voice qualities: tone, audibility, and articulation.**

Voice Mail Greetings

Your own voice mail greeting is also important because that greeting often creates the first impression of you and your organization. As you compose and deliver your greeting, think about your own experiences listening to someone else's voice mail greeting. Choose the positive characteristics of those greetings, and apply these tips.

- **Record a short "professional" greeting without background noise.** *Do not* use gimmick openings.
- **Project a positive image through your voice qualities: tone, audibility, and articulation.**
- **Include your name and organization name.** Let callers know they have reached the correct person or department.
- **Change your greeting to indicate your availability.** Inform callers of absences, and give them options to leave a message or to contact someone else who can provide assistance.

Timely Tip

Do not say anything in voice mail that you would not say in person or put in writing. Most systems allow messages to be saved and forwarded.

- **Encourage callers to leave a detailed message to avoid a series of callbacks.**
- **Let callers know that you check your voice mail regularly.** Then do so, and act on your messages as soon as possible.

For privacy or security reasons, you may not want to include your name on your personal voice mail or answering machine. Provide at least a telephone number, so callers know they have connected with the correct number.

Section 4: CONFERENCING AND VOICE RECOGNITION

Technology makes audioconferencing, videoconferencing, and voice recognition increasingly convenient.

- Audioconferencing and videoconferencing move "meetings" to the participants.
- Videoconferencing is an integral component of distance learning environments and online courses.
- Voice recognition moves steadily into the mainstream as business and industry realize more and more uses for this technology.

Conferencing

Simple **audioconferencing** (voice only) has been used in business for many years and is best suited for conversations among three or four people when visuals are not important. However, audioconferencing can be arranged to accommodate many participants. Telephone companies and other companies offer audioconferencing services to meet the needs of a particular situation.

Videoconferencing has moved beyond the television–telephone connection to one of the fastest-growing segments of the computer industry. **Videoconferencing** today includes the use of computer networks to transmit audio and video data, such as slides, documents, and animations. **Streaming media,** an Internet transfer technique, is the live flow of digital information that allows users to see video and hear audio files without lengthy download times. This kind of web-enabled conferencing allows participants in different locations to interact as though they were sitting in the same room. Participants can speak to each other, the facilitator or leader can track who is participating, and the conference can be recorded for later replay or delivery to a different audience.

Videoconferencing has many uses, including sales meetings; training sessions; product development, introduction, and updates; and educational courses. Some organizations use their own videoconferencing equipment; others contract with outside firms.

Audioconferencing and videoconferencing offer these benefits:

- Cost and time savings (less travel, reduced set-up time)
- Quick communication
- Ability to reach audiences at many locations

Voice Recognition

Voice recognition is constantly being improved. Users input the spoken word through a microphone into the computer; **voice recognition** software then converts the spoken words into written words. Voice recognition technology is especially beneficial for individuals with physical challenges because they can dictate information into the computer for conversion into written words. Other voice input uses include automating data entry tasks and voice printing for identification purposes. Many cell phones respond to simple voice commands.

Summary

Technology makes gathering and disseminating information faster and easier than ever before. The Internet contains a vast amount of information that is located using search engines and sorted for relevance by applying web evaluation criteria. The integration of tools, such as computers, telephones, and software, has resulted in increased use of e-mail, facsimile, voice mail, videoconferencing, and voice recognition to deliver messages all over the world. As a result, senders must often create and deliver messages quickly, so skilled communicators are in demand. Tools alone do not produce effective messages—*you* are the critical component.

You analyze the situation by asking yourself, *"How would I feel if I received this message as . . . ?"*

You create a message using appropriate language skills, the CBO approach, and the six *C*s of effective messages.

You choose a transmission mode that will best achieve the desired result.

As a communicator today, you need to understand both the principles of effective communication and the characteristics of electronic communication tools. Prepare and deliver an effective message—one that best conveys your intended meaning—using a transmission mode that is the most appropriate for the situation.

Complete Communication Skills Development 4, pages 135–136. For additional adjective review, see the Reference Guide, pages 419–420.

Ethics in Action

Access http://brantley. swlearning.com. Analyze the Ethics in Action for Chapter 4.

Exercises

4 - 1

Directions: Read summaries about different search engines at these sites:

http://library.albany.edu/internet/engines.html
http://www.searchengineshowdown.com

Based on the summaries, choose two search engine sites (at least one site should be different from those listed on page 104), and complete these tasks on a separate sheet of paper *for each site*:

1. Record the URL for each site you visit.
2. List key features of each homepage.
3. Activate some of the options; take notes.
4. Study the advanced search techniques; take notes.
5. Search on a topic using the techniques you learned; take notes on the engine's ease of use, productive keywords, and site features.
6. Use your notes to write one or two paragraphs about each search engine. Comment on ease of use, relevance of the features, search techniques and results, and your overall impression of the site. Be prepared to discuss your findings in class.

Exercises

4 - 2

Directions: Search for a professional organization that represents your career area. Use more than one search engine if necessary. Evaluate the site for its value as a professional resource. (Refer to Table 4-3, Web Site Evaluation Criteria, page 107, as needed.) Be prepared to discuss your findings in class. Record information in the following format:

Purpose
Audience:
Primary purpose:
Evident biases:

Authorship/Sponsorship
Responsibility for content:
Link to host/sponsor:
Contact information:

Currency
Creation date:
Revision date(s):

Reliability
Links to other resources:
Workable links:

Content
Logical organization:
Appropriate writing style; clarity:
Grammar usage; spelling:
Benefit(s) of membership:

4 - 3

Directions: Write one or two paragraphs responding to this statement: *Seek permission from a receiver before sending an attachment to an e-mail.*

Exercises

4 - 4   **Directions:** Search for emoticon and e-mail abbreviation sites. Use keywords such as *e-mail emoticons, emoticons,* and *e-mail abbreviations*. Create *three* sentences for display to the class, and use at least *ten* emoticons and/or abbreviations. (Do not use the emoticons or abbreviations shown in Tables 4-4 and 4-5, pages 110 and 111.)

4 - 5   **Directions:** Write informative e-mail subject lines for the following situations. If necessary, supply details to make the subject lines clear.

    a. A coworker knows that you frequently travel by air. She is planning a trip to Hong Kong. The flight is 14 to 16 hours, so she has asked you for some tips to make her air trip more comfortable. You are responding with information.

    b. You are sending your assistant URLs from which to access and print information about e-mail etiquette. The information will be used to develop company e-mail etiquette policies.

    c. As the president of a volunteer board of directors for a local humane society, you need a board member to proofread the monthly newsletter. This message will be e-mailed to all board members.

    d. The voice mail system at work will be upgraded next weekend, and users will not be able to leave or access messages for a short period. Your message informs users of the interruption in voice mail services.

    e. The "Ergonomically Sound Workplace" seminar has four openings. As the employee program coordinator at your firm, you are notifying employees of this opportunity.

Exercises

4 - 6

Directions: Write a paragraph responding to this statement: *Instant messaging is where e-mail was ten years ago.*

4 - 7

Directions: Key the following paragraph on the computer. Run the spell checker. Record the words that are highlighted, and decide whether to accept or reject suggested changes. Make note of but do not change any grammar checker suggestions. Print the copy and proofread; then write the correction above each error.

A article dated December 41 suggest that you be through when you

chose a knew telephone system for you're business. Although many factor

need too be considered, to factors our specially important.

Project you companys growth over the next year and the next for years.

For example, due you plan to move ore ad employees? Also, consider equipment

purchases that will utilize the system's capabilities; and lists any equipment

you think will bee connected to your telephone system.

4 - 8

Directions: Write one to two paragraphs about a recent experience that you had with someone's company voice mail. Summarize the content of the message, and explain your impression of the person and firm based on the message.

TechLinks

Internet
Challenge

4-1 Directions: Go to http://riceinfo.rice.edu/armadillo/acceptable.html for links that relate to acceptable use policies; or use a search engine to search on *acceptable use policies*. Visit two or three sites. On a separate sheet of paper, list the sites (URLs) you visited. For each site, record actions that are not permitted as well as penalties that may be involved as a result of inappropriate Internet use.

4-2 Directions: In the course of your business day, you may have telephone conversations with people from other countries. Translation services, including telephone translations, are available when you need assistance.

Search for translation services sites. Use keywords and phrases, such as *language translation* or *translation services*, to find a similar site. Activate each service link to determine what is available. Write a summary of your findings.

InfoTrac

Directions: Using the InfoTrac subject search, locate these two articles:
"First Mandarin Voice-Activated Web Search Launched"
"Lemonade your typist? (Under my Skin)"
After reviewing both articles, choose one and prepare a summary of the article contents. Identify the article by including the name of the article in quotation marks, the publication's title (underlined or italicized), and the author's name. Section 13 of the Reference Guide shows sample citation formats.

WebTUTOR
Advantage

Directions: Access your WebTutor Advantage product. Complete the short-answer portion for Chapter 4 and send the answers to your instructor.

Case Studies

4 - 1

Communication Situation: Dr. Li is out of the office for the next two weeks. You, as Dr. Li's assistant, are responding to the questions in the e-mail message, Illustration 4-1, page 114.

Task: Use search engines and search methods to find information about typical business hours and appropriate conversations in China. Print the information to use as a reference; indicate your choice of keywords. Complete the e-mail screen on the following page. Explain that you are responding on behalf of Dr. Li, and provide the requested information. Refer to the netiquette and format guidelines presented on pages 110–114 if necessary. Send your response to Clarice M. Brantley-Miller at cmbrantmil@pcola.gulf.net. Use this e-mail address for yourself: *yourname*@pcola.gulf.net, substituting your own name for *yourname*.

Case Studies

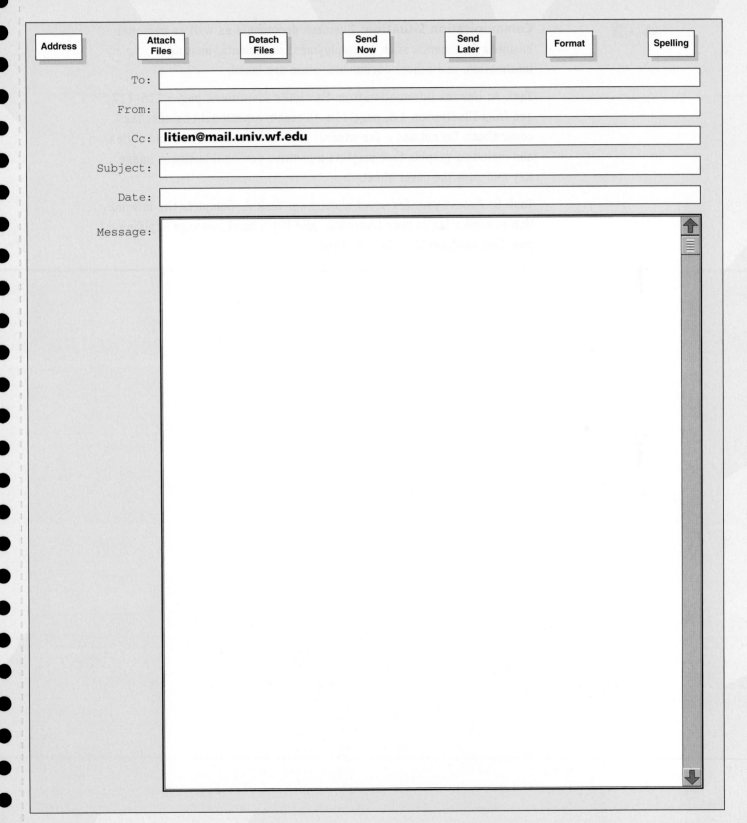

Cc: **litien@mail.univ.wf.edu**

Case Studies

4 - 2

Communication Situation: Business documents as well as personal-business documents, such as employment documents, insurance information, and school documents, often are faxed.

Task A: Use the information from Facsimile Identifiers, pages 116–117, and from Illustration 4-3, page 118, to create a personal-business fax cover sheet. Do not use a fax wizard. Use readable font sizes and styles, and include a graphic that projects a positive personal-business image. Key and save the cover sheet.

Task B: Access your fax cover sheet from Task A. Complete the information to send a fax to your instructor, and key a brief message explaining your font and graphics choices. Print.

Communication Skills Development 4

NAME_____

Part A — Adjective Usage

Directions: Of the words given in parentheses in each of the following sentences, underline the correct adjective.

1. Make environmental issues one of your (principal, principle) concerns.

2. The decision to recycle is a (personal, personnel) choice.

3. Does your town sponsor (hazard, hazardous) waste collection days?

4. Environmentalists are concerned because (improperly, improper) drainage of wetlands has depleted available waterfowl habitats.

5. (Accessive, Excessive) irrigation can leach nutrients away from plant roots and increase the chances of polluting groundwater.

6. Plastic rings that hold six-packs of beverages together are one of the (more, most) dangerous hazards to sea creatures and birds.

7. Hopefully, we will have (fewer, less) environmental disasters than we did last year.

8. You will find Internet sites that provide (up-to-date, up to date) information about environmental protection legislation.

9. Are you making (a, an) honest effort to recycle in your household?

10. Using a ceramic mug rather than a disposable cup is the (good, better) choice.

11. Oil spills cause some of the (worse, worst) environmental damage.

12. The *Exxon Valdez* oil spill was one of the (more, most) studied environmental tragedies in history.

13. To become less dependent on oil, we must conduct (further, farther) research on alternate energy sources.

14. One of the (most easy, easiest) ways to conserve water is to repair leaks around pipe joints and fixtures.

15. Water your lawn after dusk when (less, lesser) water is needed because of the lower evaporation rate.

16. Xeriscaping, a landscaping approach designed to conserve water and protect the environment, requires (less, lesser) fertilizer.

17. Xeriscaping incorporates seven basic (principals, principles) that lead to saving water.

18. If mishandled, household (hazard, hazardous) waste—paints, batteries, pesticides, and oils—can be dangerous to your health and to the environment.

19. The (EPAs, EPA's) Office of Air and Radiation has primary responsibility for regulating combustors and incinerators because air emissions from combustion pose the (greater, greatest) environmental concern.

20. Modern landfills are (well-engineered, well engineered) facilities that are designed and operated to ensure compliance with federal regulations.

Part B Skills Application

Directions: In the following memo, underline each error in spelling and in noun, pronoun, verb, and adjective usage. Write the correction above each error. (Ordinarily, memos are single spaced. In this memo, extra space has been added for you to insert corrections.)

MMC Morris Manufacturing Company

Interoffice Communication

April 17, 20—

TO: All Employees

FROM: Herbert S. Weiss, Vice President

SUBJECT: Exchange Program with China

Three of our employees has been invited to participate in a exchange of personal

with our new facility in Tianjin, China, for too months this summer. The exchange

involve employes whom have not had experience with foriegn travel or with the

costumes of other cultures. Employees was selected from departments that had

jobs interchangeable with them in Tianjin.

The visitors from Tianjin speaks limited english, so listen to the audiotape in the

library too learn a few courtesy chinese phrases. Also, the visitors will be living

with some of our employee's; so please enclude them in social activitys, such as

ballgames and picnics. Remember that they are separeted from there family's.

The principle purpose is to have an successful exchange so that more of our

St. Louis staff will want to participate. Contact me for additional information.

nl

Visit the Interactive Study Center at http://brantley.swlearning.com

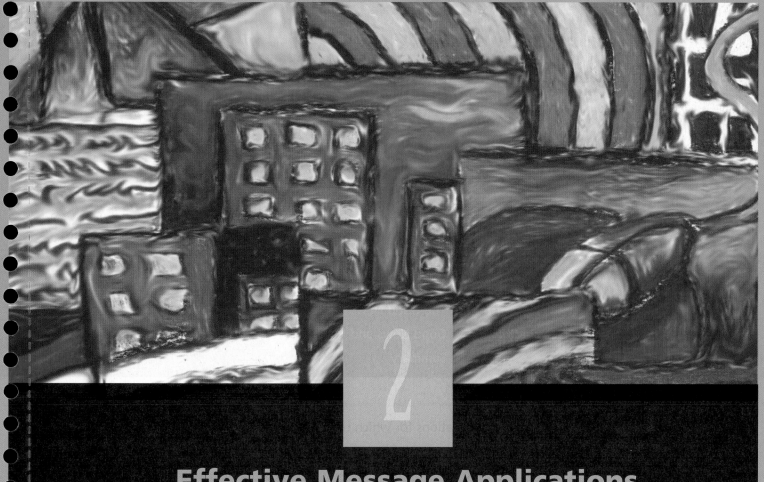

2

Effective Message Applications

Chapter 5

Good News and Neutral News Messages

Learning Objectives

1 Identify situations for which the good news strategy is appropriate.

2 Analyze good news and neutral news messages to verify that they reflect the six Cs of effective messages, acceptable message formats, and the good news strategy.

3 Prepare good news and neutral news messages by applying the CBO approach and the good news strategy.

COMMUNICATION PERSPECTIVES

Delivering Good News

In my 28 years of experience in the transportation industry, I became very adept at delivering bad news. My practice started with "solatium" payments to South Koreans whose livestock had been run over by army trucks and concluded with discontinuance of credit for delinquent customers in an intermodal (piggyback) transportation company.

However, I also conveyed the good news to customers when we were able to favorably process a claim for damages to their freight. In that situation, I needed a little down-home advice from one of our sales representatives.

In my opinion, the primary message should be that our company was the "good guy" and that we needed to keep the "bad guy," the customer, from repeating the mistakes that contributed to the damage. Only after I delivered the cautionary lecture, spelling out what needed to be done to prevent damage in transit, did I write that the claim was going to be satisfied.

One day, when I talked with a salesman who had grown up in rural Iowa, he asked why I insisted on "icing the cake with dog food." He then explained to me that by stressing the negative I was negating any positive reaction from the customer. The good news was delivered, but the customer had a bad taste in his or her mouth.

Even though perfection did not occur after that lesson, I did learn to start with the good news no matter how great the urge was to deliver a lecture. I worked on including the cautionary instructions in the form of attachments and even videotapes. I also referred to specific pages or sections in the letters. I left the lecture to the experts and enjoyed being the nice guy for a change.

Bill Hargrave, Instructor
College of Business
State University of West Georgia

Section 1: THE GOOD NEWS STRATEGY

Most businesspeople understand the value of goodwill to their success. Build goodwill by recognizing and addressing the concerns of receivers and by conveying consideration, politeness, and respect.

Messages that result in yes answers or positive responses are **good news messages**. You may write good news messages to give or ask for information. You may write **neutral news messages**, sometimes referred to as routine messages, while you wait for circumstances or conditions to change that would allow you to write a more positive response. However, both good news and neutral news messages follow the same strategy. A **strategy** is an appropriate plan to apply as you develop business messages.

Apply the good news strategy to build and maintain goodwill in all messages, whether the message is written or spoken. Examples of good news messages include the following:

- Thank-you messages
- Congratulatory messages
- Recommendation messages
- Inquiries and replies
- Requests and responses
- Orders and acknowledgments
- Routine claims and adjustments

Plan a Message Using the CBO Approach

Remember that the Communication-by-Objectives (CBO) approach offers three steps for writing effective messages. The first step helps you to plan a message, the second step helps you to compose a draft, and the third step guides you to complete a message. Give particular emphasis to the four planning activities as you prepare a good news or neutral news message.

Identify the Objective

The *why* of a good or neutral news message is the news. Use a positive or neutral statement to state the news. Place the statement in the opening paragraph to get the receiver's attention immediately. Compose the information so that the receiver will want to continue reading your message and will react favorably to other ideas you may suggest.

If you are replying to a message, review the original message several times and underline the questions to be answered. Begin your reply with the answer to one of the questions.

When you are initiating the communication, ask yourself, "What do I want the receiver to know or to be able to do after reading my message?" By determining a clear objective, you will avoid wordy, impersonal, and overused statements such as the following expressions:

Examples:

- In response to your message . . .
- I want to tell you . . .
- If we can be of further assistance . . .

Consider the case of Sarah Rosenzweig, the credit manager of City Department Store. Sarah has approved a credit request from Robert Samuel Brooks. Sarah's objective is to tell Robert that CDS has approved his credit request. In Illustration 5-1, page 141, notice how Sarah meets her objective and builds goodwill by including in the credit approval letter other details related to the objective.

Visualize the Audience

The characteristics of your audience and your message determine which message form and transmission mode will best fit your good news or neutral news communication situation. Review Illustration 1-2, Message Form, in Chapter 1, page 10, to determine whether you should write or speak your good news or neutral news message.

Once you have chosen the appropriate message form, you must select a suitable transmission mode. Review Illustration 1-3, Message Transmission, in Chapter 1, page 13, to determine which transmission mode to use for your good news or neutral news message.

Spoken Message Forms

If you determine you need a spoken message form, review speaking and listening skills in Chapter 1, pages 14–17. Consider transmission modes such as a face-to-face meeting, a telephone call, a video or an audiotape, or a video broadcast.

Written Message Forms

If you determine you require a written message form, consider transmission modes such as an e-mail, a memorandum, or a letter.

City Department Store

CREDIT DEPARTMENT

Blackhawk Mall • P.O. Box 7700
Wilmington, DE 19803-7700
Telephone: 302.555.0110/Fax: 302.555.0111

March 7, 20—

Mr. Robert Samuel Brooks
4911 Mayfield Road
Newark, DE 19713-4911

Dear Mr. Brooks

Begins with the good news: Credit is approved.

You have been approved for a City Department Store charge account. To activate your enclosed CDS Value Card, call our credit security line at 1-800-555-0196. Once your card is activated, you may begin using your CDS Value Card immediately.

Notes the credit terms; offers helpful information.

Safeguard Your Credit, the enclosed booklet, outlines our credit terms on pages 3 through 6. Pages 7 through 10 offer suggestions on how to use your credit wisely. For your convenience and security, you may report a lost or stolen credit card by calling the toll-free number printed on the back cover of the booklet.

Includes some sales and promotional ideas.

By using your CDS Value Card within the next 30 days, you will save an extra 10 percent on any purchase over $125. Watch the advertisements included in your monthly statements for additional savings.

Leaves future action to the receiver.

For questions about using your CDS Value Card or about our credit terms, please call me at 302.555.0110.

Sincerely

Sarah Rosenzweig

Sarah Rosenzweig
Credit Manager

gc

Enclosures: CDS Value Card
              Safeguard Your Credit

Illustration 5-1 **Credit Approval Message**

E-mail The hallmarks of e-mail are speed, informality, and lack of privacy. Consider the expectations of your audience carefully before you choose to transmit your message by e-mail.

Memorandum Within an organization, you may speak to coworkers and use electronic mail to communicate. You may also send coworkers written documents. These **intracompany** (within an organization) documents, called memorandums (or memos), may be concise messages that follow a set format. A memorandum is most appropriate when a message is job-related and when your audience works for the same company you do.

Letter In your job, you also may use written documents to communicate with people in other organizations. These written **intercompany** (between or among companies) messages, called business letters, vary in length but follow standard formats. The Format Guide provides examples and explanations of memorandum and business letter formats. Business letters serve a variety of purposes and represent you and your employer to the community.

Timely Tip

Use polite phrases. Successful managers find time to say *please* and *thank you*.

Respect and Empathy

Refer again to Illustration 5-1, page 141. Since this was Robert's first credit card, observe how Sarah tactfully included specific information about wise credit use. However, Sarah chose her words carefully to ensure diplomacy.

Show respect and empathy for your receiver. Emphasize *you* instead of *I* or *we*. Continue to visualize your receiver throughout the message. Speak directly to the receiver, and say exactly what you mean. Consider the following two openings for a congratulatory message:

Examples:	**Opening**	**Discussion**
	It is a pleasure to congratulate you on winning the contest.	This opening begins with the often misused pronoun *it*, resulting in a wordy phrase. The receiver does not appear important.
	I want to congratulate you on winning the contest.	The emphasis is on *I* instead of *you*. Of course you want to congratulate the winner; why else would you write the message?
	Congratulations! You won the contest.	Focus is on the receiver, and the tone is positive.

Gather Supporting Information

Supporting information helps you achieve the message objective. Include enough details to ensure clarity, completeness, and correctness. For example, when you congratulate someone, include the *what, when, where,* and *how* facts about the person's accomplishment. These details provide the supporting information that personalizes messages, convinces receivers, and helps accomplish your objective.

Culture View

Russia

The largest country in the world in terms of area, Russia, is slightly less than 1.8 times the size of the continental United States. The Russian Federation, the conventional long form for the country name, crosses 11 time zones. The two most populated cities are Moscow, with approximately 11 million residents, and St. Petersburg, with 5 million residents.

Compulsory education is free for citizens between the ages of 7 and 17; literacy is almost 100 percent. Russian, the official language, uses the Cyrillic alphabet. The alphabet consists of 33 letters: 21 consonants, 10 vowels, and 2 letters without sounds—soft sign and hard sign.

Even though communication technology is developing rapidly in Russia, the conventional telephone system is often unreliable. Since telephone books are not widely distributed in certain areas, the use of business cards is common. On your business card, include your full name, title, and any university degrees you have earned printed in English on one side and translated into Russian (with Cyrillic text) on the reverse side. When you hand someone your business card, present the card with the side printed in Russian facing the recipient.

During a business presentation, use clear, concise wording. You will not need special visuals. Even though you may use English in a presentation, you should print promotional material and other documentation in Russian. Remember this advice: Russians often place a great deal of confidence in your professional competence and experience.

Written messages lack voice tone or facial expressions. Therefore, word choices are critical to communicate your message effectively. Gather information about your receiver's background, such as age, profession, and education. Use the background information to help you write a positive message that addresses your receiver's concerns.

Organize the Information

Prepare an outline that uses the good news strategy. This strategy is based on the direct pattern, with the message objective (good news) followed by supporting and closing information. The good news strategy focuses on the receiver from the beginning to the end of the message.

To follow the good news strategy, organize the message as follows:

1. State the good or neutral news.
2. Provide adequate details or descriptions.
3. End pleasantly.

Illustration 5-2, page 144, shows how the good news strategy compares with the direct pattern.

Compose a Draft Using the CBO Approach

Apply the CBO approach by expanding the completed outline information into a message draft. Choose words and construct sentences that reflect the *you* attitude. Assemble paragraphs that have clear topic sentences and pertinent supporting sentences. Place the good or neutral news message at

Illustration 5-2 **Comparison of the Direct Pattern with the Good News Strategy**

Direct Pattern	Good News Strategy
I. Good, Neutral, or Routine News	Good or neutral news
II. General Information Supporting I	Adequate details
A. Specific Information Supporting II	or descriptions
1. Details supporting IIA	
2. Details supporting IIA	
B. Specific Information Supporting II	
III. Friendly Ending	Friendly ending

the beginning of the message. Use short paragraphs appropriately sequenced to keep the receiver's attention.

State the Good or Neutral News

Good news messages improve **human relations**, the way people respond to each other. Placing the good news at the beginning of the message sets the stage for positive human relations to develop between the writer and the receiver.

Good news or neutral news messages may include suggestions or ideas to support the message objective. Be careful, however, to avoid trite or wordy expressions. Be certain that you check for the six Cs of effective messages: courtesy, clarity, conciseness, concreteness, correctness, and completeness.

Provide Adequate Details or Descriptions

Once you have stated the good or neutral news, give enough details to ensure clarity. Include ideas that are helpful to the receiver, or present information that will promote sales of your products or services.

Some good news or neutral news messages may require only two paragraphs; for example, a thank-you for a gift or a commendation for someone who has served as a volunteer. Other messages may need three or more paragraphs; for example, notifying the winners of a contest. The winners need a written confirmation that explains what the prizes are and where, when, and how the prizes will be awarded.

End Pleasantly

The ending of a good news or neutral news message provides another occasion for you to build goodwill with the receiver. Conclude good news or neutral news messages with a positive statement. When possible, give the receiver an opportunity to take action. Note the pleasant endings in Illustration 5-3, page 145, and Illustration 5-4, page 146.

Complete a Message Using the CBO Approach

Proofread, edit, and revise your message. Make sure your good news or neutral news message achieves your objective, focuses on your audience, and follows the good news strategy.

Illustration 5-3 **Neutral News E-Mail Message**

| Address | Attach Files | Detach Files | Send Now | Send Later | Format | Spelling |

To: banderson@history.us.gov

From:

Subject: Records Management Policies Manual (RMPM)

Date: 11 November 20— 15:55:54 EST

Message:

States the neutral news. Offers extra details.

Ends with action required by reader.

Betty, to receive the latest version of the RMPM, submit your request to me by e-mail office@library.us.gov or by fax (202.555.1211). Please indicate whether you prefer a diskcopy or a hardcopy.

Submit your requisition by December 1, and you will have the material available in time to meet your January 15 project deadline.

Catherine Reginald, Director
Library Educational Services

Check for the six *C*s of effective messages. Refer to the Format Guide to ensure format accuracy. Use appropriate special references (address directories or company records) and general references (a dictionary or thesaurus) to verify content accuracy. Ask someone else to proofread your draft and your completed message. Repeat the process as often as necessary to produce a final message.

The Checklist for Preparing a Good News or Neutral News Message will help you evaluate your good news and neutral news messages.

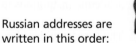

Culture Frame

Russian addresses are written in this order:
(1) country; (2) city; (3) street address and last name of the recipient.

FRIENDLY TRAVEL SERVICES

83 North Gale Drive
Marquette, MI 49855-2900
906.555.0120
http://www.friendlytravelservices.com

May 21, 20—

Ms. Mary O'Boyle
Student Travel Club
Terryton College
86 Norwich Road
Houghton, MI 49931-3492

Dear Ms. O'Boyle:

States the good news. Thank you for communicating with Friendly Travel Services. Friendly Travel Services welcomes the business of student organizations. In fact, more than 80 academic institutions in Michigan plan their travel needs through us.

Provides details. The Russian cities about which you specifically requested information—St. Petersburg and Moscow—are prime student vacation locations. The enclosed brochure describes the available student packages. The brochure also identifies departure dates, hotel accommodations, and price lists.

Ends pleasantly. Please call me at 906.555.0120 to book a trip, discuss group discounts, or make special arrangements.

Sincerely,

Leota Kornovich

Use a courtesy title to help the receiver know how to address a response.

Mrs. Leota Kornovich
Agent

bp

Enclosure

Illustration 5-4 **Good News Message**

Both personal and business situations occur that require you to write good news or neutral news messages. When a friend earns an award or achieves a goal, you write a note that expresses congratulations. When someone helps you or grants you a favor, you send a thank-you message. Likewise, in business situations, you will respond to people and react to occasions with messages that follow the good news strategy.

Good news and neutral news applications follow the good news strategy by stating the good or neutral news, providing adequate details, and ending pleasantly. Section 2 contains applications for thank-you messages, congratulatory messages, recommendation messages, inquiries and replies, requests and responses, orders and acknowledgments, and claims and adjustments.

Timely Tip

To convey a more personal tone, prepare handwritten thank-you notes for family, friends, and business associates.

Thank-You Messages

Thank you is a universal good news expression in all languages. This phrase ranks next to *please* as a powerful term in verbal communication. Even when you have said *thank you* to someone, take the time to prepare a thank-you message. A thank-you message is a strong foundation for maintaining friendships and goodwill.

In thank-you messages, make the receivers feel important. Avoid the appearance of a form message. Convince the receivers that you have only them in mind. You also can compose a message offering praise by adapting the good news strategy for a thank-you message. Apply the good news strategy.

1. Begin with the good news.
2. Offer extra details.
3. End with emphasis on the receiver.

Illustration 5-5 was mailed to a number of conference participants. Using the receiver's name in both paragraphs personalizes the message.

Illustration 5-5 **Thank-You Message**

GRACIAS

Merci Beaucoup

Your participation made a difference!

Spasibo

Ms. Davidson, thank you for participating in the International Business Conference at the Green Tree Resort in Vicksburg. Your comments and materials provided "value added" for all the attendees.

Ms. Davidson, you may periodically check our web site http://www.intleducation.ms.edu for information about future conferences. You also may call our office (1-601-555-1964) to request a copy of the yearly conference calendar.

Steven S. Bates

Steven S. Bates
Conference Coordinator

Dankeschön

شكراً

Grazie

Congratulatory Messages

Most people do not expect to receive congratulatory letters or notes. Therefore, congratulatory messages often make a major impression and build goodwill quickly. Notice how Illustration 5-6, page 149, applies the good news strategy.

1. Begin by offering congratulations for a specific accomplishment.
2. Provide extra details that clearly show your sincerity.
3. End with emphasis on the receiver.

Illustration 5-6, page 149, shows a congratulatory message that a college dean wrote to a student.

Recommendation Messages

When you apply for employment or when you are a candidate for a benefit or an award, you may ask others to prepare recommendation letters for you. *Ask* is a key term because you should request permission from others before listing their names as references on any form. Make certain that you seek recommendations from people who can attest to your skills and position-related aptitudes.

You may have occasions to prepare recommendation letters for others. However, many businesses now require employees to follow specific guidelines, such as having someone in the Compliance Department approve the message, before a recommendation letter is transmitted. When you are able to write a positive recommendation message, apply the good news strategy.

1. Identify the candidate and the job or benefit sought.
2. Provide facts relevant to the position or benefit sought.
3. Close with an offer of further information.

Illustration 5-7, page 150, shows a positive recommendation message that an associate dean wrote for a former student.

When you are unable to prepare a favorable response, you would apply the bad news strategy as shown in Chapter 6, pages 178–182.

Inquiries and Replies

Have you ever wanted to obtain more information about a product, a city, a park, or a campground? Such questions form the basis for inquiry messages. **Inquiry messages** ask the receiver for information. **Reply messages** answer inquiry messages.

Inquiries

Since most receivers consider inquiries about their products or services to be good news, use the good news strategy to prepare an inquiry. Business inquiry messages may relate to price quotations, terms of payment, guarantees, or delivery arrangements. Inquiry messages provide opportunities

CITY COLLEGE OF
MINNEAPOLIS
School of Business

796 North 58th Avenue
Minneapolis, MN 55430-5544
Telephone: 612.555.0148
Fax: 612.555.0149
E-mail: busadmin@mail.ccm.mn.edu

May 1, 20—

Miss Eileen Wells
315 Brook Lane
Minneapolis, MN 55416-1315

Dear Eileen

States the objective.

Congratulations! You earned the prestigious Campus Leader Award in the School of Business. You will receive the award at the Honors Day assembly on May 27 at 3:30 p.m. in Radford Hall.

Provides extra details.

You have maintained an outstanding record of academic achievement and service contributions. The judges made numerous positive comments about your serving as the student representative to the Greater Minneapolis Chamber of Commerce.

Emphasizes the reader.

Eileen, please encourage your family members and friends to attend the assembly and to join you at the reception that immediately follows the program.

Sincerely

Alexander Nalder

Alexander Nalder, Dean

bd

Illustration 5-6 **Congratulatory Message**

MACON STATE UNIVERSITY
College of Business

1000 College Boulevard
Lafayette, LA 70504-1000
Telephone: 337.555.9822
Fax: 337.555.9820
http://www.msu.la.edu

March 15, 20—

Mr. Wayne Moorer
Creative Productions
8250 North Acadian Drive
Metairie, LA 70006-4400

Dear Mr. Moorer

Identifies the candidate and the job sought.

Please accept this letter as my recommendation for Cassandra Boyles who has applied for the administrative assistant position with Creative Productions.

Provides facts relevant to the position sought.

Cassandra was an outstanding student at Macon State University. She graduated with a grade point average of 3.869 out of a possible 4.0. Cassandra captured first place in statewide competition for Ms. Future Business Executive and placed in the top ten in the nation in this category. She also served as vice president of public relations for Beta Gamma Sigma, the honor society for the College of Business. As a peer tutor in the Office Administration Department, Cassandra often suggested viable solutions to challenges that arose in the department.

Closes with an offer of further information.

Cassandra Boyles will make an excellent addition to the staff at Creative Productions. You may call me (337.555.9822) to discuss Cassandra's qualifications.

Sincerely

Martha Kelly

Martha M. Kelly, Associate Dean
wp

Illustration 5-7 **Positive Recommendation Message**

to build or maintain goodwill. In both personal and business inquiries, apply the good news strategy.

1. Begin with a specific question or direct statement.
2. Include adequate details and additional questions.
3. End with clear directions for the receiver.

Illustration 5-8 provides an example of a business inquiry. Use the same strategy for a personal inquiry. See the Format Guide for correct personal message format.

Replies

Effective communication is a two-way process. The reply to an inquiry message completes the communication cycle. When you receive an inquiry, prepare a complete, courteous, and prompt reply. Whenever possible, show respect for the person making the inquiry: Reply within five working days. When you reply to an inquiry, apply the good news strategy.

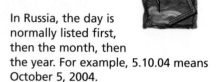

Culture Frame

In Russia, the day is normally listed first, then the month, then the year. For example, 5.10.04 means October 5, 2004.

1. State the good news by answering questions and emphasizing the *you* attitude.
2. Include any additional pertinent information.
3. End with a goodwill statement.

Illustration 5-9, page 152, is the reply to the inquiry in Illustration 5-8.

Illustration 5-8 **Memo Inquiry**

American Exchange Program

Southeast U.S. Chapter
PO Box 1515
Atlanta, GA 30301-1515

http://www.americanexchange.com
Office: 404.555.1271
Fax: 404.555.1272

MEMORANDUM

TO: Bill Williams, AEP National Headquarters
FROM: Wilma Thomas, Southeast U.S. Chapter Coordinator
DATE: February 10, 20—
SUBJECT: Russian Vocabulary

Begins with a specific question.

What Russian words should I ensure that our students know before they leave the United States in August?

Includes adequate information and additional questions.

Since you have coordinated the Eastern Europe exchange program for American Exchange during the last three years, do you have any vocabulary lists or language tapes that I can distribute? Can you suggest other sources of language and cultural information that our students might find helpful?

Gives directions.

Please send your response to me at our Atlanta office.

Illustration 5-9 **Memo Reply to Inquiry**

American Exchange Program

National Headquarters
PO Box 321-B
Chicago, IL 60690-0321

http://www.americanexchange.com
Office: 312.555.1777
Fax: 312.555.1771

TO: Wilma Thomas, Southeast U.S. Chapter Coordinator
FROM: Bill Williams, AEP National Headquarters
DATE: February 15, 20—
SUBJECT: Russian Vocabulary

Accents the you attitude. Answers questions.

The students participating in the August program will spend two weeks in San Francisco at a language camp prior to their departure from the United States. However, you may want them to learn the following Russian expressions ahead of time:

Good morning	Dobraye ootro
Good afternoon	Dobriy den'
No	Net
Yes	Da
Please	Pozhalusta
Thank you	Spasibo

Provides helpful information.

On February 14, I sent to you by Express Mail a set of language tapes we purchased. Expect the tapes to arrive before February 26. Two recommended web sites are the following: http://www.roxana.spb.ru/russian.htm and http://www.executiveplanet.com.

Ends with a goodwill statement.

Wilma, let me know if you have any more questions about Russia. Based on my experience, your students will have an interesting, exciting exchange program.

Requests and Responses

A **request** message asks for information, approval, permission, cooperation, or assistance. By asking for information, requests open the door for future business. **Responses** to requests provide a good opportunity to establish goodwill and promote business.

Requests

For a routine request or a request that you expect to be fulfilled, use the good news strategy.

1. State the major request in the first sentence. You also may use a subject line. The subject line lets the receiver know what the message is about. However, do not rely on the subject line alone.
2. Make the request clear with additional details.
3. End courteously. Close with the action you expect the receiver to take.

Illustration 5-10, page 153, is an example of a request message that uses a subject line and the good news strategy. This message is prepared in the simplified format.

Winston State Park and Resort

112 Plantation Road • Clearwater, Florida 33756-0112
Telephone: 727.555.7753 or 1.800.555.7750
Fax: 727.555.7750
E-mail: winstonparkinfo@state.fl.us

21 March 20—

Mr. Frank Bilbo
Sales Manager
Kittrell FIshing Supplies, Inc.
1256 River Road
Eufaula, AL 36072-1256

Uses a subject line (optional).

FISHING SUPPLY CATALOG

Starts with a specific request.

Mr. Bilbo, please send me a copy of your most recent catalog. The Winston State Park and Resort hosts a bass fishing tournament each year. This year 300 invitations will be mailed for the tournament that is scheduled for June 10.

Gives facts needed to obtain a complete answer.

When the tournament ends, fishing lures will be distributed to the top 20 winners. The budget for purchasing the lures is $2,000. Please include any suggestions you have, including specific items that I can purchase at bulk prices.

Ends courteously. Indicates what action the reader should take.

Mr. Bilbo, please contact me at **1-800-555-7750** and indicate when an order must be received for you to guarantee delivery before the June 10 competition.

Rogerio Liang

ROGERIO LIANG, ACTIVITIES DIRECTOR

jp

Illustration 5-10 **Request Message**

Responses

Writing a yes response to a request takes planning if the message is to sound warm and sincere. Writing a no response takes additional planning to build or maintain goodwill. (See Chapter 6.) When granting a request, follow the good news strategy.

1. State the good news first. Provide an answer to the request in a subject line and/or the first sentence.
2. Include any additional pertinent information in the second paragraph.
3. End with a goodwill statement. Request action from the receiver.

Illustration 5-11, page 155, uses the good news strategy in granting a request. The response approves the request that was made in Illustration 5-10.

Orders and Acknowledgments

An **order message** asks for goods or services and may be either spoken or written. An **acknowledgment** is a written confirmation for an order.

Orders

Orders for services include reservations for rooms or transportation, utility connections, or appointments. Printed order forms are often used for ordering merchandise. If an order form is not available, you may write an order message on plain paper or letterhead stationery.

Check for accuracy whether you order in person or by telephone, Internet, printed order form, fax, or letter. Follow the good news strategy in order messages.

1. Use direct language in the first sentence. Use phrases such as *Please ship* or *Please deliver*. Direct statements assure the seller that you want to buy. Avoid indefinite statements such as *I would like to* or *If possible*.
2. Give complete details. Indicate catalog numbers, quantities, descriptions, prices, totals, and other information that will assist the seller in filling your order promptly and correctly.
3. Include payment information and shipping instructions. Indicate when you expect to receive the delivered goods.

Illustration 5-12, page 156, shows an order letter for merchandise. Observe how the letter follows the good news strategy.

Kittrell Fishing Supplies, Inc.

1256 River Road • Eufaula, AL 36072-1256

Telephone: 334.555.7888 or 1.800.555.7999

Fax: 334.555.7889

http://www.kittrellfishing.com

March 25, 20—

Mr. Rogerio Liang
Activities Director
Winston State Park and Resort
112 Plantation Road
Clearwater, FL 33756-0112

Dear Mr. Liang:

Answers the request in the beginning of the message.

A copy of our most recent catalog that shows lures and other fishing equipment is enclosed. The prices of lures that are sold at bulk prices to fishing tournament organizers are shown below.

Includes detailed information.

Inventory Number	Item Description	Bulk Price	Individual Price
FSS-01	Flat Sugar Shad-Tennessee	$59.99/10 pieces	$6.99 each
FSS-03	Flat Sugar Shad-Gizzard	$59.99/10 pieces	$6.99 each
SS-01	Shallow Sugar Shad Lures	$62.50/10 pieces	$7.25 each
SS-02	Alabama Sugar Shad Lures	$62.50/10 pieces	$7.25 each
RSS-01	Rattlin Sugar Lures-Homer	$65.00/10 pieces	$7.50 each
RSS-08	Rattlin Sugar Lures-Chrom/Black	$65.00/10 pieces	$7.50 each

I am willing to work with you on pricing discounts for items from the regular catalog as well as the bulk-priced lures listed above.

Requests action from the reader. Ends with a goodwill statement.

Please call our toll-free number, 1-800-555-7999, or contact me via e-mail at *fbilbo@kittrellfishing.com* to order your lures and other tournament supplies. You may expect delivery within seven business days after your order is received.

Sincerely,

Frank Bilbo

Frank Bilbo, Sales Manager

vab

Enclosure

Illustration 5-11 **Response to Request**

Computer Training Center

900 Oceanfront Boulevard
Melbourne, FL 32937-0900
Telephone: 407.555.0139
Fax: 407.555.0140
E-mail: astro@melbo.ocean.net

June 11, 20—

Satellite Academic Software
Sales Division
113 Levin Road
Hanover, NH 03755-1113

ORDER FOR SCIENTIFIC SOFTWARE

States request. Identifies source.   Please ship me the following software packages, which were advertised on page 92 in the May issue of the *Collegiate Computer Journal*.

Gives full details.

Number	Quantity	Description	Price	Total
CI-6675	1	Biology Bundle	$762	$762
MA-2004	5	Mathplot	50	250
	Total			**$1,012**

Asks for reader response.   A $1,012 check is enclosed. May I expect delivery of these items by June 20?

Lorraine Cookson

LORRAINE COOKSON, DIRECTOR

je

Enclosure: $1,012 Check

Illustration 5-12 **Order Letter**

Acknowledgments

Reputable companies fill orders as soon as possible. A prompt shipment serves as an acknowledgment for most orders. When the order is from a new customer or is an unusually large order from a regular customer, send an acknowledgment message. The intent of an acknowledgment message is to provide information on delivery status and to encourage future orders. Promptly prepare a courteous acknowledgment message that applies the good news strategy.

1. Indicate that the product was sent or that the service was approved. State when the buyer should receive the merchandise or may begin using the service.
2. Describe quality features of the product or service. You also may describe another closely related product or service in which you feel the customer may be interested.
3. Encourage future orders.

Observe how the good news strategy is applied in Illustration 5-13, page 158. Note how the writer uses the *you* attitude to tailor the sales information to suit the receiver's needs.

An explanation for a delayed order to an established customer is a neutral news message. You may use a printed form or note similar to Illustration 5-14, page 159.

Routine Claims and Adjustments

A **claim** message asks for an adjustment. For example, you may request a refund of money, a replacement, or an exchange of merchandise because you are dissatisfied with the service or product. (Nonroutine claims, in which you must include a persuasive argument, are discussed in Chapter 7.) An **adjustment** message accepts the validity of the claim. The adjustment grants a refund of money, a replacement, or an exchange of merchandise.

Routine Claims

Businesses expect customers to communicate when goods or services are unsatisfactory. Consider claims against a guarantee, warranty, or contractual agreement neutral news messages because they are routine. Use the good news strategy as a guide.

1. Begin with a specific problem statement and request an adjustment.
2. Give a complete and concise description of the claim, including all essential facts.
3. End courteously with a suggestion for prompt action.

Satellite Academic Software

113 Levin Road
Hanover, NH 03755-1113
Telephone: 1-603-555-0150/Toll-Free: 1-800-555-0127/Fax: 1-603-555-0159
E-mail: ama@sas.com

June 15, 20—

FAX TRANSMITTAL: 407-555-0140

Ms. Lorraine Cookson, Director
Astro Computer Training Center
900 Oceanfront Boulevard
Melbourne, FL 32937-0900

Dear Ms. Cookson:

Answers what, how, and when about the order.

Your order for software packages (one *Biology Bundle* and five *Mathplots*) has been shipped by Quick Mail Service. You should receive your software packages by June 17.

Shows appreciation. Gives brief sales information.

Thank you for ordering from Satellite. You may be interested in a new learning module just released as a supplement to *Biology Bundle*. The learning module contains five hands-on experiments that allow students to see biological principles in living organisms. Each experiment has three difficulty levels. You may choose the levels that fit your students' capabilities. For current *Biology Bundle* users, the introductory price of the module is $29.95. You will find that our products are high-quality and have the lowest prices.

You may pay for your order by personal check, credit card, or institutional purchase orders. You may receive a replacement or full refund for any order returned with your receipt within 30 days of the shipment date.

Encourages future orders.

For your convenience, you may place an order by calling 1-800-555-0127, or you may fax your order to 1-603-555-0159. You may also make direct requests from our homepage on the World Wide Web: http://www.sas.order.com. By using any of these ordering methods, you will receive your order within 48 hours.

Sincerely,

Anne M. Cadenhead

Anne M. Cadenhead, Sales Representative

sw

Illustration 5-13 **Faxed Order Acknowledgment (shown without fax cover sheet)**

Illustration 5-14 **Printed Order Acknowledgment**

Thank you for your order!

TO:

FROM:

DATE:

You should receive your order for _____
within _____ days.

Adjustments

Adjustment messages that respond positively to claims are good news messages. Present an adjustment plan that the customer will be able to understand and follow easily. If you are replacing an item, state exactly what the customer should do with the original item.

When you grant a claim, write an adjustment message that applies the good news strategy. Use the opportunity to present additional sales information to the customer. For example, you may reassure the customer that you have quality products. You also may introduce a related item or service.

1. Grant the request in a subject line and/or in the first sentence.
2. Provide the necessary details about the adjustment. Give a clear explanation of any forms the customer needs to complete. Avoid the words *grant* and *claim*. Use positive words.
3. End with a cordial, open invitation for future business. Further action will be the receiver's responsibility.

Illustrations 5-15 and 5-16, pages 160–161, show a routine claim message and an adjustment approval message.

Illustration 5-15 **Routine Claim Message Sent by E-mail**

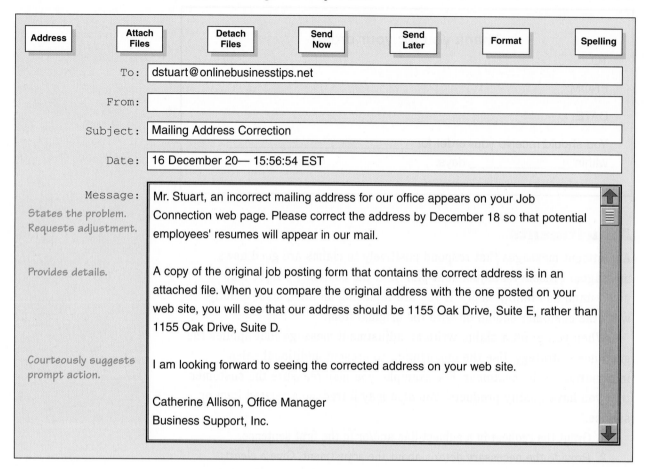

| Address | | Attach Files | | Detach Files | | Send Now | | Send Later | | Format | | Spelling |

To: dstuart@onlinebusinesstips.net

From:

Subject: Mailing Address Correction

Date: 16 December 20— 15:56:54 EST

Message:

States the problem. Requests adjustment.

Mr. Stuart, an incorrect mailing address for our office appears on your Job Connection web page. Please correct the address by December 18 so that potential employees' resumes will appear in our mail.

Provides details.

A copy of the original job posting form that contains the correct address is in an attached file. When you compare the original address with the one posted on your web site, you will see that our address should be 1155 Oak Drive, Suite E, rather than 1155 Oak Drive, Suite D.

Courteously suggests prompt action.

I am looking forward to seeing the corrected address on your web site.

Catherine Allison, Office Manager
Business Support, Inc.

Illustration 5-16 **Adjustment Approval Message Sent by E-mail**

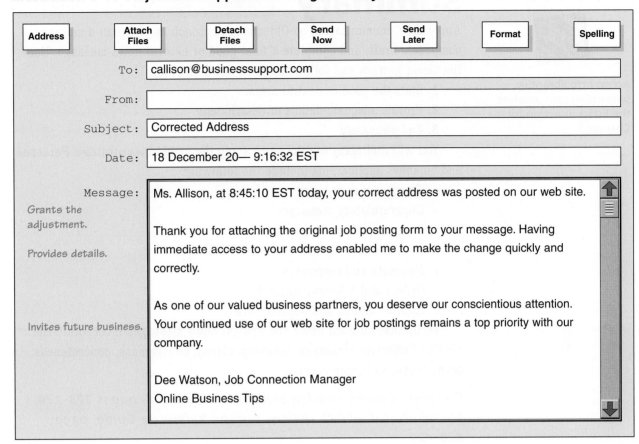

Address		Attach Files		Detach Files		Send Now		Send Later		Format		Spelling

To: callison@businesssupport.com

From:

Subject: Corrected Address

Date: 18 December 20— 9:16:32 EST

Message:

Grants the adjustment.

Provides details.

Invites future business.

Ms. Allison, at 8:45:10 EST today, your correct address was posted on our web site.

Thank you for attaching the original job posting form to your message. Having immediate access to your address enabled me to make the change quickly and correctly.

As one of our valued business partners, you deserve our conscientious attention. Your continued use of our web site for job postings remains a top priority with our company.

Dee Watson, Job Connection Manager
Online Business Tips

Summary

Apply the Communication-by-Objectives approach as you plan a message, compose a draft, and complete a final good or neutral news message. Use the direct pattern and follow the good news strategy.

1. State the good or neutral news.

2. Provide adequate details or descriptions.

3. End pleasantly.

You will find many occasions to apply the good news strategy. Personal and business applications include the following:

- Thank-you messages
- Congratulatory messages
- Recommendation messages
- Inquiries and replies
- Requests and responses
- Orders and acknowledgments
- Routine claims and adjustments

Verify that all good news and neutral news messages incorporate the six *C*s of effective messages: courtesy, clarity, conciseness, concreteness, correctness, and completeness.

Complete Communication Skills Development 5, pages 173–174. For additional adverb review, see the Reference Guide, pages 420–421.

Exercises

5 - 1   **Directions:** Collect samples of actual business messages. Examine the messages to determine whether the writer built and maintained goodwill. Highlight sentences that you consider goodwill statements.

5 - 2   **Directions:** In a brainstorming session, identify situations for which good news or neutral news messages are appropriate. Discuss how goodwill can be built and maintained in each situation.

5 - 3   **Directions:** Think of a teacher who made a favorable impact on your life. Then prepare a handwritten thank-you message to the teacher thanking him or her for being a positive influence in your life. State what you are doing now. Your final message should follow the Checklist for Preparing a Good News or Neutral News Message.

Internet *Challenge*

5-1 Directions: Search online sites for information related to telephone communication in St. Petersburg, Russia. Topics should include calling from hotels, private telephones, pay phones, and cellular phones. Then use a Venn diagram to compare and contrast telephone communication in St. Petersburg, Russia, with telephone communication in a large city in the United States. Refer to Chapter 3, page 81, for a discussion on comparing and contrasting information. Prepare to discuss your diagrams in class.

5-2 PART A Directions: Do an online search to locate the e-mail addresses for members of the U.S. House of Representatives for your state. Choose one representative to whom you will communicate. Using the Internet and library resources, identify specific legislation that you want the representative to support.

PART B Directions: Plan, compose, and complete an e-mail request message. Apply the CBO approach and the good news strategy. Then prepare your final request message asking the representative to support the specific legislation you identified in Part A. Your final message should follow the Checklist for Preparing a Good News or Neutral News Message and the specific strategy for request messages.

InfoTrac

Directions: Using the InfoTrac keyword search, locate an article on recommendation letters by Kenneth C. Petress. Write or key a summary based on the points that you will observe when you request recommendation letters, including how you will rank your skills, traits, and experiences for writers to emphasize. Prepare to discuss your summary in class.

WebTUTOR **Advantage**

Directions: Access your WebTutor Advantage product. Complete the short-answer portion for Chapter 5 and send the answers to your instructor.

Case Studies

5 - 1

Communication Situation: You are the program coordinator for the computer lab at Weston Scientific Research (2250 Stemmons Freeway, Dallas, TX 75207-2250; office telephone: 214.555.1200; fax 214.555.1222; web site: http://www.westonscientific.com). Cristina Hancock, the technical support person for Computer Tech Max for the north Texas area, donated over 40 hours to help you organize the annual computer workshop for high school business technology teachers in the Dallas area. Ms. Hancock provided printed and electronic materials to be distributed at the workshop; she also attended to answer participants' questions. As a result, attendance at the workshop increased 50 percent over last year. More than half of the participants reported on their workshop evaluations that they had increased their computer knowledge base and would be able to use the information in their classrooms.

From Ms. Hancock's business card, you know that she has a master's degree in computer science; she is a certified computer tech support professional with Computer Tech Max (293 Lee Avenue, Dallas, TX 75206-2930).

Task A: Plan a thank-you message to Ms. Hancock. Use the good news strategy for the thank-you message; and apply the CBO step, Plan a Message. Provide additional details to complete the message.

Determine the Objective: State the objective of the message.

Visualize the Audience: Consider the following criteria, and list information you should consider in visualizing your audience.

- **Age:**

- **Profession:**

- **Education:**

- **Cultural or language differences:**

- **Other:**

Case Studies

List Supporting Information: Generate ideas, words, and phrases using brainstorming, nonstop writing, or bubble writing.

Organize the Information:

a. Identify the strategy you will use for this message.

b. Organize the information in an outline, using either the traditional or the indented outline format.

Task B: Review your completed outline. Compose a draft of your thank-you letter.

Task C: Complete the message. Date your message March 1. Your final letter should reflect the six *C*s of effective messages and acceptable message format.

Case Studies

5-2

Communication Situation: You are the assistant credit manager at City Department Store (Credit Department, P.O. Box 7700, Wilmington, DE 19803-7700; telephone: 302-555-0110; fax: 302-555-0111; web site: http://www.citydeptstore.com). As part of your responsibilities, you review the credit limits of existing customers. You decide whether CDS will raise a customer's credit limit depending on each customer's credit rating, payment history at CDS, and frequency rate for using the CDS Value Card.

Based on her record, you have decided to raise the credit limit of Gloria Mendez (37 Abilene Way, Marshalltown, IA 50158-3700) from $1,500 to $3,000. Ms. Mendez has been a reliable customer for seven years and has responsibly handled a series of increases in her credit limit.

CDS is running a special promotion between September 1 and December 31 for a select group of charge-card customers like Ms. Mendez. The promotion allows customers six months of interest-free financing on any item priced over $299. In addition, these preferred customers do not have to make any payments during the six-month period. If the customers pay the full purchase price at the end of six months, no interest is charged. If the customers choose not to pay the full purchase price at the end of the initial six months, a standard payment plan begins and customers are charged interest only from that point on.

Task: Plan, compose, and complete a congratulatory message to Ms. Mendez. Apply the CBO approach and the appropriate good news strategy. Explain the promotional program. Invite Ms. Mendez to take advantage of the six months of interest-free financing. Date your letter September 14. Your final letter should reflect the six *C*s of effective messages and acceptable message format.

Case Studies

5 - 3

Communication Situation: You visited the web sites of your largest competitors and discovered that they provide hats, mugs, and clipboards as sales incentives to their sales staff. According to their web sites, they purchase these materials from A-1 Promotions, 1137 Grand Boulevard, Wilmington, DE 19803-1137. The telephone number is 302.555.0110; the fax number is 302.555.0100; the e-mail address is aonepromotions@abc.com. Ms. Michi Saga is the marketing manager for A-1 Promotions.

You are the general manager of Pete's Auto Parts Plus (2201 State Street, Dover, DE 19901; telephone 302.555.8940; fax 302.555.8944; e-mail: petesautoparts@providerpostbox.com).You are interested in providing sales incentives for the 36 staff members in the Pete's Auto Parts Plus branches located in Delaware and Maryland. You need to know the types of items, the cost of each item, and the delivery schedule offered by A-1 Promotions. Add other relevant information needed for your inquiry.

Task: Plan, compose, and complete an inquiry message to Ms. Michi Saga. Apply the CBO approach and the appropriate good news strategy. Date the message November 2. Your final letter should reflect the six *C*s of effective messages and acceptable message format.

5 - 4

Communication Situation: Review Case Study 5-3. Ms. Saga assigned you, the assistant marketing manager, the task of writing a form message that can be mailed to potential buyers.

Include these facts in the form message:

- A print catalog is enclosed. The items may be viewed online at http://www.aonepromotions.com.
- Prices range from $2.50 for a mug to $18.25 for a sweatshirt.
- Bulk prices are available when 25 or more of the same item are purchased.
- The cost includes shipping by Northeastern Ground Shippers.
- Orders are delivered within 14 business days inside an 850-mile radius of Wilmington, Delaware.

Case Studies

Task: Plan, compose, and complete a reply message. Apply the CBO approach and the appropriate good news strategy. Provide details you consider helpful or necessary to complete the message. Date the letter November 9. Use parentheses to indicate the sections that the writer should personalize when each individual message is prepared. Your final message should reflect the six *C*s of effective messages and acceptable message format.

5 - 5

Communication Situation: The state medical adviser has strongly recommended that the college centralize the student medical records, including immunization records. Previously, files were kept in the Student Service Center (SSC) and in the First Aid Center (FAC).

Assume you are the health coordinator for the Office of Student Health of Central University (300 Pine Hollow Road, Wichita, KS 67214-3306). Your office is located in Room 2 of the Medical Annex. Your telephone number is 316-555-0126, extension 37. Your fax number is 316-555-0166, and your e-mail address is medannex@centraluniv.edu. You must collect student health files from the SSC and the FAC by March 1. Your office will maintain complete health records for all students.

Your department head expressed concern for the confidentiality and security of the records during the moving process. You have spoken with the supervisor of campus mail, Don Yajima, and have arranged for special secure handling of the student health files. Don has volunteered to answer questions about appropriate packaging and delivery arrangements. He can be reached at extension 33.

Task: Plan, compose, and complete a request message. Apply the CBO approach and the appropriate good news strategy. Provide additional details to complete the message. Direct your request to L. J. Anderson, Director, Student Service Center, and to Eduardo R. Malcom, Director, First Aid Center. Date the message February 5. Your final message should reflect the six *C*s of effective messages and acceptable message format.

Case Studies

5 - 6

Communication Situation: Assume you are L. J. Anderson, Director of the Student Service Center at Central University (300 Pine Hollow Road, Wichita, KS 67214-3306). Your telephone number is 316-555-0126, extension 42. Your fax number is 316-555-0164. Your e-mail is ssc@centraluniv.edu.

Task: Review Case Study 5-5. Plan, compose, and complete a yes response to the health coordinator's request for student medical records. Apply the CBO approach and the appropriate good news strategy. Provide details you consider helpful or necessary to complete this message. Date the message February 12. Your final message should reflect the six Cs of effective messages and acceptable message format.

5 - 7

Communication Situation: Members of the Allied Health Club want to sell SUPRA Food Supplement packages as a fundraising activity. The packages are listed in a brochure of fundraising products from Community Fitness Center in Mobile, Alabama.

You are the treasurer of the Allied Health Club. You have been asked to fax an order for 200 packages at $6 each (includes the cost of shipping) to the Community Fitness Center, 111 North Water Drive, Mobile, AL 36602-1110. The fax number is 334-555-0151. The brochure offers two methods of shipping for the same cost: Coast Trucking or United States Postal Service.

Task: Plan, compose, and complete an order message. Apply the CBO approach and the appropriate good news strategy. Date the message April 20. Indicate that the Allied Health Club's tax-exemption number is H-19-714; because the club is tax exempt, no sales tax should be charged. Request that the Community Fitness Center ship the packages by Coast Trucking to you at the Allied Health Club, Marietta College, Building 17, 200 Woodmere Drive, Marietta, GA 30067-2017. The telephone number for the Allied Health Club is 770-555-0144; the fax number is 770-555-0145, and the e-mail address is allied@mail.marietta.cc.ga.edu. Also prepare a fax cover sheet to the Community Fitness Center. Your final message should reflect the six Cs of effective messages and acceptable message format.

Case Studies

5 - 8

Communication Situation: Assume you are the sales manager for fundraising products at Community Fitness Center in Mobile, Alabama.

Task: Plan, compose, and complete an acknowledgment of the order from the Allied Health Club. Apply the CBO approach and the appropriate good news strategy. Provide details you consider helpful or necessary to complete this message. Review Case Study 5-7 for the addresses you need to complete your message. Date the message April 24. Your final message should reflect the six Cs of effective messages and acceptable message format.

5 - 9

Communication Situation: Assume you are Regina Butler. You live at 9076 Montgomery Road, Cincinnati, OH 45224-9065. Your e-mail address is rbutler@webboxesonline.com. On September 29, you order the **Slim Away the Pounds** weight loss program that was advertised on television. The advertisement was sponsored by the AAA Weight Loss Clinic (330 South 13th Street, Lincoln, NE 68508-8500; telephone: 402.555.7474; fax: 402.555.1847). You ordered the weight loss program because your high school reunion is scheduled in three months, and you have 25 pounds to lose. You placed a telephone order with Deborah McIntire, the sales representative. You gave your Visa credit-card number to pay $24.95 for the program. Deborah McIntire shipped you the videotape, a 20-page diet instructional manual, and a sample AAA Weight Loss chocolate and nut snack bar. On October 10, you received your shipment. When you tried to view the videotape, you discovered that the tape was blank.

Task: Plan, compose, and complete a claim message. Apply the CBO approach and the good news strategy. Date your message October 10. Your final message should reflect the six Cs of effective messages and acceptable message format.

Case Studies

5-10

Communication Situation: Assume you are Deborah McIntire, sales representative for the AAA Weight Loss Clinic (330 South 13th Street, Lincoln, NE 68508-8500; telephone 402.555.7474; fax 402.555.1847; e-mail: dmcintire@midlands.com.

On October 10, Regina Butler (9076 Montgomery Road, Cincinnati, OH 45224-9065; e-mail address: rbutler@webboxesonline.com) mailed you a claim message stating that she received a blank videotape.

Task: Plan, compose, and complete an adjustment message. Apply the CBO approach and the good news strategy. Date your message October 15. Your final message should reflect the six *C*s of effective messages and acceptable message format.

Communication Skills Development 5

NAME_____

Part A   Adverb Usage

Directions: In each of the following sentences, underline the correct adverb of the words given in parentheses.

1. When you cannot hear callers (clear, clearly), let them know (immediate, immediately).

2. The traditional telephone is changing (drastically, drastic).

3. Car phones are used (wide, widely) by businesspeople.

4. Make a special effort to drive (safe, safely) while using a phone.

5. A pleasant phone manner can create a (remarkably, remarkable) positive impression.

6. Use concise, courteous language, (especially, especial) when leaving voice mail messages.

7. Speak (directly, direct) into the receiver at your normal rate of speech.

8. Speak (natural, naturally); emphasize ideas by varying your tone of voice.

9. Respond to voice mail messages within a (reasonable, reasonably) short time.

10. (Always, All ways) identify yourself either with your name or with your name and the name of your department or company.

11. When you use a cellular phone, check to make certain that the batteries are (full, fully) charged.

12. (Don't never, Never) hesitate to ask for the spelling of a name.

13. Be (real, really) sensitive to security issues when giving information to callers.

14. A customer service coordinator would do (good, well) to offer assistance to callers.

15. Do (not, not never) leave a call without an explanation to the caller.

16. Offering to call back is (more, most) helpful than keeping the caller on hold for several minutes.

17. Do not terminate a call (too, to) (abrupt, abruptly).

18. Avoid using a cellular phone (inappropriate, inappropriately) in public places such as restaurants and theaters.

19. Be sure, (to, too), that the directories in your office are the latest editions.

20. A manager should operate the phone equipment as (well, good) as the administrative assistant.

Part B Skills Application

Directions: In the following memorandum, underline errors in noun, pronoun, verb, adjective, and adverb usage and spelling. In the space provided, write the correction for each error. (As you have learned, simplified memos should be single-spaced. In this memo, extra space has been added for you to insert corrections.)

Interoffice Communication
NOVA Business Systems
17 Main Street • Carlsbad, NM 88220-2222
505-555-0173 • Fax 505-555-0179

1 November 20—

All Employees

PRODUCTIVITY IMPROVEMENT

Edward M. Spencer, Total-Quality-Management consultant from Dayton, Ohio, will discuss a stradegy for improving productivity at the regular scheduled monthly seminar on November 8 in the conference room. To insure clearity, please review the definition for productivity that were developed by Mr. Spencer and I.

The appripriate definition states that productivity is effectiveness in bringing about results, benefits, or profits to achieve organization objectives while maintaining employee satisfaction. NOVAS goal is to improve both productivity and employee satisfaction. Please plan to participate in the seminar on November 8 from 3:30 to 5:15 p.m.

Belinda Williamson

Belinda Williamson

Vice President

gc

Chapter 6

Bad News Messages

Learning Objectives

1 Analyze bad news messages to verify that they reflect the six Cs of effective messages, acceptable message formats, and the bad news strategy.

2 Prepare bad news messages by applying the CBO approach and the bad news strategy.

COMMUNICATION PERSPECTIVES

Delivering Bad News

One of the hardest things I do in my professional life as a radiation oncologist is deliver bad news. Sometimes I have to tell my patients their cancer has recurred. For others, I must reveal that all treatment options have been exhausted and that no other interventions would be useful. Occasionally, this discussion includes how and when they might die.

I was never instructed on how to speak to gravely ill or dying patients in medical school. Medical students essentially learned how to deliver bad news through careful observation of their mentors, just as they observed and learned how to set a fractured ankle.

I have always believed that providing details to my patients was essential. Sharing statistics seems logical, as many patients now have access to the Internet and can locate information easily. Patients can become depressed after reading this information, and the depression can make my job even more difficult.

When I begin to speak to a patient, I try to put myself in his or her position. I know this sounds like a cliché, but I try to become a spectator and imagine how I would want to be treated if I had a life-threatening illness. I am honest when asked about technical details. I see no point in holding back unpleasant information to protect from further anguish.

I prefer to have family members present when patients receive bad news. Family members may give the patient support and alleviate some stress during this emotionally charged conversation. These discussions are always conducted in private, which can be a challenge on busy hospital wards. I maintain eye contact with my patient and have boxes of tissues available. When needed, I am silent; thus, giving the patient time to ask questions. To limit interruptions, arrangements are made to have my calls answered by staff members.

My role as oncologist caretaker includes assessing emotional, social, and cultural needs while trying to provide hope. I reassure my patients that I will provide comfort or palliative care when no cure is possible; and that if I do my job well, they will not have pain.

Unfortunately, life-threatening illnesses, and all of the uncertainties and grief that come with the illness, threaten one's ability to find joy in life. As a physician, I try to help patients and their families recognize that they can still experience great moments of happiness during illness.

The essence of medicine should be to preserve health for those who are well, to care for the sick and the suffering, and to comfort the dying. These responsibilities demand that I remain truthful, show compassion, offer encouragement, and foster appropriate measures of hope. Despite 15 years of clinical experience, delivering bad news is still the hardest thing I have to do.

Joanne L. Bujnoski, DO
Medical Director
Center for Cancer Care
Sacred Heart Hospital

Section 1: THE BAD NEWS STRATEGY

Realistically in business, occasions will arise when you must say *no*. Coworkers, employees, or students will ask you to write recommendation letters; but based on legal or ethical issues, you are unwilling to provide a recommendation. People will make requests that you are unable to answer or fulfill. Companies or individuals will make mistakes that must be corrected. However routine these situations may appear to you, the requests are important to the people making them.

Whether you completely or partially refuse a request, the **refusal message** follows the bad news strategy. By following the bad news strategy and the Communication-by-Objectives (CBO) approach, you can plan a positive message that implies or states a refusal. The message focuses on the receiver's point of view. Messages that follow the bad news strategy include refusals for the following:

- Recommendations
- Requests
- Adjustments
- Credit
- Orders

Plan a Message Using the CBO Approach

The Communication-by-Objectives (CBO) approach includes three steps for writing effective messages. The first step directs you to plan a message, the second step helps you to compose a draft, and the third step guides you to complete a message. Give particular emphasis to the four planning activities as you prepare a bad news message.

Identify the Objective

Think of what you want to accomplish with the message. You want to write a refusal message that maintains goodwill. As you refuse a request, show a benefit or at least suggest an alternative. The following example indicates what a credit manager may communicate to a salesperson when a prospective client's credit request must be refused.

Example: Because the Smith & Reynolds contract is important to you, please establish a cash account until the company's credit history improves.

Visualize the Audience

Know the receiver's profile, the sensitivity of the situation, and the anticipated reaction to the bad news. Examine the situation from the receiver's viewpoint. As you carefully visualize the receiver, you should become more empathetic. As a result, you can more effectively determine your tone, word choice, and explanation for the request refusal.

Review Illustration 1-2, Message Form, in Chapter 1, page 10, to determine the most appropriate message form. Will the receiver react more positively to a bad news message that is written, spoken, or a combination of written and spoken? Also review Illustration 1-3, Message Transmission, in Chapter 1, page 13, to determine which transmission mode to use for your bad news message.

Gather Supporting Information

Information that provides additional documentation or support helps you achieve your message objective. In your refusal, use relevant facts that the receiver will understand. Obtain as much information as possible about your receiver's background, such as age, profession, and education.

Brazil

As a Portuguese-speaking country surrounded by Spanish-speaking countries, Brazil maintains a distinct culture. Therefore, observe the following verbal and nonverbal cues when you communicate with Brazilians:

- Speak Portuguese, not Spanish!
- Wear colors others than green and yellow because these are the colors of the Brazilian flag. When visitors wear the green and yellow combination, they may become the object of mockery.
- Maintain unbroken eye contact during conversations.
- Listen carefully because Brazilian fast-paced conversations are filled with animation, frequent interruptions, and nonconfrontational exclamations such as "no."
- Prepare to stand closely in front of others, even during casual conversations.
- Shake hands with everyone in the group, both upon arrival and upon departure.
- Address your Brazilian contact by title. Use first names after you are invited to do so.
- Show patience when discussing bad news because Brazilians consider aggressive business attitudes offensive.

As you become more accustomed to communicating with Brazilians, remember to remain flexible and patient. Communication effectiveness improves as you develop a deeper understanding of the country's culture and values.

Organize the Information

Use the bad news strategy as you organize the message. This strategy follows the indirect pattern—the explanation for the decision precedes the bad news. As a result, you attempt to prepare the receiver for the refusal.

The bad news strategy has five parts. You may develop each part into a separate paragraph, or you may choose to combine the parts into a three-paragraph message. Frequently, parts two and three are combined for a middle paragraph, and parts four and five are combined for the ending paragraph. To follow the bad news strategy, organize the message as follows:

1. Begin with a neutral or pleasant statement that relates to the receiver.
2. Explain the reason(s) for the refusal.
3. State or imply the refusal.
4. Offer an alternate solution or action (if possible).
5. End with a positive, friendly statement.

Review the comparison of the indirect pattern with the bad news strategy, as shown in Illustration 6-1, page 179.

Compose a Draft Using the CBO Approach

Apply the CBO approach and follow the indirect pattern as you compose a message draft. Incorporate the five parts of the bad news strategy into the message.

Illustration 6-1 **Comparison of the Indirect Pattern With the Bad News Strategy**

Indirect Pattern	Bad News Strategy
Opening	Begin with a neutral or pleasant statement that relates to the receiver.
Explanation	Explain the reason(s) for the refusal.
Main Idea	State or imply the refusal.
Additional Information	Offer an alternate solution or action if possible.
Closing	End with a positive, friendly statement.

Begin With a Neutral or Pleasant Statement

The best guideline for a bad news message is to start pleasantly. The message begins with a **buffer**, a neutral or pleasant statement. The statement contains positive words that relate to the receiver's request.

Choose words carefully to soften the negative news and to avoid misleading the receiver into thinking that a yes answer will be in the next paragraph. Thus, the buffer should establish a common bond between the receiver and you.

Timely Tip

Successful communicators choose their words carefully.

Examples:

Buffer	**Discussion**
Thank you for your interest in attending the International Hotel Management seminar.	The statement expresses appreciation.
You are entitled to quality products and service.	The sentence expresses agreement.

Explain the Reason(s) for the Refusal

When you must refuse a request, explain why you cannot do what the receiver wants before you state the refusal. By offering logical reasons for your refusal, you mentally prepare the receiver for the bad news.

Avoid the excuse of company policy as the reason for a refusal. If a company policy is the reason for the refusal, explain the policy and the logic.

In a bad news message, you may use the passive voice to describe a situation. In the following examples, the passive voice is diplomatic and encourages goodwill, while the active voice is accusatory:

Examples:

Active Voice	**Passive Voice**
The consultant did not provide a user's manual for each employee.	A user's manual was not provided for each employee by the consultant.
The team leader made a decision that resulted in lower sales.	A decision was made that resulted in lower sales.

After you have stated an adequate reason or reasons for the refusal, the next step is to say no.

State or Imply the Refusal

State the refusal concisely in a positive tone. If appropriate, use the passive voice to cushion the bad news. Notice the difference in how the human resources director informed a job applicant of the bad news.

Example:

Active Voice/Negative Tone	Passive Voice/Positive Tone
I did not select you for the tour guide position because our firm requires fluency in at least one foreign language.	Since our firm requires fluency in at least one foreign language, another applicant was selected for the tour guide position.

Negative words often sound accusatory. When negatives are unavoidable, precede the negative words with transitional terms. In most cases, when you prepare refusal messages, you should avoid negative words, such as those listed in Table 6-1.

Table 6-1 Negative Words

cannot	error	regret
damage	fault	shocked
defective	impossible	sorry
delay	inconvenience	unable
dissatisfied	negligence	unfortunately
don't	never	wrong

A refusal may be implied rather than explicitly stated when you emphasize what can be done rather than what cannot be done. When you accentuate what you can do for the receiver, you lessen the potential negative impact of a bad news message. Compare the tone in these examples:

Example:

Cannot Do—Negative Tone	Can Do—Positive Tone
You will not be allowed to return the phone after the 30-day trial period.	You may return the phone within the 30-day trial period.
Your lawn maintenance contract prohibits our applying products more frequently than twice a month.	Your lawn maintenance contract allows us to apply products twice a month.
I cannot deliver the information because you did not specify what you need.	Please call me (800.442.9937), describe what you need, and I will locate the information for you.

Offer an Alternate Solution or Action (If Possible)

The rule for bad news messages is to use positive language. Whenever possible, offer a constructive suggestion, a substitute, a counterproposal, or an alternate course of action. Explain how the receiver may benefit. When appropriate, include a resale statement. A **resale statement** gives a reminder about the company's products or services. Compare the following situations that indicate what cannot be done with alternate solutions that suggest what can be done:

Examples:	Situation	Alternate Solution
	A customer requests a camera lens attachment that is no longer available.	Recommend a similar attachment; provide an online address where available products are described.
	Temporary laborers arrive to help harvest the tomato crop. However, assistance is not needed because the crop was damaged from unusually heavy rainfall.	Suggest that the laborers seek employment in nearby locations to help harvest other crops. Offer to call farm managers to verify that laborers are needed.

When you are unable to offer an alternate solution, give a suggestion for future situations. For example, you may be able to respond positively to a request at a later time. This offer will help create a positive feeling between the receiver and you even though the current request was refused.

End With a Positive, Friendly Statement

Always end a bad news message with a positive, friendly statement to ensure your willingness to help in some way. *If* and *when* statements may imply that you expect further trouble. Therefore, avoid trite phrases such as these:

Examples:　If I can be of further help, please contact me.

　　　　　　When you have additional questions, please let me know.

Close with action required from the receiver. A receiver-oriented closing suggests that you expect to retain the receiver's goodwill. The following examples of closing paragraphs indicate how the receiver will benefit:

Examples:　Please send an e-mail message (cpbrantley@earthlink.net) or call me at 850.555.0114 to schedule an appointment to discuss startup costs for your business. You will then be ready to prepare your business plan.

　　　　　　Please answer all the items on Form 36A, and our agency will review your credit request.

　　　　　　You may expect to receive your order within ten days after you have signed the payment agreement.

Complete a Message Using the CBO Approach

Follow the CBO approach as you proofread, edit, and revise your message. Use the bad news strategy to develop any refusal message. Verify that your message contains the six *C*s of effective messages: courtesy, clarity, conciseness, concreteness, correctness, and completeness.

Continue to revise for format and content accuracy until you produce an acceptable final message. Refer to the Format Guide to verify format accuracy.

The Checklist for Preparing a Bad News Message will help you evaluate your bad news messages.

CHECKLIST

Checklist for Preparing a Bad News Message

1. **Does your bad news message:**
   - Accomplish the objective?
   - Relate to your target audience?
   - Include supporting information?
   - Organize contents in the indirect pattern?

2. **Does the draft of your bad news message:**
   - Begin with a neutral or pleasant statement?
   - Explain the reason(s) for the refusal?
   - State or imply the refusal?
   - Offer an alternate solution or action (if possible)?
   - End with a positive, friendly statement?

3. **Does your final bad news message:**
   - Incorporate the six Cs of effective messages?
   - Send the message you intend?
   - Reflect ethics and credibility by providing adequate, objective information?
   - Look and/or sound professional?

Section 2: BAD NEWS APPLICATIONS

Both personal and business situations may require you to write bad news messages. Occasionally, friends or charitable organizations may request you to volunteer time or to contribute money. When you are unable to fulfill these requests, you prepare a request refusal message. Likewise, in business situations, you apply the bad news strategy to write refusal messages that maintain goodwill.

Section 2 discusses bad news applications for refusal messages in these situations:

- Recommendations
- Requests
- Adjustments
- Credit
- Orders

Each type of refusal follows the bad news strategy.

Recommendations

Consider both potential legal and ethical issues when you are unable to provide a positive recommendation. Take time to think about your spoken or written response before you prepare an unfavorable recommendation message. Giving a spoken rather than a written poor recommendation offers you no protection against potential lawsuits.

One choice is to speak directly to the person who requested the recommendation and indicate why you cannot provide a positive response. Responses that an instructor may give students who have asked for recommendations are shown in the following examples:

Examples: I suggest that you obtain a recommendation from another instructor in whose class your attendance and grades have been better than in my course.

While I am happy to write a letter for you, based on your performance in my class, I could not speak as strongly for you as might another instructor.

A second choice is to submit a written message that is known as a "name, rank, and serial number" reference. The message provides only the employment dates and omits any references to poor performances or unsatisfactory evaluations.

The third choice is to prepare and transmit an unfavorable written recommendation. If an inquiry comes from a prospective employer without a request from the person applying for the position, decline to comment until you have verified that your former employee, coworker, or student wants you to provide a recommendation. When you decide to provide an unfavorable recommendation message, follow the suggestions in Illustration 6-2, page 184. The suggestions show how the unfavorable recommendation message pattern correlates with the bad news strategy.

Illustration 6-3, page 185, is an example of an unfavorable recommendation message.

Unfavorable Recommendation Messages	Bad News Strategy
Indicate that your message is a response to the applicant's request.	Open with a neutral statement that relates to the receiver.
Explain in what capacity you have known the applicant.	Offer an explanation.
Limit comments to objective statements; omit opinions or value judgments.	State or imply the unfavorable recommendation (the main idea).
Consider legal and ethical issues.	Offer an alternate solution or action if possible.
Mark the message as confidential; do not share the information contained in the recommendation with anyone other than the prospective employer.	End with a positive statement.

Request Refusals

When a business must refuse a request for contributions, use of facilities, preferential treatment, or special discounts, someone must write a **request refusal**.

To compose a request refusal message, visualize the receiver, consider the receiver's needs, and maintain the *you* attitude. Apply the bad news strategy.

1. Begin with a pleasant or neutral statement that relates to the receiver.
2. Give at least one reason for the refusal.
3. Imply or state the refusal (the main idea).
4. Offer a helpful solution or suggestion.
5. End with a positive statement without reference to the refusal.

Illustration 6-4, page 186, gives an example of a request refusal message written in response to a scholarship request. Note the positive tone and the implied refusal.

Adjustment Refusals

As discussed in Chapter 5, **adjustment messages** are replies to claim messages. When circumstances prevent your granting an adjustment, promptly compose an adjustment refusal message that follows the bad news strategy.

Begin the adjustment refusal message with a buffer. Then explain why you cannot grant the adjustment so that the receiver will understand your decision. Keep the tone of the refusal as positive as possible. After making the refusal, you may include a resale statement or an offer to help the receiver.

Bayside Technology
3739 Lamont Road
Santa Fe, TX 77510-3700
Telephone: 409.555.1224   Fax: 409.555.1200   http://www.baysidetech.com

May 15, 20—

Mr. Carlos Hernandez
Human Resources Director
Nova Enterprises
1650 Los Gamos Drive
San Diego, CA 92108-1650

Dear Mr. Hernandez:

Indicates that the message is a response to the applicant's request.

ANDREW MARSHALL'S EMPLOYMENT RECORD

At the request of Andrew Marshall, Bayside Technology Corporation provides you with his employment documentation.

Explains in what capacity you have known the applicant.

Andrew Marshall worked from June 10 to December 15, 2003, as a beta tester. He was assigned to Team B, one of three teams under my supervision. On his peer evaluations, he received a 2.5 rating on a scale from 0 to 5.

Provides objective statements.

Between September 30 and December 1, Mr. Marshall was absent from work four times without having filed a leave request. He did not call or offer an explanation for his absences. All four absences were on Fridays. He left the firm at Bayside Technology's request.

Considers legal and ethical issues.

During their first year of employment, employees receive evaluations from their supervisors at the end of 3, 6, and 12 months. Since the employees retain copies of their supervisors' evaluations, you may ask Andrew Marshall to share that information with you.

Marks the message as confidential.

Employee information is considered confidential. Even though Mr. Marshall signed a disclosure consent form, please discuss with him with whom you may share the information contained in this message.

Sincerely,

Michele Gunner

Michele Gunner
Business Operations Leader

lk

Illustration 6-3 **Unfavorable Recommendation Message**

FRANKLIN DAVIS FOUNDATION

Franklin Davis College
Bradee Hall
Greenville, SC 29611-3869
Telephone: 864.555.0178   Fax: 864.555.0107   http://www.franklindavis.edu

December 3, 20—

Miss Sharon Fremont
31 West Garden Beach Drive
Greenville, SC 29605-3869

Dear Miss Fremont

Begins with a buffer.

Thank you for applying for a Franklin Davis Foundation scholarship for the semester that begins in January.

Gives basis for refusal. Implies refusal (main idea).

Each application was carefully evaluated for eligibility according to foundation guidelines. To be eligible for scholarship consideration, an applicant must be a full-time student with a 3.5 grade point average.

Offers suggestion. Ends positively.

Please consider reapplying for a Franklin Davis Foundation scholarship in August. Include another copy of your college transcript with your new application to verify your student status and grade point average.

Sincerely

Steven H. McCutchen

Steven H. McCutchen
Foundation Director

wt

Illustration 6-4 **Request Refusal Message**

An offer to help will promote goodwill. If receiver action is needed, provide clear directions. End courteously, without reference to the refusal and without an apology. For adjustment refusal messages, apply the bad news strategy.

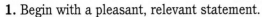

1. Begin with a pleasant, relevant statement.
2. Give a factual basis for the refusal.
3. Imply or state an impersonal refusal (the main idea).
4. Include a resale statement and/or an offer to help.
5. End pleasantly; emphasize receiver action when needed.

Illustration 6-5, page 188, provides an example of an adjustment refusal message in response to a claim. Recently, staff members from the Advanced Computer Training Company planned and conducted a computer-training program for 40 Best Western Data Systems employees.

George Culbertson, a purchasing agent for Best Western Data Systems, asked for a contract cost adjustment because three employees from Best Western Data Systems had not scored as well as he had anticipated on their computer certification test. The adjustment request was refused because 37 of the employees earned an overall B average on the certification test.

Credit Refusals

Credit requests may involve someone asking for a loan, a credit card, an extended line of credit, or a credit purchase. In any case, you review the applicant's current and past credit record. Sometimes the response to a credit request may be a **credit refusal**. You may refuse credit, or you may suggest some modified arrangement of the customer's request.

Suggesting a modification allows you to consider answering the request with a positive response later. An applicant's credit record may improve with either an increase in income or a decrease in debt. In either situation, you want to be helpful and retain the person as a cash customer.

Your task is to compose a credit refusal message that uses a buffer to establish a good feeling, shows reasons why you are refusing, refuses in a positive manner, suggests how the receiver can improve the conditions, and invites a later application. The best ending promotes a cash purchase.

For credit refusal messages, apply the bad news strategy.

1. Begin with a pleasant, timely buffer.
2. Give reasons for the refusal, but leave the way open for credit extension.
3. Imply or state the refusal (the main idea).
4. Make a counterproposal; if appropriate, introduce a cash plan.
5. End with attention on the receiver's benefits.

Illustration 6-6, page 189, shows an example of a credit refusal message. Timothy Allen, who will graduate next May with an accounting degree from West Tallahassee College, applied to City State Bank for a $3,000 loan. He listed First Mutual Bank as his only credit reference and Main Street Bakery as his employer. City State Bank requires credit applicants to have at least three credit references.

ADVANCED COMPUTER TRAINING COMPANY

200 Old Moss Street
Tucson, AZ 85702-2000
Telephone: 520.555.0147   Fax: 520.555.0143
http://www.advcom/bus/tuc.html

December 7, 20—

Mr. George Culbertson
Purchasing Agent
Best Western Data Systems
36 Manitoba Avenue
Tucson, AZ 85730-3036

Dear Mr. Culbertson

Begins with a buffer.

You are correct to expect quality programs correlated to your company's computer-training needs.

Explains conditions.

Our customized educational programs are designed to ensure maximum investment of time and money. Your employees' skills and productivity were enhanced as a result of the high-quality training. Because 37 of your employees earned an overall B average and increased their computer skills, their value to your company has increased.

Implies refusal. Includes resale.

Between now and January 2, you may register your employees for a specially designed two-hour review course at a discounted rate of $35 each. As a symbol of your employees' commitment to improved computer skills, certificates of achievement for 37 employees are enclosed.

Offers help. Asks for reader response.

Please call me (555.0147) to discuss further customized courses for your company.

Sincerely

Raymond Peterson

Raymond Peterson
Educational Director

wt

Enclosures

Illustration 6-5 **Adjustment Refusal Message**

CITY STATE BANK

341 Maystone Street
Tallahassee, FL 32304-3341
Telephone: 850.555.1114
Fax: 850.555.1100
http://www.citystbk.fl.com

March 11, 20—

Mr. Timothy Allen
6120 Wexford Lane
Tallahassee, FL 33581-8120

Dear Mr. Allen

Begins with timely, related buffer.   Attending college and working at the same time requires energy, commitment, and dedication. You have obviously planned and organized your goals carefully as your graduation is planned for next May.

Gives reason for refusal and implies refusal. Opens way for future credit.   Establishing a credit history also takes time and careful planning. To obtain a $3,000 loan at City State Bank, you need at least three credit references. When you have built a credit history with two references in addition to First Mutual Bank, please consider City State Bank for your loans.

Offers alternate suggestions.   You may qualify for a government-insured loan; these loans are available for college expenses through the Commercial National Bank (555.5000). You also may obtain an application for the local Accounting Association's scholarship by contacting Randle Irwin at 555.7712.

Ends with attention on reader's benefit.   Mr. Allen, accounting is a wise career choice. Best wishes for a successful senior year in your accounting classes.

Sincerely

Alyce H. Barnhart

Alyce H. Barnhart
Vice President

rm

Illustration 6-6 **Credit Refusal Message**

Order Refusals

Timeliness is important when you respond to a customer's order. You should ship the products as soon as possible. If you cannot fill the order immediately, you must communicate with the customer, either with a spoken or written message. Some businesses may prefer to use electronic mail.

A company may refuse an order for the following reasons:

- The order had incomplete instructions.
- The customer has not received credit approval and has not offered to pay cash.
- The merchandise is not available, and an alternate product is not accessible.
- Orders for the requested merchandise are filled only through another distributor or retailer.
- The sale is illegal.
- The product is temporarily out of stock.

When you do not have what the customer ordered or you are unable to sell to this person, you compose an **order refusal**. Order refusal messages are brief.

For order refusal messages, apply the bad news message strategy as follows:

1. Begin with a buffer; the opening statement may identify the order by date, number, and description.
2. Ask for needed information if the order was incomplete; give a reason for the refusal if the order will be delayed or will not be filled.
3. State or imply the delay plan or the refusal (the main idea).
4. Offer a resale or an alternate solution.
5. End with a positive statement.

Illustration 6-7, page 191, gives an example of an order refusal. Malcolm Hopkins, office manager for TAB Products, ordered check forms that are temporarily out of stock. Note the alternate solution offered.

MODERN OFFICE SUPPLIES AND EQUIPMENT

P.O. Box 150   Council Bluffs, IA 51501-1500
Telephone: 712.555.0152   Fax: 712.555.0115
http://www.mose/gnn/wic/bus.coun.html

November 12, 20—

MR MALCOLM HOPKINS
OFFICE MANAGER
TAB PRODUCTS
605 HOLSTON DRIVE
COUNCIL BLUFFS IA 51501-5060

NOVEMBER 10 ORDER

Begins with a buffer. Identifies the order.

Mr. Hopkins, thank you for your November 10 order for 1,000 Y-39 check forms. The Y-39 format has proved useful to you and many other customers.

Gives a reason for the delay.

Because the demand for the Y-39 check form was unusually great during September and October, our stock is temporarily depleted. You may expect to receive the Y-39 forms by December 5.

States the delay plan. Offers an alternate solution.

While the forms you requested are being prepared, I asked our branch office in Des Moines to mail you 200 M-90 check forms. The M-90 will adapt to your printer and will allow you to print your November payroll.

Ends with a positive statement.

You will receive the 200 M-90 check forms by Quick Mail Service no later than November 15. You then will receive 800 Y-39 forms to complete your order.

Quang Vo

QUANG VO, SALES MANAGER

cp

Illustration 6-7 **Order Refusal Message (shown in Simplified Format)**

If the merchandise is temporarily out of stock, you may send a short message that allows the customer a choice to accept delayed delivery or to cancel the order. Illustration 6-8 shows a sample printed card that may be personalized for each customer.

Illustration 6-8 **Out-of-Stock Order Refusal**

DATE:

TO:

FROM:

Your satisfaction is our main concern. The following merchandise is temporarily out of stock.

Item Number   Description

The anticipated delivery date for your order is _____.

Please call 1-800-555-9004 to indicate your preference:

_____ ship as soon as items are available

_____ cancel order

Ethics in Action

Access http://brantley. swlearning.com. Analyze the Ethics in Action for Chapter 6.

Summary

Compose a bad news message when you are unable to grant or approve a request. The objective of a bad news message is to say no and still maintain goodwill. Apply the CBO approach and the bad news strategy to write a positive refusal.

The bad news strategy prepares the receiver for the refusal. Begin the message with a neutral or pleasant statement (a buffer). Then explain the reasons for the refusal before you state or imply the refusal. Include an alternate solution or action when possible, and end with a positive statement.

Messages that follow the bad news strategy include refusals of recommendations, requests, adjustments, credit, and orders. Verify that all bad news messages incorporate the six *C*s of effective messages and follow acceptable message formats.

Complete Communication Skills Development 6, pages 201–202. For additional preposition review, see the Reference Guide, page 421.

Exercises

6 - 1

Directions: In the space provided, revise each of the following sentences, changing the active voice to the passive voice to avoid an accusing tone.

1. Rachel misplaced the ink cartridge.

2. Margo omitted the latest specifications in the semiannual report.

3. The new employee deleted our most important files.

4. The advertising department did not post the bid request on the World Wide Web.

5. You packaged the documents out of sequence.

6. The hardware specialist installed an extremely slow modem.

7. You mailed the report to the wrong listserv.

8. The computer manager created the web page with the wrong URL.

9. Your assistant mailed the package by regular mail instead of overnight delivery.

10. Kim did not include a financial analysis for the quarter in her report.

Exercises

6-2

Directions: In the space provided, revise the following negative statements to make them positive statements.

1. Customized learning material cannot be exempt from meeting fair use guidelines.

2. Do not violate even one of the four factors in the fair use test.

3. Copyright law does not destroy a balance between the rights of copyright holders and the rights of the public.

4. Even when you are given permission to duplicate material, you cannot make copies for more than one course.

5. Instructors are prohibited from charging students for more than the photocopying expenses.

6. Do not forward e-mail messages without the originator's permission.

7. Never use a corporate logo as a link; provide the URL instead.

8. Do not forget to properly cite web resources.

9. Instructors cannot make multiple copies of copyrighted material more than nine times in one class term.

10. The length of time material appears on a server cannot exceed the duration of a course.

Exercises

6 - 3

Directions: Research legal and ethical guidelines that should be observed in preparing and transmitting unfavorable recommendation messages. Review both print and electronic sources, including the Family Educational Rights and Privacy Act (commonly referred to as the Buckley Amendment) that was revised in 1988. You also may interview local human resources directors.

In the space provided, write a summary of your findings; prepare to discuss your summary in class.

Exercises

6 - 4

Directions: Review the paragraphs of an unfavorable recommendation message. In the space provided, revise the paragraphs. Your final message should follow the bad news strategy for unfavorable recommendation messages and reflect the six *C*s of effective messages.

Mrs. Barbara Webb worked with Ensley Network from March 6, 2002, to February 19, 2003, as my executive assistant. Mrs. Webb was one of our older employees of Mexican-American ancestry.

On numerous occasions, she asked others for assistance in order to accomplish tasks that were specifically assigned to her. In addition, she routinely avoided performing duties outlined in her job description, particularly if she felt the duties were beneath her. Understandably, this behavior caused discord in the office. On the annual peer evaluation, she only scored 2.0 on a 5-point scale. During her exit interview, Mrs. Webb said, "I do best working under direct supervision on projects with clearly defined deadlines."

Mrs. Webb was most productive when she worked on projects by herself. She does, however, possess excellent computer skills; she assisted in a project undertaken by our office to reorganize our membership database.

During a downsizing of Ensley Network, Mrs. Webb left the firm at Ensley Network's request. Please contact our human resource officer, Dee Smith, should you need any further information.

Even though Ms. Webb signed a disclosure consent form, employment records are confidential. Therefore, please obtain her permission before you share the information contained in this message with others in your firm.

Internet *Challenge*

6-1 Directions: Locate a business-related user group, newsgroup, bulletin board, or open forum on the Internet; post a request for sample letters containing bad news messages. Print copies of the messages. On a separate sheet of paper, summarize your findings. Share the printed messages and your summary in class.

6-2 Directions: Search online sites for information helpful to doing business in Brazil. On a separate sheet of paper, write a short article summarizing three concepts businesspeople should know if they plan to work in Brazil. Try the following key phrases in your search:
- Brazilian business etiquette
- Business in Brazil
- Working in Brazil

Share your summary in class.

InfoTrac

Directions: Using the InfoTrac keyword search, locate an article about passive voice by C. Edward Good. After your read the article, write or key a summary that describes when the passive voice is preferred. Prepare to discuss your summary in class.

Directions: Access your WebTutor Advantage product. Complete the short-answer portion for Chapter 6 and send the answers to your instructor.

Case Studies

6 - 1

Communication Situation: You are the public relations director for Datatron, Inc. (72 Ticonderoga Avenue, Tucson, AZ 85730-3036; telephone: 520.555.0117; fax: 520.555.0119; web site: http://www.datatron.tucson.net). Mrs. Anna J. Hadley, President, Board of Directors, Samaritan Retirement Community, 100 Heavenly Drive, Tucson, AZ 85730-0100, has requested a $500 contribution. Datatron has contributed to the fund drives in previous years because the Samaritan Retirement Community serves senior citizens in your business area.

All charitable donations are planned before Datatron's fiscal year begins on July 1. Mrs. Hadley's request was received on September 1.

Task A: Plan a request refusal message to Mrs. Anna J. Hadley. Use the bad news strategy for request refusals; and apply the CBO step, Plan a Message. Date the message September 5. Provide additional details to complete the message.

Determine the Objective: State the objective of the message.

Visualize the Audience: Consider the following criteria, and list information you should consider in visualizing your audience.

- **Age:**
- **Profession:**

- **Education:**

- **Cultural or language difference:**

- **Other:**

List Supporting Information: Generate ideas, words, and phrases using brainstorming, nonstop writing, or bubble writing.

Organize the Information:
a. Identify the strategy you will use for this message.

Case Studies

b. Organize the information in an outline using either the traditional or the indented outline format.

Task B: Review your completed outline. Compose a draft of your request refusal message.

Task C: Complete the message. Follow your outline, and use the bad news strategy to prepare your request refusal message. Provide details necessary to complete this message. Your final message should reflect the six *C*s of effective messages and acceptable message format.

6 - 2

Communication Situation: You are the senior staff designer with Northwestern American Interiors (125 Apple Avenue, Seattle, WA 98113-3324; telephone: 206.555.1719; fax: 206.555.1700; web site: http://www.nwamerinteriors.com). The design firm specializes in commercial interior design projects. You have just completed the design and implementation of the interior renovations of a locally owned restaurant called The Seattle Diner. Two weeks preceding the completion of the project you were notified that the eight tabletop jukeboxes you ordered were no longer being manufactured. Therefore, the jukeboxes were unavailable for installation in the final stage of the renovation. You have located a vintage full-sized jukebox in excellent condition for the same price as the original eight tabletop jukeboxes for the restaurant.

You have received an adjustment request from Mr. David R. Stevens, owner and manager of The Seattle Diner that is located at 396 Williamson Avenue, Seattle, WA 98117-3960. Mr. Stevens has asked for a reduction in the final invoice from Northwestern American Interiors because of the last-minute change made to the original design plan.

Task: Plan, compose, and complete an adjustment refusal message. Apply the CBO approach and the appropriate bad news strategy. Provide details you consider helpful or necessary to complete this message. Date the message December 7. Your final message should reflect the six *C*s of effective messages and acceptable message format.

Case Studies

6 - 3

Communication Situation: You are the business office manager for the Palm-N-Sun Resort Hotel (543 Starfish Drive, Miami, FL 33140-4461; telephone: 786.555.1886; fax: 786.555.1800; e-mail: businessoffice@palmnsun.resort.net). You have received a credit application from the board of directors for the Middle Tennessee Business Professionals Association. The directors want to hold their annual meeting at your resort. You have reviewed the Association's credit history and the credit request for an amount up to $12,500. Based on previous meetings of a similar size, the amount of credit necessary to successfully host the meeting is on target. Unfortunately, however, the Association has hosted only one previous annual meeting at a resort in Orlando, Florida. The Palm-N-Sun Resort Hotel requires three hotel/resort credit references for new guests whose banquet and event costs will exceed $3,000.

Task: Plan, compose, and complete a credit refusal message. Apply the CBO approach and the appropriate bad news strategy. Provide details you consider helpful or necessary to complete this message. The address for the Middle Tennessee Business Professionals Association is PO Box 321, Murfreesboro, TN 37133-3210. Your final message should reflect the six *C*s of effective messages and acceptable message format.

6 - 4

Communication Situation: You are the sales manager for Specialty Paper Products. Your e-mail address is specpro@gulf.com. Michael Hamilton, office manager for Mail It Now, a one-stop shop that provides copying, packaging, and mailing services, ordered by e-mail 25 boxes of custom paper (item no. CV967) at $25 per box from Specialty Paper Products. The cash order totals $722.50, including tax and shipping.

Mr. Hamilton requested that the order be charged to the shop's credit card. Mail It Now is a repeat customer for Specialty Paper Products. The CV967 custom paper is listed in your current catalog at $25 per box for *cash purchases* plus tax and shipping. Credit purchases cost $26.75 per box plus tax and shipping. Since the $25 price is for cash purchases, you must refuse Mr. Hamilton's credit order.

Task: Plan, compose, and complete an order refusal message. Apply the CBO approach and the appropriate bad news strategy. Transmit the information as an e-mail message. The e-mail address for Mail It Now is minow@shore.com. Use the current date. Provide helpful or necessary details to complete this message. Your final message should reflect the six *C*s of effective messages and acceptable e-mail format.

Directions: In each of the following sentences, underline the correct preposition or prepositional phrase of the words given in parentheses.

1. The artists selected a time most convenient (for, to) the editor's schedule.

2. The editor asked, "Will you be angry (about, with) me after the decision is made?"

3. Oday asked, "What time is convenient (for, to) you to meet with us?"

4. The computer template appears (behind, in back of) the index.

5. You must choose (among, between) the traditional and the online version.

6. The publisher agreed (to, with) the outline for the new student workbook.

7. She wants to be independent (of, from) her husband's income.

8. They walked (in to, into) the next room to meet the production editor.

9. However, the authors readily decided to follow the bad news strategy (in, into) their counterproposal.

10. To prepare the publisher for their refusal, the authors provided an explanation (for, about) the refusal before the actual refusal was stated.

11. The publisher was especially intrigued (by, with) the authors' creative alternatives for the contract terms.

12. (Beside, Besides) proposing an advance on royalties, the authors included a request for a grant to purchase new multimedia systems.

13. Their letter ended with a positive statement appropriate (for, to) the situation.

14. After discussing contract issues with their colleagues, the authors planned their approach by applying information gained (from, off) similar cases.

15. Their analysis involved a comparison of the advantages (to, with) the disadvantages.

16. The editorial management team listened intently (at, to) the authors' concerns.

17. After careful consideration of the authors' dilemma, the project editor agreed (on, with) the authors' newly proposed writing schedule.

18. Because each author wanted to write only two chapters, the writing responsibility for the remaining chapters would be divided (among, between) three freelance writers.

19. The authors agreed to work closely (on, with) the freelance writers to establish consistency in style.

20. All writing team members must discuss any deviations (away from, from) the approved plan.

Part B   Skills Application

Directions: In the following e-mail message, underline errors in noun, pronoun, verb, adjective, adverb, and preposition usage and spelling. Write the correction above each error. (Ordinarily, e-mail messages are single-spaced. In this e-mail message, extra space has been added for you to insert corrections.)

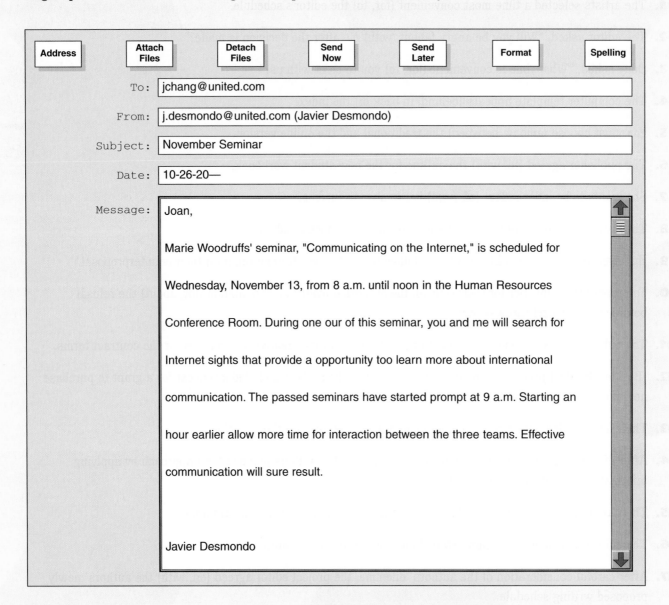

| Address | | Attach Files | | Detach Files | | Send Now | | Send Later | | Format | | Spelling |

To: jchang@united.com

From: j.desmondo@united.com (Javier Desmondo)

Subject: November Seminar

Date: 10-26-20—

Message:

Joan,

Marie Woodruffs' seminar, "Communicating on the Internet," is scheduled for

Wednesday, November 13, from 8 a.m. until noon in the Human Resources

Conference Room. During one our of this seminar, you and me will search for

Internet sights that provide a opportunity too learn more about international

communication. The passed seminars have started prompt at 9 a.m. Starting an

hour earlier allow more time for interaction between the three teams. Effective

communication will sure result.

Javier Desmondo

Chapter 7

Persuasive Messages

Learning Objectives

1 Discuss situations when persuasion may be necessary.

2 Discuss the role of ethical persuasion when preparing persuasive messages.

3 Explain receiver benefits, descriptive language, and appropriate appeals as they relate to the persuasive strategy AIDA.

4 Identify unique characteristics of donation requests and sales messages, and discuss how those characteristics encourage favorable responses.

5 Prepare effective persuasive messages by implementing the CBO approach and the persuasive strategy AIDA.

COMMUNICATION PERSPECTIVES

The Power of Persuasion

The Susan G. Komen Breast Cancer Foundation was founded on a promise made between two sisters—Susan G. Komen and Nancy Brinker. Suzy was diagnosed with breast cancer in 1978, when it was rarely discussed in public and little was known about the disease. Before she died at the age of 36, Suzy asked her sister to do everything possible to bring an end to breast cancer. Nancy kept her promise by establishing the Susan G. Komen Breast Cancer Foundation in 1982 in Suzy's memory.

Nancy's promise became a reality in large part because of her ability to communicate her vision, her passion, and her mission to others. Her gift of articulation enabled her to open doors that had been shut, to open ears that didn't want to hear, and to bring recognition where there had been denial.

She traveled the country compelling people with the statistics that while 59,000 Americans had died in the Vietnam War, 339,000 American women died of breast cancer during that same time. But no one protested *their* loss—no one spoke up for these women. And, as she says, "That silence became my cause . . . and in 1982 the cause became the Komen Foundation. I had found the way to keep my promise to Suzy."

Twenty years later, the Komen Foundation and its Affiliate Network are global leaders in the fight against breast cancer through support of innovative research and community-based outreach programs. Today, we celebrate the power of a promise and how a single person's vision can change the lives of millions.

Powerful and persuasive communication can, indeed, make a difference in this world.

Barbie Casey
Communications Coordinator
The Susan G. Komen Breast Cancer Foundation

Section 1: THE PERSUASIVE STRATEGY

Instructions, directives, and routine requests within organizations are typically written in the direct pattern. These kinds of messages require little persuasion because employees are expected to perform their job tasks without being persuaded. The direct pattern is also used for correspondence outside an organization when quick agreement is expected.

However, when you ask someone to go beyond the routine—do a favor, respond to a complaint, pay an overdue bill, or buy a product—you may be asking for more than a receiver wants to do. You may need to persuade the receiver to do what you ask, so you prepare a **persuasive message**.

Typical persuasive messages ask the receiver to do the following:

- Donate time, money, or knowledge
- Support an activity or cause
- Cooperate to resolve an issue or pay a bill
- Purchase a product or service (sales message)

A persuasive message follows the persuasive strategy **AIDA** (**a**ttention, **i**nterest, **d**esire, **a**ction) and explains how the receiver benefits from fulfilling a request—*before* the request is made. When explanations and reasons are presented before the main idea (which is the actual request), receivers are more likely to consider the value of the entire message, continue reading or listening, and respond favorably.

Timely Tip

When you know a receiver prefers the direct approach, use the direct approach; and adapt the persuasive strategy AIDA by presenting the main idea as the attention-getting opening.

Persuade Ethically

As you prepare a persuasive message, remember that you are trying to influence a receiver's actions or beliefs. Sometimes the word *persuasion* is negatively associated with dishonest practices, such as misleading people into buying something they cannot afford or do not need or want. Thus, to persuade ethically is an important responsibility. Repairing the damage done by unethical messages or activities is difficult and sometimes impossible. Credibility is lost, and relationships are destroyed.

Ethical persuasion means that you give the receiver the information that he or she needs to make an *informed decision* about the value of your request or your product. You must make every effort to avoid words and analogies that cause misunderstandings and distort the truth.

You also want to be perceived as *credible* (worthy of trust). Include facts, name sources, and add relevant proof in your message to gain credibility. Communicate ethically.

- Provide information that can be confirmed.
- Choose clear, straightforward words. Do not set out to mislead someone.
- Show knowledge about the subject of your message so that your audience can identify with what you are saying.
- Do not omit information that people need to make informed decisions.

Plan a Message Using the CBO Approach

You prepare a *persuasive* message because the receiver may be reluctant to comply; therefore, planning is especially important. Begin by completing the Communication-by-Objectives (CBO) planning activities.

Identify the Objective

Usually, the objective of a persuasive message is clear: You want to persuade the receiver to respond favorably to your request by taking some kind of action.

Sometimes you may be unsure of what you want. For example, you are not satisfied with the tile recently installed in the foyer of your home. Do you want a replacement? a reimbursement? Think carefully about your objective. Once you clarify the objective, you will be able to include relevant, supportive information.

Visualize the Audience

What you know and what you can learn about your receiver, your target audience, will help you address the receiver's needs and wants in a persuasive message. Receiver age, education, interests, profession, marital status, and other background information provide clues about what motivates the receiver. Learning as much as you can about your receiver also enables you to make better decisions about message form and transmission mode. (If necessary, review the characteristics of various message forms and transmission modes in Chapter 1.)

Mexico

Mexico and the United States are close geographically, but significant differences separate the two countries culturally. In addition, the regions of Mexico are separated by differences in business culture. Business culture in the four main regions of Mexico ranges from a dynamic, modern orientation to business in and around urban Mexico City to virtually no modern-day business structure in the paternalistic and class-influenced southern region.

Regardless of region, however, personal friendships are important to successful business relationships in Mexico. Personal friendships help develop contacts and form networks among businesspeople and government officials. In fact, interpersonal skills may be considered more important than professional expertise. Thus, building and maintaining personal relationships that emphasize trust and compatibility are worth the effort.

Gather Supporting Information

As part of the planning process, you generate ideas and select those that are pertinent to your objective. Some ideas emerge as key ideas and are often called **central selling points** (especially when referencing sales letters). The remaining ideas are expanded to support, explain and develop, central selling points. All the information in your message must relate to the objective, confirm the validity of your request, and ethically persuade the receiver to respond favorably. Information that provides clear and convincing answers to *what, when, where,* and *how* are imperative to accomplishing the message objective.

Organize the Information

The indirect pattern of organization and the persuasive strategy AIDA positively influence the receiver by providing an explanation *before* the actual request. The AIDA strategy is designed to:

- Attract the receiver's favorable <u>**attention**</u>, and promote further reading or listening.
- Build the receiver's <u>**interest**</u> by implying or expressing receiver benefits.
- Encourage the receiver's <u>**desire**</u> to respond favorably by using an appropriate appeal, addressing receiver concerns, and describing with vivid words.
- Request and motivate the receiver to take <u>**action**</u> by making a response quick and easy.

Table 7-1 shows the relationship between the indirect pattern of organization and the persuasive strategy AIDA.

Table 7-1 Comparison of the Indirect Pattern and the Persuasive Strategy AIDA

Indirect Pattern	Persuasive Strategy AIDA
Opening	Attention-getting opening to encourage further reading or listening
Explanation	Key points and receiver benefits; leads to main idea
Main Idea	The request
Additional Information	Continued explanation of benefits to confirm validity of request
Closing	Action-oriented closing with easy, dated response; motivational incentives

Compose a Draft Using the CBO Approach

Continue with the CBO approach by applying the AIDA strategy to compose a draft of your persuasive message. Present a convincing explanation before you make your request.

Attract Attention

The opening of a persuasive message has two purposes: to attract the receiver's favorable **attention** and to encourage further reading. The opening should be brief (one to four lines), *you* oriented, and relevant to the content of the message. Successful openings are sometimes stated in one sentence and include thought-provoking questions, agreeable statements, compliments, immediate requests, facts, and proverbs or quotations.

Open-Ended, Thought-Provoking Question

An **open-ended, thought-provoking question** arouses curiosity and requires more than a yes or no response. The receiver must continue reading or listening to get the details.

Examples:

What are you waiting for?	*Discussion* — A blunt question encourages the receiver to look for the answer in this message asking for blood donors.
How many lives will you save today?	A thought-provoking question opens a message requesting funds for children's relief programs.

Agreeable Statement

An **agreeable statement** is one with which a receiver is likely to agree, so you are able to establish a common interest.

Timely Tip

A well-written one-line opening is an excellent technique for attracting favorable attention.

Examples:

The number of families seeking a kind face and a helping hand doubles during the holidays.

You will find no shortage of advice about how to run your business!

Discussion

Most receivers will agree that shelters and food pantries experience increased visits during the holiday.

Business owners likely receive lots of unsolicited advice and can relate to the opening of this sales message.

Compliment

A **compliment** begins a message positively by recognizing a receiver's expertise or accomplishments.

Examples:

You have worked hard to ensure that the Ripon City Council makes environmentally sound development decisions.

Your credit record is enviable.

Discussion

Recognition of the receiver's hard work will catch the receiver's attention in a message requesting a keynote speaker.

A compliment to the receiver's past payment record begins a collection letter.

Immediate Request

When an **immediate request** opens a message, the request is "superficial." The receiver must continue reading or listening. An immediate request opening does *not* present the main idea. The main idea—the *real* request—appears after the explanation.

Examples:

Register for a $1,000 shopping spree today!

Make a promise.

Discussion

The receiver must continue reading to learn the details. The main idea, which is a request to open an account, appears after the explanation.

An immediate request piques the receiver's curiosity and encourages the receiver to continue. The main idea, which is a request to purchase tickets for a charity event, comes later.

Startling Fact

A **startling fact** that can be easily verified may capture a receiver's attention.

Examples:

Fifty years of service to the community—and still going strong!

An estimated 500,000 will die from cancer this year—about 1,300 people every day!

Discussion

A strong statement of fact opens a message requesting contributions for a homeless shelter.

Dramatic statistics begin a request for cancer research donations.

Proverbs or Quotations

Proverbs or **quotations** often capture a receiver's attention because the sayings have a familiar or relevant theme.

Examples:

"Eat to live, and not live to eat."

Treat the earth well: it was not given to you by your parents, it was loaned to you by your children.

Discussion

Benjamin Franklin's quote opens a message selling a weight-control program.

This Native American proverb opens and sets the theme requesting support for environmental protection laws.

Build *Interest* and Encourage *Desire*

The interest and desire paragraphs present the explanation by building on the opening theme of the message. The key points of your message (referred to as *central selling points* in a sales message) present and expand supporting information. In these paragraphs, you convince the receiver of the value of your request *before* you make the actual request.

Receivers respond favorably for a variety of reasons, including concern about themselves or someone close to them, interest in what you have to offer, or the opportunity to help someone. The more you know about your audience, the better able you are to include information that reflects the receiver's interests.

The length and detail of your explanation depend on how much information you believe the receiver needs to know. You build interest in your request and encourage desire to respond favorably by presenting receiver benefits, using an appropriate appeal, addressing receiver concerns, and choosing descriptive words.

Receiver Benefits

Interest and desire are created by implying or expressing receiver benefits. Receiver benefits are *direct* or *indirect*. **Direct** or *explicit* benefits are

Timely Tip

When preparing the explanation, remember that you may be requesting someone to do something that primarily benefits you, such as buying your product or service.

expressly stated and obvious, such as guarantees, monetary compensation, or favorable publicity. Depending on your message, you may not have many direct benefits to offer. More likely, you will rely on **indirect** or *implied* benefits, such as personal satisfaction or enhanced reputation. Whether direct or indirect, the receiver benefits must be clearly recognizable.

Examples:

	Discussion
Museum membership entitles you to ■ Free admission ■ Gift shop discounts ■ Educational workshop discounts ■ Guest passes	An easy-to-read list emphasizes direct receiver benefits soliciting museum membership.
Only with help like yours have we been able to carry out our mission. Once again, the future of The Sanctuary is in your hands.	The importance of the receiver's past and future monetary contributions is clearly implied in this donation request.

Culture Frame

Subjective feelings influence Mexican business culture. Therefore, emotional appeals, especially those that promote honor and family pride, will aid in achieving the message objective.

Appeals

As a sender, you convince receivers to do what you ask by using an emotional appeal, a rational appeal, or a combination appeal.

Emotional appeals relate to ego and status and arouse feelings such as pride, anger, and love. Emotional appeals are especially successful for seeking donations or support when you cannot offer tangible receiver benefits. Instead, you emphasize the indirect benefits that result from responding favorably, such as a sense of accomplishment or satisfaction or fulfillment of a moral responsibility.

Examples:

	Discussion
Prompt payers like you are the exception. In fact, your excellent payment record enabled you to receive additional credit.	These statements in a collection letter appeal to the receiver's pride.
Twelve special people like you created a relay team to drive Phoebe across the United States to a sanctuary where she will never again be abused.	This emotional appeal in a request for volunteers implies that only "special" people will volunteer for difficult tasks.

Rational appeals focus on the receiver's sense of logic and intellect. Increases, decreases, size, speed, durability, and finances are examples of direct or tangible reasons for a receiver to respond favorably. Warranties or guarantees, free samples, and statistical information are often part of rational appeals.

Discussion

Power-Built brakes are backed by a 15-year warranty—the best warranty in the business.	A sales letter promotes the product warranty to confirm the logic of the purchase.
As an Ortega-Carter charge customer, you receive an additional 10 percent discount on *all* your purchases *and* advance notification of our sale events.	A message promoting charge accounts indicates that *only* charge customers will save additional money.

A **combination appeal** targets a receiver's emotions as well as the receiver's sense of reason. Most persuasive messages use a combination appeal. For example, a nonroutine claim message incorporates the rational appeal when chronologically and objectively presenting the events that led to the claim. In the same example, when seeking the desired action in the claim message, an emotional appeal focuses on the receiver's sense of fair play and desire for customer satisfaction. Sales messages often use a combination appeal to help receivers achieve a balance between what is wanted and what is needed.

Examples:

Discussion

Because of your excellent selection, I always stop at Nelly's Boutique first. However, after asking for assistance three times and getting no response, I finally left your store and spent $150 in a competitor's store.	In this claim message, the first appeal is to the receiver's sense of pride (emotional). The details (rational) lead to the reason for shopping elsewhere.
When chosen with care, gifts help cement international business relationships. The gifts show that you are a thoughtful person.	Cementing international relationships (rational appeal) and being perceived as a thoughtful person (emotional appeal) are used in this sales message.

Receiver Concerns

An important consideration when developing the explanation paragraphs is to anticipate receiver concerns or objections. You anticipate by "putting yourself in the receiver's shoes." Determine possible objections; then offer positive information to address those concerns *before* the receiver has an opportunity to raise them. You can reduce receiver resistance by addressing receiver concerns.

Quickly scan each issue, zero in on what you need, and put the information to use fast!	**Discussion** Action words tell the receiver that finding important information in a specialized newsletter is fast and easy.

Descriptive, Concrete Words

Descriptive, concrete words help build mental images for your receivers. Vivid language, analogies, metaphors, stories, and evidence help to clarify your ideas and connect the content of your message to something familiar to the receiver: in other words, translating facts into receiver benefits. Typically, *positive* descriptive words create interest and desire.

Examples:

League members have collected more than 100,000 signatures in fewer than four weeks.	**Discussion** Concrete language tells receivers what has been accomplished in a short time in this request for support.
Native American, Spanish, and western pioneer influences create a unique experience for you and your family. The beauty and adventure of the Phoenix Mountain Reserve and the casual yet sophisticated style of Scottsdale offer boundless opportunities for exploration and entertainment.	Vivid language helps the receiver build a visual image of the area and creates interest in visiting this vacation destination.

Sometimes *negative* descriptive words are used successfully in persuasive messages to achieve the desired effect. Those preparing claims and charitable donation requests find that appropriate negative words used sparingly can emphasize the seriousness or inconvenience of a situation and thus encourage a favorable response.

Examples:

Today, off-color remarks can upset coworkers so much that you can be fired or even dragged through the courts.	**Discussion** Blunt, descriptive words in a sales message encourage the purchase of training videos to identify and eliminate sexual harassment situations.
Of the last six flights from Milwaukee to Denver, four have been delayed more than three hours. These delays have forced us to reschedule meetings, meals, and presentations, which resulted in a loss of money and goodwill.	Presenting evidence adds legitimacy to a nonroutine claim letter.

Final-stage collection messages, which are organized in the direct pattern, also use negative descriptive words to tell a receiver that this is the last opportunity for payment before formal collection proceedings begin. Collection messages are discussed on pages 220–223.

Example:		*Discussion*
	Your failure to pay your bill, which is 120 days overdue, leaves us no choice. You can expect a small claims court action within the next two weeks.	In this collection message, *failure, overdue,* and *small claims court action* are negative descriptive words used to encourage payment.

Call for Action

The closing of a persuasive message courteously but confidently asks the receiver to take a specific action. To encourage a prompt, favorable response, action closings restate key receiver benefits; offer incentives, such as gifts or reduced prices, when appropriate; and limit a response time when time is important. Providing an easy way to respond is critical, so the closing includes contact information: toll-free telephone or fax number, an e-mail address, or a stamped, addressed response card.

Examples:		*Discussion*
	This is your chance to be heard! Register your opinion by March 1 between 9 a.m. and noon by calling the Opinion Hotline at 800.555.0186.	This closing provides complete contact information.
	Contact Ruso DeShane by May 1 to choose a payment plan that meets your financial needs. You can reach him between 9 a.m. and 4 p.m. Monday through Friday at 800.555.1234.	A courteous closing in a collection message presents a resolution and makes action easy.

Finalize the Message

Edit, proofread, and revise until you are satisfied that the message reflects the six Cs and that the content is accurate and says what you intend. Ensure that you have chosen a message form and transmission mode that are appropriate for the situation. Prepare your final message; but before sending the message, review your message using the Checklist for Preparing a Persuasive Message, on page 214.

Checklist for Preparing a Persuasive Message

1. Does your persuasive message:
- Accomplish the objective?
- Relate to your target audience?
- Identify key ideas and include relevant supporting information?
- Organize contents in the indirect pattern?

2. Does the draft of your persuasive message:
- Attract attention with a specially designed opening?
- Build interest and encourage desire by explaining reader benefits, incorporating an appropriate appeal, addressing receiver concerns, and using descriptive words?
- Present the main idea—the request?
- Close by asking for action (dated, if helpful), offer appropriate motivational incentives, and make responding easy?

3. Does your final persuasive message:
- Incorporate the six Cs of effective messages?
- Send the message you intend?
- Reflect ethics and credibility by providing adequate, objective information?
- Look and/or sound professional?

Section 2: **PERSUASIVE APPLICATIONS**

Persuasive messages are divided into two broad categories: nonroutine requests and sales messages. The cover letter in an employment message package, discussed in Chapter 8, is also considered a persuasive message.

A nonroutine request may be prepared for an audience of one or an audience of thousands. Most charitable donation requests and sales messages are form letters because they are mailed to hundreds or thousands of people. However, even a message prepared for mass mailing can appear individualized when you compose a receiver-oriented message and when you use software to incorporate personalized information, such as a receiver's name and address.

Timely Tip

Unusual formats, writing styles, and language mechanics are *not* appropriate for typical business messages.

Nonroutine Requests

Nonroutine requests ask for support or cooperation. Because they ask people to do something out of the ordinary, the messages are organized in the indirect pattern and incorporate the persuasive strategy AIDA. Nonroutine requests, especially messages asking for monetary donations, often use unusual formats, writing styles, and language mechanics to attract and maintain attention. (See Technique and Writing Style, page 234, for more information.)

Requests for Support

When you seek support for a cause or an activity, you are usually asking for a donation of time, money, or knowledge. Your objective is to convince the receiver that your request is worthy of a favorable response. The likelihood of a receiver responding favorably is increased when you follow these guidelines.

1. Begin with an attention-getting statement that encourages continued reading.
2. Choose an appropriate appeal. Discuss the key points that show the situation is of consequence and that the situation can be solved or controlled with the receiver's help. Imply or express receiver benefits.
3. Lead to the request, which is the main idea of the message. Present additional details, including receiver benefits.
4. Close by stating the action you want, and give an easy way for the receiver to respond.

Illustration 7-1, page 216, asks for support; Illustration 7-2, page 217, requests a donation of knowledge and time; and Illustration 7-3, page 218, requests a donation of money.

Requests for Cooperation

Requesting an adjustment, making a claim because of an unusual circumstance, and requesting a past-due payment are nonroutine requests because you need to convince a receiver that cooperation is beneficial.

Claim Messages

Claim messages are also called **complaint messages** or **adjustment requests**. You ask for an adjustment because you are dissatisfied with a product, a service, or a situation. When a situation is obvious, you assume that the receiver wants to resolve the problem; so you use the direct pattern and the good or neutral news strategy to compose your message. (Review Routine Claims and Adjustments in Chapter 5.)

Sometimes a situation is not obvious, and resolution will result in considerable expense or inconvenience to the receiver. In those cases, you will likely use the indirect pattern and the persuasive strategy AIDA to encourage a favorable response. Such circumstances include repairs after warranty expiration, repeat product or service problems, travel delays, and inaccurate bills.

Begin by assuming that your receiver will help if you present adequate information to justify your request. When possible, go to the source of the problem; and try to resolve the issue through discussion.

Timely Tip

Many times you may need to persuade receivers to help even when they cannot participate in person.

567 Mountain View Road
Trinidad, CO 81082
March 31, 20—

Attention: Council President Kevin Moy
City Council
Town Hall
100 Freedom Square
Trinidad, CO 81082

Dear Council Members:

Attracts the receivers' attention with a compliment. As a resident of Trinidad for nearly 30 years, I firmly believe that City Council's wise decisions have helped to preserve our small town. We move forward but at a comfortable pace.

Uses a rational appeal to review an issue that receivers must address. Next week, you will vote on an important rezoning issue: Starburst Entertainment Inc. wants to build an amphitheater and a 1,000-car parking lot near the corner of Highway 350 and I-25. The promoters plan to schedule musical groups for outdoor concerts from June through August; and they expect to draw concert goers from as far away as Denver, Amarillo, and Santa Fe. Estimates indicate that the city may receive more than $30,000 a year in taxes from this amphitheater.

Indicates understanding of tax benefits but uses descriptive words and references a similar situation to emphasize possible negative consequences. Prepares receivers for the request. Yes, the new taxes would help our tight budget; but we also must consider the impact of such an amphitheater on our small town. You may already know that Star Entertainment built another amphitheater in Redmond, Washington. Redmond's civic leaders have been struggling ever since to reduce the noise level during concerts and property damage after concerts. The heavy metal music can be heard in backyards—even inside homes—for miles around the amphitheater. Cars, trucks, and SUVs park on nearby residents' lawns; and throngs of people walk through yards into the early morning. Call Redmond Mayor Lisa Henderson at 425-555-0095. She can explain the issues that have risen around Redmond's amphitheater. Also, ask her about the traffic on concert nights.

Makes the request and reminds receivers of their responsibilities as elected officials. Please vote to stop this rezoning and continue your excellent job of managing this city. Your "no" vote will show your commitment to keeping Trinidad a wonderful place to live and do business.

Uses a courtesy title to help the receiver know how to address a response. Sincerely,

Mrs. Terry Smithson

Mrs. Terry Smithson

Illustration 7-1 **Request for Cooperation (Personal-Business Letter)**

VALLEY UNIVERSITY SYSTEM

Kohler School of Business
1200 West Sheffield Way
Monterey, CA 93940

December 2, 20—

Mr. Kaleb Kaiser
San Francisco Chronicle
4155 North Pacific Street
Petaluma, CA 94952

Dear Mr. Kaiser

Attracts attention with reference to the receiver's achievements.

The "Employment Corner" in the *San Francisco Chronicle* is at the top of my "to read" list. I also assign your column as weekly reading for my management students. All of us appreciate your style and your employment advice.

Builds interest by continuing with opening theme.

Your column is popular because you give good advice and because you incorporate important communication principles in your messages: courtesy, clarity, conciseness, concreteness, correctness, and completeness.

Uses rational appeal to provide supportive details that lead to the main idea.

These same communication principles are stressed in a booklet, "To Be Employed—or Not," that is being prepared for our employment-bound graduates. This practical guide will contain candid tips on how to prepare, follow through, and interview. Because of your effective communication ability, please contribute your thoughts about communicating clearly and effectively when seeking employment.

Implies enhanced reputation to encourage a favorable response.

The booklet will contain vignettes contributed by others like you—effective communicators who can testify to the need for communication skills. The 250- to 300-word vignette would relate a personal experience that demonstrates the importance of writing and/or speaking effectively. Your insight on completing job applications, preparing for and participating in interviews, or preparing employment follow-up messages will make a positive difference in emphasizing the need for communication skills at all occupational levels.

Asks for action and provides dated response time. Makes final "plea."

Your response by December 20, 20—, will help keep this project on track. You may reach me at 831.555.8002 or at oquinn@ksb.vus.edu for additional details. Please say *yes*.

Sincerely

Therese O'Quinn

Therese O'Quinn, Ph.D.
Dean, Student Life Services

Phone: 831.555.2511   Fax: 831.555.2623   Web site: www.vus1200.edu

Illustration 7-2 **Request to Donate Knowledge and Time**

Moving Forward
Arthritis Training Team

P.O. Box 892
Chandler, AZ 85224

May 1, 20—

Dear Mr. and Mrs. Ward

What did you do this morning when you got out of bed? stretch to work out the kinks? get dressed? help your kids get ready for school? eat breakfast and hurry off to work?

Imagine how different your morning routine would be if a little stretching did not get your muscles moving or if you could not get dressed because you couldn't bend your fingers. Think about how you would help your children or hurry off to work if your hip joints were so swollen that you walked only with great difficulty?

Arthritis, a disease of the joints, comes in more than 100 forms and affects one of every three people in the United States. You may already know how devastating this disease can be.

Arthritis is not for "Adults Only." Unfortunately, 285,000 children in the United States suffer from arthritis. Lindsey, for example, is only 14; but her juvenile rheumatoid arthritis causes painful swelling of her joints; and her medications have weakened her immune system. Still, neither the pain nor the medications slow her down. In fact, she hopes to swim competitively some day—after a cure is found for her disease.

You can help find that cure, and **you** can help the Juvenile Arthritis Foundation (JAF) continue to offer programs and services by sponsoring me in the 10-Mile JAF Marathon on June 15. I am running because I can run, and I want to be a part of finding a cure. Together, **you** and I can help kids like Lindsey move through life and accomplish her goals with less pain.

Let's make arthritis a disease of the past. **Please** sponsor me by sending your tax-deductible contribution TODAY in the enclosed envelope.

Sincerely

Shawna Talavara

Shawna Talavara

Enclosure

Draws reader into message and attracts attention with thought provoking questions.

Begins with an emotional appeal using vivid language and the you attitude to build mental images and stimulate further reading.

Moves to a rational appeal by including facts. Continues with descriptive language to reduce resistance. Encourages empathy. Leads to the main idea, which is the request. Implies the benefit of personal satisfaction in helping many people. Uses print mechanics to emphasize the you orientation. Motivates action and makes the action easy.

Illustration 7-3 **Request for Donation of Money**

If the situation is not resolved, prepare a written message for someone in a position of higher authority. The guidelines for preparing an effective persuasive claim message are applicable to *both* spoken and written messages.

1. Begin the message with a courteous, attention-getting opening, such as a compliment or an agreeable statement.
2. Clearly, calmly, and precisely provide details in chronological order. Describe inconveniences you suffered and negative feelings that resulted from the situation.
3. Include pertinent information, such as model numbers and dates, to support your case. Reference *copies* that you are enclosing to substantiate your claim (receipts, warranties, and similar documents).
4. Appeal to the receiver's sense of fairness, ethical or legal responsibility, and value of maintaining goodwill. When appropriate, as in claim and collection messages, state or imply consequences if a receiver does not respond favorably.
5. Close with a reasonable request; provide an action date. Do not try to make money; be satisfied with the compensation for legitimate expenses and inconvenience.
6. Consider the details.
   - Key your message.
   - Address the message to a specific person.
   - Keep the message short (preferably one page) and focused.
   - Include your contact information (phone number and e-mail address).
   - Sign the letter.
   - Proofread for correct grammar, spelling, and content.

Timely Tip

Send only copies of verifying paperwork. Do not send originals.

The following examples show parts of a traveler's claim letter following the CBO approach and the persuasive strategy AIDA. The message opens with a compliment.

Example: TransOceanic Airlines has been my favorite airline for almost ten years.

The explanation presents the sequence of events that led to the claim. Using negative descriptive words to relate the problem may be necessary, so the receiver clearly understands the inconvenient circumstances. A calm, objective presentation of details strengthens your case and encourages the receiver to find a positive resolution. A hostile message causes the receiver to be defensive, and you lose credibility. Remember, your objective is to get favorable action.

Timely Tip

A hostile message may result in inaction.

Example: The beverage cart was not secured; and when the plane encountered turbulence, several glasses of soda spilled on me. Needless to say, I was uncomfortable for the last 40 minutes of the flight because I had to sit in a damp suit. My intentions to go directly to a scheduled meeting were delayed. Instead, I waited for my luggage (in a damp suit), hailed a cab to the hotel, and changed into dry clothing. As a result, I was an hour late for an important client meeting.

The explanation also implies a loss of business or other undesirable consequences if the situation is not resolved favorably. At the same time, assure the receiver that a favorable response will maintain goodwill.

Example: Business associates often ask me to recommend an airline because I log more than 70,000 flight miles annually. I want to continue recommending TransOceanic Airlines.

After explaining the situation, the time is right to ask for action. Typically, the closing paragraph clearly presents a statement of action—*what* and *when*.

Example: Please reimburse me $81 ($32.50 for one-hour dry-cleaning service and $48.50 for cab fare). Receiving that reimbursement by April 2 will convince me that TransOceanic Airlines will remain my first choice when I travel by air.

Illustration 7-4 is a request for an adjustment. The sender is asking for a refund beyond a refund date. Since the resolution may set a precedent for future refunds, the sender uses the indirect pattern and the persuasive strategy AIDA.

Collection Messages

Collecting money for the products or services that you sell is critical to the operation of a business. The collection process begins when a person or organization is extended credit and does not pay within the stated payment period. A systematic collection process shows a receiver that you are serious about collecting money. The collection policies and practices of an organization must reflect state regulations and the criteria established by the Fair Debt Collection Practices Act of 1978, a federal law enacted by Congress as part of the Consumer Credit Protection Act.

Collection messages are prepared to collect money and to maintain goodwill. Implement these guidelines:

- Assume that the receiver intends to pay.
- Follow federal and state collection regulations.
- Send collection messages at regular intervals.
- Use an appropriate organizational pattern and message strategy for each collection stage.

Collection messages are prepared in three stages: initial, middle, and final; and the organizational patterns correlate with each stage. Two to three messages may be sent at regular intervals (a week or two apart) during each stage, but company policy determines the length of the entire collection process.

When someone does not pay a bill, you assume the person forgot or has encountered a temporary shortage of funds. An **initial-stage** collection message is a routine *reminder* and is written in the direct pattern. Initial-stage collection messages appear as a brief message or sticker on a customer's bill, a preprinted collection card, or a form letter. Illustration 7-5, page 222, shows a clever initial-stage collection card that incorporates the theme of the business.

Timely Tip

The opportunity to collect money after 90 days is greatly diminished.

230 Fortune Drive
Aurora, CO 80012
September 12, 20—

Director Pablo Ruiz
State College Admissions Office
125 Lee Grant Grande Parkway
Denver, CO 80209

Director Ruiz

State College's online admissions procedures and evening and weekend classes make returning to school much easier for the working student.

I have completed two classes each quarter for the last ten quarters, maintaining a 3.5 GPA. Last June, I enrolled in Economics 240 and Computer Science 280 for the fall quarter. Both courses are requirements for a business communication major.

However, my mother was recently diagnosed with cancer and must begin aggressive chemotherapy. Her condition is serious, and she will need my help daily. I also must work full-time and parent my two school-age children. Needless to say, I am unable to concentrate on these two classes.

I have carefully budgeted both money and time so that I could complete the remaining classes for my degree and finally achieve my career goal. Although the final date for a full tuition refund was September 1, please make an exception based on these unusual circumstances. I am working diligently to help my mother through this crisis, reduce everyone's anxieties, keep my job, and return to school in January.

Unfortunately, many of us are part of the "sandwich generation," with responsibilities for both children and parents. A refund minus an administrative fee (perhaps 10 percent) would help me and others understand that the college is willing to work with us to resolve legitimate special circumstances.

Please grant this request so that I may earn my degree and support the college as a member of the State College Alumni Association. You may reach me at 720-555-8205 (work) or 720-555-1445 (home).

Sincerely

Carolanne Hempstead

Carolanne Hempstead

Illustration 7-4 **Request for an Adjustment**

Illustration 7-5 **Initial-Stage Collection Message**

We looked all over . . .
The Pampered Pet

. . . but we couldn't find your check.

If one or two initial-stage messages do not result in payment, call the customer to determine the problem. Sometimes a phone call will resolve payment issues. When calls do not resolve the problem, continue with the collection process.

The **middle-stage** collection message follows the indirect pattern and incorporates the persuasive strategy AIDA. You still assume that the receiver wants to pay, but you also assume that something has happened to interrupt a timely payment. The objective of the middle-stage message is to get the receiver to pay the bill or to maintain communication with the receiver. Thus, personalize the message when possible. A personalized message gives you greater opportunity to express concern for the receiver's credit rating and ability to buy products as well as to present payment options. Using the passive voice during this stage helps avoid an accusatory tone.

Middle-stage collection messages open with a positive or neutral statement to promote continued reading. A combination appeal typically is most successful. Present the tangible benefits that will remain available if the account is paid. Tangible benefits include discounts, charge purchases, and special offers. Appeal to a sense of fairness (you received the product; please pay the bill) or sense of pride (you can maintain your good credit reputation by paying this bill). The explanation leads to the request for payment and references the amount owed and the number of days the account is overdue. Also include payment options if available, such as smaller payments or more time.

The closing courteously asks for payment and makes action easy by including an addressed payment envelope and complete contact information. Illustration 7-6, page 224, is a personalized middle-stage collection message.

Use the following guidelines to prepare an effective middle-stage collection message.

1. Open with a positive or neutral statement that encourages further reading.
2. Use the combination appeal to explain objectively without accusation.
3. Point out the benefits of complying with the request.
4. Make the request. Offer payment options if possible.
5. Provide a courteous close that calls for action (payment or contact). Make action easy by providing contact information.

A **final-stage** collection message is organized in the direct pattern even though the message contains bad news. The direct pattern is appropriate because you have already made several requests for payment and your receiver has not responded with a payment or an explanation.

Final-stage collection messages are assertive but not defamatory. The tone should be businesslike and firm. Most final-stage collection messages are form letters with individualized information inserted. In addition to including the amount owed and the number of days past due, the messages stress the negative consequences of nonpayment, such as collection agency intervention or small claims action. See Illustration 7-7, page 225, for an example of a final-stage collection message. A message at this stage is an ultimatum and incorporates the following plan:

1. Open with the main idea—the consequences of nonpayment.
2. Briefly restate details leading up to the final collection attempt. Be specific about the consequences, and provide the date on which collection proceedings will begin.
3. End with a neutral closing. Provide one more opportunity to avoid drastic action if payment is made immediately.

Sales Messages

The main objective of sales messages, of course, is to persuade receivers to buy something. In large companies, sales messages are created by sales or marketing specialists. However, small businesses may rely on the talents of employees who are not specialists in those areas; so you may find yourself creating a sales message for your employer. You may also prepare sales messages for your own business or for an organization to which you have made a commitment.

 **The Pampered Pet**

128 Highway G   Phone: 704.555.0157
Union Grove, NC 28689   www.pamperedpet.com

May 18, 20—

Mr. Ronald Aring, Jr.
Pet Club Supplies
PO Box 78
Pleasant Garden, NC 27313-0078

Dear Mr. Aring

Opens with a positive statement to encourage further reading.

You have earned a fine credit reputation in the past five years because of your prompt payments.

Reminds receiver of benefits of a good credit reputation.

In fact, your credit reputation has enabled you to purchase quality pet supplies at significant discounts and to participate in manufacturer-sponsored promotions. As a result, Pet Club Supplies has increased its visibility in the community as well as its potential for increased profits.

Provides account details. Leads to the main idea (overdue account) and reinforces the importance of receiver's success.

Keep the momentum going! What can we do to help you bring Pet Club Supplies' account up to date? The current balance is $3,298 and 50 days past due. The success of your business is important to us and to the pet owners who rely on Pet Club Supplies for top-notch products and personalized service.

Calls for action and makes response easy. Suggests possible payment option if necessary.

The most beneficial solution is to send your check for the full amount in the enclosed postage-paid envelope. If you need to make other payment arrangements, we can work together to find a satisfactory payment plan. Please call me at 704-555-0157 by May 25.

Sincerely

Mai Bozosi

Mai Bozosi
Credit Office

lk

Enclosure

Illustration 7-6 **Middle-Stage Collection Message**

The Pampered Pet

128 Highway G
Union Grove, NC 28689

Phone: 704.555.0157
www.pamperedpet.com

July 15, 20—

Mr. Ronald Aring, Jr.
Pet Club Supplies
PO Box 78
Pleasant Garden, NC 27313-0078

Dear Mr. Aring

Gets to the point in the opening sentence.

If we do not receive full payment of your account by July 20, Fullerton Collection Agency will begin collection proceedings.

Briefly restates details.

The account balance of $3,298 is more than four months past due, and you have not responded to any of our messages.

Makes a last collection attempt. States consequences.

You may still avoid collection proceedings by paying the full amount to Pampered Pet by July 20. After July 20, you must contact Fullerton.

Sincerely

Mai Bozosi

Mai Bozosi
Credit Office

lk

Enclosure

Illustration 7-7 **Final-Stage Collection Message**

Sales messages come in many forms, such as letters, commercials, billboards, brochures, flyers, and e-mail messages. Whether or not you actually compose a sales message, your understanding of the sales strategy is important because all business messages have an element of sales. All business messages *sell* an image of you and your company.

Sales messages are either solicited or unsolicited. When someone inquires about a product or service, your response to that inquiry is a **solicited** sales message because someone has solicited (asked for) information. In this situation, the potential customer has provided you with some knowledge of your audience. You know the customer's name and geographical location, and you also know that the customer is interested in your product or service. A solicited sales message may be a form message or an individually prepared response.

An **unsolicited** sales message *is not* written in response to a specific inquiry. A business initiates an unsolicited sales message, usually a form message, to sell a product or a service. Through a merge process, the message may appear personalized and begin with *Dear Mrs. Vealey*; or the letter may be generic and begin with *Dear Friend* or *Dear Preferred Customer.*

Sales messages follow this plan:

1. Attract attention with an attention-getting opener. Successful openers include questions, quotations, or startling statements.
2. Build interest and create desire in the explanation paragraphs by choosing an appropriate appeal to present receiver benefits. Use descriptive words, emphasize central selling points, and enhance with supportive details. Anticipate receiver objections and questions, and include information to reduce concerns about a purchase. (Techniques to reduce receiver resistance include testimonials from users, satisfaction guarantees, and so on.)
3. Lead to the request, which is the main idea of the message. Present additional details including receiver benefits.
4. Close by telling the receiver what you want and by motivating the receiver to act with a limited-time offer or free gift. Make the action easy by providing immediate contact information, such as a postage-paid reply card, phone number, or web address.

Technique and Writing Style

By design, sales messages "violate" the rules of typical effective business messages. Sales messages often exceed one page, include gimmicks such as gifts and free offers, and employ a variety of print mechanics.

> *Examples:*   *You* be the judge. Enjoy this issue of SPACE CADET absolutely *free.*
> Are *you* ready to save **$$big bucks**??

Sales messages frequently incorporate a casual writing style and ignore standard grammar and punctuation rules. Contractions, dashes, exclamation marks, and ellipsis marks are used liberally as are sentence fragments.

Timely Tip

To accomplish their objective, donation request messages generally use the same techniques and writing style as do sales messages.

Examples: Two months FREE—TRY US!

Hot off the press!

Audience and Product

To create interest and desire for what you have to offer, you need to know your audience and your product. Then you can emphasize the features that will have the greatest appeal to a particular audience. (Review ethical persuasion on page 205.) Sending sales messages without having a good knowledge of your audience or your product is neither productive nor cost effective.

Target Audience. Even when you send an unsolicited sales message, you can take steps to learn more about your potential customers—your **target audience**. You can gather information about your audience through surveys; or you can purchase information from other sources, such as marketing research firms, which specialize in gathering facts about various populations. Additional sources of information can be obtained from professional organizations, credit card companies, and sometimes educational institutions. Once you identify receiver characteristics (age, education, occupation, cultural background, interests, and so on), you have a better understanding of how to market your product or service. For example, targeting fitness club members to receive sales messages about exercise and fitness equipment is likely to generate more purchases than selecting names randomly from a telephone book.

Product Appeal. You will be most convincing when you know the characteristics of your product, so investigate before you compose. Carefully analyze your product or service, and identify its selling points and receiver benefits. Selling points are *product focused* and receiver benefits are *receiver focused* as shown in Table 7-2.

Timely Tip

Direct print sales messages are expensive; that is why planning is critical.

Table 7-2 Selling Points and Receiver Benefits

Selling Points (Product Focused)	Receiver Benefits (Receiver Focused)
Ports of call include New Orleans, Natchez, Vicksburg, and Memphis.	Cruise the Lower Mississippi in September and save $1,500 on a six-night vacation package.
Credit cards, airline tickets, and luggage are covered.	You are covered up to $100,000 if your credit card, airline ticket, or luggage is lost or stolen.

As you list the selling points (features) of your product, one or two features usually emerge as dominant and are referred to as the **central selling point(s)**. The **central selling points** are features that you believe will most effectively influence your receiver to buy what you have to sell. To determine the central selling point, decide what sets your product or service apart from a competitor's similar product or service.

Then present your explanation by choosing the appeal that best relates your product to the receiver's needs and wants. Most sales letters use a combination appeal. Emphasize the central selling point(s), and include the other features that support and enhance the central selling point. Anticipate receiver objections and questions, and respond by using descriptive words to show your product's value to the receiver. Reduce opportunity for resistance by including money-back guarantees, gifts, testimonials (quotes from satisfied users), awards, and other techniques that will set the receiver's mind at ease about the purchase. (See Build Interest and Encourage Desire, pages 209–210, in this chapter.)

Examples: "I was so pleased with Xye-Brite. My monitor remained static-free—even during the dry winter months."

—Bo Boehmer, Rhinelander, Wisconsin

Charlie Ate a Bug received the prestigious Pelchy Elementary Reader Award for three consecutive years.

Your membership guarantees deeply discounted rates (at least 50% off) and no blackout dates at any of our 750 hotels worldwide. *Aurora Vacation Network responds to your lifestyle*!

If you think price will be an obstacle, de-emphasize the price in any of these ways:

- Omit the price from the message, and include the price in a separate enclosed card or brochure.
- Position the price in the middle of a paragraph, a position of de-emphasis.
- Break the price into "manageable" increments, such as *three payments of $39.95.*
- Relate price to receiver benefits, such as savings and bargains.

Motivation

The purpose of the closing, the final paragraph, is to motivate the receiver to act favorably and quickly. Be specific about what you want the receiver to do, set a time limit, and make the action easy. To make action easy, provide a postage-paid card or envelope, a toll-free telephone number, or an e-mail or web site address. Offering an additional discount or gift if action is taken by a certain date may motivate people to respond quickly.

Many sales letters include a postscript (P.S.) because a reader's eye is drawn to that final line. A postscript is a good place for a final inducement to respond positively. Illustration 7-8, page 230, incorporates several sales message techniques, including a postscript.

Examples: Act quickly! This offer expires May 1. Call 1-800-555-0142 or fax your order to 1-800-555-0146 NOW.

Open a checking account at any CityFed Bank by June 15. You will receive absolutely *free* checking for six months!

P.S. You earn **5,000** bonus points if you sign up for service by October 1.

Online Sales Messages

Increasing numbers of businesses use e-mail to promote their products and services. Delivery is efficient and less expensive than print messages, and e-mail offers ready-made opportunities to cultivate ongoing relationships with clients. However, unsolicited materials and sometimes objectionable materials plague e-mail delivery. This *spam* clogs e-mail systems, irritates receivers, and results in ill will. To avoid these criticisms, prepare e-mail sales messages for current customers or prospects *who have given you permission* to e-mail sales messages. This is called **opt-in**.

When a company elects to use e-mail for sales purposes, companies must consider both the similarities and differences between e-mail sales messages and traditional print sales messages. For example, the six *C*s of effective messages are critical to both types of messages: *courtesy, clarity, conciseness, concreteness, correctness,* and *completeness*.

A major difference, though, is how the message is organized as shown in Illustration 7-9, page 231. E-mail sales messages are best prepared in the direct pattern, and the AIDA strategy is reorganized to orient readers quickly to the message content and to fit space limitations. The following guidelines are useful for preparing e-mail sales messages.

1. Create a headline for the message with an attention-getting subject line.
2. Prepare a *you*-oriented, personalized message to recipients who have "opted-in."
3. Keep the message short by focusing on one or two central selling points. Limit text to one or two screens. When receivers need more detail, refer them to the web site or physical location.
4. Offer something special to online users only.
5. Provide an easy way to respond. Include a hot link so the receiver can take action directly from the message. Also include a toll-free telephone number and a facility address (if you have a physical site).
6. Give the receiver an opportunity to be removed from the mailing list.
7. Respond to customers within 24 hours.

The Clean Team—Winning Peace of Mind for You!

www.TCT.com   Phone: 215-555-9003

September 6, 20—

Addresses the family.

The Williams' Family
12 Banek Way
Philadelphia, PA 19103

Uses a one-line opening to grab attention.

Greetings

You can have a clean house—without lifting a finger!

Explains the central selling point, the rotational cleaning system. Expresses receiver benefits.

We can help *you*, just as we've helped hundreds of other Philadelphia families during the past two decades by making sure your home is always fresh and clean. Roto-Clean, our specially designed rotation system for busy households, keeps your home in top shape. Here's how the system works:

On the first visit to your home, we give the whole house a general cleanup with an indepth cleaning of your *bathrooms* and *kitchen*. On the second visit, we clean everything again but do an indepth cleaning of your *living room* and *bedrooms*. Each time, your *whole house* gets a general cleanup with special attention to designated areas.

Provides details to create interest. Uses indentions, symbols, and print mechanics to emphasize specific services and to help build desire for the services.

These tasks and others are always included in our **general cleanup plan**:
- ✓ Cleaning and disinfecting tile walls, bathtubs, showers, sinks, and toilets
- ✓ Wiping appliances and cabinet/vanity tops
- ✓ Washing floors and vacuuming carpets
- ✓ Shining mirrors and fixtures
- ✓ Dusting furniture and removing cobwebs

Indepth cleaning includes these special touches:
- ✓ Scrubbing tile grout
- ✓ Disinfecting floors
- ✓ Handwiping baseboards, doors, and cabinet fronts
- ✓ Small-brush cleaning around faucets, drains, and other hard-to-clean places
- ✓ Vacuuming window coverings and cleaning lampshades

Uses positive descriptions to address potential staffing and cost concerns.

You will find our staff pleasant, efficient, and willing to "go that extra mile." They are carefully trained, bonded, and insured.

Motivates receiver action with limited offer and easy contact.

You get a great cleaning staff *and* reasonable rates. In fact, the first cleaning visit is 50 percent off with a six-month contract! Take advantage of this limited offer by calling me today at 215-555-9003 or by visiting our web site at www.TCT.com.

Sincerely

Sylvia Sanders

Sylvia Sanders
President

P.S. Let's make an appointment, so I can tell you how little you will spend to keep your house clean and to keep a "piece" of your mind!

Illustration 7-8 **Sales Message**

Illustration 7-9 **Online Sales Message**

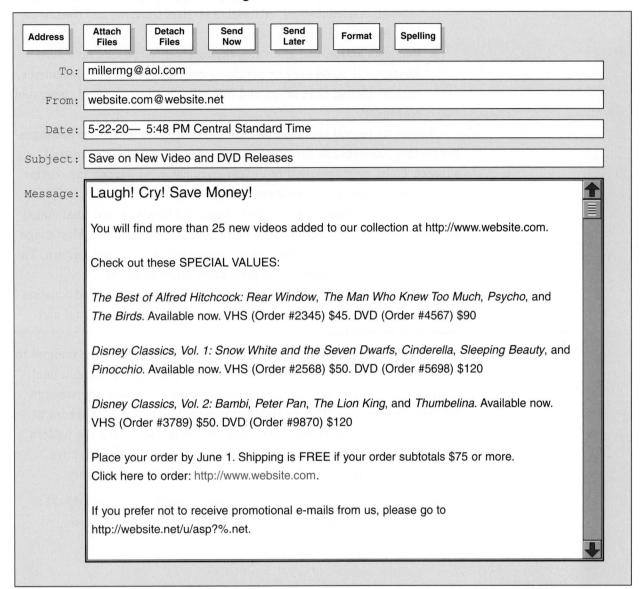

| Address | Attach Files | Detach Files | Send Now | Send Later | Format | Spelling |

To: millermg@aol.com

From: website.com@website.net

Date: 5-22-20— 5:48 PM Central Standard Time

Subject: Save on New Video and DVD Releases

Message:

Laugh! Cry! Save Money!

You will find more than 25 new videos added to our collection at http://www.website.com.

Check out these SPECIAL VALUES:

The Best of Alfred Hitchcock: Rear Window, The Man Who Knew Too Much, Psycho, and *The Birds*. Available now. VHS (Order #2345) $45. DVD (Order #4567) $90

Disney Classics, Vol. 1: Snow White and the Seven Dwarfs, Cinderella, Sleeping Beauty, and *Pinocchio*. Available now. VHS (Order #2568) $50. DVD (Order #5698) $120

Disney Classics, Vol. 2: Bambi, Peter Pan, The Lion King, and *Thumbelina*. Available now. VHS (Order #3789) $50. DVD (Order #9870) $120

Place your order by June 1. Shipping is FREE if your order subtotals $75 or more.
Click here to order: http://www.website.com.

If you prefer not to receive promotional e-mails from us, please go to http://website.net/u/asp?%.net.

Summary

Persuasive messages may ask for more than the receiver wants to give; therefore, persuasive messages are organized in the indirect pattern and incorporate the persuasive strategy AIDA. Persuasive messages show the value of the request and explain receiver benefits *before* making a request.

Persuasion involves influencing receiver actions or beliefs; thus, senders must practice *ethical persuasion* by providing the receiver with the kind of information that he or she needs to make an informed decision.

The persuasive strategy AIDA accomplishes the following:

- Attracts **attention** with openings that promote continued reading or listening.
- Builds **interest** and creates **desire** to convince the receiver of the value of responding favorably. Interest and desire are generated by

Ethics in Action

Access http://brantley.swlearning.com. Analyze the Ethics in Action for Chapter 7.

presenting receiver benefits, using an appropriate appeal (emotional, rational, or combination), addressing receiver concerns and objections, and choosing descriptive words.

■ Requests **action** and motivates the receiver to respond favorably. Response is made easy by providing contact information. Incentives, such as limited-time offers and free gifts, motivate prompt, favorable responses.

Nonroutine request messages and sales messages are persuasive messages. Nonroutine requests ask for donations of time, money, knowledge, and support. Claim messages that represent circumstances beyond the routine also follow the persuasive strategy AIDA.

A collection message series (first-stage, middle-stage, and final-stage) has two objectives: collecting money and maintaining goodwill. First-stage and final-stage collection messages are organized in the direct pattern. The middle-stage message follows the persuasive strategy AIDA.

Sales messages are solicited or unsolicited. Sales messages and donation requests often use unusual techniques and writing styles to attract and keep receiver attention.

Online sales messages (e-mail sales messages) have become integral to many sales and marketing efforts. Online sales messages and traditional print sales messages have similar characteristics with some adjustments for delivery by e-mail. These adjustments include receiver willingness to accept e-mail sales messages, the length of the message, and the pattern of organization used for the message. However, the six *C*s of effective messages are critical for all sales messages, regardless of delivery.

Complete Communication Skills Development 7, pages 249–250. For additional conjunction review, see the Reference Guide, page 422.

Exercises

7 - 1   **Directions:** Analyze billboard, television, radio, newspaper, and magazine advertising. Think about what causes you to listen to or read ads. Note the characteristics that attract your attention; for example, color, phrases, music, and pictures and graphics. Write a memo to your instructor explaining which characteristics attract your attention; describe why.

7 - 2   **Directions:** Visit http://www.manythings.org/proverbs/. Click a selection from "More than 230 Common Proverbs Sorted Alphabetically," pages 1–16. Choose two different proverb activities, and complete one page from each choice. Identify a few proverbs that could be used in persuasive messages, and be prepared to discuss your choices in class.

7 - 3   **Directions:** Analyze this quote by Joseph Conrad ("A Familiar Preface," 1912). "He who wants to persuade should put his trust not in the right argument, but in the right word. The power of sound has always been greater than the power of sense."

What do you think the writer means? What is your interpretation of this quote? How does this relate (or not relate) to today's persuasive messages? Compose a summary based on your thoughts. Be prepared to discuss your interpretation in class.

7 - 4   **Directions:** List five descriptive, concrete terms for each of the following topics: (1) the school you attend, (2) the program or class in which you are enrolled, and the (3) city or town in which you live.

Exercises

7 - 5

Part A

Directions: Use different approaches to write two attention-getting openings for each situation. Add details as necessary. Save your responses to complete Parts B and C.

Situation 1: A request for volunteers to help build houses for people with limited incomes who could not otherwise afford a house.

Opening:

Opening:

Situation 2: A request for donations of computers.
Opening:

Opening:

Part B

Directions: Write three or four interest and desire sentences for each situation in Part A. To convince the receiver to do what you ask, use descriptive words and add details as necessary. Be prepared to discuss how your explanatory sentences encourage the receiver to act favorably. Save your responses to complete Part C.

Situation 1 Explanation:

Exercises

Situation 2 Explanation:

Part C

Directions: Use your responses to Parts A and B to write one action ending for each of the situations. Add details as necessary.

Situation 1 Ending:

Situation 2 Ending:

Exercises

7 - 6

Part A

Directions: Collect two requests for donations of time, knowledge, money, or cooperation. Analyze each message according to the following information requested below. Be prepared to discuss your findings in class. Save the messages, your analysis, and your summary for Case Study 7-5.

a. Target Audience: Identify the target audience. Consider the topic of the message and the language used to give you "clues" about the audience.

b. Opening: Explain whether the opening encourages you to continue reading. Why or why not?

c. Interest and Desire Paragraphs: Explain whether the appeal(s) and receiver benefits are appropriate for the content and audience. Identify potential receiver concerns, and explain how concerns are addressed. Underline persuasive language; discuss which words influence you. Does the explanation lead you to the main idea?

d. Closing: Comment on the action requested. Is the response easy? Is the receiver motivated to respond favorably? Why or why not?

e. Techniques and Writing Style: Comment on the appropriateness of the writing style and on the techniques, such as length, inclusions, and print mechanics.

f. Appearance: Explain how the overall appearance of the message negatively or positively influences you.

Part B

Directions: Choose one of the messages from Part A. Use your analysis of the message to write a memorandum or an e-mail to your instructor. Summarize why you believe the message will or will not achieve its goal. Identify the characteristics that you think have the most positive or negative influence.

Exercises

7-7

Part A

Directions: Revise the following openings to nonroutine claim letters to incorporate the persuasive strategy AIDA.

Opening 1: I was not happy with the instructor who taught the Business Management 101 philosophies class last semester.

Opening 2: The wallpaper that you recommended is not holding up.

Opening 3: My cell phone reception leaves a lot to be desired.

Part B

Directions: Compose a closing for each of the openings in Part A. Determine an appropriate action, and provide the necessary details to prepare the closing.

Ending 1:

Ending 2:

Ending 3:

Exercises

7 - 8

Part A

Directions: Collect two sales messages. Analyze each message according to the information requested below. Be prepared to discuss your findings in class. Save your analysis and summary to complete Case Study 7-12.

a. **Target Audience:** Identify the target audience. Consider the topic of the message and the language used to give you "clues" about the audience.

b. **Opening:** Explain whether the opening encourages you to continue reading. Why?

c. **Interest and Desire Paragraphs:** Identify what you believe to be the central selling points. Explain whether the central selling points and receiver benefits are appropriate for the product. Identify potential receiver concerns, and explain whether the concerns are addressed. Underline persuasive language; discuss which words influence you.

d. **Closing:** Comment on the action requested. Is the response easy? Is the receiver motivated to respond favorably? Why or why not?

e. **Techniques and Writing Style:** Comment on the appropriateness of the writing style and on the techniques, such as length, inclusions, and print mechanics.

f. **Appearance:** Explain how the overall appearance of the message negatively or positively influences you.

Part B

Directions: Choose one of the messages from Part A. Use your analysis of the message to write a memorandum or an e-mail to your instructor. Summarize why you believe the message will or will not achieve its goal. Identify the characteristics that you think have the most positive or negative influence.

Internet
Challenge

7-1 Directions: Identify two or three companies. Conduct a search for the ethics policies of those companies. Search using keywords and phrases, such as *ethics policy of [insert company name]*.

At each company's web site, link to information about how ethics are incorporated into the organization. Does an ethics committee exist? Is advertising guided by specific ethical policies? Can employees safely report unethical conduct?

1. Link to the company ethics company. Print the policy.
2. Highlight words, phrases, or paragraphs that you believe are ethically important.
3. Based on your readings, prepare a summary of your findings. Provide the following information:
   a. Is the code written for employee? consumers?
   b. Explain what the code covers. Is the code understandable? specific?
   c. Include significant features of the code?

7-2 Directions: Search for information about business practices in Mexico. Use keywords and phrases, such as *business in Mexico, business practices in Mexico,* and *business etiquette in Mexico.* Prepare a one-page list of helpful etiquette tips for the first-time business visitor.

InfoTrac

Directions: Using the InfoTrac keyword search, locate articles on advertising bloopers. Retrieve the article "Avoid Translation Bloopers." Read the article and any links. Read a second article that references international translations. Prepare a summary based on the two articles. Identify each article by including the name of the article in quotation marks, the publication's title (underlined or italicized), and the author's name. Section 13 of the Reference Guide shows correct notation formats.

WebTUTOR Advantage

Directions: Access your WebTutor Advantage product. Complete the short-answer portion for Chapter 7 and send the answers to your instructor.

Case Studies

7 - 1

Communication Situation: The Student Life Office of your college sponsors a Life After Graduation breakfast each spring. The buffet breakfast, to be held April 15, is open to students of the college who will graduate with an associate degree in any of the business programs. Approximately 200 students attend, and 3 or 4 former graduates of various programs give brief presentations about how their academic preparation prepared them for their career choices.

You are a committee member for the Life After Graduation breakfast, and you are responsible for securing speakers. Contact Chanda Barr, Weyerson and Riley, 4879 West Olin Road, Anaheim, CA 92807-0883. Ms. Barr graduated three years ago with an associate degree in instructional design. She is employed in her field at a local firm.

Task A: Plan a persuasive message to Chanda Barr. Use the persuasive strategy AIDA and apply the CBO step, Plan a Message, to invite Ms. Barr to give a five- to seven-minute presentation. Date the message March 1. Provide additional details to complete the message.

Determine the Objective: State the objective of the message.

Visualize the Audience: Consider the following criteria, and list information you should consider when visualizing your audience.

- **Age:**

- **Profession:**

- **Education:**

- **Cultural or language difference:**

- **Other:**

Case Studies

List Supporting Information: Decide on an appeal. Generate ideas, words, and phrases using brainstorming, nonstop writing, or bubble writing.

Organize the Information:
  a. Identify the strategy you will use for this message.

  b. Organize the information in an outline using either the traditional or the indented outline format.

Task B: Review your outline. Compose a draft of your persuasive letter.

Task C: Complete the message. Date your message March 1. Your final letter should reflect the six *C*s of effective messages and acceptable message format.

Case Studies

7-2

Communication Situation: The Austin Business Education Network sponsors a two-day learning experience for more than 300 area high school students and their instructors. This Business Ethics Forum will be held on April 16 and 17 at the Slide Park Convention Center. Local business leaders host a variety of ethics-oriented activities, such as an ethics computer simulation, the development of a decision-making framework, role playing, and discussion groups. The keynote speaker is Donald Sprague of Global Works Corporation, who will talk about conducting business in a global market.

You are the development assistant for the Austin Business Education Network, and you must ask Lucy Mejias, an area businesswoman, to facilitate a discussion group. She is employed at VanBank, Delaney, and Associates, 85 West Post Road, Austin, TX 78727-2986.

Task: Plan, compose, and complete a persuasive message to Ms. Mejias asking her to facilitate a discussion group that focuses on fiscal responsibility versus ethical responsibility. Explain the purpose of the forum. Tell her that more than 1,500 students and instructors have attended since 1998 and that the response has been overwhelmingly positive. Also, give her the details about the various activities offered during the two days as well as when her discussion group meets (April 17 from 1 to 3 p.m.). Include your contact information, which is the Austin Business Education Network, 2750 Riley Road West, Austin, TX 78727-0293. Your phone is 512-555-0165 and your fax number is 512-555-0135. Date the letter January 9. The final message should reflect the six *C*s of effective messages and be prepared in acceptable business letter format.

7-3

Communication Situation: More than 30 students have registered for tutoring assistance in English grammar, foreign languages, math, and computer programming. Staffing the school tutoring program with qualified tutors is the responsibility of the Student Senate. You are the chairperson of the Student Senate Tutoring Committee.

Task: Plan, compose, and complete a persuasive memorandum to qualified students asking them to donate time and knowledge. This will be a form message that will be distributed by instructors to those who qualify. Tutors are paid $8 per hour. Tutors must have a minimum 3.5 grade point average, and they must be available at least four hours per week.

Case Studies

The budget can only accommodate a limited number of paid positions. Apply the CBO approach and the persuasive strategy AIDA. Explain the program, and invite qualified students to apply. Date the memorandum September 15. The final message should reflect the six Cs of effective messages and acceptable memorandum format.

7-4

Communication Situation: The Children's Center at Grant College offers an after-school program called Partners With Kids for children ages 5 to 11 years whose parents are at work or school. The program operates year round from 2:30 until 6 p.m. The children are cared for by qualified caretakers who are assisted by students from Grant's early childhood program. The environment is safe and comfortable; and the program includes sports, music, and art opportunities and guided study time. Partners With Kids is a nonprofit organization, and area residents are the main source of operating revenue. You have volunteered to write this year's fundraising letter.

Task: Plan, compose, and complete a form letter that can be personalized. Apply the CBO approach and the persuasive strategy AIDA. Explain the program, and provide the details necessary to convince receivers to contribute money to this cause. The Children Center's address is 5368 West Gavine Boulevard, Mobile, AL 36688-6743; the telephone number is 334-555-0160. Date the letter April 12. You are writing the letter for the director, Madeline Bertuzzi. Your final message should reflect the six Cs of effective messages and acceptable message format.

7-5

Communication Situation: Use one of the letters collected for Exercise 7-6.

Task: Revise the message by applying the CBO approach and the persuasive strategy AIDA. Convince the receiver to respond favorably to your request for a donation of money, time, knowledge, or cooperation. Your final letter should reflect the six Cs of effective messages and acceptable message format.

Case Studies

7-6

Communication Situation: Identify a nonprofit organization in your area that interests you. Research the organization and gather facts that you can use to prepare a donation request letter.

Task: Design a letterhead for the organization. Then plan, compose, and complete a donation request letter for your chosen organization. Apply the CBO approach and the persuasive strategy AIDA. Provide details about the organization that will persuade receivers to contribute money. Sign the letter as the volunteer fundraising coordinator.

7-7

Communication Situation: Some issues that concern the general public at all levels of government include the environment, taxes, health care, education, and crime. Choose an issue that is important to you, and determine an action that you want taken, such as voting for or against current pending legislation or resolving a dangerous issue. Use the Internet, the library, and other sources to study the issue so that you have a solid knowledge base to support your request. As assigned by your instructor, prepare either a letter or an e-mail to a government official.

Task: Plan, compose, and complete a persuasive message to a specific government official. Apply the CBO approach and the persuasive strategy AIDA to convince the official to support your request by taking a specific action. Your final letter should reflect the six Cs of effective messages and acceptable message format.

7-8

Communication Situation: Several customers at your small, independent grocery store have recently returned packages of Green Line vermicelli because the packages contained a white dust. A check of the pasta packages in the store revealed several packages contain the dust. The supplier is Worldwide Pasta. Until this experience, you have been satisfied with the products from Worldwide; but now your customers are beginning to wonder if the food you sell is safe to eat.

Case Studies

As store manager for Healthy Harvest (7813 Peterson Avenue, Denver, CO 80210; telephone: 303-555-1889; fax: 303-555-1888; web site: http://www.healthyharvest.com), you are asking Worldwide for a refund of $389, which includes shipping costs and reimbursement for packages that customers have returned. However, when you check your contract with Worldwide, you discover that you are required to report problems within 15 working days. Your records show that you received this shipment over a month ago. You believe the dust is harmless; nonetheless, customers are concerned. You also believe Worldwide might reject your request.

Task: Plan, compose, and complete a claim message to Worldwide Pasta. Apply the CBO approach and the persuasive strategy AIDA. Express your concerns, and provide details that are helpful and necessary to complete this message. Ask Worldwide about the dust. Persuade the company to replace the pasta and to check its products more carefully. Address your message to Gabriel Masselli, Worldwide's president, at 67 Executive Way, Minneapolis, MN 55407. Your final letter should reflect the six *C*s of effective messages and acceptable message format.

7 - 9   **Communication Situation:** Identify a situation that *you* would like resolved.

Task: Plan, compose, and complete a claim message to address the situation you want resolved. Apply the CBO approach and the persuasive strategy AIDA to convince the receiver to respond favorably to your claim. Arrange the sequence of events so that the receiver will understand why the situation needs resolution. Your final letter should reflect the six *C*s of effective messages and acceptable message format.

Case Studies

7-10

Communication Situation: Identify a local business. Gather information about the business so that you can prepare a first-stage collection message.

Task: Plan, compose, and complete a first-stage collection message for the business you identified. Prepare the message as a "stamp" to include on a bill or a reminder card. See Illustration 7-5 for an example.

7-11

Communication Situation: Using the business from Case Study 7-10, write a middle-stage collection letter to Patrick Casey, who has an account balance of $456 that is 60 days past due. You have sent Mr. Casey reminders, but he has not responded. He has paid promptly for five years. You want to keep him as a customer, but you want him to pay his bill. Send your letter to Mr. Casey at 4567 East Ravinia Street. Add a city, state, and ZIP Code.

Task: Plan, compose, and complete a middle-stage collection letter to Mr. Casey. Apply the CBO approach and the persuasive strategy AIDA adapted for middle-stage collection messages. Point out the benefits of paying the bill, and offer payment options. Use the current date. Your final message should reflect the six *C*s of effective messages and acceptable message format.

7-12

Communication Situation: Rewrite one of the sales messages that you analyzed in Exercise 7-8.

Task: Use the information you collected in Exercise 7-8 to revise one of the sales messages. Apply the CBO approach and the persuasive strategy AIDA. Use the current date. Your final letter should reflect the six *C*s of effective messages and acceptable message format.

Case Studies

7-13

Communication Situation: Choose a product or service that you like. Research the product or service. Assume that you are the sales representative for this product.

Task: Plan, compose, and complete a sales message. The message should be written as a form letter that can be personalized. Apply the CBO approach and the persuasive strategy AIDA to convince receivers to buy your product or service. Use techniques and a writing style appropriate for your product or service.

Communication Skills Development 7

NAME_____

Part A   Conjunction Usage

Directions: Underline the conjunction(s) in each of the following sentences.

1. You may need to use persuasion when you want someone to do a favor for you.

2. Rational appeals focus on logic, and emotional appeals focus on feelings.

3. A donation request message may ask not only for money but also for materials.

4. When a person or an organization is extended credit and does not pay within the stated payment period, begin a systematic collection process.

5. An effective collection message is designed to collect money and maintain customer goodwill.

6. Because you want to keep the lines of communication open, use the persuasive strategy AIDA to write a middle-stage collection message.

7. Neither harsh words nor threats in a claim message bring satisfactory results.

8. Both emotional and rational appeals are used to create receiver interest and desire.

9. An opening paragraph may consist of one sentence or several sentences.

10. Before you write your sales message, determine your target audience.

11. Colorful brochures and free gifts stimulate interest in a product or service.

12. If action is easy, the receiver is likely to respond favorably.

13. Negative descriptive words may achieve the desired receiver reaction if you use the words appropriately.

14. You must convince the receiver of a persuasive message that responding positively is beneficial.

15. Although you may be angry, remain calm while you present your claim.

16. Notice that people react defensively when you approach them angrily.

17. Put aside your complaint letter for 24 hours so that you have time to calm down before you mail your letter.

18. Claim letters have greater impact than you may think.

19. Both initial-stage and final-stage collection messages follow the direct pattern of organization.

20. Proofread your persuasive message for format and content accuracy until you produce a final copy.

Part B   Skills Application

Directions: In the following draft of a sales letter, underline errors in noun, pronoun, verb, adjective, adverb, preposition, and conjunction usage. Also, underline spelling errors. Write the correction above each error. (Ordinarily, letters are single-spaced. In this letter, extra space has been added for you to insert corrections.)

Dear Museum Friend

Joins us for an Mexican holiday!

You're holiday begin in Mexico City, the capitol of Mexico. Our stops in

Mexico City includes the Basilica of Our Lady of Guadalupe and the

National Palace. You will also enjoy a performance buy the Ballet

Folklórico and shoping in the colorfull craft markets. Than we will travel

to Mazatlan wear you can sun yourselfs on one of Mexicos longer

beaches, visit art gallerys in colonial downtown, or travel to a

outlying village.

Visit the museum travel office on the corner of Water Street or Wisconsin

Avenue on October 18 at 6 p.m. for a "taste" of Mexico. Call Marla too let

her now that youll be their.

Chapter 8

Job Searches, Résumés, and Cover Letters

Learning Objectives

1 Develop a job search strategy by analyzing your interests, evaluating your job-related skills and abilities, and researching employment opportunities.

2 Consult a variety of sources to research job descriptions and employment opportunities.

3 Use the CBO approach and the persuasive strategy AIDA to prepare résumés that accurately and persuasively present your qualifications in formats that accommodate traditional paper and electronic transmission.

4 Prepare effective cover letters to accompany traditional paper résumés or online résumés implementing the CBO approach and the persuasive strategy AIDA.

COMMUNICATION PERSPECTIVES

Ask for Help

When I was job hunting some years ago, I forgot two basic rules of communication: Know your audience and target your message to them. As an older professional, my work history stretched back a few decades; yet I hadn't changed the chronological format of my résumé since I was a young college graduate. Twenty years of chronology can be boring. I was sending out three to five résumés weekly and getting no calls from employers. At last, I responded to a recruitment agency ad, where a wise recruitment counselor reviewed my résumé. She asked if I'd like to try a functional format résumé and gave me a sample. As I plugged my work life into functional categories, my strengths jumped off the front page of my new résumé. The revised format made it easy for busy HR staff to see my qualifications, and I started getting called for interviews the following week. Another great wisdom learned: Ask for help if you are stuck!

Jane Martell
HR Manager
Department of Pediatrics
Medical College of Wisconsin

Section 1: THE JOB SEARCH

Skill requirements and job responsibilities change rapidly due to technology, corporate mergers, downsizing, and a global economy. As a result, people change jobs frequently; and many change careers.

Finding a job that is right for you is important because you spend most of your waking hours doing your job or attending work-related functions. Opportunities for finding a job that satisfies you personally and professionally will increase if you implement this job search strategy:

1. Analyze your personal characteristics.
2. Determine and evaluate your job-related skills and abilities.
3. Research job descriptions and employment opportunities.

Recruiting and training are expensive, so employers want candidates with the best skills for the wages offered. Use the many sources available to prepare yourself so that you "stand out" from other applicants.

Personal Characteristics and Skills

Begin the job search by analyzing your personal characteristics and evaluating your job-related skills and abilities. Think about the courses you like and do well in, and consider how you spend your leisure time. Complete skill inventory and personality tests offered by college counseling centers as well as free tests available on the Internet. Compare the results. What are the common factors? Comment on your reactions to the test evaluations.

Remember, personality tests and skill inventories are simply tools; they may not accurately reflect who you are. Sometimes, however, test evaluations give you new ideas about yourself that may broaden your job search perspective. Looking closely at what you have to offer helps you match your abilities and temperament to the requirements of a job.

Employment Opportunities

The *Occupational Outlook Handbook*, a U.S. government publication, is a good place to begin gathering general information about jobs. The

Timely Tip

A **job** is perceived as an activity performed regularly in exchange for payment. A **career** is a broad reference to a field of related jobs. For example, being an *accounts payable manager* is the job; *accounting* is the career.

Timely Tip

When the market has more candidates than job openings, employers are selective.

Handbook lists job titles, related occupations, typical work environment descriptions, job requirements, average salaries, and employment outlooks. The book is available online and in most libraries. Another print source is the *Jobs Rated Almanac*, which ranks jobs by factors, including current salaries, future prospects, career outlook, and physical demands.

Employment projections, wages, and other statistics are available at the U.S. Department of Labor site: http://stats.bls.gov/. The site also provides links to state information. Regional information is available through the various state departments of labor.

Networking, companies, job experiences, college career centers, publications, employment agencies, and the Internet are excellent sources for career and job information.

Networking

Networking is often considered the most valuable source of job information. Networking means talking to people about potential employment.

To help you visualize job contacts, prepare a networking list. Begin with a clean sheet of paper; place your name at the top. Below your name, list four or five different employment contact *categories* across the page. School, family and friends, employers, professional affiliations, social and professional clubs, employment agencies, and the Internet are examples of employment contact categories. Once you have identified categories, list contacts, such as department names and people's names. Brainstorm. Think outside the box. The people whose names appear in more than one category are likely to have greater knowledge of employment opportunities because they have exposure to more people.

People Connection

Begin with friends, relatives, acquaintances, professors, and company employees. Let them know you are looking for a job. Someone usually knows something about a job opening somewhere.

Memberships

Membership in a professional association (career-focused) shows commitment to your profession. Memberships in community-focused organizations show commitment to your community. These memberships also provide employment information and opportunities. Many professional associations operate online job boards for members; sometimes the job boards are open to nonmembers of the same profession. Employers post openings on association job boards because the audience is targeted to people with specialized backgrounds. Some professional associations work closely with student affiliates, so membership as a student is a wise career move.

Before joining, attend a few meetings of organizations that reflect your career and interests. Join one or two that have professional and personal

Timely Tip

Polish your communication skills and develop up-to-date contacts by networking.

appeal. As a member, make yourself known in the organization by doing the following:

- Initiating conversations with members
- Identifying the "movers and shakers," and looking for opportunities to work with them
- Volunteering for committee work

Informational Interviews

An **informational interview** is another technique that expands your professional network. An informational interview gives you firsthand occupational information, introduces you to a company, and builds your confidence for job interviews. You initiate an interview for the purpose of obtaining information.

1. Identify a company and a position of interest.
2. Contact the company to arrange the interview.
3. Develop a list of questions to ask (job duties, work environment, skills needed, and so on).
4. Conduct the interview.
5. Follow up with a thank-you message.

Companies

Targeting a company at which to apply is another way to find a job. You can check for openings online or at a company's physical facility. Apply whether or not openings are listed, so your employment information is on file. Attend job fairs where recruiters are available to discuss job prospects. Most companies want an applicant pool for openings as they occur. Investigate federal, state, and local government positions, which may require the completion of a civil service exam. Exam information can be obtained from the appropriate government office.

College Career Centers

In addition to offering testing services and career advice, college career centers usually offer free employment services to students and graduates. Firms like to list positions with colleges because candidates can be recruited from specific programs and because professors may know potential candidates. Most colleges also arrange campus job fairs and interviewing sessions where company recruiters actively seek job candidates. Take advantage of these free services by registering with your college career center.

Career-Related Experiences

Paid work or nonpaid work enhances your employment possibilities. Part-time jobs, internships, and volunteer positions that relate to your career are excellent ways to gain experience and to introduce yourself to prospective employers. Contact your college, companies, and professional associations for intern opportunities; also network and search the Internet for relevant programs.

Newspapers and Professional Publications

Newspaper employment advertisements are helpful sources of information. In addition to job openings, newspaper ads show various job titles and descriptions that you can use when preparing employment messages.

Newspapers divide employment advertisements into categories, such as office/clerical, health, managerial, professional, and technical. Positions may be advertised in more than one category. For example, other titles for *medical administrative assistant* might be *medical receptionist* or *staff assistant*; and positions could be listed in both the *Office/Clerical* section and the *Health Professions* section.

Professional magazines and newsletters may list job openings, but the jobs are usually filled before the print publication is distributed. As organizations turn to e-mail and web sites to advertise job openings, information will be timely.

Employment Agencies

Employment agencies may conduct business in person or over the Internet. For-profit agencies charge the employer (or sometimes the candidate) a fee for matching a candidate to a job. The fee structure varies as does the candidate's contractual obligation. If you use an employment agency, carefully check the reputation of the agency. Ask others for recommendations, and confirm an agency's reputation with your local Better Business Bureau. Also investigate government agencies that operate free employment services.

Sometimes companies hire temporary employees. If the candidate fits an open position, he or she is offered a permanent job; otherwise, the candidate may be terminated.

The Electronic Connection

The Internet has profoundly affected the job market. Company web sites, bulletin boards, and newsgroups list employment opportunities. Job information for both the applicant and the employer is globally accessible 24 hours a day.

A résumé database service is an electronic connection. As an applicant, you provide information to a résumé database service. Your information is entered into a résumé bank. Employers looking for qualified applicants provide the résumé database service with keywords on which to conduct a search. The objective is to match company keywords with applicant qualifications and produce potential job candidates. See pages 265–266 for more information about keywords.

Two popular URLs that contain timely career advice and articles, job search tools, résumé posting services, and links to additional sources appear below. Many other sites can be accessed using keyword searches.

http://www.jobweb.org
http://www.ajb.dni.us/

Timely Tip

A wealth of employment information exists on the Internet, including job-seeking strategies, document preparation, and job postings.

Employer Information

Investigating potential employers not only helps you decide who to contact for job opportunities but also gives you topics for discussion during interviews. Request information directly from companies that interest you. Company web sites, brochures, newsletters, and annual reports tell about company history, products and services, and growth projections. Informational interviews with company employees are also valuable sources of information.

Standard and Poor's Register of Corporations, Fortune Magazine, Jobs Rated Almanac, and similar publications include facts about large companies (location, size, products, officers, and growth).

Culture View

Australia

Australia promotes well-being for the whole of society, which is reflected in extensive social welfare programs for its citizens.

Australians view self-importance negatively and are wary of authority and of those who consider themselves "better than others." Their conversations are direct and literal, and they expect the same in return.

When you conduct business in Australia, avoid pretentious titles and overblown presentations (which may make you a subject for ridicule). Australians value a straightforward, modest approach. Downplay your knowledge and expertise, and let your accomplishments speak for themselves. Emphasis is on ability, not on rank.

Section 2:   THE RÉSUMÉ

After your personal analysis and employer investigation, you prepare employment messages that demonstrate why you would be an asset to an organization. Initial employment correspondence typically consists of a résumé and an accompanying cover letter. You should prepare at least two versions of your résumé: a traditional paper copy and an electronic version.

Plan the Résumé Content

The CBO approach provides the framework for an effective résumé: Plan the résumé content, prepare the résumé draft, and complete the résumé.

The **objective** or **purpose** of preparing a résumé and a cover letter is to obtain a timely interview. Therefore, use the AIDA strategy to attract a receiver's *attention* in you as an employment candidate, create *interest* in and *desire* for your skills and abilities, and encourage a receiver to take *action* to interview you. (Review the AIDA strategy in Chapter 7.)

Timely Tip

Employers assume that your résumé and cover letter are examples of your best work. Therefore, create a positive first impression with these messages.

Get started by creating a résumé master list. A master list is a source of information from which to build and customize your résumé for each employer and position. To create a master list, record each job in order of occurrence, along with tasks you performed and skills you demonstrated. Provide educational details, and include school- and work-related achievements. Once you have compiled the list, sort for job relevancy.

Visualize your audience and customize your résumé accordingly. Your résumé is usually screened by personnel in the human resources department and then forwarded to the hiring manager for review—if the résumé created a positive impression.

Identify experiences and skills desired by the employer, choose tasks and skills from your master list that relate to the employer's requirements, and highlight them on your résumé. Computer software makes modifying easy and enables you to emphasize through description and position what is most applicable to the position for which you are applying.

Example: Matt Martinelli graduated with a computer-aided drafting degree. His drafting position lasted 12 years. A job layoff and a questionable job market convinced Matt to retrain for a computer programming career. When he applies for a computer programming position, Matt emphasizes his programming degree by listing relevant coursework and projects. When a potential job requires drafting experience with a knowledge of programming, Matt emphasizes his drafting experience and lists supporting computer programming information.

Gather supporting information so that your résumé is a personal statement about *you*.

- Tell who *you* are
- Communicate the kind of job *you* want
- Show that *you* can do the job
- Distinguish *you* from other applicants

When you buy a product, you look at the list of product features; and you analyze how those features meet your needs and wants. The résumé is a marketing tool that relates the good things about you (the product) to the prospective employer (the buyer). Employment recruiters scan a résumé for about 30 seconds to determine whether an applicant should be interviewed. Critique the information you include on your résumé by asking yourself this question: *Does the information on my résumé relate to the job?*

After gathering information for the résumé, you must group related facts. Apply the persuasive strategy AIDA as you compile information. Include, arrange, and emphasize information that will persuade the receiver to grant an interview. Begin the résumé with a *heading*. Add a *job objective*. List and organize your facts into *work experience* and *education*. Include other sections, such as *skills, achievements, honors, professional certifications,*

Timely Tip

Employers look for people who can effectively perform the tasks of the position. Make sure your employment messages clearly reflect what you can do for the employer.

Timely Tip

Every résumé should relate how an employer will benefit from hiring you.

and *memberships* if they are needed. Keywords (see pages 265–266) as part of your descriptions are increasingly important. List *references* on a separate page and present them upon an employer's request.

Follow these standard format guidelines when you prepare your résumé:

- *Do not* use personal pronouns such as *I, me, you,* and *my*.
- Use descriptive phrases (not sentences) that begin with strong action verbs to tell what you did.
- Punctuate the phrases as though they are sentences.
- Maintain parallel structure within your descriptions.
- Present information within each section in a consistent format.
- Omit the articles *a, an,* and *the* whenever possible.

Example: Developed web sites for eight companies. Wrote code for new version of radiology software.

Résumé Heading

The heading contains complete contact information: name, address, home telephone number, and e-mail address and fax number (if applicable). Sometimes a temporary address and phone number may be added if you are a college student. *Do not* include telephone or fax numbers or an e-mail address from your current place of employment as a means of contacting you. Suggesting that you can be reached at your current job does not send a positive message to a potential employer.

When your *relevant* information fills more than one page, begin each subsequent page with your name and page number so that the document is clearly identifiable if separated from the opening page. An example of a second-page heading follows.

Example: Kira Randall   Page 2

Job Objective

A **job objective** (or **goal**) follows the résumé heading. This is a one- to three-line *employment-centered* statement that indicates your employment interests *and* weaves in how the organization will benefit from hiring you. Other suggested titles for this section are *Professional Objective* and *Employment Goal.*

Some experts believe that a job objective restricts an applicant's opportunities and that specific goals should be discussed in a cover letter or during an interview. However, many recruiters strongly advocate the inclusion of a job objective. From an employer's viewpoint, a job objective helps determine what kind of match to make between what you have to offer and what is available. A job objective also tells employers that you have given thought to your career direction.

From a personal perspective, writing a job objective causes you to focus on your strengths and how you would like to use those strengths in

Timely Tip

Do not use the word résumé on the résumé.

your work. An objective also helps you arrange the remaining information in your résumé.

Wording a job objective can be challenging. Avoid trite wording, such as *entry level*, *challenging position*, *opportunity for advancement*, and *progressive organization*. Also avoid vague wording, which may be misinterpreted and eliminate you as a job candidate. Objectives similar to the following examples give the recruiters enough information to make connections to available positions.

Timely Tip

Compose an employment-centered objective that aligns with each position for which you are applying.

Examples:

Vague Job Objectives	**Informative Job Objectives**
Accounting position in real estate firm.	Supervisory accounting position with emphasis in real estate acquisition and appraisal.
Position in medical records.	Part-time coding position in medium- to large-sized medical facility for an experienced coder with an opportunity for future full-time employment.

When you respond to an advertisement or when you believe a title is understood by receivers, writing the job objective is easier.

Example: **Job Objective:** Obtain a geriatric nursing assistant position within Auburn Health Systems.

Summary of Qualifications

Some job candidates use a summary of qualifications in addition to or as a replacement for a job objective. A **summary of qualifications** summarizes your strongest and most relevant skills and abilities. Positioning this information near the beginning of your résumé attracts the receiver's attention and gives an overview of what you have to offer. The title for this section reflects its content. Other title possibilities are *Capabilities* or *Relevant Skills and Abilities*. See Functional Résumé, page 265, for more suggestions.

Examples:

Relevant Qualifications:
- Nine years providing administrative support for corporate VPs
- Strong written communication skills as evidenced in composing and editing monthly company newsletters
- Proven organizational skills managing personal and professional schedules for six cardiothoracic surgeons

Overview of Qualifications:
Progressive responsibilities performing financial audits of major retail and manufacturing clients. Considerable audit experience in limited partnerships, qualified partnerships, and joint ventures.

Timely Tip

Ask yourself: *What can I do or what do I know that I can use on the job regardless of job type?*

Follow the job objective or summary with *your most important qualification*, which is usually your experience or education. Use concrete words and action verbs to tell how your educational, work, and personal experiences can satisfy job requirements.

Work Experience

Timely Tip

Emphasize facts most related to the position.

Employment (or *Work*) *History* is commonly used as a heading for this section. Other common titles are *Professional Experience*, *Related* (or *Relevant*) *Experience*, and *Additional Experience*.

Employers are most interested in experiences that relate to the job for which you are applying. You may divide your experiences into related experience and additional experience. Unpaid, job-pertinent experiences, such as volunteering or interning in your field, also are appropriate for this section.

Refer to your master résumé list. Organize job entries from the most recent employment to the least recent employment, and include this information:

- Company name, city, and state
- Dates of employment (month/year)
- Status, if part-time (otherwise, full-time is assumed)
- Job title, significant duties, and accomplishments

Employment information can be presented in various arrangements. Once you decide on an arrangement, use the same arrangement for each entry.

Examples: November 1999–Present. Track time reports, balance cash receipts and adjustments, make daily bank deposits, enter expenses, and run monthly reports. Accounting Assistant, County Parks System, Milwaukee, WI

Payroll Assistant   County Parks System, Milwaukee, WI Tallied time reports, entered employee data, ran bi-weekly payroll checks, ran and distributed monthly reports. (Full-time Summers 2003 and 2004)

Short-Term or Unrelated Work Experiences

Short-term work experiences or unrelated experiences often develop desirable skills and attitudes that are applicable to other jobs and careers. Short-term experiences deserve inclusion, but length of time and place of employment should be de-emphasized. One technique is to combine experiences. Whether your experiences are short-term or unrelated to the position sought, emphasize the transferable skills that will help you perform the targeted job. Communication skills and decision-making skills, for example, are highly valued by employers.

Examples: Developed patience and tact working with a diverse population while conducting telephone surveys. Demonstrated the ability to work under pressure in quantity-oriented environments. Applied excellent organizational skills by preparing and assembling a 25-page training manual for new employees. Employed by telemarketing firms in Denver, Colorado (2002–2004)

Operated in-home childcare business for three- and four-year-old children. Developed and implemented monthly plans for educational instruction, physical activities to promote small and large muscle development, and balanced meals. Prepared progress checklists for each child, and conducted parent conferences quarterly. September 2000 through October 2005.

Timely Tip

Accomplishments and activities that are job related may be listed in the employment section of your résumé or in a separate section.

Job Descriptions

Describe your job tasks and responsibilities with concrete words, action verbs, and short phrases. Use present tense verbs for current jobs and past tense verbs for previous jobs. Table 8-1 is a sampling of action verbs.

Table 8-1 Action Verbs

adapted	directed	originated
administered	distributed	performed
advised	documented	planned
analyzed	edited	prepared
answered	eliminated	presented
arranged	established	programmed
assembled	evaluated	published
assessed	expanded	received
assisted	forecasted	recorded
attained	identified	reduced
audited	implemented	reorganized
built	improved	represented
clarified	increased	researched
collaborated	indexed	resolved
collected	initiated	restored
compiled	installed	revised
completed	instructed	sold
computed	integrated	solved
conducted	interpreted	sorted
constructed	investigated	summarized
coordinated	led	trained
created	maintained	transcribed
decreased	managed	translated
delivered	negotiated	updated
deposited	networked	worked
designed	ordered	wrote
developed	organized	

Also, use the jargon of your field appropriately. Employers are especially interested in learning about your communication skills, your leadership and decision-making skills, and your dependability. When possible, quantify your accomplishments.

Examples: Opened, annotated, and distributed mail for six franchise managers.

Designed follow-up form that was adopted into 22 branch offices for help desk reps.

Maintained lab equipment for three professors.

Education

Education, *Academic Experience*, *Educational Preparation*, and *Professional Training* are suggestions of other titles for the education section. If you are a new graduate, a career changer, or a student, you want to show that you have acquired new knowledge and skills. Relevant training programs and seminars may be included in this section. Professional certifications may be listed here or emphasized in a separate section. Individual *relevant* courses also may be listed.

Present educational details in reverse chronological order. Include the following information for each entry, and arrange the information in a consistent format.

- Graduation and/or attendance dates (month/year)
- Degree (major and minor fields of study), diploma, and certificates

Examples: **Associate Degree in Environmental Services Management,** Augusta Technical College, Augusta, GA (August 2001 to August 2003)
Education and training included methods for cleaning interior and exterior building surfaces, identification and reduction of workplace hazards, industry regulatory requirements, work measurement tools, and personnel recruitment strategies.

March 2004 to December 2004. Completed 40 hours of seminars conducted by the University of Texas—Austin: Small Business Budgets; Small Business Plans for the 21st Century; and Grant Writing for Nonprofits.

A grade point average (GPA) may be used as a screening device, so include only GPAs of 3.0 or above. Indicate the grading scale and whether you are reporting your overall GPA or the GPA in your major only. Include graduation honors.

Examples: 3.5 (4.0 scale)   *or*   3.7 in major (4.0 scale)
Graduated cum laude with BA in French

Timely Tip

Educational or job-related awards and proficiencies may be listed within their respective sections, or they may be listed in a separate section for emphasis.

Accomplishments and Activities

Your accomplishments and activities provide clues about your personality, attitude, and how you will fit into an organization. When you have more than two awards, honors, special skills, and organizational involvements, list them in a separate section for emphasis. Otherwise, place the information in a related section as previously discussed.

Titles for this section will vary based on what you include. Title ideas are *Honors and Awards*; *Accomplishments*; *Scholarships and Awards*; *Professional Affiliations* or *Memberships*; *Professional Certifications*; *Professional Development*; *Community* or *Collegiate Activities*; *Special Skills*.

Accomplishments and activities that deserve recognition include:

- Receipt of scholarships and awards
- Proficiencies in specific skills or equipment operation
- Competencies in foreign languages
- Full or partial financing of one's education
- Completion of career-related class projects
- Certifications or licensures
- Volunteering
- Memberships and leadership roles in professional, school, and community organizations

Be sure to include those extras that connect to your career or to the job you are seeking. Quantify achievements when possible.

Examples: Received Boston Globe Inc. Employee of the Year Award for the development of safety checklists that reduced shop accidents by 21 percent in the first six months.

Co-captain of Temple University's champion debate team for the years 2001, 2002, and 2003.

Mobile library volunteer (ten hours weekly) at Children's Hospital of Southeastern Wisconsin, Milwaukee, WI. Recruit and schedule BookMobile volunteers; inventory and order books for patient mobile library.

Extensive European travel. Fluent in French language; well versed in French culture and history.

Silent auction chair for the 7th Annual "Beat Breast Cancer" Picnic. Net auction profit: $42,300.

References

Professional references are people other than personal friends who can comment positively on your capabilities. Past and present employers, colleagues, instructors, and others who can give reliable testimony about your abilities and achievements are good sources.

Timely Tip

Accomplishments and activities often provide evidence about work-related skills.

Timely Tip

Add references to the résumé itself only when an employer requests that format or when the addition of references enhances the appearance of a short résumé.

Timely Tip

Whenever you think
your references will be
checked, alert the
individuals that they may
be contacted.

Before you include names on a reference page, always ask the individuals if they are willing to answer questions about your job-related qualifications. Graciously accept that someone may not want to be a reference or that companies may not allow someone to provide information.

Prepare a standalone reference page with the same heading that appears on your résumé. Include complete contact information as provided by each individual: name, occupational title, complete address, telephone number, and/or e-mail address.

Normally, you will not submit a reference sheet until you meet for an interview. Companies usually check references after an interview, not before.

Information to Exclude

Personal information does not belong on a résumé. Although laws prohibit job discrimination based on age, gender, race, national origin, religion, or marital status, this type of information may be used as a screening device. Remember that your résumé will be screened by someone who will have his or her own viewpoint. Do not eliminate yourself from consideration because of someone else's biases and before you have the opportunity to present your qualifications in person. (Refer to Chapter 9, Table 9-2, for illegal interview questions.)

Prepare the Résumé Draft

Your résumé should present an accurate "report" of your skills, abilities, education, work experience, and accomplishments. Today's job market is results oriented. Present accurate information, and emphasize how your individual qualifications relate to the job you are seeking. Package your information in a style that best represents *you*.

Timely Tip

Misrepresentations and
lies are embarrassing.
They destroy credibility
and careers.

Ethical Considerations

Most employers conduct background checks to verify the accuracy of the information you supply, and they may request school transcripts. Even though people have been hired and have performed well on the job, they are often fired when distortions on their résumés or applications are discovered.

In the last few years, people in prominent positions, such as college coaches, have been fired as a result of résumé exaggeration or outright lying. Employment dates, education, grades, and job descriptions are the areas most frequently exaggerated. *Do not* put yourself in the position of explaining why you have false information in your employment documents.

Résumé Style

Which style is best for you? Your background and job goals will help you decide which résumé style best emphasizes your qualifications. The **reverse chronological** résumé, the **functional** résumé, and the **combination** résumé are three organizational patterns.

Reverse Chronological Résumé

The reverse chronological résumé is popular among recruiters because employment and academic histories are easy to find. The format is simple and direct: Events in each section are listed from the most recent occurrence to the least recent. Those who have considerable relevant experience in their field and those who are seeking career advancement based on a previous record of progressive responsibilities often use the reverse chronological style.

The reverse chronological order focuses on past events rather than on future possibilities. Thus, the style is not as beneficial for candidates who lack related work experience or who have gaps in work history because the missing information is quickly noticed.

Kira Randall, the candidate presented in Illustration 8-1, page 270, has updated and expanded her skills in a career-related area. She is seeking a position that will utilize her newly acquired skills and her relevant computer experiences. Her reference sheet, Illustration 8-2, page 271, is prepared on a separate page.

Functional Résumé

People who lack work experience (such as recent college graduates) and people who have changed jobs frequently or have employment gaps find the functional résumé useful. The functional arrangement emphasizes the candidate's skills and abilities and minimizes work history or training.

Transferable skills and abilities, desired by most employers, may be grouped into broad categories with titles such as *Summary (Overview) of Qualifications* and *Skills and Capabilities*. Technical or job-specific skills may be grouped into categories with titles such as *Technical Skills*, *Sales and Marketing Skills,* or *Negotiating*. These descriptive categories may replace or immediately follow the job objective. William Klein, a recent college graduate, uses a functional résumé to highlight skills that he believes will be desirable to a nonprofit organization. William's résumé, shown in Illustration 8-3, page 272, emphasizes transferable skills because his work experience and degree are unrelated to the position he is seeking.

Combination Résumé

A combination résumé incorporates the best features of the functional and the reverse chronological résumés. The combination résumé highlights skills and abilities *and* presents a work history. This style is appropriate for almost everyone *except* someone who has a poor work record or no work experience.

Keywords

Keywords are nouns and phrases that reflect professional jargon, descriptively relate technical skills, and highlight job-related accomplishments. Keywords are especially important for Internet résumés, but they are also

Timely Tip

Many large companies scan and store résumé data in a computer database. Applicant information can be accessed quickly to respond to targeted job openings.

valuable additions to paper résumés. Keywords attract a recruiter's eye (whether the recruiter is a human or a computer) and quickly answer "who" and "what" about an applicant.

Paper or electronic résumés may be scanned and converted into a searchable database. Then computer software looks for words in the résumé that match position-specific keywords designated by the employer. Technical skills, industry-specific keywords, and transferable skill keywords such as *teamwork*, *organizing*, and *planning* are usually in the employer's keyword vocabulary. Job categories that contain matching keywords are identified. Applicants are identified for interviews based on the number of keywords that match, or applicant information is stored for future reference.

When your résumé is in a résumé database, employers can look for information in different ways; for example, searching for keywords that represent a specific experience. Think about how employers might search. What keywords describe your skills and support the jobs you are seeking? Knowing your career goals and characteristics about various jobs in your field assist you in determining keywords that have the best opportunities for a match. Choose concrete words to define your experience, skills, and professional achievements.

The Morales résumé, Illustration 8-4, page 273, opens with a job objective as well as a summary of relevant skills. Keywords are scattered liberally throughout the résumé to attract positive attention to Silvia Morales's skills.

Arranging important employment terms in a keyword summary is a good technique. A keyword summary follows the résumé heading or job objective and includes industry jargon and abbreviations; significant responsibilities; special skills, abilities, and awards; interpersonal skills; fields of study; academic degrees; and professional designations or certifications, such as CPA and CMT.

Examples: Project Manager. A+ Certification. CCNA and CCNP certifications. Problem solver. Client support. Hardware selection. User documentation. 5 years of training experience. Spanish fluency. AITP member. BS Management Information Systems. University of Michigan.

Account Representative. Strong communication skills. Customer service. Budget analysis. Team player. Maryland Association of Accounting Professionals. Associate Degree in Banking and Finance.

A keyword summary follows the heading in the Dimos résumé shown in Illustration 8-5 on page 274.

Computer-Friendly Résumés

Job seekers investigate job availability, post job inquiries, and submit resumes by the computer. Employers use the computer to post job openings and to screen and track applicants.

Be prepared to respond to varying employer requirements by having on hand at least two different formatted versions of your résumé: traditional paper and computer-friendly. After you have prepared a traditional paper résumé, modify the résumé to a format that accommodates Internet transmission and scanning. Regardless of transmission mode, résumés have the same goal: to get you an interview. Computer-friendly résumés are free of graphics, unusual font styles, and other print mechanics, such as underlining and italics.

Internet Résumés

Internet résumés include e-mail résumés and résumés posted online.

E-mail Résumés

Although you want to submit your résumé in its most visually appealing form, you will find that transmission and format requirements vary from company to company. A traditional paper résumé, prepared with a word processing program, does not always transmit well over the Internet. Also, a résumé on a screen may look different when printed on paper.

Prepare the electronic version of your résumé as an ASCII (ASK-ee) text file (plain text) for the best chance of readability on the receiver's end. E-mail résumés require special formatting to ensure the best outcome.

- Provide an e-mail subject line that clearly identifies the purpose of the message. Supply a job title or use other descriptive terms to alert the receiver that this is a legitimate message.
- Include a cover message that tells the receiver why you are making contact. Cover messages are important because résumés lose their visual appeal when they are converted to ASCII files.
- Send a traditional paper copy of your employment messages when possible.

Online Posting

Before you prepare an online résumé, visit several résumé database sites. Gather information about confidentiality, services, and fees.

Confidentiality, control over who has access to your employment information, is an important consideration. Posting online may open your résumé to many viewers, some of whom are an unintended audience. Find out who can access your information. Public databases are exactly that—open to the public. Even if you post with a private résumé service, you may not be able to restrict who looks at your information.

You also need to know about the services and fees. What are the requirements for posting? What services do you receive? How easily can you update information on your résumé? What are the costs associated with posting and updating?

After investigating a few résumé database services, you will be in a better position to make informed decisions about posting online. Always read the site guidelines carefully before submitting your employment material. In other words, *think before you post.*

Timely Tip

ASCII stands for American Standard Code for Information Interchange.

Timely Tip

Many firms will not accept files attached to an e-mail message because attachments often pass computer viruses.

Once you decide to post your résumé online, format your document for the best online appeal.

The Elena Dimos résumé, Illustration 8-5, page 274, has a simple layout and plain font with no unusual print mechanics. The résumé, with its wide margins, keyword summary, capital letter titles, and industry jargon is designed for searchable databases, online posting, and Internet transmission.

Hypertext Résumés

A hypertext résumé provides links to another location that houses samples of your work. In other words, the receiver of an online résumé can click on hypertext and be directed to your personal web site and to files that may include animation, sound, color, and other enhancements that are not ordinarily represented in a résumé. Hypertext résumés are not for everyone, nor do they impress all employers. Hypertext résumés may be effective when the position requires a demonstration of creativity or a specific level of technical expertise.

Some job candidates are using *web portfolios* to showcase their talents. Check with a potential employer before submitting a hypertext résumé or a web portfolio. Like hypertext résumés, web portfolios are not automatically a desirable format for presenting qualifications.

Fax Résumés

Job seekers also use facsimile machines to transmit employment correspondence at the request of employers. Many of the formatting techniques that enhance a paper résumé can be used effectively for a fax résumé. Always remember, though, to use 1 to $1\frac{1}{2}$-inch margins and avoid script fonts and fonts that are unusually light or dark.

Prepare a cover letter to accompany your fax résumé. Also prepare a separate fax cover sheet to transmit both your résumé and cover letter to the employer. Before faxing your documents to an employer, fax to a friend; and evaluate the clarity.

Complete the Résumé

Once you are satisfied with the résumé content, turn your attention to the "whole package." Your résumé and cover letter may be the first contact an employer has with you as a potential employee, so create a positive impression.

Appearance

No matter what transmission mode you use, your résumé must be perfect: no typos, spelling errors, or stains. Employers use résumés as screening devices. Appearance does count! In fact, employers rank résumé appearance almost equally to content in importance.

Traditional paper résumés that are mailed, not scanned, are prepared with word processing software. You can enhance the appearance of your document with a variety of options that are available. For example, bolding, blocking, centering, underlining, shading, and bulleting as well as font

Timely Tip

Some résumé database services provide an electronic form to input text into specific fields. The information is then submitted and added to the service's database.

sizes and styles can produce eye-catching copy. Use the techniques selectively because you do not want the print features to overwhelm the résumé content. Also provide adequate white space (areas free of text or graphics), which makes reading easier. White space consists of top and bottom margins (1 to $1^1/_2$ inches) and areas between sections or items.

Purchase quality matching paper and envelopes for your employment message series: résumé, cover letter, and any follow-up correspondence. The best stationery colors are white, buff, light blue, and grey. Black is the favored ink choice. Print your résumé on a quality laser printer. Customizing your résumé to each position is preferable; but if you send a generic résumé for mass mailing, use a high-quality photocopier to produce copies on the stationery.

When you prepare a résumé for transmission over the Internet, the ideal situation is to prepare your résumé according to the instructions provided by the employer. Use the guidelines presented in Table 8-2 and seek formatting advice from a specialized reference.

Table 8-2 General Format Guidelines for Computer- and Fax-Friendly Résumé Preparation

Guidelines	E-Mail or Online Posting	Scannable	Fax
Prepare as an ASCII file (plain text).	✓	✓	
Use a one-column format.	✓	✓	
Use a 65-space line; begin lines at the left margin.	✓	✓	
Use standard fonts in which the letters do not touch (Courier, Times New Roman, Arial, for example).	✓	✓	✓
Use at least a 10- or 12-point font size. (10-point in some font styles is too small.)	✓	✓	✓
Avoid italicized and decorative fonts.	✓	✓	✓
Do not use vertical or horizontal lines, graphics, or boxes.	✓	✓	
Do not use shading.	✓	✓	✓
Avoid bullets and symbols, such as ampersands (&), percents (%), and pound signs (#).	✓	✓	
Use these symbols for emphasis: all capital letters, asterisks (*), hyphens (–), and plus signs (+).	✓	✓	
Print on high-quality white paper using a laser or ink-jet printer. (Fax copy does not have to be high quality paper.)		✓	✓
Send only originals in a flat envelope. Do not fold or staple.		✓	
Send yourself and a friend a copy to evaluate clarity and visual appeal.	✓	✓	✓

Kira M. Randall

47 Taylor Trail   330.555.2446
Akron, OH 44310   krandall@core.com

<table>
<tr><td><p align="left">States specific position and identifies up-to-date skills.</p><p>Presents education before work history to show how new degree relates to position qualifications.</p></td><td>**Position Objective**</td><td>IT technician position that utilizes state-of-the-art knowledge of .NET Framework, e-security, and database management.</td></tr>
<tr><td></td><td>**Education**</td><td>Associate of Arts Degree, Computer and Information Sciences Programming Specialization
University of Akron, Akron, Ohio
June 2002 to December 2004</td></tr>
</table>

States specific position and identifies up-to-date skills.	**Position Objective**	IT technician position that utilizes state-of-the-art knowledge of .NET Framework, e-security, and database management.
Presents education before work history to show how new degree relates to position qualifications.	**Education**	Associate of Arts Degree, Computer and Information Sciences Programming Specialization University of Akron, Akron, Ohio June 2002 to December 2004
		Bachelor of Science Degree, Computer Science Education Kent State University, Kent, Ohio September 1990 to August 1994
Arranges education and jobs by order of occurrence.	**Work History**	**Supervisor of Computer Services** St. Vincent High School, Akron, Ohio September 1999 to June 2002
Emphasizes computer-related responsibilities. Uses past tense action verbs.		*Responsibilities*: Updated software and hardware as budget allowed. Conducted in-house computer skills training for administrators and staff. Developed training materials and computerized maintenance and inventory schedules. Supervised hardware repairs. Resolved user hardware and software issues.
		Teacher Cuyahoga Falls High School, Cuyahoga Falls, Ohio September 1994 to June 1999
		Responsibilities: Taught computer science to college-bound students. Conducted basic equipment maintenance and repair.
	Professional Affiliations	Ohio Technical Teachers Association September 1994 to June 2002

Illustration 8-1 **Reverse Chronological Résumé**

Kira M. Randall

Uses same heading format as résumé.

47 Taylor Trail   330.555.2446
Akron, OH 44310   krandall@core.com

References

Provides complete reference contact information in consistent arrangement.

Mr. Chikara Enami
Supervisor, Kushkin Computer Laboratory
University of Akron Main Campus
Akron, OH 44301
cenami@uamc.edu

Lists two references with knowledge of candidate's new skills.

Mr. Kevin Houseman, Instructor
Kushkin Computer Laboratory
University of Akron Main Campus
Akron, OH 44301
khouse@uamc.edu

Includes one reference with knowledge of candidate's job skills and work ethic.

Sr. Dorothy Harris
Principal, St. Vincent High School
15 North Maple Street
Akron, OH 44303
330.555.8719
dharris@stvincenths.edu

Looks pleasing to the eye.

Illustration 8-2 **Standalone Reference Page**

William C. Klein

1245 Timber Ridge Drive
Brookfield, WI 53045

Phone: 262.555.2345
E-mail: wmcklein@homebase.net

Indicates area of
interest and states
transferable skills.

Position Objective

Seeking a development position in a nonprofit organization that will benefit from strong
language skills and ability to work effectively with diverse populations.

Key Competencies

Provides keywords
likely to attract
receiver's attention.

Written and spoken communication skills. Ability to adapt to variety of situations as
experienced by living and traveling abroad. Highly developed organizational skills.
French language fluency; well versed in French culture. Significant cultural exposure
through extensive travel in Europe and China.

Education

Provides educational
background.

Bachelor of Arts, University of Tennessee, Knoxville, TN
Emphasis: French Language with focus in World Business
Graduated cum laude May 2004

University of Rennes II, Rennes, France
Completed a semester of junior year in France. January–June 2003

Work Experience

Arranges work
experience by job
title and provides
brief description
of tasks.

Language Assistant. Villeneuve-sur-lot, France
Led group discussions with high school students. Developed materials, conducted oral
exams, evaluated student progress. October 2004–May 2005

Discussion Leader. Community Cultural Center, Villeneuve-sur-lot, France
Volunteered weekly to hold conversational English classes. Developed materials for
adults interested in specialized terms for travel and banking. January 2005–May 2005

Sales Associate. Boston Store (Carson Pirie Scott), Wauwatosa, WI
Part-time during high school and college. June 1999–Present

Reader and Proofreader. Knoxville, TN
Dictated material from print text to tape. Proofread and organized documents for dyslexic
MBA student. September 2002–May 2003

Achievements

Phi Theta Kappa member, collegiate national honor society. Blood Donor: University of
Tennessee and Blood Center of Southeastern Wisconsin since 1999.

Illustration 8-3 **Functional Résumé**

Silvia Morales
14 Silver Street
Denver CO 80209

smorales@home.net   303.555.9289

Employment Objective

States position and presents skills that emphasize job-related qualifications.

Position as health information management technician utilizing coding and reimbursement experience and training.

Summary of Relevant Skills

Highlights skills using keywords appropriate for professional field. Positions keywords throughout the résumé.

Uses adjectives in column layout to describe relevant and desirable personal characteristics.

Offer a combination of practical experience and current training. Familiar with health information systems, including ethical and legal aspects and regulatory requirements. Skilled in abstracting, verifying, coding, and indexing medical data. Ability to retrieve and compile health data for reimbursement review, quality assessment, and other needs.

- detail-oriented
- resourceful

- problem solver
- tactful

- multitasking
- highly motivated

Educational History

Working toward a Bachelor of Science degree in Health Information Management
    Regis University, Denver, CO   2003 to Present

Associate of Applied Science Degree, Health and Wellness
    Emphasis: Health Information Specialist
    Community College of Denver, Denver, CO   Graduated 2003

Employment History

Uses action verbs and keywords to describe tasks.

1999–Present   Administrative Assistant
             Office of Dr. Albert Hart, North Aurora, CO

Maintain and compile health records for more than 600 patients. Ensure appropriateness and adequacy of health care documentation. Code and classify diagnoses and procedures for reimbursement. Process insurance claims.

1996–1999   Order Coordinator
             Data Tech, Inc., Denver, CO

Processed customer orders. Arranged subcontractor scheduling for timely completion. Worked with customers and subcontractors to resolve issues.

Illustration 8-4 **Combination Résumé**

Elena Dimos

1002 Fitzwater Quarry Road
Roslyn, PA 19001
215.555.0174
Elena.D@athome.com

KEYWORD SUMMARY

HTML codes and tags including DHTML, XML, Java, CSS, ASP, and Javascript. Knowledge of TCP/IP, DNS, NT, and IIS. Experience using SQL server. Self-starter. Team oriented. Temple University honor student.

CAREER OBJECTIVE

Seeking full-time position in web development where strong background in web technologies, energy, and creativity will aid in the design and maintenance of web sites to positively represent an organization.

EXPERIENCE

Project Intern assigned to Cross Wiring Corporation, Trenton, NJ. Key developer on team responsible for designing, testing, implementing, and supporting the web infrastructure using HTML, ASP, ASP.NET, Javascript, VBScript, and Flash. Involved from beginning to completion of "Look and Touch" prototype. January 2004–September 2004.

Lab Assistant in Computer Science Lab, Temple University, Philadelphia, PA. Assisted students enrolled in introductory computer science courses. August 2002–December 2003.

EDUCATION

Temple University, Philadelphia, PA. Computer Science major. Completed 90 credits. GPA: 3.5. Temple University Honor Roll. Expected graduation June 2005.

Illustration 8-5 **Computer-Friendly Résumé for Searchable Databases and Internet Transmission**

The Final Copy

Compare your résumé with the Checklist for Preparing a Résumé below to assist you in assessing its effectiveness. Proofread and edit. Have someone else proofread your document. Proofread again until you are absolutely sure you have a perfect copy.

Timely Tip

Proofread! Proofread! Proofread!

Checklist for Preparing a Résumé

1. Does your résumé:
- Accomplish the objective?
- Relate to your target audience?

2. Does the draft of your résumé:
- Provide complete contact information?
- Offer a concise, informative job objective or summary of qualifications?
- Reflect a style that best promotes your salability?
- Present information as phrases and use parallel structure?
- Use descriptive words, including keywords and action verbs, to provide relevant details?
- Include achievements, honors, and activities that enhance your salability, if relevant to the position?
- Include a correctly formatted separate reference page?

3. Does the final version of your résumé:
- Utilize a format that ensures clarity on the receiving end?
- Send the message you intend?
- Reflect ethics and credibility by providing adequate, objective information?
- Look professional?

Section 3: THE COVER LETTER

The résumé is a compilation of facts—a product list about *you*. The **cover letter** or **application letter** is the persuasive message that accompanies a résumé—a sales letter about *you*. Thus, you will apply the CBO approach and the persuasive strategy AIDA to explain how your qualifications can benefit an employer and how you differ from other applicants. A well-written cover letter is often as important as a résumé.

Cover letters, like sales letters, are solicited or unsolicited. When you know a position is open, you write a **solicited** cover letter; and you provide

Timely Tip

The cover letter is an example of your communication skills.

concrete information that directly relates to the open position. When you are unsure whether an opening exists, you write an **unsolicited** cover letter. Whether the cover letter is solicited or unsolicited, your opening encourages further reading by showing that you know something about the company and/or by telling how your knowledge, skills, and abilities will benefit the company.

Plan the Cover Letter

Apply the CBO approach and begin by planning your message. Ultimately, you want to develop a basic cover letter that can be modified and tailored for each employer and position.

Identify the Objective. The cover letter and résumé are an employment message package. The main objective of this package is to persuade the receiver to grant an interview, which you will do by relating what you have to offer to what the employer needs. The cover letter also introduces the résumé.

Visualize the Audience. When you know something about an organization's mission, products and services, or expansion plans, you are better able to visualize your audience and customize your message. Web sites, newspaper articles, annual reports, and company brochures provide helpful information.

Gather Supporting Information. Supply information that supports you as a candidate for the job. Elaborate on those abilities and characteristics that help the receiver understand your value to the workplace.

Although you use personal pronouns (*I*, *me*, and *my*) to describe your accomplishments, limit their use; and tie-in your offerings to the employer's needs. The following receiver-focused examples will appeal to an employer more than the sender-focused statements.

Timely Tip

Remember, your employment messages are likely to have a dual audience: the human resources department, which screens the applicants, and the department, which has the open position.

Examples:	**Sender Focus**	**Receiver Focus**
	I believe that my computer skills will benefit you.	You will find that my computer skills enable me to enter data quickly and accurately.
	I have received awards for my responsible attitude toward work, and I can have the same work attitude at O-hi Corporation.	You can count on me to be on the job every day as evidenced by the Perfect Attendance and Employee of the Month awards I received at O-Hi Corporation.

Organize the Information. Organizing your information before beginning your draft is critical so that you present your best selling points. Begin with an outline. The cover letter is a persuasive message, so follow the persuasive strategy AIDA to group information. Remember that the

AIDA strategy encourages a favorable response—and you want an interview! Table 8-3 outlines cover letter content.

Table 8-3 Cover Letter Outline

I. Attract Attention in Opening
   A. Use Opening Appropriate for Situation
      1. Summary of qualifications
      2. Personal referral
      3. Advertisement or posting
      4. Combination
      5. Other relevant statement
   B. Mention Specific Job or Area of Interest
II. Create Interest and Desire in Explanation
   A. Discuss Qualifications from Reader's Viewpoint
      1. Education and/or training
      2. Work experience
      3. Positive personal attitudes, qualities, transferable skills
      4. Achievements and awards
   B. Reference Résumé
III. Request Action in Closing
   A. Request Interview
   B. Provide Contact Information

Compose a Cover Letter Draft

A cover letter should reflect your personality and your individuality as well as relate to an employer's needs. Prepare each cover letter individually; do not distribute a generic cover letter.

When possible, direct the cover letter to a specific person; and confirm the correct spelling of the receiver's name by calling the company. A salutation such as *Dear Human Resources Manager* is appropriate when you cannot confirm a person's name. The first receiver is typically someone in human resources (HR) because the HR department screens applicants based on their initial employment messages. After your employment information is reviewed, your résumé and cover letter may be forwarded to one or more department managers.

Attract Attention

Attract the receiver's attention in the opening of the cover letter. When you know a position is open, you mention the position in the opening (solicited cover letter). Otherwise, you refer to an area of interest and the possibility of an opening (unsolicited cover letter). In either case, present information that encourages the receiver to read further. Popular techniques for opening a cover letter include a summary of qualifications, a personal referral, a reference to an advertised position, or a combination of approaches.

Examples:

Summary of Qualifications

Five years of experience in web development, enthusiasm, and motivation to keep my skills current have prepared me to assume the responsibilities of Web Development Supervisor as advertised in the March 1 *Floridian Key*. (solicited)

Prior experience in public sector accounting and leadership roles in community organizations will enable me to make significant contributions in the budget and finance areas of your respected nonprofit organization. (unsolicited)

Personal Referral

On the recommendation of Anna Chu, my instructor at Tucson Community College, I am applying for the part-time occupational therapy assistant position. (solicited).

Naris O'Sullivan, program coordinator at your Santa Fe branch, suggested that I present my qualifications for an administrative assistant or similar position that may be open in any of your three Albuquerque clinics. (unsolicited)

Response to Advertised Position

The job notice you filed with Pelcher Business College indicates the need for a receptionist in the School of Dentistry. Courses at Pelcher have prepared me for this position. (solicited)

According to the November 15 *Trenton Times*, you are seeking a manuscript proofreader with a BA in English and two years' experience. I can offer both the experience and education you seek. (solicited)

Combination

Will computerized billing experience, accurate keying skills, and an attention to detail qualify me for the Account Rep I position that is open at Medi-Services Billing? (solicited)

Are proven telephone and in-person communication skills, familiarity with resort operations, and fluency in Spanish desirable qualities for front desk staff at Mayflower Hotels? (unsolicited)

Stimulate Interest and Encourage Desire

A cover letter is a persuasive message. Therefore, the explanation paragraphs create interest in and desire for you as a job candidate. Employers want to know what you can do for them. These tips will be helpful as you prepare your cover letter:

- When possible, research the potential employer so that your cover letter reflects an informed interest in that employer.
- Determine *your* central selling point. Then choose supporting information from your résumé. Appeal to the receiver's sense of logic by describing how your abilities can satisfy the job requirements.
- Present your qualifications in the order that best enhances your salability. For example, if your education most directly relates to the job being sought, position that discussion close to the beginning of the message.
- Explain what you can do for the company as a result of your training or experience (*you* attitude).

Examples:	**Uninviting Explanations**	**Persuasive Explanations**
	I speak Japanese.	Your Japanese travelers will find my Japanese language skills helpful in interpreting instructions, messages, and directions.
	My previous experience makes me a qualified candidate based on the job description.	My experience in staffing, scheduling, budget management, and resource allocation will provide your firm with a highly productive office manager.

Most of the time, your explanation will focus on the value of your education or experience. Sometimes, however, valuable skills and capabilities are developed through involvement in professional, school, or community activities. Participation in these kinds of activities indicates not only your interests, skills, and attitudes, but also your willingness to accept responsibilities outside the workplace.

Example: As a member of Horticulturists USA, I participated in state and national competitions. These competitions taught me to "think on my feet." I had to respond quickly and effectively to a series of case problems. The ability to organize my thoughts rapidly will be helpful as a customer service representative for Financial Investing Partners.

In the explanation paragraphs, you refer your reader to your enclosed résumé for additional details.

Examples: You will see from my enclosed résumé that I have three years' experience preparing South American cuisine.

As my résumé shows, my background includes the software experience you seek.

Ask for Action

Courteously, but assertively, ask for an interview in your last paragraph. Let the reader know when and how to contact you. An employer is more likely to respond favorably if you have made responding easy. End with contact information: your telephone number, voice mail, and/or an e-mail address. If you are difficult to reach, tell an employer when you are available. Employers avoid frustration when they know your availability.

Examples: Please consider me for the Patient Access position. I can be reached at 555-0169 between 3 and 7 p.m. (after class and before work) to schedule an interview.

I will appreciate meeting with you to discuss how my skills match the responsibilities of the job. Because of my current work schedule, I am most easily reached by e-mail mschmidt@net.net or by voice mail 610-555-0193.

Prepare yourself for a call from a potential employer. Practice answering the phone. A simple greeting is sufficient: "Shawn O'Brien speaking." Educate family members on how to answer the telephone politely and how to take accurate messages: "Heller residence. Ali speaking." Your answering machine or voice mail message also must be brief and professional. Review guidelines in Chapter 4, pages 122–124.

Complete the Cover Letter

Complete a customized cover letter in acceptable business letter format. Cover letters are one page, and they are printed on stationery that matches the résumé. The cover letter must be free of wrinkles and ink or smudge marks. Finally, your signature must be legible and neat.

Examine the cover letters shown in Illustrations 8-6 through 8-9, pages 282–285. Then use the Checklist for Preparing a Cover Letter on page 281 to prepare and evaluate your own cover letter. You want to be sure that your final message represents you effectively to a potential employer.

Kira Randall has prepared a solicited cover letter, Illustration 8-6, page 282, based on a personal referral by a former instructor. Kira's letter provides persuasive information that relates her skills and experiences to the employer's needs and correlates with her résumé, Illustration 8-1, page 270.

William Klein's cover letter, Illustration 8-7, page 283, is unsolicited. He personalizes the message with anecdotes about the Zoological Society, and he explains how transferable skills will make him a valuable addition to the staff. The cover letter accompanies William's résumé, Illustration 8-3, page 272.

To create interest and desire in her as a potential employee, Silvia Morales presents concrete examples of how her experience and training will benefit Northwest Family Physicians. Silvia's solicited cover letter as shown in Illustration 8-8, page 284, responds to a newspaper ad and accompanies her résumé, Illustration 8-4, page 273.

The last cover letter, Illustration 8-9, page 285, is Elena Dimos's response to an inquiry about her online résumé. The employer requested a paper résumé but provided only a post office box number for replies. Elena's résumé, Illustration 8-5, appears on page 274.

Distribute Initial Employment Messages

Submit your employment messages as you are instructed by an employer. If you are not told how to submit the résumé and cover letter, consider the situation; and decide which delivery method is the most appropriate: postal mail, fax, hand delivery, or e-mail.

If you are sending your résumé and cover letter as an attachment, clearly reference the position you are seeking in a subject line. Briefly indicate your interest in the position and refer to the attachments in the body of the e-mail message. If you have been directed to send your résumé within the body of an e-mail message, precede the résumé material with a summarized version of your cover letter.

CHECKLIST

Checklist for Preparing a Cover Letter

1. Does your cover letter:
- Accomplish the objective?
- Relate to your target audience?
- Include supporting information?
- Organize contents in the indirect pattern and follow the persuasive strategy AIDA?

2. Does the draft of your cover letter:
- Attract favorable attention by beginning with a summary of qualifications, a personal referral, a response to an advertisement or posting, or a combination of techniques?
- Emphasize your most important qualifications?
- Include information that supports your candidacy for the position?
- Relate your qualifications to receiver benefits?
- Request an interview?
- Include complete contact information?

3. Does the final version of your cover letter:
- Incorporate the six Cs of effective messages?
- Send the message you intend?
- Reflect ethics and credibility by providing adequate, objective information?
- Look and/or sound professional?

---

47 Taylor Trail
Akron, OH 44310
January 10, 20—

Mr. Henry Stevenson
Human Resources Department
ODE Logistics Inc.
300 Prince Street
Cuyahoga Falls, OH 44221

Dear Mr. Stevenson

Opens with personal referral from a previous instructor. Compliments employer.

Dr. Mary Rombach, one of my former instructors at the University of Akron's Kushkin Computer Laboratory, recommended that I apply for the IT technician position that is open at ODE Logistics. Your company is a leader in inventory management and warehouse logistics and requires knowledgeable, skilled employees.

Addresses job requirements by summarizing key abilities in bulleted list.

With a B.S. degree in Computer Science Education and an A.A. degree in Computer and Information Sciences, I offer
* A strong background in database management and e-security
* Up-to-date programming skills
* Excellent organizational and communication skills gained from eight years of teaching and supervising

Continues to develop interest and desire by relating education and experience to employer needs. Refers to résumé for supporting details.

Dr. Rombach explained that you are looking for someone who can manage all your PCs, printers, and modems and coordinate your networking, e-mail system, and firewall protection. As you can see from my enclosed résumé, I not only have been responsible for similar tasks but also have taught others to manage many of them.

Previous experience and formal training have helped me gain valuable troubleshooting skills. In addition, I am accustomed to working with people with varying levels of computer knowledge. This knowledge and practical application will enable me to coordinate and maintain the IT systems at ODE and to solve user problems quickly.

Requests an interview and provides contact options.

I would appreciate the opportunity to explain how my background relates to ODE's needs. Please call me at 330.555.2446 or e-mail me at krandall@core.com.
.

Sincerely

Kira Randall

Kira Randall

Enclosure

Illustration 8-6 **Cover Letter for Kira Randall**

1245 Timber Ridge Drive
Brookfield, WI 53045
June 10, 20—

Ms. Nina Clark
Zoological Society of Milwaukee
10005 W. Bluemound Road
Milwaukee, WI 53226

Dear Mr. Clark

Please consider me for a development or similar position within the Zoological Society. I offer strong organizational and communication skills, a team orientation, and an enthusiasm for the Zoo.

My family has maintained a membership in the Zoological Society for many years; and I have enjoyed numerous special events, such as the opening of the Australian exhibit, the wolf exhibit, summer campouts, and Platypus dinners. When I visit zoos elsewhere, I quickly conclude: "There's no place like home."

What I have learned formally and informally can be utilized to further the Zoological Society's goals. My academic and personal experiences enable me to meet, converse, and work with varied populations, which will aid in developing membership. In addition, living and traveling abroad have taught me to be flexible, to make decisions, and to assume responsibility. These abilities can be put to good use planning and carrying out the variety of activities sponsored by the Society. My enclosed résumé provides details for your review.

You will find that my background and motivation will assist in promoting the Society's work. I would like to be a part of the Society's family and contribute to its growth. Please contact me by phone at 262.555.2345 or by e-mail at wmcklein@homebase.net to schedule an interview.

Sincerely

William C. Klein

William C. Klein

Enclosure

Illustration 8-7 **Cover Letter for William Klein**

14 Silver Street
Denver, CO 80209
April 16, 20—

Mr. Chris Carmen
Office Manager
Northwest Family Physicians
555 Rock Road
Denver, CO 80222

Dear Mr. Carmen:

You are seeking a person with insurance reimbursement and A/R experience for the medical billing position advertised in Sunday's *Denver Post*. My experience and training meet those requirements.

Four years with Dr. Albert Hart have provided me with in-depth knowledge of the patient-to-payment process, which will enable me to contribute productively to your office. Among my responsibilities were medical records management, procedural coding, and insurance claims processing.

In addition to on-the-job experiences, formal education in the health information field continues to strengthen my skills, including my knowledge of medical office software.

Because Dr. Hart is retiring and closing his office, I am seeking a new position. The efficiency and professionalism of the staff at Northwest Family Physicians is well known, and I would like to join your office team.

After you compare my qualifications presented in the enclosed résumé with the requirements of the position, I would appreciate an interview. My telephone number is 303-555-9289, and my e-mail address is smorales@home.net.

Sincerely,

Silvia Morales

Silvia Morales

Enclosure

Responds to specific skills requested in advertisement. Refers to an advertised position.

Builds interest by showing how experience relates to position requirements.

Points out relevant education.

Provides explanation for seeking new position. Customizes message with statement about potential employer.

References the résumé. Asks for action by requesting an interview and providing convenient contact information.

Illustration 8-8 **Cover Letter for Silvia Morales**

1002 Fitzwater Quarry Road
Roslyn, PA 19001
February 20, 20—

Human Resources Director
P.O. Box 345B
Mount Holly, NJ 08060

Uses a generic salutation because the employer is unknown.

Dear Human Resources Director

Responds to an employer inquiry about applicant's online posting. Provides a summary of relevant background.

Thank you for responding to my résumé, which I posted online last week. The coursework I have completed at Temple University (a B.S. degree in Computer Science expected in June 2005) has prepared me for the position of a web developer for your firm.

References pertinent web development experience and desirable communication skills.

The project experience I acquired at Cross Wiring Corporation has given me valuable exposure to web development as I seek a full-time position in the web development field. Also, I have polished my "people skills" through the teaching assistant position at Temple and the intense team activities at Cross.

Introduces enclosed paper résumé. Reminds reader that applicant's skills meet job requirements. Requests interview and provides specific contact information to reduce employer frustration.

A résumé is enclosed so that you may again review how my skills and abilities correspond with the requirements of the position you e-mailed me. May I talk with you in person to discuss the responsibilities of the position and to direct you to online samples of my work? I am available after 4 p.m. weekdays at 215.555.0174.

Cordially

Elena Dimos

Elena Dimos

Enclosure

Illustration 8-9 **Paper Cover Letter Responding to Employer Inquiry**

Summary

As a job seeker, you want to secure a position that will satisfy your professional goals and meet your personal needs. An organized approach will aid you in searching for a job and in preparing effective employment messages.

1. **Develop a search strategy.** An effective search strategy involves evaluating your personal characteristics and skills. Honest answers on personality inventories and self-evaluations help you relate what you have to offer to the requirements of a job.

   Another aspect of the search strategy is to research employment opportunities by networking, investigating potential employers, contacting college career centers, participating in career-related experiences, reading newspapers and professional publications, contacting employment agencies, and using the Internet.

2. **Prepare a résumé.** The CBO approach provides the framework for an effective résumé. A résumé is a persuasive list of details that tells who you are, what you have learned and accomplished, and how your abilities will benefit an employer. A résumé begins with a heading followed by the most important qualification you have to offer. Relevant information is grouped under titles, such as the job objective, education, experience, and other achievements.

   The reverse chronological, functional, or combination are three popular résumé formats. Résumés are prepared to accommodate various modes of delivery: postal mail, e-mail, online posting, and fax.

3. **Prepare a cover letter.** A cover letter, which reflects your personality and your individuality, accompanies a résumé and relates your abilities to an employer's needs. The persuasive strategy AIDA is used to prepare a customized cover letter and to present information that attracts attention, creates interest in and encourages desire for you as a candidate, and asks for an interview.

Complete Communication Skills Development 8, pages 299–300. For additional punctuation review, see the Reference Guide, pages 430–440.

Exercises

8 - 1   **Directions:** Prepare an employment folder, preferably using a three-ring binder, in which to store the information that you gather in the Chapter 8 exercises. The information that you compile will be helpful in completing exercises and cases in Chapter 8 and Chapter 9. The information also will be helpful for your job search and interview activities.

8 - 2   **Directions:** Complete the following Informal Evaluation of Job-Related Factors. If necessary, use a separate sheet of paper to answer questions 1 through 9. Answer as objectively and completely as possible. Save the information in your employment folder to help you prepare employment messages and to prepare for interviews.

Exercises

Informal Evaluation of Job-Related Factors

Directions: Answer completely and honestly. When asked for examples, be specific in your descriptions.

1. List the areas of business or industry in which you would consider working; for example health, retail, and insurance.

2. List the most important qualifications you have to offer an employer; for example, skills, attitude, and personality.

3. What size company appeals to you for employment (small, medium, large)? Explain why.

4. Are you willing to relocate? If so, where?

5. Are you a planner, a listener, or a talker? Give at least one example that supports your answer.

6. Are you a leader or a follower? Provide an example that supports your answer.

7. Give an example of how you functioned as a member of a team. What role did you assume in the group?

8. How well do you perform under pressure? Provide an example that supports your answer.

9. Give at least one example of how you accept and use constructive criticism to improve yourself and your work.

Directions: Rate yourself on the following characteristics as they relate to the job.

	Commendable (high level)	Acceptable (just fine)	Not Acceptable (needs improvement)
Loyalty			
Enthusiasm			
Initiative			
Dependability			
Flexibility/adaptability			
Honesty			
Friendliness/tactfulness			
Self-confidence			
Team orientation			
Decision-making skills			
Communication skills (written)			
Communication skills (spoken)			
General health			
Personal appearance			

Exercises

8 - 3

Directions: From the following list, circle the adjectives that describe you. Add others if needed. Compare the words you have chosen with those you see in employment advertisements. Be prepared to discuss your choices in class. Save the list in your employment folder.

accurate	ethical	personable
alert	flexible	pleasant
ambitious	friendly	poised
analytical	hardworking	polite
assertive	healthy	professional
calm	honest	punctual
confident	imaginative	resourceful
conscientious	logical	respectful
considerate	loyal	responsible
cooperative	mature	self-confident
courteous	motivated	self-controlled
creative	neat	self-reliant
curious	open-minded	sincere
dependable	optimistic	sympathetic
dynamic	orderly	tactful
empathetic	organized	well-groomed
energetic	patient	
enthusiastic	persistent	

Additional adjectives:

_____

_____

_____

8 - 4

Directions: Create a networking list on a separate sheet of paper. Include at least four major contact categories. Provide specific details under each category. See Networking, pages 253–254, for additional information. Save the information in your employment folder.

Exercises

8 - 5

Directions: Use the print or online version of the *Occupational Outlook Handbook* to research three job titles and corresponding occupational categories that reflect your education and/or experience. The online address is http://stats.bls.gov/oco. Provide the following information for each job.

- Job title and identification code
- Job description
- General work environment
- Average salaries
- Requested or required qualifications
- Employment outlook
- Related occupations

Be prepared to discuss whether your findings reflect job titles, responsibilities, and trends in your area. Save the information in your employment folder.

8 - 6

Part A

Directions: Review employment advertisements in newspapers for three or four days. Gather information as directed below. Save the information from Parts A and B in your employment folder.

1. Cut out or copy three to five job ads with different titles that represent positions for which you qualify.

2. List the source and date for each job.

3. Highlight the titles.

Part B

Use two additional sources, such as the Internet, company postings, and school placement centers to locate three to five jobs for which you qualify. Record the URLs and job titles. Keep the information for future use.

Exercises

8 - 7 **Directions:** Visit web sites that contain career information in addition to the sites listed on page 255. Informally evaluate the site and summarize your findings in a memorandum or an e-mail as assigned by your instructor. Be prepared to discuss your findings in class. Save the information in your employment folder. Your summary should include comments on these aspects of the web site:

Visual appeal

Ease of navigating the site and finding information

Helpful, working links

Career-related topics

Overall value of site (helpful? interesting?)

8 - 8 **Directions:** Choose three job opportunities from Exercise 8-6. Investigate the employers who are advertising the positions to find the following information:

- Product and/or service offered
- Approximate number of employees
- Facility address (location)
- Any other notable organizational information

Save the information from Exercise 8-8 for Case Study 11–1, page 400, and for your job-seeking activities.

8 - 9

Part A

Directions: Write a job objective for each of the three job opportunities you chose in Exercise 8-6. The information you gathered for Exercise 8-8 also may be helpful. Save the job objectives in your employment folder.

Part B

Directions: Prepare a summary of qualifications for each of the same three jobs. Save the summary of qualifications in your folder.

Exercises

8-10

Directions: Use descriptive words, including action verbs and keywords, and rewrite the following résumé entries. Provide details to create interest in the applicant. Use parallel structure.

1. I helped develop training programs. I was active in recruiting and supervised two to three intern students. I supervised those students about every six months.

2. I did the work scheduling for the support staff work schedules. The support staff was five technicians and two radiology assistants. Coordinating vacation schedules for them was also part of my job.

3. I received congratulations for my sales record because I went over the sales quota for 12 months.

4. My volunteer work was for about four hours a week.

5. I use three different kinds of software a lot.

8-11

Directions: Choose action verbs from Table 8-1 (or add your own), and compose two résumé entries that relate to your job or accomplishments. Save your work in your employment folder.

Exercises

8-12

Directions: Use the information you gathered in Exercises 8-5 and 8-6 (and from other employment sources) to develop a keyword list.

1. Once you have listed the keywords, underline those skills and abilities you possess.
2. Use the list to guide you in preparing a keyword summary for yourself. Include skills, abilities, education, and professional jargon. Review Keywords, pages 265–266, and Illustration 8-5, if necessary.
3. Save the keyword summary for Case Study 8-4, page 298.

8-13

Directions: Revise the following cover letter information. Use descriptive words and add appropriate details to create interest in the applicant. Your revisions should reflect the six *C*s of effective messages.

1. **Opening:** The job you advertised interests me.

2. **Explanation (Interest and Desire):** I do not have any applicable work experience, but I believe I can handle the job responsibilities.

3. **Explanation (Interest and Desire):** I have taken many classes that should help me do the job.

4. **Explanation (Interest and Desire):** I improved the billing and collection time in the department.

5. **Closing:** I'd like to come in for an interview soon.

Internet
Challenge

8-1 Directions: Visit http://www.ncsu.edu/careerkey/. Familiarize yourself with the content of the site by pointing to various hyperlinks.

Click on *You*.

- Under The Career Test, choose "Take the Career Key." Log in and complete all activities.
- Under Career Exploration, choose "Jobs that Fit Your Holland Personality Type," and complete all activities.
- Under Career Decisions, choose "High-Quality Decisions," and complete all activities.

Prepare a message for your instructor based on the information you gathered. Compare your career and job choices to what you learned by reading and completing the activities at this site. Summarize how you believe this information relates to the decisions you will make. Arrange your information in the direct pattern in memorandum format.

8-2 Directions: You will be traveling to Brisbane, Australia, in July as a student member of your professional organization. Conduct searches on *Brisbane* and *Australia* to find the following information. Use the direct pattern of organization to prepare a memorandum or e-mail message as assigned by your instructor. Summarize your findings and include helpful URLs.

Climate in July:

Time Zones:

Appropriate Business Dress:

Tips for Entertaining Australians:

Few Facts About Brisbane:

InfoTrac

Directions: Using the InfoTrac keyword search, locate the article on personality tests from the *Knight Ridder/Tribune News Service*, October 21, 1997. Read the article. Then prepare a summary of the personality tests described in the article in a format assigned by your instructor. Include your opinion of personality testing based on this or other readings. Be prepared to discuss your summary in class.

WebTUTOR Advantage

Directions: Access your WebTutor Advantage product. Complete the short-answer portion for Chapter 8 and send your answers to your instructor.

Case Studies

8 - 1

Communication Situation: Use a separate sheet of paper to create a master list of résumé information about yourself.

Task: Write down everything you can think of that relates to each of the headings provided in this exercise. Highlight job-related information. Use this master list to prepare your résumé in Case Study 8-3.

- Education
- Work experience
- Activities and interests
- Honors, awards, and achievements
- Special abilities and skills
- References

8 - 2

Communication Situation: Your 18-year-old neighbor knows that you volunteer in a literacy program at the local library. He graduated from high school last week (current year), and he needs help composing a résumé for the management trainee program at the supermarket where he works part-time. You asked him to give you a list of facts about his education, work experience, and skills.

Task A: Correct grammar, word usage, spelling, punctuation, and other errors in the information he provided. The information will be used in Task B to draft résumé entries.

Part-time employment at Shop and Bag, Fort Washington, Pensylvania, from October (insert a date two years prior) to present. Work as stock boy filling shelfs and takeing weekly inventory. Work over time work nights and work weekends when needed. Filed in as cashier if a threat of bad weather cause the store to be overly busy. Took care of customer's needs when they asked for special item's. Assist assistant store manager in checking back order and special holiday item's.

High school education at Upper Dublin High School (insert present graduation date), Fort Washington, PA, with C+ average. Worked on school newspaper and serve as homeroom representive to student counsel.

My job-related traits are friendly, tackful, and hardworking; getting more self-confident as I get older; and interested in an career in retail food management.

Case Studies

Task B: Compose a draft of the information for these sections of your neighbor's résumé: Job Objective, Work Experience, Education, and Abilities.

8 - 3

Communication Situation: You have decided to prepare your résumé.

Task: Prepare your résumé in a style that best represents what you have to offer. Then choose a potential employer from Exercise 8-6. Review the employer information that you gathered in Exercise 8-8. Customize the résumé for that employer, if necessary.

Case Studies

8 - 4

Communication Situation: The employer to whom you sent a résumé in Case Study 8-3 has requested a scannable résumé.

Task: Prepare your résumé in scannable format, opening with a keyword summary. Review Keywords, pages 265–266; Illustration 8-5, page 274; and Table 8-2, page 269, for helpful information.

8 - 5

Communication Situation: The résumé you prepared for Case Study 8-3 requires a cover letter.

Task: Prepare an outline for your cover letter. Apply the persuasive strategy AIDA when organizing your information. Use the outline to complete your cover letter in Case Study 8-6.

8 - 6

Communication Situation: Prepare a cover letter based on the outline you developed for Case Study 8-5.

Task: Review the information you collected about yourself and employers in earlier exercises. Also refer to your completed résumé for helpful information. Use your outline as a guide. Apply the CBO approach and the persuasive strategy AIDA. Use an acceptable message format to prepare your final cover letter. The cover letter will accompany the résumé you prepared in Case Study 8-3.

Part A — Periods, Commas, and Semicolons

Directions: If the punctuation in the following sentences is correct, write **C** (correct); otherwise, underline the error and write the correction in the space above the error.

1. I will go to the market, to buy food.

2. Mr Levin has an appointment with our accountant today.

3. Her manuscript is too long; therefore, I edited only the first five chapters.

4. You Mrs. Chang, are one of our most valued customers.

5. The game went into overtime as you can imagine the players were exhausted.

6. Some of our students compose at the computer; others compose at their desks.

7. Karl, you have our support in this matter.

8. Attending the CBC International Conference were Dell Myers, executor director; Erin Bransom, past president; and George Wang, editor.

9. Before running Natalia always stretches for fifteen minutes.

10. Jane said that she was not ready.

11. Betsy has degrees in communication arts, and in geography.

12. Robin did not appear to work very hard, nevertheless, she always met deadlines.

13. The fax machine is in my office the other equipment is in the library.

14. We are not accepting applications for summer jobs, because we have no openings.

15. To help me fall asleep quickly I listen to soothing music.

Part B   Skills Application

Directions: Rewrite the following draft. Your revision should reflect corrections in grammar; word usage; spelling; and in the use of periods, commas, and semicolons.

Choosing References for Employer Inquiries

As your develop your employement correspondence do not over look the importants of your references. List at least three good references, carefully analyze you're choices. Determine, who can testify to your skills and abilitys. Before you contact references for permission to use therenames, prepare a outline of what you want to say to them. A outline will help you organize you're thoughts and your references will be impress with your organizational ability. You may need to summarize your personnel and professional acomplishments to remind them of your abilities. Tell your references about your employment goals. If your references clearly understands your employement goals they will be able to provides helpful infromation to employers whom call too ask about you.

Chapter 9

Applications, Interviews, and Follow-Up Messages

Learning Objectives

1 Complete a paper and an online application neatly and accurately.

2 Prepare for interviews by identifying and practicing successful interview techniques.

3 Use the Internet to locate information that pertains to employment applications, interviews, and follow-up messages.

4 Prepare effective employment follow-up messages by implementing the CBO approach and the appropriate message strategy.

COMMUNICATION PERSPECTIVES

Breaking News

- A leading job site boasts that its database contains more than 22 million résumés, yet no study shows that more than 4 percent of American job seekers are finding jobs through electronic efforts. Does this meager yield suggest that savvy searchers will master both paper résumés and e-résumés—and learn the best ways to distribute them?

- A recent investigation suggests that résumé bias is a widespread fact. Résumés with a white-sounding first name elicited 50 percent more responses than résumés with black-sounding names. Does this discrimination suggest that job seekers with black-sounding names use initials rather than names on their résumés, or must they be 50 percent better than job seekers with white-sounding names to get an equal number of job interview calls?

Let the debate begin as you study questions of communication in the job sector. Among a myriad of issues to consider: What is the best way to explain demotion? job gaps? firings? downsizings? transition from self-employment? An urgency to wrestle with vexing questions follows you throughout your working life as this recent e-mail from a reader illustrates:

"My company is going through some restructuring and all of us have to reapply for our jobs as four jobs will be cut. My reapplication letter to sell myself—skills, performance, attitude—to win my job back is to be handed to my boss by Friday of this week. Can you give me an example of a job reapplication letter?"

I can't think of a better time to learn winning strategies and contents of the self-marketing communication that you will need as you progress through the workplaces of the world.

Joyce Lain Kennedy
Syndicated Careers Columnist

Section 1: EMPLOYMENT APPLICATIONS

In addition to a cover letter and a résumé, companies require that you complete either a paper or an online application. Applications generally ask for information that may not appear on your résumé. Paper applications require a signature and date, and online applications require verification that you have completed the application fully and truthfully. Illustration 9-1, page 304, is a typical employment application.

An application may be the primary source of information about you; and like other employment messages, applications create impressions of you as a job candidate. Space is limited, so you want to be sure that you emphasize your most important qualifications.

Guidelines for Completing Applications

An organized approach to completing an application is critical. Refer to your résumé for information to complete applications. Submit your paper résumé along with the application form. When you complete an online application and you know the company's address, mail or fax a copy of your paper résumé. The employment recruiter can refer to an eye-pleasing paper résumé while reviewing your formal application.

Applications are screening tools, so they must be complete and error free to help keep you in the candidate pool. Follow these guidelines when completing employment applications:

- Plan ahead. Have your résumé with you so that you can transfer the information from the résumé to the application neatly and efficiently. Also, have your reference list available to provide the complete contact information of professional references if requested.

Timely Tip

If you go to a physical location to apply for a job, present yourself as though you might be interviewed on the spot. Dress appropriately and have your employment-related information with you.

- Read the entire application before you begin. Then follow the directions *exactly* to complete the application. For example, when an application asks for "last name first," list your last name first!
- Unless the instructions read otherwise, present employment and educational histories in reverse chronological order in the space provided.
- Complete all sections. When a section is designated as "required," you must complete that section; otherwise, you may be eliminated from consideration. Some online forms will not allow you to submit the application until all sections have been completed. On a paper application, write N/A (not applicable) in sections that do not apply to you.
- List the position you seek. Some positions require a job reference number provided in an employment advertisement.
- Check for completeness and accuracy. Confirm spelling (carry a pocket dictionary) and dates. Be sure your dates are accurate. To correct errors on a paper application (which is usually completed in ink), draw a single line through the error; then make a neat correction.
- Answer truthfully. Many employers conduct background checks.
- Sign and date the application, which affirms the truthfulness of the information you provided. Remember that a signed application form is a legal document. If you are hired and an employer finds out that you have misrepresented information, you can be dismissed for breach of trust—even years later.

Guidelines for Completing Online Applications

In addition to the preceding guidelines that apply to both paper and online applications, here are tips specific to online applications.

- When possible, print and study a copy before completing the online application.
- Notify an employer when you experience technical difficulties completing an online application.
- Allot enough time to complete all sections of the application. Some online applications allow you to begin, save, and return to complete the application later. Check to see if that option is available.
- Submit your application before the closing date. Otherwise, the volume of applicants trying to submit an application might be high; access may be difficult.
- If you are able to print, keep a copy of each online application to use as a reference in interviews.
- To ensure clarity on the receiving end, key your information rather than copying and pasting from an existing résumé. Currently, the copy and paste technique does not always result in an easy-to-read transfer.
- Click the Submit or Send button *once*.

Timely Tip

Some organizations accept both paper and online applications; some organizations accept only online applications.

Town Center Employment Application

Town Center is an Affirmative Action and Equal Opportunity Employer

No question on this form is asked for the purpose of limiting or excluding any applicant's consideration because of race, color, sex, creed, national origin, age, marital status, disability, religion, veteran status, sexual orientation, or status in regard to public assistance, or membership or activity in local commission.

Date _____

Personal Data

Full Legal Name _____
First _____ Middle _____ Last

Present Address _____
Street _____ City _____ State _____ Zip
Phone ( ) Area _____ Number

Permanent Address _____
(If different than above)
Street _____ City _____ State _____ Zip
Phone ( ) Area _____ Number

E-mail Address _____
Daytime Phone ( ) Area _____ Number

Social Security Number ___ — ___ — ___
Are you at least 16 years of age? ☐ Yes ☐ No

Are you a U.S. citizen or national, permanent resident, a refugee, an asylee, or authorized to work under the amnesty provisions of U.S. immigration law? ☐ Yes ☐ No

Interests

Position title(s) and **posting number(s) (required)** _____

Date availale to begin employment: _____

Availability: (Please check all that apply)
☐ Full-time ☐ Day ☐ Night ☐ Temporary
☐ Part-time ☐ Evening ☐ Weekend ☐ Summer Only
How long? _____

Would you be unable to come to work on certain days? If so, specify: _____

Sourcing

From what source(s) did you learn of the position(s)? Specify your source selection(s) below and name **specific source(s)** for each selection. Example of specific source would be the exact name(s) of a college, internet site, newspaper, etc.

☐ Career Fair _____
☐ College Recruiting _____
☐ Direct Mail or Poster _____
☐ Employee Referral _____
☐ Former Employee _____
☐ Friend Referral _____
☐ Internet _____
☐ Internship _____
☐ Journal _____
☐ Newspaper _____
☐ Radio _____
☐ Recruiting Firm _____

Related Skills

Indicate any office equipment with which you are proficient: _____

Indicate computer equipment and software with which you are proficient: _____

Other: _____

Licensure Data

Professional Licences/Registrations	Expiration Date (month, date, year)	State	Number
Current			

Education Data

Name of School	City/State	Major/Degree	GPA	Graduation Year
Last High School				
Vocational School				
College or University				
Additional Education				

Have you ever been employed by any Town Center entity? ☐ Yes ☐ No
Where? _____
From _____ To _____ (mo/yr)

Reason for leaving _____

Job title _____ Name when employed _____

Please fill out completely with most recently held positions listed first. Do not omit unrelated work experience. Include military service if applicable. You may attach an additional page if you have more relevant work history. **Resumes are accepted but are not a substitute for this section.**

Employment History

Most Recent Employer	Address		Work Performed
	City	State	Zip
Telephone Number ( )	From: To:	Job Title	Salary
Your Supervisor's Name	Reason for Leaving		May we contact your current employer at this time? ☐ Yes ☐ No

Previous Employer	Address		Work Performed
	City	State	Zip
Telephone Number ( )	From: To:	Job Title	Salary
Your Supervisor's Name	Reason for Leaving		

Previous Employer	Address		Work Performed
	City	State	Zip
Telephone Number ( )	From: To:	Job Title	Salary
Your Supervisor's Name	Reason for Leaving		

Have you ever been convicted of a crime (excluding parking and petty misdemeanor traffic tickets)? *Conviction doesn't necessarily ban from employment.* ☐ Yes ☐ No
If Yes, describe in full: _____

Please read carefully and sign below

I understand this application may be shared with any Town Center affiliated entity. I hereby authorize investigation of all statements contained in this application. I release Town Center from any and all liability resulting from such investigation. I affirm that all information contained in this application is true and complete and that any misrepresentation, falsification, or willful omission herein shall be sufficient reason for dismissal and/or refusal of employment. I understand that employment is subject to satisfactory reference reports, satisfactory completion of a pre-employment medical examination and authorization for employment in the United States.

I understand that all conditions of employment, including but not limited to, hours, benefits, and salary are subject to change by Town Center at any time without prior notice to employees, subject to its obligations under the terms of any currently effective collective bargaining agreement. I also understand that employment at Town Center is at will employment and may be terminated at any time by either party. I further understand that I am required to abide by all rules and regulations of Town Center.

I certify that the information provided above is true and complete to the best of my knowledge. I have read and understand the statements in the paragraphs above. By signing here, I am also verifying information on my resume.

Date: _____ _____
Applicant's Signature

Illustration 9-1 **Employment Application**

After you submit an application or a résumé, develop a follow-up pattern. Check on positions for which you applied once every seven to ten days. You want to be consistent, but you do not want to be a nuisance. Courteously identify yourself and ask about the status of your application.

Example: This is Angela Frier. I submitted an application for the Visitor's Center representative position about ten days ago. Can you tell me the status of the position?

Follow-up calls are another networking technique, especially if you talk with the same person each time you call. An inquiry, conducted professionally, tells a receiver that you are serious about your job search.

Section 2:   EMPLOYMENT INTERVIEWS

The objective of the résumé and the cover letter combination and the employment application is to persuade a prospective employer to grant you an interview. Assume that your initial employment messages have accomplished this objective and that you have been contacted for an interview. Just as you carefully planned and completed your written employment messages, you must now plan and carry out your spoken employment message: the **interview**.

The following discussion focuses on a traditional face-to-face interview with additional information about telephone interviews. Chapter 8, page 251, introduced you to the informational interview, which is a networking technique by which you expand your contacts in a specific industry. Conduct an informational interview with a human resources representative or a department manager where you would like to work. (An informational interview may lead to a job interview should an opening arise.)

Culture View

South Africa
South Africa is a multilingual nation where most South Africans speak at least two languages. Sorting through applications must present challenges! The country recognizes 11 official languages: Afrikaans, English, Ndebele, Northern Sotho Tsonga, Tswana, Southern Sotho, Swazi, Venda, Xhosa, and Zulu. Zulu is spoken by the largest number of speakers, followed by Xhosa. In addition, Funigalore, a combination of the different languages, has evolved so that people of various language backgrounds can communicate with each other.

Timely Tip

Prepare for an interview just as a salesperson prepares for a product demonstration.

Before the Interview

Begin preparing for an interview while you are conducting your job search. Study the techniques presented in this chapter, and read additional articles about interviewing so that you are knowledgeable and confident by the time an interview takes place.

Personal Information

Review your personal information. Compare your qualifications with what you know about the job. Identify the qualifications that best meet the requirements of each job, and be able to explain how your skills and abilities match the employer's needs. List some keywords that will remind you to emphasize those qualifications.

Salary Information

Determining a salary range for the type of position you are seeking helps you respond to employment ads that request your salary requirements. If you don't respond to a salary question on an application or résumé, you may be eliminated as a candidate. When salary is requested, providing a number that falls in the middle of the range is probably the safest option. Remember, too, that online applications may not transmit if required information is not supplied.

Research salaries wherever you seek a position. Gather regional and local salary information from college career centers, local employment agencies, job postings, and state departments of labor. Much of the information is available online.

You must also compare your current and anticipated expenses with the salary range you determined. A comparison helps you understand whether your salary expectations are reasonable and whether the salary offered is equitable.

An interviewer may ask you about your salary expectations, so practice possible responses. First, try to defer discussion about salary until you are reasonably sure that you will be offered a position that you want.

Example: "May we carefully review the responsibilities of the position before we talk about salary?"

An interviewer may insist that you respond to a salary question; here is one suggested response:

Example: My investigation shows that salaries for similar positions in the Milwaukee area range from $xxx to $xxx; however, I am open to discussing the salary you are offering for this position.

Salary is an important consideration for most people. Ideally, a recruiter will provide salary and benefit information during the interview. When you are offered a job but you do not know the salary, you will have to ask. Practice your approach.

Example: I am very interested in the position. My qualifications and the opportunity you offer seem to be a good fit. Now that I have an idea of the job responsibilities and company expectations, please explain the salary structure for this position.

If the salary offered is lower than what you want or expect, *do not* immediately refuse; and *do not* make negative remarks. Other job factors, such as flexible schedule, health insurance, and tuition reimbursement, may offset a lower salary. Ask for time (24 to 48 hours) to consider the offer.

Example: Thank you for the offer. I am very interested in this position. However, this is an important decision; and I would like time to review the responsibilities and the salary. May I call you with an answer tomorrow?

If you decide to refuse based on salary, politely explain your decision.

Example: This position is exactly what I am looking for, and I know that I could do a good job for you; but based on my research, the salary is lower than what I expected.

When you want the position but the salary is too low, seek an opportunity to negotiate. Most companies have a range in mind; and the range is based on experience, education, and demand. Negotiation may be expected.

Example: This position is exactly what I am looking for, and I know that I could do a good job for you; but based on my research, the salary is lower than what I expected. May we discuss the salary?

Employer Information

Before interviewing, compile and review information about a prospective employer. Familiarize yourself with the organization's products/services, locations, philosophies, and growth record. Chapter 8 suggested several ways to gather information about a prospective employer, such as company web pages, annual reports, and employee interviews.

Typical Interview Questions

Anticipate questions the interviewer may ask and objections the interviewer may raise. Prepare positive responses, and study them carefully. Questions may relate to your future goals or to specific on-the-job situations. Interviewers today often ask for concrete examples that demonstrate your skills and abilities. For example, you may be asked to explain a real-life situation that demonstrates how you handle pressure.

Practicing responses to typical questions, such as those shown in Table 9-1, page 308, helps you answer questions calmly and logically. Thinking ahead about how to explain gaps in employment, lack of training, and so on, gives you time to word your answers to achieve the best effect. Practice

Timely Tip

Do not make a salary question the first question that you ask. First, ask about job responsibilities, company expansion plans, or other employer related topics.

Table 9-1 Typical Interview Questions

Why do you want to work for this company?	What courses did you like best (or least)?
Do you prefer working independently or as part of a team?	What makes you think that you are the right person for this job?
What is your salary expectation?	What did you like best (or least) about your last job? Why?
Why should I hire you?	
What do you want to be doing in three years?	What do you perceive are your weaknesses?
Are you a team player?	Did you ever have a conflict with a boss (or some other person)? How did you handle the situation?
How did your education prepare you for this job?	If I asked someone to describe you, what would that person say?
You completed (name of course). What did you learn?	

your answers with friends; record yourself. Are your responses clear? Do you sound confident?

Inappropriate Interview Questions

Federal and state laws prohibit an employer from asking questions that may result in discrimination based on sex, marital status, age, race, color, religion, or native origin. Study the questions in Table 9-2, page 309, so you are prepared to respond if an interviewer asks you an inappropriate question. Practice collecting your thoughts before responding, and consider the following three options:

- **Answer the question, knowing that the question is inappropriate.** Of course, you may voluntarily answer any question. Consider the intent. One inappropriate question may be an unintentional interviewer error. Two or more such questions should signal your concerns about the ethics of this company. The interviewer should know better.
- **Tell the interviewer that the question is inappropriate and that you refuse to answer.** Refusing to answer an inappropriate interview question is within your rights. You must quickly decide whether you want to work for this employer because your response may result in a lost job opportunity. If you refuse to answer a question, provide a courteous, firm response.

   Example: Because asking about my marital status is unrelated to my ability to perform the job and is not an appropriate question, what job-related information can I provide?

- **Rephrase to make the question job relevant.** This approach shows that you can take control of a situation and respond positively. The question, "Do you have any children?" suggests that the interviewer is concerned that you may not be able to handle the multiple responsibilities of a job and a family. The following is a polite, job-focused response.

Table 9-2 Examples of Illegal Interview Questions

What May Not Be Asked	What May Be Asked
What is your age?	Are you old enough to work?
Are you married?	Do you use illegal drugs?
How many children do you have?	Are you able to work second shift?
Where were you born?	Are you authorized to work in the United States?
What religion are you?	What is your social security number?

Example: Maintaining a high grade point average and working full time demonstrates that I am able to handle multiple responsibilities.

Questions for the Interviewer

Being informed about the employing organization and knowing something about the job that you are seeking create a positive impression. Develop three or four questions to ask the interviewer based on information you gathered during your employer investigation. Asking questions about topics such as job responsibilities, career paths, and company expansion plans shows the interviewer that you have initiative and that you have prepared for the interview.

Interview Materials

Assemble materials to take to the interview, including at least two print copies of your résumé and references. The résumé serves as a reminder of what to emphasize during the interview. If your interviewer does not have a print copy, you can provide one at the interview.

Consider writing key points on a note card to remind you of questions to ask. You may have a portfolio to share. A portfolio usually includes samples of work that show your capabilities. Examples of content include relevant class projects, academic transcripts, and certificates of achievement. Some people include letters of recommendation.

Interview Appointment

Confirm the interview date, place, time, and the pronunciation of the interviewer's name. Repeat the interviewer's name until you can say the name correctly without hesitation. Call to verify the name, if necessary. Arrive at least 15 minutes early (consider travel and parking time). Make a practice trip to the interview destination if you are unfamiliar with the area.

Appearance

You may have only one chance to make a good impression. Keep in mind that appropriate attire differs from one region of the country to another and from one industry to another. What may be considered appropriate in one situation may be

Culture Frame

Business dress in South Africa is conservative. Women wear wool or cotton blend business suits during the cooler months of April through August and cotton or linen suits during the warmer months. Men wear wool suits all year.

inappropriate in another. Even when you know casual clothes are acceptable in a firm, *do not* wear casual clothes for an interview. Dress conservatively, and be sure that your clothes are clean and pressed. Typical attire for men is a suit or sport coat and slacks with a white or light colored shirt and matching tie. For women, a business suit (skirt or slacks) is appropriate. Neutral colors are preferred. Minimal, simple jewelry is acceptable.

Make sure that you are well groomed and clean. Pay attention to details, such as clean nails and freshly shined shoes. Do not wear cologne or perfume because many people suffer from allergies. The interviewer's attention should focus on your employment qualifications, not on your appearance or your personal hygiene.

During the Interview

You have arrived with your materials in hand. Your dress and your demeanor project an image that you are qualified and competent. Check in courteously with front desk personnel. Upon meeting the interviewer, smile, offer a confident greeting, and pronounce his or her name correctly.

Example: Good morning, Ms. Chau. I am Lana Portonelli.

Let your enthusiasm and energy show when you respond to questions about your work and schooling. Be prepared to explain anything you included on your résumé. Emphasize how your qualifications have prepared you for the job responsibilities, and give concrete examples of how you can fulfill the requirements of the position and contribute to the company.

Timely Tip

Everyone you come in contact with during an interview is watching and judging you.

Your responses to interviewer questions and the topics you initiate during an interview provide insight into your personality, maturity, and work attitude. Be yourself; answer questions honestly. If you are asked about former or current employers, refer to them positively. *Do not* make negative statements about other employers, or the interviewer may assume that you will talk about future employers negatively.

When you are given the opportunity, ask pertinent questions about the company and the position based on the employer research you conducted prior to the interview.

Body Language

Be aware of your *body language* during the interview. Body language sends strong messages to interviewers, so you want the messages to be positive. Follow this advice:

- Do not chew gum or smoke.
- Assume a posture that reflects self-assurance and alertness.
- Try to relax, but do not slouch.
- Maintain eye contact with the interviewer. Eye contact indicates confidence and reinforces listening. Remember that not all cultures consider direct eye contact a positive signal.

Interview Closure

The last two or three minutes of a job interview can be very important. These techniques will help you exit an interview successfully:

- Watch for signs that the interview is drawing to a close. An interviewer usually signals the end of the interview by standing up, making a concluding statement, and shaking hands.
- Smile pleasantly and express appreciation for the interview.
- Ask about the action that will follow and how you can learn about your status as a candidate.
- Clarify any follow-up activities the interviewer expects from you. If a second interview is arranged, jot down the date, time, place, and name of the person conducting the interview. List additional information you need to provide, such as credentials. Verify your notes before you leave.
- If you are interested in the job, say so! Interviewers are impressed with an expression of interest.
- As you leave, use the interviewer's name when you express appreciation for the interview.

Avoid actions that may cause you to be rejected as a job candidate. Among the most common reasons for rejection: being late for the interview, dressing too casually, revealing confidential information about a former or current employer, and asking about benefits and salary at the beginning of the interview.

Telephone Interviews

Telephone interviews are becoming a popular screening device to determine whether you should be called in for a face-to-face interview. If an interviewer calls you spontaneously (not scheduled) and the timing is not good for you, provide a brief explanation and ask to reschedule.

Example: Thank you for calling. I am very interested in talking with you, but I am on my way to work. May we reschedule for tomorrow?

Most of the suggestions for face-to-face interviews apply to telephone interviews, so study all interview information carefully. As you plan and prepare for a telephone interview, observe these additional tips:

- Record a professional, concise message for your answering machine or voice mail. (See Chapter 4, Voice Mail Greetings, pages 123–124.)
- Check messages two to three times daily during your job search.
- Have your résumé and other job-related correspondence within easy reach, along with a notepad, pencil, and calendar for recording information.
- From the information you gathered about each employer, highlight key details about the company (products, services, reputation) and the job (job duties and requirements).

- Select an "interview" room in your home where you will not be disturbed during an interview.
- Decide what to wear for the "interview." Your mental mindset is important. The significance of a telephone interview is reinforced when you dress as though you are interviewing face-to-face.
- When you know a telephone interview is to take place, ask for the interviewer's name. Keep the name(s) visible for reference during the interview.
- Conduct a mock interview over the telephone with a friend or family member.
- Talk while sitting *and* while standing to determine which position gives you the clearest projection. Use good posture whether you sit or stand.
- Smile while you practice your responses. A smiling response is usually recognizable over the phone.
- Ask your practice buddy for a candid assessment of your telephone manners, ability to project your personality, and clarity of responses. Make the necessary adjustments.

Each conversation with an employer is an opportunity to sell yourself. Create a positive image by following these suggestions:

- Turn off the call waiting feature.
- Answer the phone professionally and enthusiastically.
- Never put an interviewer on hold.
- Write down the name(s) of the interviewer(s).
- Speak clearly, energetically, and courteously. Also remember that nonverbal communication is important. *Do not* eat, drink, smoke, chew gum, or do anything else that interferes with your speaking ability.
- Allow the interviewer to lead the conversation.
- Answer in short sentences, which are better understood on the phone.
- Ask for clarification if you do not understand something the receiver said. Provide clarification if you sense your listener does not understand something you said.
- Request a few seconds to prepare a response to an unexpected question so that your response is more effective.
- Send a thank-you message after the interview.

After the Interview

After the interview, send a thank-you note with a concise, personalized message. Sending a thank-you note is a task that most applicants ignore; thus, you have an opportunity to remind an interviewer of your skills as well as your business manners. The message should be sent immediately after the interview because the thank-you is a gentle reminder of you and your skills. Thank-you messages are discussed in detail in Section 3: Follow-Up Messages.

Also fulfill any requests that were made during the interview, such as providing additional materials. File your interview notes in an employer folder, so they are easily accessible for reference.

When a hiring decision will be made within a day or two of your interview, consider e-mailing or faxing a thank-you message within a few hours of the interview to ensure that the interviewer will receive the message before the decision is made.

Other important messages in the employment process include follow-up inquiries and thank-you, acceptance, job refusal, and resignation messages. A follow-up inquiry checks the status of an application or résumé. A thank-you message expresses gratitude to the people involved in an interview. An acceptance message says "yes" to an employment offer, whereas a refusal says "no." A resignation letter formally notifies an employer that you are leaving your current position. Follow the CBO approach to **plan**, **draft**, and **compose** your message.

Use the good news/neutral news strategy to prepare follow-up inquiries as well as thank-you, acceptance, and resignation messages. Use the bad news strategy to prepare job refusals. Whether your message is good news or bad news, always end with a positive statement.

Proofread, edit, and revise your message until you are satisfied that the message reflects the six Cs of effective messages and that the content of the final message is accurate and says what you intend. Use the Checklist for Preparing Follow-Up Messages as a guide. Confirm that the format and transmission mode are appropriate for the situation.

Checklist for Preparing Follow-Up Messages

1. **Does your message:**
   - Accomplish the objective—inquire, thank, accept, refuse, or resign?
   - Relate to your target audience?
   - Include supporting information?
   - Organize contents in the pattern appropriate for the message?

2. **Does the draft of your message:**
   - Begin with an opening appropriate for the strategy (good news for follow-up inquiries, thank-you, acceptance, and resignation messages; bad news for refusal messages)?
   - Provide adequate details relevant to the situation?
   - End with a positive, friendly statement appropriate for the situation?

3. **Does the final follow-up message:**
   - Incorporate the six Cs of effective messages?
   - Send the message you intend?
   - Reflect ethics and credibility by providing adequate, objective information?
   - Look and/or sound professional?

Follow-Up Inquiry

Inquire about your employment documents if you have not received a response within two weeks of submitting a cover letter and résumé or application. A courteous follow-up indicates initiative and confidence. Generally, a telephone call is appropriate to ask whether your employment materials were received or to ask about the status of a position for which you applied. When you write a **follow-up inquiry**, such as Illustration 9-2 on page 315, use the direct pattern and the good news strategy. Keep the message brief.

1. Begin with the main idea: the inquiry.
2. Explain your interest in the position; mention the date that you submitted your initial employment correspondence. Briefly restate how your qualifications will benefit the firm. Indicate that you are enclosing another copy of your cover letter and résumé.
3. End the message with a request for an interview.

Thank-You Letter

Regardless of your interest in a position, prepare a **thank-you letter** after an interview. A written message is a matter of courtesy and a gesture of goodwill. In addition, a thank-you message sets you apart from applicants who have not followed the interview with such an acknowledgment.

Use the direct pattern and the good news strategy to write a brief thank-you message. Address the letter to the person who conducted the interview. William Klein's letter shown in Illustration 9-3, page 316, thanks the interviewer and expresses interest in the position.

1. Begin with the main idea: a thank you. Extend appreciation to everyone involved in the interview.
2. If you want the job, briefly restate how your qualifications will benefit the firm. Include relevant information that may not have been presented in the interview, and offer to provide additional information.
3. End the message by expressing your interest in the position.

Even when you are not interested in the position, write a thank-you message. You never know when another position that interests you may open. Express your appreciation for time spent and include positive but noncommittal comments about the organization. Elena Dimos is not interested in the position for which she interviewed. Thus, her thank-you letter shown in Illustration 9-4, page 317, closes with a noncommittal statement.

Timely Tip

Sometimes follow-up messages may be e-mailed or faxed, depending on the situation.

47 Taylor Trail
Akron, OH 44310
January 25, 20—

Mr. Henry Stevenson
Human Resources Department
ODE Logistics Inc.
300 Print Street
Cuyohoga Falls, OH 44221

Dear Mr. Stevenson

Inquires about the position.

Have you chosen interview candidates for the IT technician opening at ODE?

Relates position description to applicant's skills.

The job description called for someone with an IT-related degree, database management experience, and programming skills. ODE also is seeking someone with communication and organizational skills. I possess both the technical and interpersonal skills you are seeking.

Although I mailed a cover letter and résumé on January 10, additional copies are enclosed for your review.

Emphasizes what the applicant can offer to the employer. Requests an interview and provides contact information.

You will find that my qualifications are a good fit. May we schedule an interview so that I can show you samples of my work and provide you with additional details of my training and experience? My phone number is 330.555.2446, and my e-mail is krandall@core.com.

Sincerely

Kira Randall

Kira Randall

Enclosures: Cover Letter
　　　　　　Résumé

Illustration 9-2 **Follow-Up Inquiry**

1245 Timber Ridge Drive
Brookfield, WI 53045
June 28, 20—

Ms. Nina Clark
Zoological Society of Milwaukee
1005 W. Bluemound Road
Milwaukee, WI 53226

Dear Ms. Clark

Thanks the
interviewer and
compliments the
staff.

Thank you for interviewing me yesterday for the development position. The Zoological Society is nationally known, and now I know why! The enthusiasm and energy of the staff are clearly visible; I appreciated the opportunity to see what goes on behind the scenes.

Reminds
interviewer of
applicant's relevant
qualifications.

During the interview, you emphasized that the person you hire must have excellent communication skills. You also indicated that the new employee must be able to put in long hours during special events. You will find that I have the skills and the "get-up-and-go" to work special events effectively.

Closes with a
"personalized"
statement of
interest in the
position.

Please consider me for the development position. I have been a zoo fan since childhood, so promoting the zoo is easy for me.

Sincerely

William C. Klein

William C. Klein

Illustration 9-3 **Thank-You Letter**

1002 Fitzwater Quarry Road
Roslyn, PA 19001
March 15, 20—

Ms. Therese Krakowski
Nardelli Plumbing Incorporated
PO Box 3458
Mount Holly, NJ 08060

Dear Ms. Krakowski

Opens directly with a thank-you statement.

Thank you for the March 12 interview for the web developer position at Nardelli Plumbing.

Compliments the firm.

The firm is making its mark statewide and earning a well-deserved reputation for quality and efficiency. Based on the materials we viewed, the marketing department is doing a great job getting the Nardelli name out to contractors.

Closes with an expression of appreciation but does not mention interest in the position.

I appreciated your willingness to walk me through the warehouse and to share details about the company's operations and growth plans.

Sincerely

Elena Dimos

Elena Dimos

Illustration 9-4 **Noncommittal Thank-You Letter**

Acceptance Letter

You will usually accept employment by telephone or in person. On occasion, though, a company will ask that you write an **acceptance letter**. When you accept in writing, organize the message in the direct pattern and follow the good news strategy. Illustration 9-5 on page 319 is an acceptance letter.

1. Begin with the main idea: the acceptance.
2. Provide goodwill statements, such as your commitment to doing a good job or your enthusiasm for this opportunity.
3. End courteously, perhaps with a confirmation of the starting date and time.

Refusal Letter

You may need to write an employment **refusal letter** when you decline an offer of employment. Remember that the company took time to interview you and that you were chosen because your personal qualities and professional skills met the company's needs. Although your objective is to refuse the position, you want the employer to remember you favorably. Use the indirect pattern of organization and the bad news strategy to write a refusal message. Illustration 9-6, page 320, courteously refuses the company's job offer.

1. Begin with a buffer. A buffer may be an expression of appreciation for the job offer, a compliment, or some other neutral statement.
2. Provide an orderly explanation that prepares the receiver to accept your implied or expressed decision.
3. Imply or state the main idea: the refusal.
4. Provide additional information to neutralize the unfavorable news.
5. End by restating your appreciation for the offer or by adding some other goodwill statement.

Resignation Letter

When you accept a new position, you may have to resign from your current position. Whether or not your employer requires an official written resignation, preparing a written resignation is good business practice. Leave a job gracefully, pleasantly, and professionally. Typically, you will tell an employer of your decision to leave. Then, you will confirm your departure with a resignation letter similar to Illustration 9-7, page 321. Write a resignation letter in the direct pattern, and use the good news/neutral news strategy because you are simply confirming what you have already told your employer. Send a copy to your supervisor as well as to the human resources department of your current employer.

1. Begin with the main idea: the confirmation of your resignation.
2. If appropriate, briefly explain your reason for leaving. Include the resignation date and other pertinent details. You may also offer to assist in the transition process.
3. End with an expression of appreciation for your work experience at the company.

14 Silver Street
Denver, CO 80209
May 1, 20—

Mr. Chris Carmen
Office Manager
Northwest Family Physicians
555 Rock Road
Denver, CO 80222

Dear Mr. Carmen:

Thanks the interviewer and accepts the offer.

Thank you! I accept your offer for the medical billing technician position.

Includes statements of goodwill and confirms details.

This new position presents coding and records management opportunities that I am prepared to undertake. As you suggested, I will stop in Monday to complete the employment paperwork.

You indicated that I should begin working on May 20. The May 20 start date gives me adequate time to complete my responsibilities at Dr. Hart's office.

Closes positively and restates the acceptance.

I look forward to joining the staff at Northwest Family Physicians on May 20.

Sincerely,

Silvia Morales

Silvia Morales

Illustration 9-5 **Acceptance Letter**

1002 Fitzwater Quarry Road
Roslyn, PA 19001
April 15, 20—

Ms. Therese Krakowski
Nardelli Plumbing Incorporated
PO Box 3458
Mount Holly, NJ 08060

Ms. Krakowski

Thank you for offering the web development-marketing position that I interviewed for last month.

Nardelli Plumbing's growth, based on its fine operation, is evident; and the offer to join the team is appreciated.

As I reviewed my notes from the interview, I realized that many of the tasks focus on advertising campaigns. Since my primary interest is web development, I will continue to seek a position with that emphasis.

Ms. Krakowski, thanks again for offering me the opportunity to work with Nardelli. Please keep me in mind as Nardelli opens positions with a web focus.

Cordially

Elena Dimos

Elena Dimos

Illustration 9-6 **Refusal Message**

14 Silver Street
Denver, CO 80209
May 2, 20—

Dr. Albert Hart
7894 West Alpine Terrace
North Aurora, CO 80222

Begins with confirmation of the resignation and the effective date.

Dear Dr. Hart

As you and I have discussed, my resignation is effective May 16.

Expresses appreciation for opportunities, training, and support throughout employment.

Offers to help.

Thank you for the opportunities you have given me to develop my skills during my tenure in your office. You have supported my efforts to continue my education, and you have enabled me to apply what I learned.

You can be sure that I will help prepare the office for closing during the next two weeks. I am also available to help you on weekends and evenings during June to ensure that everything is in order for your retirement.

Closes with sincere expression of appreciation and best wishes.

Thank you, Dr. Hart, for your guidance and encouragement. Enjoy a happy, healthy retirement.

Sincerely

Silvia Morales

Silvia Morales

Illustration 9-7 **Resignation Letter**

Summary

To fulfill your career aspirations, you must proceed through each step of the job search process until you secure the job you want. Chapter 9 presents information on completing applications, participating in interviews, and preparing follow-up messages.

Employment applications are used as screening devices; thus, applications should be complete, truthful, and error free. The résumé and reference list help you transfer information to a job application easily and efficiently.

The objective of an interview is to secure the position. Considerable preparation takes place before the interview. Preparation involves reviewing personal and employer information, gathering salary information, practicing responses to typical interview questions, developing appropriate questions for the interviewer, compiling interview materials, confirming the interview details, and determining your professional image. During an interview, employer impressions are influenced by your appearance, nonverbal communication, and your answers to questions. Telephone interviews may precede a face-to-face interview. Successful telephone interviews involve additional rules specific to a telephone format. After the interview, you are wise to send a thank-you message.

Other important messages in the employment process include follow-up inquiries and thank-you, acceptance, job refusal, and resignation messages. Each message follows the CBO approach, applies the appropriate message strategy, and incorporates the six *C*s of effective messages to promote and maintain goodwill between you and an employer.

Complete Communication Skills Development 9, pages 333–334. For additional punctuation review, see the Reference Guide, pages 430–440.

Ethics in Action

Access http://brantley.swlearning.com. Analyze the Ethics in Action for Chapter 9.

Exercises

9 - 1

Directions: Download the application form available on the text support web site: http://brantley.swlearning.com. Click on the Student Resources link to access the form. Print the form. Follow the instructions on the employment application and apply the guidelines presented in Chapter 9 to complete the application. Be prepared to discuss the format of the application and any concerns you had providing information.

9 - 2

Directions: Determine a job for which you qualify. Using a minimum of five sources, investigate salaries to determine a salary range for your geographical area. Sources may include people working in the field, newspaper ads, job postings (including online postings), your college career center, employment agencies, and Internet references. The information you gathered in Chapter 8 may be helpful. Indicate the job titles you researched, prepare a list of salaries and sources, and determine a salary range. Be prepared to discuss your findings in class. Keep this information for Exercise 9-3, Part B.

Exercises

9-3   ## Part A

Directions: List your monthly expenses using the following personal expense inventory as a guide. Add other expenses as necessary. If you are sharing or contributing to expenses, including rent/mortgage, food, and so on, list your share of the cost.

Estimate of Monthly Expenses		Amount
Housing	Telephone	
	Utilities (heat, electricity, etc.)	
	Other (be specific)	
Travel	Car payment	
	Car maintenance (tires, oil changes)	
	Bus passes	
Food		
Child care		
Clothing		
Insurance	Auto	
	Health	
	Co-pay; deductibles	
	Life	
	Renter	
	Home	
	Other (be specific)	
Entertainment		
	Vacation	
	Hobbies	
	Sports	
	Other (be specific)	
Loans/Expenses		
	Credit card	
	School loans	
	Other loans	
Charities		
Savings		
Other (be specific)		

TOTAL MONTHLY ESTIMATE: _____

Exercises

Part B

Prepare a memorandum or an e-mail message as directed by your instructor. Compare your expenses with the salary range you determined in Exercise 9-2.

9-4

Directions: One method of tracking employment opportunities is to prepare a tracking sheet for each employer you contact.

Design a tracking sheet. The tracking sheet should include space for the company name, address, phone number, and contact person. The form should also provide space to record dates, the names of people you contacted, interview activity, and so on. A sample tracking sheet is provided. The left column consists of the kind of information to record; the right column shows user notes.

Employer contact	XYZ Corporation, 458 E. Burleigh, Milwaukee, WI 53210 414.555.4444 Fax: 414.555.4422
Résumé/application sent Follow-up date/action Follow-up date/action	Paper résumé sent Feb. 2 2/15 Checked HR with Steve. No action yet. 2/25 Checked HR. Talked with J.R. Résumé sent to acctg. supervisor
Interview Follow-up date/action Follow-up date/action	3/1 in Room 256. 10 a.m. with B. Pipps 3/3 Sent thank you to B. Pipps, acctg. supervisor 3/10 Checked hiring status. No decision yet.

Exercises

9 - 5

Directions: Prepare a list of five questions that are appropriate to ask an interviewer. The information you compiled about employers in Chapter 8 may be helpful. Be prepared to present your list to the class.

9 - 6

Directions: Refer to two current sources other than this text to gather information about proper dress for an interview. List the sources, summarize the information, and include what you will wear to an interview. Be prepared to discuss your interview wardrobe in class.

Internet
Challenge

9-1 Directions: Conduct a search for interview bloopers (funny mistakes job candidates make on interviews). Compile a list of three to five bloopers, and prepare in a format designated by your instructor. Be prepared to discuss your list in class. Save the information for use in Chapter 10.

9-2 Directions: Choose one of the following topics, and search online for information about conducting business in South Africa. Prepare a summary in a format assigned by your instructor. Be prepared to present your findings in class.

- Addressing people
- Conducting oneself appropriately in public
- Making and keeping appointments

InfoTrac

Directions: Using the InfoTrac keyword search, locate an article on telephone interviews. Read the article and prepare a summary of important points in a format assigned by your instructor.

Directions: Access your WebTutor Advantage product. Complete the short-answer portion for Chapter 9 and send your answers to your instructor.

Case Studies

9 - 1

Communication Situation: Maura O'Donnell is a 22-year-old recent graduate from the College of New Jersey in Trenton, New Jersey. She lives with her parents and three siblings. Her brothers are ages 19 and 17; her sister, 14. Maura majored in management and is interested in becoming a manager-trainee for a pharmaceutical or medical supply company. Her hobbies include jazz dancing, playing tennis, surfboarding, gardening, and participating in the church choir. Maura was on the Dean's List all four years of college and she worked part-time during her college years to help pay for her personal expenses. Her supervisors and many professors have congratulated her on her leadership ability and her cooperative attitude. Maura is engaged to be married in three months.

Task A: What should Maura mention when she responds to the statement, "Tell me about yourself."

Task B: How should Maura respond to the following illegal question? "I see you are not wearing a wedding ring. Do you have plans to marry in the near future?"

Case Studies

9 - 2   **Communication Situation:** Choose three questions from Table 9-1, Typical Interview Questions, page 308. Identify five additional interview questions from another current source.

Task: Write your responses to the eight questions based on your personal, educational, and employment background. Be prepared to discuss your responses in class.

9 - 3   **Communication Situation:** Noah Martin is preparing to interview for a junior accountant position with a large chemical company. Noah is nervous about the interview. He dropped out of high school in the eleventh grade because of poor attendance and a lack of interest in his classes. He worked at a few odd jobs for awhile, and he finally sought assistance. After two years of counseling, Noah "turned over a new leaf." He studied for the GED exam and passed in one try.

He then enrolled in Montgomery County Community College. Unfortunately, he was in an auto accident during his first semester. Noah withdrew from school to spend one year in physical therapy. The therapy led to a full recovery and enabled him to return to college to finish his studies. Noah will graduate next month with an associate degree in accounting. He is now ready to begin his accounting career.

Task A: If the interviewer asks, what explanation can Noah give for dropping out of high school and leaving college for a year?

Case Studies

Task B: What can Noah say to impress the interviewer about his passing the GED exam, his initial enrollment in college, and his return to college to earn his degree?

9 - 4

Communication Situation: During an interview for a position that you want, you are asked, "What religion are you?"

Task: Prepare a response to the question.

9 - 5

Communication Situation: You recently interviewed for a position in which you are interested. The information you compiled for some Chapter 8 exercises and cases may provide helpful background.

Task: Apply the CBO approach and the appropriate strategy to prepare a thank-you message for your interviewer. You are interested in the position. Add details necessary to complete this message, such as specific comments about the company's growth or exciting marketing plans. The final message should reflect the six Cs of effective messages and acceptable message format.

Case Studies

9 - 6

Communication Situation: You have been offered a position with one of the companies where you interviewed. You have decided to accept the position. After telephoning your acceptance, you must send a written confirmation. Case Study 9-5 may provide helpful information.

Task: Apply the CBO approach and the appropriate strategy to plan and develop an acceptance message. Add details as necessary to complete the message, such as confirmation of starting date. The final message should reflect the six *C*s of effective messages and acceptable message format.

9 - 7

Communication Situation: You have been offered a position that you do not want. The information you compiled for Chapter 8 exercises and cases may provide helpful background information.

Task: Apply the CBO approach and the appropriate strategy to plan and develop a refusal message. Add details as necessary to complete the message. The final message should reflect the six *C*s of effective messages and acceptable message format.

9 - 8

Communication Situation: You must resign from a job you currently hold.

Task: Apply the CBO approach and the appropriate strategy to plan and develop a resignation letter. Add details as necessary to complete the message.

Part A Colons, Quotation Marks, and Apostrophes

Directions: Make corrections to the colons, quotation marks, and apostrophes as needed in the following sentences. If the punctuation is correct, write **C** (correct) in the space provided.

1. We need the following items copy paper, toner, and labels.

2. When I evaluate compositions, I find that these words are often misspelled *accumulate,* and *separate*.

3. He asked, Can you attend our next business meeting?

4. After losing the game, the team member's left the stadium quickly.

5. Our motto is "Safety is our priority."

6. When Cherlyn s desk will arrive is anyone s guess.

7. I recommend that you read the article, South Africa's Deserts, Savannas, and Mountains.

8. Where is you're dictionary?

9. Tomorrow's game should be the best of the season.

10. A voice exclaimed, Stand up!

11. Return these books to the library *South Africa as the Cradle of Civilization, Cultural Traditions in South Africa,* and *An Archeologist s Delight*.

12. She is a perfect example of a "woman of valor."

13. On the way to the concert, we passed Darcie Ross's house.

14. Did Leonard actually say, I prefer paper messages over e-mail ?

15. W. Somerset Maugham wrote in *The Summing Up,* It is well to remember that grammar is common speech formulated.

Part B   Skills Application

Directions: Revise the following draft. Your revision should reflect corrections in grammar; word usage; spelling; and periods, commas, semicolons, colons, quotation marks, and apostrophes.

Dear Mr. Grafman;

Thank you for requesting the article Preparation for a Informational Interview that appeared in last months online newsletter, *The Career Journal*.

At the top of page 2, you will fine the following statement by Ms. Formicheli The beauty of the informational interview is that you introduce yourselve to a company and you get information about the work enviroment at the same time.

As to your questions concerning tips for telephone interviews, and in-person interviews at job fairs visit www.thecareerjournal.xyz.com. Youll find helpfull links to video clips and exerpts of recent articles.

Please contact me when you need assistence as you build you're liberry of career materials' and expands your knowledge of career opportunitys.
Sincerly

Chapter 10

Visuals and Presentations

Learning Objectives

1 Select visuals appropriate for the communication situation.

2 Design meaningful and ethical visuals for written reports and spoken presentations.

3 Use the CBO approach to prepare effective spoken presentations.

COMMUNICATION PERSPECTIVES

Know Your Customer

New York Stock Exchange Rule 405, also dubbed the "Know Your Customer" rule is a vital component of the comprehensive examination required for licensure in the securities industry. What the rule means is that only after certain essential facts have been gathered about a client's financial suitability can recommendations be offered by a registered representative. Failure to abide by the dictates and spirit of Rule 405 may result in forfeiture of license and possible legal liability.

Early in my career, I learned valuable lessons derived from Rule 405 that can be applied as a communications tool for presentations to large audiences as well as to one-on-one interactions. How can you learn more about your customer? Ask the right questions and make a concerted effort to hear both the answers and the manner in which the answers are given.

I have learned that being an effective communicator means being an attentive listener, and being an attentive listener is a continual process that begins with initial preparation and carries through to actual delivery of a message.

As part of the initial preparation, I research (as much as can be learned or anticipated) backgrounds, demographics, careers, and educational levels of the audience. Once I compile the information, I consider how the information should influence the organization and depth of my presentation. Most importantly, I try to put myself in the role of the listener, not the presenter, during an oral presentation. Ironic as that may seem, I am reminded to be attentive to my body language, tonal inflections, and other signs that help me gauge audience reaction. Also, the process taught me to be flexible as I speak—maybe cutting a little here or expanding a little there.

Over the years, I believe I have become a better listener and thus a more capable speaker. The "proof of the pudding" is sometimes reflected in the question and answer period, which is always welcome feedback. Sometimes an audience member tells me after a presentation: "Though I was one of many in the audience, I felt you were speaking to me."

Rule 405 served as more than an adequate reminder that the art of good listening, though sometimes humbling, is essential to good communication.

Larry Kjosa
V.P. Investments
Morgan Stanley

Section 1: VISUALS

Visuals, sometimes called **visual aids**, simplify and reinforce concepts, attract attention, emphasize important points, and summarize discussion. By guiding receivers through a presentation, visuals help the receivers understand your message and help increase their retention. Visuals are especially helpful when you are communicating with an audience of diverse backgrounds.

Visuals enhance both written reports and spoken presentations. When you choose visuals, you must consider (1) the purpose of your message and (2) the format(s) that will show the information meaningfully and accurately.

Audio aids also may be used effectively during presentations. However, this chapter presents an overview of commonly used visuals; specifically, overhead transparencies, computer-generated slides, tables, and graphs. For detailed information about these and other presentation aids, consult a specialty reference.

Popular Presentation Aids

Used correctly, visuals can dramatically improve the professionalism of your presentation. Two types of visuals often used in conjunction with spoken presentations are overhead transparencies and computer-generated slides. Observe these basic design principles for both media:

- Show simple, topic-related content
- Ensure adequate margins (at least three-quarters inch on all sides)
- Group similar items and maintain consistent format
- Provide logical visual flow (top to bottom or left to right)

Overhead Transparencies

Text or graphics may be prepared on an acetate transparency and projected. Transparencies are usually black and white, but color production is available. The main advantages of using transparencies are that they can be rearranged quickly if necessary, and equipment is available in most meeting rooms. Some facilities provide electronic overhead projectors, so presenters can prepare "transparencies" on paper rather than on acetate film. The main disadvantages of using transparencies are that (1) some images, especially photographs, do not reproduce well; (2) any changes result in reproducing the transparency; and (3) color transparencies, which are pleasing to the eye, are expensive.

Transparency projection works best for groups under 150, and the audience should be positioned close to the projection screen.

Incorporate these transparency design guidelines:

- Limit each transparency to one topic represented by keywords and keyword phrases.
- Use a combination of upper- and lowercase letters for easy reading.
- Choose a plain font style. Avoid italics and script letters if readability is affected.

Timely Tip

Visuals convey powerful conscious and unconscious messages.

- Use a readable font size. Some references suggest a minimum 18- to 20-point size.
- When using multiple transparencies, prepare *all* transparencies in either landscape or portrait orientation. Switching directions is disorienting to the audience.

Computer-Generated Slides

Computer-generated slides, such as those created with PowerPoint software, enable you to display text and graphics on a monitor or on a large screen. Computer-generated slides, when they are not overused, add interest and professionalism to your presentation through layout, color, sound, animation, artwork, and other special effects. The key is to *not* let the slides upstage your presentation.

Most presentation software packages come with templates that make slide preparation easy. **Templates** are "packaged" formats with predefined color schemes, backgrounds, font styles, and layouts. Templates can also be customized to suit professional needs. For example, Mason Brick Company created a template using a specific color scheme, font style, and brick-look background for presentations to customers. The brick look is a subtle marketing technique for their products and services.

Prepare your slides with these four design elements in mind: content, readability, special effects, and color.

Content

Visuals often contain too much information. Effective visuals are short and to the point. Simplify your visuals by covering one topic per slide using keywords and phrases; group related information.

Whatever appears on the slide, including graphics, clip art, and photographs, must relate to the information being presented. Although pictorial representations add interest, their primary purpose is to increase audience comprehension. Illustration 10-1 on page 339 is a good example of using keywords and phrases to emphasize important points.

Readability

To achieve the best readability, maintain as much "nontext" space as possible (adequate margins and space between lines). Choose a *sans serif* font (without lines on the ends of each letter), and use a combination of upper- and lowercase letters for text. References suggest font sizes of 24 to 36 points for headings and 18 to 24 points for text. Avoid italics and script if readability is affected. Limit font styles to three or fewer because too many styles can be distracting.

Information arranged horizontally is easier to read, and the 7 × 7 Rule is a helpful guide: *Seven words per line and seven lines per slide.*

Special Effects

Today's most popular software allows you to enhance your slides by adding special effects. Audio, animation, Internet connections, and video clips are special effects that can be incorporated into computer-generated slides.

Illustration 10-1 **Computer-Generated Slides**

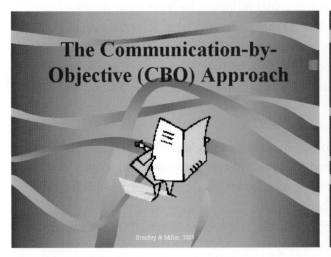

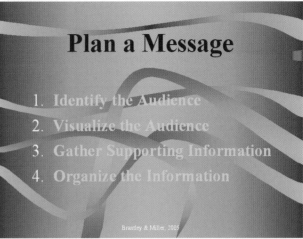

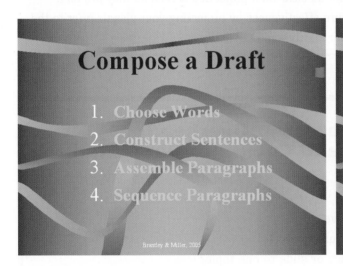

Special effects are great attention getters, but they should be used sparingly to maintain their impact. Only use pictures or special effects that further the purpose of your message, not detract from your message—*less is usually better*. Audio effects, for example, must be used with care because sound is quickly perceived as "silly" if the sound is not relevant to the message.

Animation features let you dictate how and when information is presented on the slide. Options such as fade-in, dimming, and bouncing let you establish how you want words or pictures to transition on or off the screen. You are able to introduce one key point at a time to allow the audience to focus on each point as you provide the explanation. For the best results, choose one subtle technique to be used cautiously in your presentation.

Color

Color is a major visual influence because color sends messages. The meanings derived from color vary among cultures, so research your audience. You want to choose colors that capture audience attention, increase audience retention, and ultimately send your intended message. Follow these four color rules:

- Use five or fewer colors.
- Use the same color for similar elements: make all first-level headings one color, all second-level headings another color, and so on.
- Use contrasting colors: dark letters on a light background and light letters on a dark background.
- Avoid reds and certain shades of green for letters. These colors are difficult to read when projected.

Sometimes slides are not as clear on a projection screen as they are on a computer monitor. Ensure effectiveness by projecting your visuals *prior* to the presentation to check for clarity and readability.

CHECKLIST

Checklist for Preparing Overhead Transparencies and Computer-Generated Slides

1. **Does your visual:**
   - Accomplish the objective?
   - Relate to your target audience?
   - Limit each transparency or slide to one topic?
   - Use keywords or keyword phrases appropriate for the audience?
   - Accommodate cultural differences in graphic representations?
   - Consider the various meanings derived from color? (slides)

2. **Does the format of your visual**
   - Display words and graphics for readability?
   - Use adequate font size?
   - Incorporate special effects sparingly?
   - Follow the 7 × 7 Rule? (slides)
   - Use contrasting colors for text and background? (slides)

3. **Does final visual message:**
   - Incorporate the six *C*s of effective messages?
   - Send the message you intend?
   - Reflect ethics and credibility by providing adequate, objective information?
   - Look professional?

Tables and Graphs (Charts)

Tables and graphs often accompany written and spoken presentations because the visuals enable audiences to grasp complex data, such as numerical data, at a glance. Tables represent detailed, specific information. Graphs, also called charts, quickly present information for comparison or visualization of trends. Bar, line, and pie graphs show trends or relationships among variables. Although graphs present information in a more comprehensible form, they are less accurate than tables. Sometimes a graph is accompanied by a table to provide the details. Flowcharts, on the other hand, present information that occurs in stages or steps.

Table and graph titles should tell the viewers what to look for by using descriptive titles.

Example:	Nondescriptive Title	Descriptive Title
	January through June Sales	Sales Increases January through June

Label all legends, column headings, and section headings clearly and concisely. When the information in your table or graph comes from another source, include a source line under the visual at the lower left corner. A source line appears in Illustration 10-2.

Considerable study and careful construction are needed to ensure that your visuals present information accurately and ethically. Ethical visuals include all relevant data and omit irrelevant data. Ethical visuals also maintain an accurate scale of measurement and indicate important outside influences on data, such as who sponsors the information.

Timely Tip

Position each visual close to its discussion.

Timely Tip

Consecutively number illustrations in a written report: Illustration 1, Illustration 2, Table 1, Table 2, and so on.

Tables

A table, such as Illustration 10-2, consists of columns and rows of data. The data may be words or numbers. A table provides an easy-to-read format for detailed or tedious information. The following guidelines help you achieve a readable format.

Illustration 10-2 **Table**

Table 1. Leading Lenders to Regional Businesses January 1–December 31, 2004			
Lender	**Rank**	**Amount Lent (Millions)**	**Number of Loans**
First Citizen's Bank	1	$56.4	267
American Bank	2	50.0	225
Tri County	3	48.6	192
Bridgewater Bank	4	31.5	201
First Bank Savings	5	22.5	175

Source: Bay County Financial News, April 2005

- Use clear, concise titles and column heads that reflect content.
- Use understandable units, and specify the unit you are using (dollars, percentages, and so on). Abbreviate units, such as $, %, and lb., when possible. Use the same unit to express all items in a column.
- Round off numbers when possible for easier reading.
- Maintain adequate white space between rows and columns.

Bar Graphs

The bars in a bar graph represent statistical information in a variety of formats. Bars are arranged vertically or horizontally; and they may appear as single, grouped, or stacked components. A bar graph compares one item to another, shows changes over time, and shows a correlation among items.

Both bar and line graphs are composed of a vertical and a horizontal axis that intersect at right angles. The x-axis is the horizontal line; the y-axis is the vertical line.

Follow these guidelines when you construct bar graphs.

- Begin each axis at zero, and label each axis.
- Arrange the bars in chronological order.
- Construct all the bars with the same width and place them close together to allow comparisons.
- Confirm that the space between the bars is smaller than the width of the bars.
- Distinguish bars by color, shading, or pattern.
- Use a legend to show which bar represents which element.

A **multiple bar graph** groups two to four bars to compare quantities. Illustration 10-3 shows cell phone sales of three popular brands for October through December.

A **stacked bar graph**, shown in Illustration 10-4, page 343, is broken into segments and shows how different components contribute to the whole. Each segment is labeled for clarity.

Illustration 10-3 **Multiple Bar Graph (Vertical)**

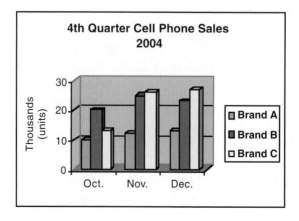

Illustration 10-4 **Stacked Bar Graph (Horizontal)**

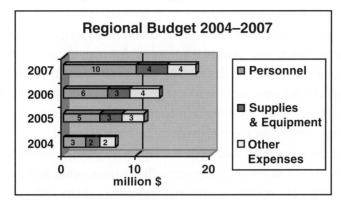

Line Graphs

Illustration 10-5 shows a multiple line graph. Usually, a line graph compares two or more sets of figures. (Sometimes a line graph can consist of only one line.) Create effective line graphs:

- Divide the horizontal axis into equal units in a logical order from left to right.
- Divide the vertical axis into equal units from the least at the bottom to the most at the top
- Label the horizontal axis and the vertical axis. When numbers are used, begin each axis at zero.
- Use no more than three lines on one graph. (If the lines cross each other, even three lines may be too confusing.)
- Avoid placing numbers along the lines. The lines themselves show trends.

Illustration 10-5 **Multiple Line Graph**

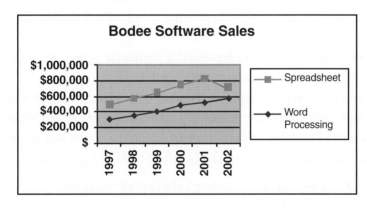

Pie Graph

A pie graph is a 360° circle divided into "slices" or segments. Illustration 10-6 shows how a pie chart compares the size of the parts to the whole.

Incorporating the following format suggestions helps you construct meaningful pie charts:

- Start at the 12 o'clock position with either the largest percentage or the percentage you want to emphasize. Arrange the remaining segments clockwise in descending size or some other logical order.
- Divide the pie into six or fewer segments. If necessary, combine smaller parts into an *Other* or a *Miscellaneous* category.
- Provide a different color or pattern for each segment.
- Label each segment, and keep the labels horizontal. Indicate the value of each segment, and ensure that values equal 100 percent.
- For emphasis, explode a part (pull out a part of the pie).

Illustration 10-6 **Pie Graph**

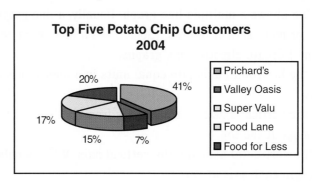

Top Five Potato Chip Customers 2004

- Prichard's
- Valley Oasis
- Super Valu
- Food Lane
- Food for Less

41%, 20%, 17%, 15%, 7%

Flowchart

A flowchart, such as in Illustration 10-7, page 345, links boxes and other shapes to show the steps in a process from beginning to end. The steps in the process may consist of pictorial representations or standardized geometric shapes.

When you construct a flowchart using standardized shapes, follow these basic guidelines:

- Use a specific shape to represent a particular action. Specified shapes typically represent certain actions.
- Keep the chart as simple as possible with adequate white space.
- Label each step either inside or immediately next to the shape.
- Connect the items in the flowchart according to the sequence in which the steps occur—usually left to right or top to bottom.

Visuals for an Intercultural Audience

Because the U.S. workforce is diverse and because business is conducted in many countries, the people with whom you communicate represent a variety of cultures and languages. The audiences for spoken and written messages will include coworkers, customers, vendors, and business partners with varying backgrounds and English language abilities.

Illustration 10-7 **Flowchart**

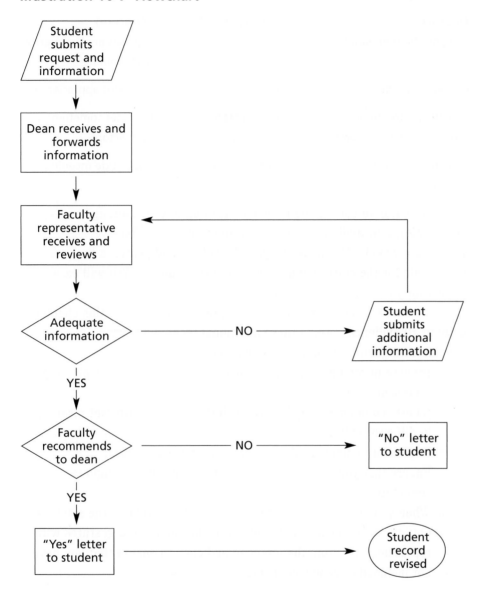

Visuals offer communication advantages in today's global environment because graphic representations overcome language barriers by simplifying complex information and by representing terms that are difficult to translate.

In addition to the words you choose, however, you must ensure that your visuals send the message you intend. For example, other than some scientific and mathematical symbols, symbols are not globally standardized. Images, how people or body parts are depicted, are not universally accepted; and the meanings of gestures and colors vary from culture to culture.

Culture Frame

Pointing with a finger is considered rude in India; Indians point with their chin. Also, feet are considered unclean; apologize if your shoes touch another person.

Gesture	Country	Meaning
Tugging, flicking earlobe	Italy	Signifies another person is effeminate
Pinching earlobe	Brazil	Expresses appreciation
Thumb and forefinger forming a circle (OK gesture)	United States	Indicates something is satisfactory
Thumb and forefinger forming a circle	Germany and Brazil	Has a rude meaning

Your goal is to convey the intended meaning of your message. Researching your audience enables you to prepare nonoffensive, informative visuals. Use images, symbols, colors, and gestures that are appropriate for the culture and country of your audience. You will earn respect for your firm and for yourself.

The formatting guidelines for visuals presented earlier in this chapter apply to all audiences. Apply these additional techniques when communicating with intercultural audiences.

- Prepare uncomplicated visuals; use simple words and simple graphic representations.
- Choose colors carefully because colors represent different meanings in different cultures.
- Represent humans as abstract figures (outline figures).
- Ensure that your symbols and graphics do not have religious connotations.
- When you use symbols, provide a legend that explains the symbols.
- Confirm your choices of images, symbols, colors, and gestures with representatives from the intended audience to ensure that you have not included offensive elements.

Timely Tip

When possible, prepare visuals with words in both English and the language of the audience.

Knowing how to prepare and deliver a spoken presentation, a *speech*, is a valuable skill. Regardless of country or culture, the CBO approach and the six *C*s of effective messages are as important for spoken presentations as they are for written messages.

Plan a Message

Follow the same planning steps to prepare a spoken presentation as you do to prepare a written message.

Presentations are prepared to inform or persuade. When you give a presentation, you are likely to know or you can obtain information about your audience, such as cultural and educational background and level of interest. The more you know about your audience, the better you can anticipate and address audience reactions.

Your presentation must consist of relevant, accurate information that assists the audience in understanding your message. How you organize the information depends on the content of the message. Persuasive messages typically use the persuasive message strategy AIDA and the indirect pattern or organization. Presentations that contain bad news usually follow the bad news strategy and indirect pattern of organization. Good news or neutral news presentations follow the good news/neutral news strategy and direct pattern of organization.

Outline your presentation; include notations for visuals. Review and modify the outline until you are satisfied with the order of your presentation.

Compose a Draft; Complete the Final Message

Compose a draft of your message. After editing and revising, compose your final message.

Typical presentations consist of the **introduction**, which prepares the audience to listen; the **text** or **body**, which provides the details; and the **closing**, which brings the message to an end.

Introduction

The **introduction** attracts the attention of the audience, relates content to audience needs, and establishes your credibility as a presenter.

Draw the audience into your presentation with your opening statement. Effective openings relate to the topic of the presentation. Some opening techniques are presented here:

- Open with a personal experience. Anecdotes help audiences identify with you.
- Tell a humorous story or joke. Using humor to make fun of yourself may be helpful in establishing rapport with the audience. Be sure that your joke is not offensive.

Timely Tip

Effective speakers use outlines or small note cards with key points to guide them during presentations.

- Give a startling statistic or statement.
- Begin with a meaningful or inspiring quotation.
- Ask a rhetorical question. A rhetorical question does not require an answer but does get the audience to think about your topic.

Example: Should all unwanted animals be euthanized?

Text

The **text** or **body** of the report consists of the details. Restrict coverage to five or fewer main points and support each point with adequate but not excessive explanation.

Spoken presentations are for a *listening* audience—prepared for the ear, not the eye. To maintain audience interest, limit your presentation to fewer than 25 minutes; and relay the information in a logical, simple order. Outlining the text is invaluable because you can easily visualize the flow of information.

Several options to sequence the text of your presentation are available. Chapter 3, pages 80–81, discussed these four typical arrangements: time, logic, cause and effect, and comparison and contrast. You may also sequence by main points, by priority, and by topic.

When you have several points to cover, begin by listing the **main points**. Then cover each point in detail.

Example: Updating stockholders on important company projects.

If you have taken or plan to take a particular action that necessitates explanation, present your reasons in order of **priority**, beginning with the least important and leading to the most important reason. Audiences usually remember the last point they hear.

Example: Changing long-term suppliers.

You may organize the body of your report by **topic**. Discuss each topic separately.

Example: Presenting the safety features of cars organized by brand of car.

Closing

The **closing** (also known as the **terminal section** or **end**) of a presentation is a position of emphasis. People remember best what they hear (and *see*) *first* and *last*. The end of a presentation should emphasize what you want the audience to do or remember: Usually you will alert the audience that you are heading toward the end of your presentation with a statement such as "In conclusion . . ." or "To summarize . . ."

Closings may summarize main points, ask for audience action, or conclude with a brief anecdote or an inspiring story that reinforces the purpose of your message.

Once you have finalized the content of your message and you have developed presentation visuals, turn your attention to the method of delivery and to the listening experience.

Method of Delivery

The delivery of your message can be impromptu, extemporaneous, textual, memorized, or a combination of these methods.

Impromptu delivery is spontaneous, such as when you respond immediately to a customer complaint or when you are asked for your opinion during a meeting. In these situations, you cannot rehearse your response; but you can prepare by anticipating possible involvement.

Extemporaneous delivery sounds spontaneous but is actually the result of considerable practice. This method of delivery is the most common for most presentations. Extemporaneous delivery usually allows you to modify your presentation based on audience reactions. For example, you can respond to a listener's request to clarify a complex point if necessary.

Extemporaneous speakers use presentation aids, such as note cards, an outline, overhead transparencies, computer-generated slides (with speaker notes), or other aids to ensure coverage of important points.

Textual delivery involves reading verbatim (word for word) from a script. Government officials and company executives often use textual delivery to ensure accuracy and to avoid being misquoted by the news media, especially when reporting policies or legal issues. Too much verbatim reading is monotonous and maintaining eye contact is difficult.

Memorized delivery is word-for-word recitation without referring to any notes. Memorized delivery sounds "flat," and you may forget what comes next in the presentation.

Combined delivery is any combination of the delivery methods. For example, you may prepare most of a report for extemporaneous delivery; but you may read certain portions (textual delivery) to ensure accuracy.

A Positive Listening Experience

A presentation listening experience has two stages: *prior to the presentation* and *during the presentation*. Create a positive listening experience for your audience.

Prior to the Presentation

Prior to the presentation, address listener needs by preparing for the delivery and by considering the physical environment.

Prepare for Delivery

Practice is critical to a successful presentation.

- Rehearse in front of a mirror or videotape yourself to see how you look to an audience.
- Identify points in your notes to indicate when visuals should be displayed.

Timely Tip

Audiences remember best what they *see* and *hear*; so when possible, complement your spoken words with visuals.

- Practice with your visuals.
- If you use computer-dependent visuals, prepare alternatives, such as overhead transparencies or handouts, in the event of equipment or software malfunction.
- Vary the presentation format; that is, interject humor when appropriate, or invite audience comments.
- Present each key idea and its supporting information separately. Reinforce important points by repeating them throughout the presentation.
- Anticipate typical audience questions, and formulate answers.
- Time your delivery to stay within the limits.

Consider the Physical Environment

The physical environment influences how an audience will receive your information.

- Confirm the room arrangements. A pleasant, well-ventilated room with comfortable seating facilitates a positive listening experience.
- Determine equipment needs, and make necessary equipment reservations.
- Before presenting, confirm that the equipment works.
- Practice using the equipment until you can operate the equipment with ease.

During the Presentation

At the onset of your presentation, take a deep breath, make yourself comfortable, and greet the audience. Then apply these helpful presentation techniques:

- Vary your rate of speaking, the pitch of your voice, and your volume. Variations help you emphasize important ideas and avoid speaking in a monotone. (The average speaking rate is 140 to 150 words a minute.)
- Pronounce words clearly and correctly. Eliminate fillers such as *er, ah,* and *you know* from your presentation.
- Distribute handouts for use during the presentation if the handouts will not distract the audience from your message. Sometimes distributing the handouts after the presentation is best.
- If possible, refer to audience members by name. (Name tags help.)
- Focus on the audience. Throughout your presentation, look steadily at different members.
- Keep your delivery notes from the view of the audience. Glance quickly at your visuals, including your delivery notes, for reinforcement; but do not read them verbatim.
- Look for verbal and nonverbal clues (other than just eye contact) that demonstrate the audience is listening.

- Maintain control, and keep the audience listening. Ask the audience questions, and solicit answers.
- Move away from the podium and toward the audience when possible.
- Dress professionally and practice good grooming so that your appearance does not detract from your message.

Summary

Visuals simplify and reinforce concepts, attract attention, emphasize important points, and summarize discussion. Visuals help receivers understand a message as well as increase receiver retention. When you choose visuals, consider the purpose of your message and the format(s) that will show the information meaningfully and accurately.

Overhead transparencies and computer-generated slides often are used in conjunction with spoken presentations. Four main design elements must be considered when preparing computer-generated slides: content, readability, special effects, and color.

Tables and graphs also are used to present information because they enable audiences to grasp complex data at a glance. Tables show detailed, specific information in an easy-to-read format. Graphs (including bar, line, and pie graphs) show relationships and enable comparisons. Flowcharts present information that occurs in stages or steps.

When you prepare visuals for an intercultural audience, research the audience to ensure that the visuals are not barriers to effective communication.

The CBO approach and the six Cs of effective messages are as important for spoken presentations as they are for written messages. Methods of delivery include impromptu, extemporaneous, textual, memorized, or a combination of these methods. To attract and hold the attention of the audience, the presentation must include an interesting introduction; text that is sequenced for easy listening; and a closing that summarizes, requests action, or concludes with a reinforcing story.

A listening experience consists of two stages: *prior to the presentation* and *during the presentation*. Prior to the presentation, prepare for delivery by practicing the presentation and evaluating the physical environment. During the presentation, apply techniques that enhance your presentation.

Complete Communication Skills Development 10, pages 359–360. For capitalization review, see the Reference Guide, pages 440–442.

Exercises

10-1

Directions: Investigate presentation software. You will find descriptions of the software features online, on software boxes, and in print advertisements. Note information relevant to developing visuals. Prepare a memorandum or an e-mail message as assigned. Identify the software and discuss features that are important to presenters. Your message should reflect the six *C*s of effective messages.

10-2

Directions: Research how colors are perceived in the United States. Cite your sources. Choose two colors and prepare a two- to three-paragraph summary on how each color is used and the message that is intended. Your summary should reflect the six *C*s of effective messages.

10-3

Directions: Analyze computer-generated slides using the following list as a guide.

Content:
  a. Is each topic represented clearly by keywords and phrases?
  b. Are similar ideas grouped?
  c. Are graphics topic-related?

Readability:
  a. Is the 7×7 Rule utilized with adequate "nontext" space provided?
  b. Is the font style easy to read and limited to three or fewer fonts?
  c. Is the font size adequate?

Special Effects:
  a. What special effect(s) is used?
  b. Is the effect appropriate for the topic?

Color:
  a. Does the presentation use five or fewer visually appealing colors?
  b. Are similar elements colored the same?
  c. Are contrasting colors used for background and text?

Exercises

10-4

Directions: From the graphics listed below, choose a table or graph that best represents each of the following four situations.

table   **bar graph**   **line graph**   **pie chart**

a. To show the percentage of employees at each of four branch offices.

b. To compare the number of sick days used monthly by employees at each of four branch offices.

c. To present the company's operating costs over a four-year period for each of these categories: salaries, benefits, advertising, building rental, equipment, supplies, maintenance, and other expenses.

d. To show the trend in ticket sales for 12 months.

10-5

Directions: Read two paper or online articles that include at least one visual (excluding photographs); one visual must be different from the illustrations presented in Chapter 10. Study the visuals, and provide the following information in a format assigned by your instructor. Your final message should reflect the six *C*s of effective messages.

a. What information does the visual represent? Is the representation accurate? Why?

b. What message did the visual send to you?

c. Does the visual enhance the content of the article? Why?

d. Are the titles and labels informative?

10-6

Directions: Choose a topic from the following list and compose an opening statement using two different techniques.

Personal experience
Relevant humorous story or joke
Topic-related startling statistic or statement
Meaningful or inspiring quotation
Rhetorical question

Internet
Challenge

10-1 Directions: Research gestures in a country of your choice (other than the United States). Prepare one or two paragraphs explaining the gestures and their meanings. If a similar gesture has a different meaning in the United States, add that information to your comments. Be prepared to discuss your findings.

10-2 Directions: To facilitate discussions in a business-social situation with your peers, colleagues, or business partners from India, conduct an online search for Indian holidays and festivals. Search using keywords such as *India, holidays in India,* and *Indian festivals.* Record each URL, and take notes. Organize your notes into an outline, and use your outline to present your findings in class.

InfoTrac

Directions: Use the InfoTrac keyword search to locate articles on presentation tips. Use keywords such as *speaker tips* and *presentation tips*. Read two articles, and take notes. Follow the guidelines in the chapter to prepare either overhead transparencies or computer-generated slides based on your notes.

WebTUTOR
Advantage

Directions: Access your WebTutor Advantage product. Complete the short-answer portion for Chapter 10, and send the answers to your instructor.

Case Studies

10-1

Communication Situation: In Internet Challenge 9-1, page 327, you conducted a search for interview bloopers. Prepare the bloopers for display as computer-generated slides.

Task: Design the slides based on the key elements discussed on pages 338–340. Create a slide to represent each interview blooper. Use one or two appropriate graphics and one special effect.

10-2

Communication Situation: Analyze an existing speech. One print source is *Vital Speeches of Our Day,* which is available in most public and school libraries. Search online using keywords and phrases, such as *speeches* and *historical speeches*; print a copy of the speech.

Task: Use the copy of the speech to provide the following information. Be prepared to discuss your findings in class.

   a. Identify the introduction, text, and terminal section of the speech. Comment on the effectiveness of each section based on your readings in this chapter.

   b. Describe how the information is sequenced (time, logic, compare and contrast, main points, and so on).

   c. Identify main points. Explain whether the main points are adequately supported.

   d. Indicate who you believe is the audience. Comment on whether the speech seems appropriate for the audience.

   e. Explain whether visuals would enhance the speech. Indicate where you would position visuals. Briefly explain the content of visuals you would develop.

Case Studies

10-3

Communication Situation: Read a few articles that are class or career related. The articles should not include graphics.

Task A: Use the CBO approach to prepare a presentation based on the articles you read.

   a. Prepare an outline.
   b. Determine information that can be enhanced with visuals, and identify which visual format best represents the information.
   c. Mark the position of the visuals in your outline using keywords or sketches.

Task B: Once you have completed Task A, prepare the presentation. Use an appropriate message strategy, and incorporate the six *C*s of effective messages.

   a. Prepare a draft. Review, edit, and revise the draft as necessary.
   b. Complete the presentation.
   c. Create accompanying visuals.

10-4

Communication Situation: Select a topic from the following list. Research the topic, and prepare a five-minute presentation with visuals.
   Buying a pet appropriate for apartment living
   Purchasing a used car
   Choosing a summer or winter vacation spot
   Choosing a banking facility
   Choosing an appropriate gift for a visiting foreign client

Task A: Use the CBO approach to prepare a presentation based on your research of the topic.

   a. Prepare an outline.
   b. Determine information that can be enhanced with visuals, and identify which visual format best represents the information.
   c. Mark the position of the visuals in your outline using keywords or sketches.

Case Studies

Task B: Once you have completed Task A, prepare the presentation. Use an appropriate message strategy, and incorporate the six Cs of effective messages.

   a. Prepare a draft. Review, edit, and revise the draft as necessary.
   b. Complete the presentation.
   c. Create accompanying visuals.

10-5

Communication Situation: Select a topic that interests you and is appropriate for a presentation in your classroom.

Task A: Use the CBO approach to complete the following planning steps:

   a. Brainstorm and choose ideas.
   b. Prepare an outline.
   c. Determine information that can be enhanced with visuals, and identify which visual format best represents the information.

Task B: Once you have completed Task A, prepare the presentation. Use an appropriate message strategy, and incorporate the six Cs of effective messages.

   a. Prepare a draft. Review, edit, and revise the draft as necessary.
   b. Complete the presentation.
   c. Create accompanying visuals.

Part A Capitalization

Directions: Rewrite each sentence correcting the capitalization errors.

1. Read Chia's article, "understanding different cultural values and styles," in the january 7 issue of *journal of world communication.*

2. does your presentation include an Introduction, a Text, and a Closing?

3. schedule a meeting for the Supervisors.

4. duane ordered the model no. 2233A computer.

5. The Members will meet at 7:30 a.m. in room 25 of the bockel building.

6. laura's comments revealed her in-depth knowledge of india, pakistan, and other nations in that region of the world.

7. I plan to attend these three workshops: "understanding our biases," "valuing diversity," and "meeting the cultural challenge."

8. the conference speaker was gurpreet patel, director of communications for the rubicon company.

9. mr. amin recommended this class to all Managers.

10. keshia andres will supervise the construction of our new plant in southern india.

Part B   Skills Application

Directions: Find the errors in grammar, punctuation, spelling, and capitalization. Underline each error, and in the space provided above each error, write the correction. (Ordinarily, letters are single-spaced. In this letter, extra space has been added for you to insert corrections.)

Dear Ms Koch;

These are the results of the survay in which you participat last Fall. More than

60 percent of the 200 Desktop publishing Club members responded. their

recomendations are summarized below.

1   Write a list of words you frequent misspell.

2   Use the Dictionary to check the spelling of each word on you list.

3   Pronounce allowed each syllable of the word.

4.   Spell the word allowed several times.

5.   note any silent letters in the word.

6.   Close you're eyes, pronunce the word, and slow spell the word.

7.   Write the word from memory; check you're spelling with the dictionary.

8.   set aside 15 to 20 minutes; daily too practice your word list;

To develop spelling skills, you must want too improve, and practice; follow

these eight guidelines to begins improving your spelling today?

sincerely,

Felder Johnson

Felder Johnson, Chairperson

Education committee

Chapter 11

Reports, Proposals, and Instructions for the Workplace

Learning Objectives

1 Explain how each step of the CBO approach relates to planning and developing reports, proposals, and instructions.

2 Identify and discuss methods of collecting and organizing data.

3 Discuss the purpose(s) of formal reports, and explain various formal report parts and components.

4 Explain the purpose(s) of proposals, and discuss their characteristics.

5 Explain the variations of informal reports, their primary purposes, and their characteristics.

6 Explain the characteristics of instructions.

7 Prepare reports, proposals, and instructions by following the appropriate guidelines, implementing the CBO approach, and incorporating the six Cs of effective messages.

COMMUNICATION PERSPECTIVES

PDR: A Prescription for Retention

Psychologists describe the way people classify, interpret, and remember information as a *schema*. As a general rule, new employees may have had limited experience with ethics programs. When employees have a decision-making framework, they have a greater chance of absorbing and retaining concepts associated with new information. Absent a framework, employees have very little chance of absorbing and retaining much associated with the new information. One way to increase retention is to categorize the information. I have tried to categorize the elements of our ethics program into PDR: Prevention, Detection, and Resolution.

First, let's look at prevention. Prevention is the foundation of an effective ethics program. Skipping the prevention step will result in an inordinately high volume of cases. From my experience, cases are very labor intensive and can quickly swamp the ethics officer and the management team.

Detection is next. An effective ethics program is greatly advanced by a diligent, committed workforce. An employee population who speaks out without fear of retaliation will assist in monitoring the organization and alert management of issues in a timely fashion. Accessibility to the ethics officer is also an important element in detecting issues. At Texas Instruments, the ethics officer has standard e-mail access as well as anonymous e-mail access. Also, an 800 line and a local number for global access are both available. A separate ethics PO Box is available to ensure immediate access as well as confidential or anonymous input. Finally, the old-fashioned walk-up and knock-on-the door method is available.

Resolution is the desired final step. Resolution involves investigating and solving quickly and fairly the various cases. Resolution sends clear signals that the ethics office really is an appropriate vehicle to resolve issues that arise.

When the individual who initiated the original inquiry is known by the ethics office, a good practice is to close the loop and inform the employee that appropriate action has been taken and the case is closed. If the employee who submitted the original inquiry has remained anonymous, however, closing the loop will not be possible.

An effective resolution pattern will certainly reinforce the other two aspects of the program: prevention and detection.

©Texas Instruments, 2003

Key Factors in an Ethics Program

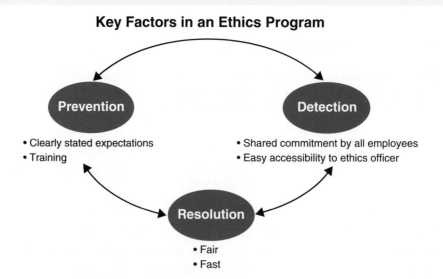

A report is a planned, organized, factual presentation of information prepared for a specific purpose and for a specific audience.

Internal reports are distributed within an organization. Internal reports move information in the following directions:

- Horizontally from peer to peer to describe activities, generate ideas, or solve problems
- Vertically upward from nonmanagement employees to management to provide the information necessary to make competent organizational decisions
- Vertically downward from management to nonmanagement employees to provide nonmanagement employees with information to carry out their responsibilities

External reports are distributed outside the organization. External reports present organizational information to clients, prospective clients, stockholders, government agencies, and the general public.

Understanding the characteristics of various reports, implementing the CBO approach, and incorporating visuals and other report presentation techniques will help you prepare effective reports for internal or external distribution.

Formality

Reports are divided into two broad categories: formal reports and informal reports. The report topic, target audience, and company preference determine whether a report will be prepared as a formal or an informal report. A **formal report** covers a complex situation or project, includes report parts and components, and typically is written in formal language. An **informal report** covers a routine or less complicated situation, includes fewer parts, and typically is written in informal language.

Function

Reports are considered informational or analytical. An **informational report** presents the facts but does not include an analysis or make a recommendation. Progress, periodic, and travel reports and minutes of meetings are examples of informational reports.

- **Progress reports** update receivers on the status of a project at various *stages*. Progress reports may tell receivers whether a project is within budget and on schedule. Progress reports are often issued during construction and research projects.
- **Periodic reports** are similar to progress reports. Periodic reports also update receivers except that periodic reports are issued at regular *intervals*, such as weekly or monthly. A monthly sales report is an example of a periodic report.

- **Travel or trip reports**, including convention and conference reports, summarize the purpose and activities of a trip.
- **Minutes of meetings** provide a record of discussions and decisions. Minutes describe what happened during the meeting without offering any interpretation of actions or decisions.

An **analytical report** provides information, presents an analysis, *and* draws a conclusion. Recommendations may be included. An analytical report is more complex than an informational report. Often, the intent of an analytical report is to describe a situation and to convince receivers that a certain solution or course of action is practical and effective. Sometimes an informational report leads to an analytical report. For example, a monthly sales report shows a drop in sales (informational). When an analysis of that data leads to a recommended change in sales procedures, the resulting report is analytical.

Feasibility reports and justification reports are examples of analytical reports.

- **Feasibility reports** evaluate two or more possible solutions to a problem and make a recommendation. For instance, a feasibility report evaluates two or more computer network systems and makes a recommendation based on the evaluation.
- **Justification reports** explain in detail the need for a purchase, an investment, additional staff, or a change in procedure or structure. For example, changes in privacy laws and the addition of four physicians to a clinic staff have increased the turnaround time for coding and processing patient records. After a thorough investigation, a report justifies the need to hire two additional employees to decrease turnaround time.

Plan a Report

You prepare a report because someone has authorized you to do so or because you have participated in or observed an activity that requires a report. By implementing the CBO approach, you carry out the planning steps to achieve your communication objective.

Determine the Objective

The focus of the report is the **problem** or **situation**—the reason you are writing.

Reports are written to summarize an event or activity, provide decision-making or policy-making information, and present evidence to request an action.

Visualize Your Audience

Reports should be written for those who will use the information in the report. The knowledge level of the audience, the anticipated reaction of the audience, and sometimes the preference of the audience influence how you present information.

Gather Supporting Information

Timely Tip

Ensure that your sources are timely, relevant, and accurate.

Decisions and policies based on a report are only as good as the information in the report. The more complex the situation, the more you must research. Information is available through primary and secondary sources. **Primary sources** are firsthand accounts, the actual participation in or observation of events. **Secondary sources** are materials that have been prepared by someone else and published. Most people begin by researching secondary sources because information about a topic usually exists somewhere.

Secondary Sources

Information from secondary sources is available both online and on paper. Secondary sources include books; journal, magazine, and newspaper articles; and encyclopedia entries. Secondary sources report or analyze information from primary sources. For example, a research team may conduct tests and record the results of the testing. At this initial stage, the data gathered from the actual event is the primary source. Once the data is published in a journal, however, the article becomes a secondary source of information.

Dictionaries, encyclopedias, manuals, and atlases are examples of secondary sources. Statistics published by state, local, and federal agencies are secondary sources. Online databases contain thousands of directories and indexes, including the *Directory of Periodicals* and the *Business Periodical Index*. Mecklermedia's web site categories thousands of Internet-accessible files by subject, including publications, mailing lists, and web sites. Both general and specialty sources are available online, on CD, and on paper.

The library is another valuable source. You can investigate paper sources, conduct online Internet searches, and be guided by librarians whose specialty is finding information. One of the most comprehensive libraries in the world is the Library of Congress, http://catalog.loc.gov/, which lists available services as well as search techniques. (If necessary, review search techniques on page 104.)

The Internet provides easy access to information. Confirm that your information is from a reputable source. For a helpful guide, consult Table 4-3, Web Site Evaluation Criteria, on page 107.

Primary Sources

Primary sources provide information from firsthand accounts or investigations, such as surveys, interviews, questionnaires, observations, and experiments. Information gathered from primary sources lends credibility to business reports. For example, when a firm considers developing a product, the firm may use surveys to gather information about customer needs and wants. Interviews with people who have considerable knowledge about a topic are also primary sources of information.

Organize Information

Preparing an outline assists you in organizing information within the report. As you position information in the outline, mark the type and location of the visuals you plan to use. Outlines enable you to look quickly at the structure of the whole report. The outline headings, especially the main headings, often become report headings. The arrangement of information depends on your audience and the report topic.

Compose a Draft

Most reports require more than one draft. Edit and revise the draft as often as necessary; pay close attention to language, readability, and appearance.

Language

Most formal reports are written in formal or impersonal language (third person), and most informal reports are written in informal or personal language (first and second person).

Examples:	**Formal Language**	**Informal Language**
	The report, which presents a comprehensive discussion of investment opportunities within the Pacific Rim, was authorized by Ms. Kolb.	At your request, I prepared an in-depth report on investment opportunities within the Pacific Rim.

Receiver knowledge dictates whether you use technical or nontechnical vocabulary. Technical vocabulary is appropriate when your receiver knows the subject matter; otherwise, nontechnical vocabulary is the better choice. Translating technical language into nontechnical language often requires additional words to ensure clarity.

Examples:	**Technical Language**	**Nontechnical Language**
	The patient suffers from arteriosclerotic and heart disease and atrial fibrillation.	The patient has thickening and loss of elasticity of the small heart arteries and irregular, rapid contractions of the upper chamber of the heart.

Readability and Appearance

The appearance of your report gives the receiver a lasting impression of you and your organization. Use visuals and headings to improve readability and appearance.

Visuals simplify and reinforce concepts and emphasize important points. Most of the guidelines for developing visuals presented in Chapter 10 are relevant to both spoken and written reports.

Headings guide the receiver through a report by dividing the report into readable portions and alerting the receiver to changes in topic. The position and format of headings indicate whether the information that follows is a major topic or a subtopic of a major topic. Refer to Headings, pages 370–371, for details.

Complete a Report

Once you have prepared a draft of your report, you are ready to look at all aspects of the report. Ensure that the report meets your objective, contains correct and unbiased content, and follows acceptable format guidelines. Confirm that your report incorporates the six *C*s of effective messages. Verify readability and evaluate overall effectiveness of any visuals that you include.

Section 2: FORMAL REPORTS

Complex situations generally require in-depth investigating and reporting. The comprehensive report that results is called a **formal report**. Formal reports include specific parts with their respective components (individually titled pages), follow detailed format guidelines, and most often are written in formal language.

Report Parts

The three main parts of a formal report are the *preliminary parts*, the *report body*, and the *supplementary parts*. The preliminary and supplementary parts include separate components, but each component is not included in every formal report. Inclusions are based on report topic, length, company policy, and possibly audience need or preference. Table 11-1 summarizes typical formal report parts, components, and order of arrangement.

Culture View

France
In France, formality is important and evident in business transactions and correspondence. Proposals are examined carefully; and the French may assertively question aspects that appear illogical. Intense discussions may follow. Proposals must be well-planned and logically organized.

Status is also important in business relationships. Professional hierarchies are strong; decisions are centralized and made at the highest level of authority. Often bureaucracy is more important than efficiency, so cultivating high-level contacts may expedite business negotiations.

Table 11-1 Typical Formal Report Parts, Components, and Order of Arrangement

Preliminary Parts	Report Body	Supplementary Parts
Title Page	Introduction	Works Cited or References
Transmittal Message	Authorization	Glossary
Table of Contents	Objective	Index
Abstract	Problem	Appendixes
	Background	
	Scope	
	Limitations	
	Research Sources	
	Order of Presentation	
	Text (Findings)	
	Summary or Conclusions	
	and/or Recommendations	

Preliminary Parts

Preliminary parts, sometimes called the **front matter**, consist of the pages that precede the body of the report. The most common preliminary parts are the title page, transmittal message, table of contents, and abstract.

The **title page** includes a descriptive report title, which reflects the purpose and content of the report; the author's name and department; date of submission; and the receiver's name.

The **transmittal message** accompanies a report and officially submits the report to the receiver. The transmittal message includes information that you would tell the receiver if you delivered the report personally. The message is organized in the direct pattern, begins with the reason the report was written, highlights important points, and offers to provide additional information as necessary. When the report is distributed internally, the transmittal message is usually a memorandum. When the report is distributed externally, the message is a letter.

The **table of contents** lists the report parts, the components within each part, and their respective page numbers. Headings in the table of contents should be exactly the same as the headings in the report.

An **abstract** is a condensed version of the report with or without conclusions and/or recommendations. Receivers often read the abstract to determine whether they want to read the entire report. Abstracts may be delivered to those who need to be aware of the report content but do not need to read the entire report. The length of the abstract depends on how much information is included.

Report Body

The **report body** contains the information and visuals that support the report objective. The body consists of three major sections: the *introduction*, the *text*, and the *terminal section*.

Timely Tip

The title of a report should be informative. For example, "How to Increase Laptop Purchases Among College Students" is more informative than "Increasing Computer Purchases."

Arrange the sections in the direct order or the indirect order as follows:

Direct Pattern: Terminal section, introduction, text

Indirect Pattern: Introduction, text, terminal section

Use the direct pattern to organize the body of the report for these situations:

- The information is favorable or routine.
- The receiver prefers the main idea immediately (whether or not the information is favorable).
- The receiver is knowledgeable about the content.

Use the indirect pattern to organize the body of the report for these situations:

- The information will be perceived as unfavorable or questionable.
- The receiver prefers the indirect pattern (whether or not the information is unfavorable).
- The receiver does not have adequate knowledge and needs explanation.

Introduction

An **introduction** orients the receiver to the content of the report by including any or all of the following elements:

- An **authorization statement** tells who requested the report.
- A **report objective** or **purpose** explains why the report was prepared.
- The **problem** describes the situation to be reviewed (focus of the report).
- The **background** explains how the reporting situation evolved.
- The **scope** relates the boundaries of the investigation (to what extent the problem was investigated).
- The **limitations** discuss restrictions on time, money, assistance, information, or other factors relating to the preparation of the report.
- The **research sources** explain the sources of primary and/or secondary information.
- The **order of presentation** orients the reader to the arrangement of information in the sections that follow.

Text

The **text**, sometimes called the **findings**, provides the details that support the report objective. The text, which includes the information that you gathered from primary and/or secondary sources, is the longest section of the report body. Headings and subheadings divide information in the text.

The text presents information in a sequence that is appropriate for the report content. You have studied sequencing in Chapter 3 (time, logic, cause and effect, and comparison and contrast) and in Chapter 10 (main points, priority, and topic). Determine the sequence that is best for your topic.

Terminal Section

The **terminal section** of an informational report presents a summary of the key points in the order that they were discussed in the text of the report. The **terminal section** of an analytical report provides conclusions drawn from a logical analysis of the information and/or **recommendations** for appropriate action based on the conclusions. The terminal section of the report body includes only information that has been covered previously in the report, not new information.

For easier reading, number conclusions or recommendations when you have more than two. If your report includes personal opinions in the terminal section or anywhere else in the report, your opinions should be clearly identified as opinions; otherwise, you will lose credibility.

Supplementary Parts

Supplementary parts, sometimes called **back matter**, are the pages that follow the report body. The most common components are a *works cited* or *references* page and an *appendix*.

A **works cited** page lists *all* of the sources that were cited in the report. The page is positioned at the end of the report body and is titled according to the citation format you use.

Information that is presented in an **appendix** is helpful but not necessary to understand the report. Examples include lengthy visuals, technical data, and data collection instruments (survey forms and questionnaires). Reports often contain more than one appendix. Appendixes are listed in the table of contents in ascending order, beginning with *Appendix A*, and labeled with a descriptive title. Refer to an individual appendix at its point of discussion in the report body.

Other supplementary parts include a glossary and an index. A **glossary** alphabetically lists and defines select terms found in the report, especially those terms that may be unfamiliar to your audience. An **index** is an alphabetical listing of all major topics and subtopics in the report.

Report-Writing Mechanics

Formatting instructions vary among report-writing references, and many organizations have their own requirements. General format information is presented here. When you need information for unusual situations, consult a comprehensive report-writing reference.

Headings

Headings help receivers to shift from one thought to another and to recognize major and subordinate ideas. Heading styles vary. Style affects position, capitalization, bolding, underlining, and spacing. Some sources describe headings using the terms such as *Level 1, Level 2,* and so on. This text uses the terms *center, side,* and *paragraph* to describe headings.

Examples of heading format and spacing appear in Illustration 11-1, page 372. Regardless of the style you choose, these simple heading format principles contribute to the readability of your report:

- Each heading level (type) may be formatted differently; but the format within each level must be the same.
- Headings within each level must be grammatically parallel as shown in the following examples:

Examples:	Noun Headings	Accounts Receivable for April 20
		Accounts Payable for April 20
		Vendor List for the Midwest
	Phrase Headings	Installing GemStone
		Creating Data Files Using GemStone
		Preparing Reports With GemStone
	Independent Clause	Enter Employee IDs
	Headings	Complete Deduction Information
		Delete Employee Records

- Limiting headings to three or fewer levels, if possible, guides the receiver easily from one topic to the next *and* gives the report a "clean" appearance.
- Each heading in the text of the report body should be followed by at least two lines of text.

Spacing and Margins

Formal reports are most often double spaced with paragraph indentions. Some organizations may require single spacing (with double spacing between paragraphs) to conserve space and/or paper.

Unless you are instructed otherwise, vertically and horizontally center the information on the title page to create a pleasing effect. Prefatory parts (other than the transmittal message) and supplementary parts are usually double-spaced. Standard formal report margins are as follows:

- 2-inch top margin on the first page of each preliminary and supplementary part and on the first page of the report body
- 1-inch top margin on subsequent pages of the report body and on subsequent pages of each preliminary part and each supplementary part
- 1-inch side and 1-inch bottom margins for all pages (side margin requirements differ for top- and left-bound reports)

Reference Citations

When you use another person's material in a report, you use *reference citations* to identify that person as the originator. Otherwise, you are **plagiarizing** (using another's words or ideas as your own), which is unethical and unfair to the original writer. **Quoting** means stating the exact

Timely Tip

A double space (DS) is equivalent to one blank line. A quadruple space (QS) is equivalent to three blank lines.

Timely Tip

Follow company format instructions when they are provided.

Memorandum

January 15, 20—

To: Business Communication Students
From: Ben Chapman, Instructor
Subject: Heading Format and Spacing

Examples of heading levels are shown below:

CENTERED HEADINGS

The title of a report is written as a centered heading. The titles of report components (prefatory and supplementary, such as the parts listed in Table 11-1) also are written as centered headings. Format the title of a report or the title of report components as follows:

- Begin the heading two inches from the top of the page.
- Key the heading in all capital letters.
- Center and bold the heading.
- Follow the heading with one blank line before keying text.

In addition, centered headings identify major sections of the report body (introduction, text, and terminal section). Format titles that identify a section of the report body in this way:

- Precede the heading with one blank line.
- Key the headings in all capital letters (some references suggest capitalizing only the first letter of each important word).
- Center but do not bold the heading.
- Follow the heading with one blank line before keying text.

Side Heading

Side headings are used when the topic under a centered heading can be divided into two or more subtopics. Format side headings like this:

- Precede the side heading with one blank line.
- Capitalize the first letter of the first word and the first letter of each major word in the heading.
- Bold all the words, and align the heading at the left margin.
- Follow the side heading with one blank line before keying text.

Paragraph headings. Paragraph headings are used when the discussion under a side heading can be divided into two or more subdivisions. Format paragraph headings by following these guidelines:

- Precede the heading with one blank line.
- Capitalize the letter of the first word only, and bold all the words.
- Indent a paragraph heading on the same line as the text, and follow the heading with a period.

Illustration 11-1 **Heading Format and Spacing**

words of someone else; **paraphrasing** is restating someone else's words in your own words. Both quoting and paraphrasing require reference citations. You must indicate in your report that you quoted or paraphrased material. Sources are documented as parenthetical citations within the report body and a listing of *all* the sources you quoted and consulted to develop the report are listed on a works cited page.

The Source Format Guidelines in the Reference Guide show example entries for both the Modern Language Association (MLA) and the American Psychological Association (APA). In addition to paper MLA and APA manuals, their respective URLs are http://www.mla.org and http://www.apa.org.

Parenthetical Citations

Parenthetical citations, sometimes called **internal citations**, appear in the report body and provide just enough information to locate the appropriate source in the comprehensive list. The citation is enclosed in parentheses and immediately follows quoted or paraphrased material. The first example citation is in APA format; the second example is prepared in MLA format. In both formats, the citation is positioned *before* the period that ends the sentence.

Examples: Installation of a grab bar has resulted in a 28 percent reduction in injuries among children ages 5 to 10 and among adults ages 70 to 85 (Frankowicz, 2004, p. 4).

                  Installation of a grab bar has resulted in a 28 percent reduction in injuries among children ages 5 to 10 and among adults ages 70 to 85 (Frankowicz, p. 4).

Works Cited or Reference Page

Details about the sources consulted and cited in the report are listed alphabetically on a separate page. The documentation format differs between MLA and APA. The Modern Language Association refers to the listing as *Works Cited*; the American Psychological Association titles the page *References*.

Pagination

Formal reports use a combination of small Roman numerals and Arabic numerals. Prefatory parts are numbered with small Roman numerals, such as ii, iii, and iv. The report body and the supplementary parts are numbered with Arabic numerals, such as 1, 2, and 3. Page numbers are usually centered at the bottom of the page or flush right at the top of the page. The transmittal message is neither numbered nor counted.

Illustration 11-2 shows select pages of an analytical formal report. The sources are documented in the MLA style on a *Works Cited* page.

QS

56 Pine Creek Road
Florence, IN 47020
October 28, 20—

QS

Ms. Joyce Whittier, Chairperson
Florence City Council
City Hall
100 State Street
Florence, IN 47020-1236

DS

Dear Ms. Whittier

DS

Acknowledges authorization and provides background information

The report that was authorized by the Florence City Council regarding the establishment of a curbside recycling program in this city is enclosed. The mayor and the Florence City Council requested that a committee of citizens be formed to study the potential for curbside recycling in our city. That committee included city residents and representatives from Florence Community College, including me. Our committee met for more than a year to learn about curbside recycling and to study programs in cities similar to Florence.

DS

Recaps report content

This report presents the benefits and costs of recycling, a description of curbside recycling programs in nearby Centerburg and other small cities, a summary of the current market for recycled items, and general guidelines for setting up a curbside program in Florence. Our committee has concluded that a curbside recycling program can quickly pay for itself. This kind of program protects our environment by reducing the amount of waste sent to our landfill, thus reducing the need to process new raw materials.

DS

Offers assistance

Our committee is ready to assist the Florence City Council in any way that we can.

DS

Sincerely

QS

Joseph Stevens

Joseph Stevens
Environmental Management Student

DS

Enclosure: Report

Omits page number

Select Page From a Formal Report—Transmittal Message

---

*equal top and bottom margins
vertically and horizontally centered lines*

Report title

ESTABLISHING A CURBSIDE

COMMUNITY RECYCLING PROGRAM

IN FLORENCE, INDIANA

QS or more

Report receiver

Prepared for:
Joyce Whittier, Chairperson
Florence City Council

QS or more

Report writer

Prepared by:
Joseph Stevens
Environmental Management Student

QS or more

Date submitted

October 29, 20—

Illustration 11-2 **Select Page From a Formal Report—Title Page**

Table of Contents page

2" top margin

1" side margins

1" minimum bottom margin

TABLE OF CONTENTS

DS

Preliminary parts:

ii

Abstract page

2" top margin

1" side margins

1" minimum bottom margin

ABSTRACT

DS

The Florence landfill will be full by 2015 if our current rate of solid waste disposal continues. Building a new landfill will be costly. The citizens of Florence need a simple and practical way to recycle more of their waste so that our current landfill does not fill so quickly. The recycling program must not add to the tax burden of Florence residents.

The United States and Indiana offices of the Environmental Protection Agency (EPA) provided statistics and other information for this proposal. The staff at the Municipal Solid Waste Disposal Facility also aided in gathering data and making projections. In addition, the Centerburg City Council provided information about the history, implementation, and effectiveness of that city's curbside recycling program.

Neighboring community recycling programs have been well received and supported by their residents. Recycled materials are sold to manufacturers for reprocessing, resulting in a small but growing profit. During the first year of its recycling program, Centerburg reduced the amount of solid waste being deposited in its landfill by 23 percent.

The Florence City Council should approve a nine-month pilot curbside recycling program. After nine months, the results should be evaluated. If indicated, the program can then be expanded to more residents.

States problem (focus of report)

Indicates sources of information

Provides brief overview of findings

Makes recommendations

iii

Illustration 11-2 **Select Page From a Formal Report—Table of Contents**

Select Page From a Formal Report—Abstract

2" top margin

1" side margins

1" minimum bottom margin

INTRODUCTION
DS

Joyce Whittier, chairperson of the Florence City Council, authorized this committee to prepare a report of the feasibility of establishing a pilot curbside recycling program in Florence.

Includes authorization, purpose, background, problem, research sources, scope, and order of presentation.

Each person in the United States generates nearly 5 pounds of solid waste every day. The recycling and composting rate is only about 1.25 pounds per person per day. The remaining 3.75 pounds of solid waste goes to landfills (Environmental Protection Agency, *Municipal*, 3). The Florence landfill, like others nationwide, is nearing its capacity. At the current fill rate, the Municipal Solid Waste Disposal Facility staff expects the landfill to be at capacity by 2015. At that time, Florence will need to have another landfill ready to receive solid waste.

Shows parenthetical citation with shortened version of long publication title. Includes one title word to distinguish brochure title from other EPA works.

Currently, limited recycling options are available to city residents. This report discusses the need for recycling, the costs involved, and potential markets for selling recycled materials. The report also describes a recycling program in Centerburg that meets needs similar to ours. The report ends with recommendations for establishing a curbside recycling program in Florence.

Although more study is necessary to determine the exact costs and savings of recycling, this report represents a first step in delaying the expensive task of building another landfill for our community.

The information in this proposal was gathered from material prepared by the Environmental Protection Agency (EPA). The committee also interviewed staff at the solid waste facilities in Florence and Centerburg as well as the committee members who are involved with the Centerburg recycling program. The Centerburg City Council generously provided considerable information about its program.

1

Select Page From a Formal Report—Introduction

1" top margin

1" minimum bottom margin

DS
CONCLUSIONS AND RECOMMENDATIONS
DS

A recycling program, such as the one being implemented in nearby Centerburg, would benefit Florence by reducing the amount of waste being dumped in our landfill and by selling materials for reuse. The program should be profitable by the end of the first year.

Ends with conclusions and recommendations, which follows text. Does not have to appear as a seperate page.

Therefore, our committee recommends that Florence institute a pilot program in the 400-home Annehurst neighborhood beginning in July 20—. In April 20—, the City Council and this committee can evaluate the results and decide whether to expand, modify, or disband the program.

The committee recommends the following actions to ensure a smooth transition into a curbside recycling program.

Numbers recommendations for easy reading.

1. Hire a manager to organize and implement the program.
2. Locate or lease a suitable area for sorting the recycled materials.
3. Contact purchasers of recycled materials to begin establishing markets.
4. Hire additional staff to implement the program.
5. Meet with sanitation workers and supervisors to explain the procedure.
6. Conduct a public relations program to increase citizen participation in the program.

15

Select Page From a Formal Report—Terminal Section

Illustration 11-2 Select Page From a Formal Report

2" top margin

1" minimum bottom margin

WORKS CITED

DS

List sources cited in the report

Burkley, Amy. A Community Guide to Curbside Recycling. Chicago:

Burnside Press, 2003.

Peters, Frank, and Associates Comp., Centerville, Indiana, Five-Year

Curbside Recycling Plan and Program Tasks: 2003–2008. Indianapolis:

State of Indiana, 2003.

Scott, Vivian, Manager of the Florence Municipal Solid Waste Disposal

Facility. Personal interview. 22 July 2004.

Suter, Jeffrey. Citizen Participation in Recycling Waste. New York: Desktop

Press, 2003.

United States. Dept. of Energy. EREC Fact Sheets: Energy Efficiency

and Renewable Energy Network. 2004. Retrieved 8 August 2004

<http://www.eren.doe.gov/erec/factsheets/savenrgy.html>.

---. Environmental Protection Agency. EPA Environmental Fact Sheet:

Municipal Solid Waste Generation, Recycling and Disposal in the

United States, Facts and Figures for 2004. 2004. Retrieved 8 August

2004 <http://www.epa.gov/osw>.

---. Environmental Protection Agency. National Solid Waste Facts,

Figures, and Recycling Rates for 1998–2004. 2004. Retrieved 8 August

2004 <http://www.epa.gov/osw>.

17

2" top margin

1" minimum bottom margin

APPENDIX B

DS

FIRMS THAT PURCHASE RECYCLED MATERIALS

DS

Association of Aluminum Recyclers
1900 19th Street NW, Suite 1400
Washington, DC 20006
Phone: 202-555-0125
Fax: 202-555-0126

International Products Association
1001 Belleview Place, Suite 800
Washington, DC 20036
Phone: 202-555-0163

International Plastics, Ltd.
1801 Chesterwood Avenue North
Oxford, NY 13830-1301
Phone: 1-800-PLASTIC

Recycling Coalition
789 Highway JK, Building 7B
Alexandria, VA 22314-2720
Phone: 703-555-0199
Fax: 703-555-0189

Metal Institute of Recycling
1890A Barnard Road
Vandalia, OH 45377-2700
Phone: 937-555-0111

20

Checklist for Preparing a Formal Report

1. Does your formal report:

- Accomplish your objective?
- Identify the problem?
- Appeal to your target audience?
- Identify main points and include supporting information?
- Inform or analyze?
- Present the report body in an organizational pattern appropriate for the situation?

2. Does the draft of your formal report:

- Include the necessary preliminary and supplementary parts?
- Include an introduction, a text, and a terminal section?
- Use vocabulary and style appropriate for the receiver?
- Include descriptive headings?
- Include appropriate visuals to clarify and emphasize important points?
- Correctly document sources?

3. Does your final formal report:

- Incorporate the six *C*s of effective messages?
- Send the message you intend?
- Reflect ethics and credibility by providing adequate, objective information?
- Have a professional appearance?

Section 3: INFORMAL REPORTS

Informal reports communicate within an organization about routine or short-term situations. Like other business messages, informal reports are prepared by following the CBO approach and by incorporating the six *C*s of effective messages.

Informal reports, especially memorandums and letter reports, consist only of the report body: the *introduction*, the *text*, and the *terminal section*. The introduction orients the receiver to the report content, and the report text includes supporting information. The terminal section, depending on whether the report is informational or analytical, presents a summary or conclusions and/or recommendations. Most informal reports are written in personal language because the writer and the receiver often know each other. Headings may be used to divide content for easier reading.

Timely Tip

Companies may require specific formats to report certain kinds of information.

Informal reports are usually five or fewer pages; and they may be formatted as memorandums, letters, and standardized forms. Minutes of meetings also are included.

Memorandum Reports

A **memorandum report (memo)** is the message form used to distribute information within an organization. The Format Guide shows how to format a memorandum.

Illustration 11-3 on page 380 is a memorandum report. The report body is arranged in the direct pattern, so the terminal section appears first. The introductory material is combined into one sentence and follows the terminal section. A descriptive subject line introduces the receiver to the report topic.

Letter Reports

Letter reports are prepared on company letterhead, formatted as business letters, and distributed outside an organization. Letter reports are written in the direct or indirect pattern depending on the objective and content of the report. A subject line orients the receiver to the report content. Illustration 11-4, page 381, is an analytical letter report.

Standardized Forms

Many companies use standardized forms to submit routine reports. The forms may be paper or online forms. Standardized forms increase the likelihood that essential information will be provided by the user and that the information will be processed quickly and efficiently. Standardized forms are designed for efficiency. They usually allow limited space to identify the details about an activity. The travel expense report and the customer contact report in Illustrations 11-5 and 11-6, page 382, are two examples of standardized report forms.

Agenda

An agenda is a brief list of items for discussion or action by the people attending a meeting. Agendas provide details of the meeting structure and topics for discussion. An agenda is prepared by the person conducting the meeting. For some groups, such as government bodies or corporate boards, an agenda is a legal document and must follow a certain format. For less formal meetings, an agenda is a meeting plan that helps organize and limit the discussion. For an example of an agenda, see Illustration 11-7, page 383.

Minutes

Minutes are a chronological record of the discussion and important actions taken during a meeting. In formal meetings where decisions are made and responsibilities assigned, someone is often appointed to take minutes. As Illustration 11-8 on page 383 shows, the minutes followed the order set in the meeting agenda. Minutes include the information presented on page 384.

MEAL-IN-A-MINUTE RESTAURANTS

To: Doug Patterson, Restaurant Operator
From: Beth Gomez, Franchising Monitor
Date: May 13, 20—
Subject: Quarterly Review—Southfield Branch

Opens with the terminal section (direct pattern)

Your restaurant has met all four of the national franchising standards. However, opportunities exist to improve in the areas of quality, staff training, and finances.

Follows with the introduction

This memo summarizes my findings and our conversations during my visit to your restaurant on April 28.

Customer Satisfaction

You are doing very well in customer satisfaction. Your restaurant maintains an average score of 90 percent as measured by the national franchising standard. As you noted, your staff focuses on both speed and accuracy of service. The satisfied customers in your restaurant during my visit attest to your success in meeting the customer satisfaction standard.

Quality

Presents detailed findings

Your team continues to improve its grill procedures and assembly speed to ensure that each customer receives a hot, fresh meal. Nevertheless, the team needs to focus on the quality of products served to customers. In particular, more attention needs to be paid to the lettuce that goes on the sandwiches and into the salads. Continue to observe team members and direct them to discard any lettuce that is limp or brown around the edges.

Staffing

Your staff includes 5 members with formal training; the remaining 17 employees must attend formal training at regional headquarters. You mentioned high turnover as the reason for so many marginally trained employees. However, lack of early formal training may be a reason for high turnover. Consider implementing formal training procedures within the first ten days of employment. The national franchise standard requires that advanced training certificates be earned by 50 percent of your working staff.

Financial Status

The financial position of your restaurant is rated "stable" according to the national standard. Your franchise payments are current and sales exceed your expenses by a margin of 5 percent. The highway-widening project in front of your restaurant appears to be affecting business. The project will be completed in six weeks.

Provides a summary and conclusion.

Early formal training and completion of highway project should result in increased sales and the target 9 percent profit.

Illustration 11-3 **Informational Memorandum in Standard Memorandum Format (Direct Pattern)**

Illustration 11-4 Informal Report—Analytical Letter Report

NOISE CONSULTANTS OF CENTRAL NEW MEXICO
3050 LINWOOD AVENUE • LA JARA, NM 87027
505-555-0180 • FAX: 505-555-0170

October 23, 20—

Mr. Robert Charles, Mayor
La Jara City Hall
8355 Valdayo Freeway
La Jara, NM 87027

Dear Mr. Charles

RESULTS OF THE COMMUNITY NOISE SURVEY

[margin note: Orients receiver to report topic]

At your request, our staff conducted a community noise survey between May 1 and September 30, 20—. The objectives of the survey were to:

[margin note: Presents authorization, problem statement, scope, and limitations]

1. Determine the average noise levels in the areas covered by the La Jara noise control ordinances.
2. Evaluate the adequacy of the current noise ordinance in addressing complaints and in preventing an increase in noise levels.
3. Develop a "noise map" of the city.

We monitored 124 sites around the city to gather the necessary data, with a nearly equal balance of residential, commercial, and industrial settings. Each site was monitored six times, three times for 45 minutes during normal working hours and three times for 30 minutes during nighttime hours. We determined how often the noise at these locations exceeded the levels set by the noise control ordinance, which is 65 dB.

[margin note: Follows with summary of findings]

We also documented and charted formal complaints submitted to the city concerning noise levels at all of the sites that were included in this study. We did not consider complaints regarding sites outside the study. Our findings are listed below:

[margin note: Numbers findings for easier reading]

1. Noise levels at residential sites (averaging 40 dB) were consistently and considerably below the limit set by the ordinance. Despite this finding, the number of complaints was highest in these areas. The complaints suggest that the ordinance is set too high and allows annoying noise levels without permitting residents to take action against the noise source or sources.

2. In commercial areas, noise levels approaching the limit were not noticeable during the day but drew complaints from business owners during the evening hours. This finding suggests that a single daytime/nighttime standard may not be appropriate for business areas.

1" top margin

Mr. Robert Charles
Page 2
October 23, 20—

DS

3. The noise levels in industrial areas exceeded the ordinance limits at least 50 percent of the time during working hours. However, no complaints are on record for the industrial areas we monitored. The lack of complaints might suggest that the noise ordinance is set too low for these areas. Incidentally, we did observe that all workers in high-noise locations were wearing ear protection, as required by OSHA regulations.

[margin note: Concludes and recommends in the ending (indirect pattern)]

Based on this study, we strongly recommend that City Council revisit the noise ordinance. The ordinance needs to be modified for different areas of the city and, in some areas, set at different daytime and nighttime limits. Specifically,

[margin note: Bullets recommendations that correlate with numbered findings]

• The levels for residential areas need to be lowered to address annoying noise levels and reduce the number of complaints.

• The levels for commercial areas need to be lower, especially during evening hours, to prevent noise from interfering with the businesses, mainly restaurants that operate during that time and require a pleasant environment.

• The noise levels for industrial areas might be raised, after the city health department ensures that companies in these areas are following OSHA regulations to protect their employees' hearing.

Please call 505-555-0180 to discuss these recommendations in more detail.

Sincerely

Daniel Merkelli

Daniel Merkelli, Director

bl

Weekly Call Plan for HighTime Textbooks

Sales Representative _Marci Graves_   Date _10/21/20—_

Call codes: T = telephone   P = in person   E = e-mail

TIME	SCHOOL	CODE	PURPOSE	REMARKS
8:00A	Milford Elementary	P	sales literature	librarian preparing book order
8:30A				
9:00A	Heritage Middle	P	deliver order	discussed new series
9:30A	Mark Twain Elemen.	T	set appt.	Wednesday, 10/26, 2:00P
10:00A	Genoa Middle	E	explain delay	promised delivery on 10/31
10:30A	Fourth St. Elementary	T	set appt.	Wednesday, 10/26, 10:30A
11:00A	North High	P	present line	call back on 10/28
11:30A				
12 NOON				
12:30P				
1:00P	Convention Center	P	set up display	
1:30P				
2:00P				
2:30P	Regional sales meeting			
3:00P				
3:30P	Walnut Springs Middle	T	confirm appt.	ok for Thursday, 10/25,
9:15A				
4:00P	Macy Elementary	E	check on order	will be ready by 10/28
4:30P				

Illustration 11-6 **Standardized Customer Contact Report**

PERFORMANCE RECRUITMENT SPECIALISTS EXPENSE REPORT

NAME	PERIOD	DATE

EXPENSES (hotel, parking, airfare, cab, other)

DATE	EXPENSE	DESCRIPTION	AMOUNT	ACCT#

MEALS AND ENTERTAINMENT DETAILS

DATE	EXPENSE	PEOPLE/RELATIONSHIP	BUSINESS PURPOSE	AMOUNT	ACCT#

USE REVERSE SIDE FOR MILEAGE REIMBURSEMENT

TOTAL CASH AMOUNT _____

SIGNATURE _____

Illustration 11-5 **Standardized Expense Report**

Minutes of the Monthly Board Meeting
Ajax Manufacturing
April 13, 20—

Present: Christina Sanchez, Charles Hall, Velma Raines, Nicholas Mitchell, Ellen Rider, Ron Hanford

Absent: Christopher Boye

Board Chair Christina Sanchez called the meeting to order at 9:10 a.m. in the company conference room. The minutes of the March 12, 20—, meeting were read and approved.

Committee Reports

Human Services: Nicholas Mitchell noted that the company had contracted with a recruitment firm to fill the position of accounting manager. He stated that the firm expects to have at least two candidates to be interviewed within ten days.

Expansion Program: Ellen Rider reported that her committee is researching available parcels of land for the proposed plant. Several municipalities are offering tax and other incentives to locate within their boundaries. She will provide a detailed comparison of those at the next monthly meeting.

HMO Selection: Charles Hall stated that his committee has met with representatives from three HMOs. The committee asked all three organizations to respond to the list of questions developed at the last board meeting. Then the committee will present its findings and recommendations to the board, ideally at the June meeting.

Old Business: None

New Business: J. Kelly—Motion: To send Nai Tarmes to the regional OSHA conference on August 10. Motion passed 6–0.

The meeting was adjourned at 11:00 a.m. The date of the next board meeting is May 18, 20—, at 9 a.m. in the conference room.

Respectfully submitted,

Richard James

Richard James, Board Secretary

Illustration 11-8 **Minutes of Meeting**

Monthly Board Meeting
Ajax Manufacturing
Thursday, April 13, 20—

AGENDA

1. Call to order
2. Approval of minutes from the March 12, 20—, meeting
3. Report from the director
4. Committee reports:
   Human Services
   Expansion Program
   HMO Selection
5. Old business
6. New business
   Appointment of a representative to the OSHA regional meeting
7. Adjournment

Illustration 11-7 **Meeting Agenda**

- Name of the group holding the meeting
- Meeting time, date, and location
- Names of people present and absent
- Status of previous minutes
- Exact wording of any motion, who proposed the motion, and the outcome of the motion
- Discussion of old business, new business, committee reports, and other pertinent announcements
- Adjournment remarks
- Name and signature of the person documenting the minutes

CHECKLIST

Checklist for Preparing an Informal Report

1. **Does your informal report:**
   - Accomplish the objective?
   - Identify the problem?
   - Appeal to your target audience?
   - Identify main points and include supporting information?
   - Inform or analyze?
   - Present the report body in an organizational pattern appropriate for the situation?

2. **Does the draft of your informal report:**
   - Contain an introduction, a text, and a terminal section?
   - Use vocabulary and style that are appropriate for the receiver?
   - Appear in a format suitable for the topic and the audience?
   - Include descriptive headings as necessary?
   - Include appropriate visuals that clarify and emphasize important points if appropriate?
   - Correctly document sources, if necessary?

3. **Does your final informal report:**
   - Incorporate the six *C*s of effective messages?
   - Send the message you intend?
   - Reflect ethics and credibility by providing adequate, objective information?
   - Have a professional appearance?

A **proposal** is prepared to persuade the recipient(s) to take a course of action, whether that action is to buy a product or service or to make a change or improvement. The persuasive techniques presented in Chapter 7, Persuasive Messages, are applicable to writing proposals because proposals are persuasive messages. Also, proposals and reports share similar characteristics. In fact, proposals are persuasive reports!

Audience

Proposals are prepared for an internal receiver or an external receiver. When you see a reason for a change or improvement inside the company or when you seek consideration for a project that you want to undertake, you will prepare an *internal proposal*. The proposal is aimed at someone who is able to make a decision to act on your proposal.

When your goal is to sell your company's product or service, you prepare an *external proposal*. Sales proposals are marketing tools by which companies gain business. The purpose, of course, is to show that your product or service will provide tangible benefits to the receiver. Many companies and government and educational agencies issue a *request for proposals* (RFP) to seek bids for upcoming projects. The RFP lists the requirements of the project. Bidders respond to specific criteria in the RFP, so the issuing company is able to compare submitted proposals efficiently and objectively.

Format

A proposal is either a formal document or an informal document. Formality is determined by the complexity of the proposal, the target audience, and company requirements. Informal proposals are usually five to six pages and are presented as letters (external distribution) or memos (internal distribution). Formal proposals cover lengthy, complex situations and are formatted like formal reports. You use as many of the report parts and components as are appropriate for your topic and coverage.

Preparing a Proposal

You plan, draft, and complete a proposal in the same way as you plan, draft, and complete a report: Apply the CBO approach and incorporate the six Cs of effective messages. Follow the same planning steps presented in Plan a Report on pages 364–366. Determine the objective, visualize your audience, gather supporting information, and organize the information. You also add elements of the persuasive strategy AIDA (attention, interest, desire, action).

Culture Frame

Education is highly regarded in France; therefore, academic credentials (especially credentials from a prestigious university) should be included on a business card.

Because the objective of the proposal is to persuade a receiver to act on what you propose, you must present receiver benefits as well as logical plans to accomplish the task. Implementing all the steps of the CBO approach is especially important because you want the receiver to do something that the receiver may perceive as costly, time-consuming, or inconvenient.

Content

Although the length of each section varies depending on the information included, all proposals contain an *introduction*, a *text*, and a *conclusion/recommendation*. Formal proposals generally include preliminary and supplementary parts.

The **introduction** includes the purpose and scope of the proposal. The introduction is where you state the problem (situation) that you propose to solve along with the proposed solution. You may include your qualifications for sales proposals.

The **text** presents the details. When you prepare a sales proposal you discuss the products or services that can solve the problem. When you seek assistance to launch a project or you indicate the need for an improvement within a company, you provide the details that support your objective. Present key points that directly relate to your objective, and stay focused. Courteously and concisely present facts and examples that support your appeal and lead to the conclusion.

Explain the background leading to the proposal. Discuss how the task will be accomplished, staffing and material requirements, anticipated costs, and approximate completion schedule.

The **conclusion** reiterates the benefits and value of responding favorably. Maintain a positive and confident tone when you request the action that you want the receiver to take.

Illustration 11-9, page 387, is an informal proposal prepared as a memorandum.

Timely Tip

Prepare ethical proposals. Do not make false claims or exaggerate outcomes.

Illustration 11-9 **Informal Proposal**

BAYFRONT PUBLISHING
INTEROFFICE MEMORANDUM

To: Caroline Brentnell
From: Charles Hall
Date: September 6, 20—
Subject: Telecommuting Opportunities

Introduces a clear, brief statement of the problem; offers a proposed solution

To meet the needs of our growing company, we plan to hire four more salespeople, another programmer, and three more support staff. However, creating more offices by dividing our limited floor space into smaller cubicles is likely to decrease morale and increase friction. No other areas of our building or nearby buildings are available for lease.

Instead of overcrowding our office space, I suggest that we investigate telecommuting opportunities for both full-time and part-time employees.

Benefits

Supports proposed solution with facts and examples

Telecommuting offers the advantages of increased productivity, reduced turnover, scheduling flexibility, and employee benefits.

Increased productivity. Studies show a 15 to 30 percent increase in productivity for staff working from home for these reasons: Travel time is reduced or eliminated, and bad weather is no longer a travel influence. Employees are more likely to continue working with minor illnesses, such as colds, rather than to take a sick day. In addition, staff with disabilities also can function more easily by eliminating commuting hassles.

Reduced turnover. Studies also indicate an average 20 percent reduction in employee turnover. Turnover is reduced because full-time telecommuters can stay on the job even when a spouse's job change requires a location change. Bayfront would reduce hiring and training costs and would benefit from retaining experienced, skilled staff.

Scheduling flexibility. Some employees have indicated a willingness to work during peak periods and to work a reduced or stand-by schedule during slow periods.

Employee benefits. Telecommuting offers commuting relief, opportunities for flexible work hours, and the opportunity to balance work and family needs.

Caroline Brentnell
Page 2
September 6, 20—

Costs

Includes a general reference to costs with mention of attached details

The costs associated with telecommuting will depend on which employees are permitted to take advantage of this opportunity. Some IT staff, for example, may not be able to telecommute because of the equipment required to perform their tasks. The nature of other jobs also may require employees to be on site. However, our sales reps already have laptops that can be connected to our system for a modest cost. Other employees may be able to perform their jobs at home but may require computer hookups. General equipment cost projections are attached to this memorandum.

Recommendation

Makes suggestion for next step in the process

I suggest that a staff-management committee be appointed to identify positions suitable for telecommuting, to conduct an interest survey, and to determine telecommuting criteria and projected costs. Telecommuting affects all employees. Therefore, participation in the committee by both management and staff members is necessary to achieve a strong commitment.

Emphasizes benefits and requests meeting

Based on my initial investigation, I believe telecommuting will enable us to enlarge our staff, increase our productivity, boost employee morale, and maintain a positive physical plant. I would like to meet with you within the next two weeks to answer any questions and discuss the details of this proposal, including the attached survey and cost projection data.

Attachments

Checklist for Preparing a Proposal

1. Does your proposal:

- Accomplish your objective?
- Identify the problem?
- Appeal to your target audience?
- Identify main points and include supporting information?
- Provide a solution?
- Present the proposal body in an organizational pattern appropriate for the situation?

2. Does the draft of your proposal:

- Appear in a format most effective for the audience?
- Include an introduction, a text, and a terminal section?
- Use vocabulary and style appropriate for the receiver?
- Include descriptive headings, if necessary?
- Include appropriate visuals to clarify and emphasize important points?
- Correctly document sources?

3. Does your final proposal:

- Incorporate the six Cs of effective messages?
- Send the message you intend?
- Reflect ethics and credibility by providing adequate, objective information?
- Have a professional appearance?

Section 5: **INSTRUCTIONS**

Timely Tip

Well-written instructions create goodwill. Poorly written instructions create ill will.

Instructions tell, and often show, a receiver how to accomplish a task. Instructions may be spoken or written; and written instructions may be formal, such as equipment assembly instructions, or informal, such as brief directions to a meeting site. Whether written or spoken, formal or informal, effective instructions save time and/or money, promote safety, or increase productivity. Effective instructions enable the receiver to complete a task successfully. Because instructions must be clear, complete, and easily understood, the CBO approach and the six Cs of effective messages are invaluable when composing instructions.

Content

Instruction length and format depend on the difficulty of the task. Some instructions are short and simple. Traffic signs are examples of one-word instructions. *Do Not Enter* is another example of a short, simple instruction.

The more complicated the task or procedure, the greater the need for detailed instructions.

Remember your target audience when you plan and develop instructions. Unless you know otherwise, assume that a receiver has not performed a particular task or has not performed the task often. Use vocabulary that is readable by a majority of your intended audience.

Evaluate the situation carefully, and anticipate possible receiver questions. Address those questions as you write the instructions because someone will not always be available to provide clarification as the receiver completes the task. Accurate instructions eliminate the need for a receiver to call you (or the company hotline) for clarification.

Instructions consist of an introduction, a list of supplies (when necessary), and the instructional steps.

Introduction

The introduction tells the receiver why the instructions were written. For simple tasks, the title of the instructions may serve as the introduction, such as "How to Replace Toner for the Apex Printer." When applicable, the introduction includes an approximate completion time or any warnings that receivers should consider *before* beginning the instructional steps. When instructions include unfamiliar terms, you may provide definitions. You might also present an overview of a complicated procedure before presenting the detailed steps.

List of Supplies

A list of supplies tells what is needed to complete the task. Not all tasks require supplies. When supplies are needed, confirm that the list is complete. List specific quantities and sizes, and organize the supplies in the order that they will be used.

Instructional Steps

The instructional steps explain how and in what order to complete the task. One technique to ensure that you include the necessary steps and appropriate details is to (1) prepare a draft of the steps; (2) record (or have someone else record) the process of each step as you complete the step; and (3) perform the procedure several times to verify that the steps are complete, correctly sequenced, and easy to follow.

Apply these guidelines when preparing instructions:
- Know your topic.
- Use short, imperative sentences and action verbs.
- Present exact measurements, distances, and times to avoid reader misinterpretation.
- Present instructional steps in a list or paragraph.
- Organize and label each step. Use numbers when steps must be performed in a specific sequence. Bullets, other identifying marks, and separate paragraphs may be used to signify each step.

- Number only actions the reader should perform.
- Break a major step into substeps if necessary.
- Group short, closely related activities into one step; and use transitional words to show relationships.
- In a long set of instructions, group related steps under descriptive headings.
- Include cautions or warnings whenever safety is at risk. Identify caution statements with all capital letters or bold colors.
- Use visuals to simplify or clarify your written description. Position each visual near the point of discussion.
- If appropriate, tell readers where to find additional tips to help them complete the task.

Notice the use of imperative sentences as shown in the following examples and in Illustration 11-10 on page 391.

Examples: Bake at 350 degrees.

Use the red "out" card to replace each file removed from the shelf.

CAUTION: Harmful if swallowed. Wash hands thoroughly after handling.

Boil 6 cups water. Add noodles. Boil 7 to 10 minutes, stirring occasionally. Drain noodles thoroughly.

CHECKLIST

Checklist for Preparing Instructions

1. Do your instructions:
- Accomplish their objective?
- Identify the desired result?
- Consider your target audience?

2. Does the draft of your instructions:
- Contain an introduction, a list of supplies, and the instructional steps?
- Present steps in correct sequence?
- Identify steps with numbers, marks, or paragraphs?
- Use imperative sentences, action verbs, and transitional words or phrases?
- Include specific information to avoid reader misinterpretation?
- Use clarifying visuals close to related steps when helpful?

3. Do your final instructions:
- Incorporate the six Cs of an effective message?
- Send the message you intend?
- Have a professional appearance that is easy to follow?

Printing a Greeting Card

After you have chosen and personalized your card, you are ready to print. Heavy paper (at least 65 pounds) works best for printed cards. Start at the Card Preparation screen, and select Print. The screen below will appear.

1. **Select a printer.**

   ❒ HP DeskJet 895 Series

   ❒ Generic/Text Only (TTY) on LPT1

2. **Select a print source.**

   ❒ Automatic sheet feeder

   ❒ Manual feed

3. **Select a paper size.**

   ❒ Letter (8½ x 11 in)

   ❒ Legal (8½ x 14 in)

   ❒ Executive (7¼ x 10½ in)

4. **Change printer setup.** (optional) [ ]

5. **Select a print format.**

   ❒ Single fold (1 page)

   ❒ Single fold (2 pages)

   ❒ Quarter fold

6. **Select the number of copies.** [1]

7. **Print!** [ ]

1. Select your printer. If your printer is not listed as an option, see page 44.

2. Select how the paper is fed into the printer. For very heavy paper (more than 65 lb), you may need to use manual feed.

3. Choose the paper size.

4. If necessary, change the printer setup. For example, if your printer is set to print in "grayscale," you will need to change the printer Properties setting to "color."

5. Check the print format. A single-fold card with one or two pages will measure 5½" x 8½". A quarter-fold card will measure 4¼" x 5½". You can choose either size.

6. Mark the number of copies you want to make.

7. If you are satisfied with your settings, click Print.

   A single-fold card will have printing on both sides of the paper. After printing one side, the screen will tell you when to reinsert the paper and print the other side.

Illustration 11-10 **Instructional List**

Summary

The CBO approach and the six *C*s of effective messages are essential to producing successful reports, proposals, and instructions.

A report is a planned, organized, factual presentation of information prepared for a specific purpose and for a specific audience. Internal reports move information upward, downward, or horizontally within a company. External reports inform clients, stockholders, government agencies, and the general public about company activities.

Reports are formal or informal. Formal reports cover complex situations, include report parts and components, and are typically written in formal language. Informal reports cover routine situations, have fewer parts, and typically are written in informal language. Variations of informal reports are memorandums, letters, standardized forms, and minutes of meetings.

Reports are considered informational or analytical. Informational reports present facts but do not include an analysis or recommendations. Analytical reports provide facts, an analysis, and conclusions and/or recommendations. Report information is gathered from primary and/or secondary sources and organized into an outline.

Proposals are persuasive reports. Proposals are prepared for internal and external use to persuade recipients to take action. External proposals are marketing tools to gain business. Proposals identify a problem to be solved, propose a solution to the problem, include background information, explain how the task will be accomplished, list staff and materials, indicate how much the costs will be, and give an approximate time of completion.

Instructions tell and/or show how to complete a task. Instructions are prepared so that users save time or money, complete a task safely, or increase productivity. Instructions include the introduction, a list of supplies if necessary, and the instructional steps. The length and format of instructions depend on the complexity of the task. Visuals may be added for clarification. The needs of the audience must be considered throughout the instructional writing process.

Complete Communication Skills Development 11, pages 407–408. For additional number review, see the Reference Guide, pages 443–444.

Exercises

11-1

Directions: Consider this statement: *Reports tend to become shorter and less detailed as they travel upward in the organizational structure.* Respond to this statement in a format assigned by your instructor. Do you believe the statement is accurate? Why or why not? Consider why reports are prepared from employees to management. Include your responsibilities as a communicator when your audience is your supervisor or other upper-level management personnel. Explain how you would determine what kind of information should be included in reports that are distributed vertically.

11-2

Directions: Locate URLs for reference sources that will be helpful in conducting research. The Web Site Evaluation Criteria, page 107, will help you determine the reliability of the URLs. Record the complete address for sources that you determine to be helpful. At a minimum, you must include <u>one</u> URL for each of the following sources:

Online library catalog
General encyclopedia
Specialty (subject) encyclopedia that reflects your career area
Dictionary
Thesaurus
Atlas
Statistical source

11-3

Directions: Find the homepage for a public library. Prepare a one-page summary in a format assigned by your instructor to explain the services offered by the library, related links, and other helpful information that you observed. Include comments about visual appeal and ease of use.

Exercises

11-4

Directions: You are assigned the following situations to investigate. Consider the topics and choose your sources of information. Explain whether primary, secondary, or a combination of the sources yield the most useful information.

a. Investigating customer satisfaction from the service department of an automobile dealer

b. Preparing questions that human resource personnel should *not* ask potential employees

c. Choosing an employment agency through which to hire temporary employees

d. Determining the efficiency of registering patients for outpatient surgeries

e. Learning about the advantages and disadvantages of employees working from home (telecommuting)

Exercises

11-5   **Directions:** Rewrite the following sentences to change the sentences from informal language to formal language. Observe the six *C*s of effective messages when composing your sentences.

1. You may find yourself in a lawsuit if a report that you write has factual errors.

2. You know that the major difference between periodic and progress reports is how often you prepare them.

3. You can use the direct pattern to organize your report body when your reader prefers to read the main idea at the beginning of a report or when your company prefers that organizational pattern.

4. You will find useful information in secondary sources, such as magazines and brochures and on the Internet.

5. Begin researching information at your library because libraries have extensive print and electronic resources.

Exercises

11-6   **Directions:** Rewrite the following sentences to change the sentences from formal language to informal language. Observe the six *C*s of effective messages when composing your sentences.

1. When illustrations are included in a report, the report must provide a clear explanation for each illustration; and the report must show that the illustration is important to the discussion.

2. Headings help writers organize the information in a report, but writers must use the same format for headings at the same level.

3. Some reports may be sent to clients outside the United States; therefore, words should be chosen carefully to avoid misinterpretation.

4. Conclusions and/or recommendations are included in an analytical report, but a summary is provided only in an informational report.

Exercises

11-7

Directions: Write the following information as headings in the grammatical form indicated in the left column. Confirm that headings are grammatically parallel.

Part A

Heading Information
doing searches for subjects on the Internet
the library as a place to find information
dictionaries that are online

Independent Clauses:

Phrases:

Nouns:

Part B

Heading Information
looking up information about a potential employer
finding job openings
how to complete online applications

Independent Clauses

Phrases:

Nouns:

Exercises

11-8   **Directions:** Choose a current topic in your career area, a topic from the following list, or a topic of your choice (with instructor approval). Brainstorm ideas about the topic; then locate and read a minimum of six articles that relate to the topic. At least three of the sources must be online sources. Note important information in the articles, and record the complete source information. You will use the information to prepare a report for Case Study 11-2.

> **Potential Topics:**   Background checks for job applicants
> Writing reports for an international audience
> Age discrimination in the workplace
> Bioethical issues, such as cloning, tissue transplants
> Advantages and disadvantages of online courses

11-9   **Directions:** Request a standardized form from an organization. Study the form, and label the areas that answer *how, who, what, when, where,* and *why.* If the form can be improved, indicate the improvements you would make. Be prepared to show and discuss your form in class.

11-10   **Directions:** Choose a set of instructions that does not exceed two pages. Preferably you will have tried the instructions. Evaluate the instructions according to the following criteria:

> Adequate introductory material
> Complete supply list
> Logical sequence of steps
> Clarity of steps (adequate detail, appropriate vocabulary for intended audience)
> Caution statements, if necessary
> Quality of visuals to enhance or clarify
> Incorporation of the six *C*s of effective messages.

Internet *Challenge*

11-1 Directions: Search online for a minimum of two articles on plagiarism, especially articles that appear appropriate for your situation as a student. Record helpful URLs. Summarize your findings in a format assigned by your instructor. Your summary should include the URLs, a definition of plagiarism, consequences of plagiarizing, and when you should cite material.

11-2 Directions: Your firm has recently purchased a firm in Bordeaux, France. You and three others will be living and working in Bordeaux for six months (January through June). Search online for information that will help you develop a positive business relationship with your French counterparts. Include helpful web addresses. Pertinent topics may include business manners, appropriate business and social dress, and business lunches. Prepare the information as an *informational* memorandum for quick and easy reading.

InfoTrac

Directions: Using the InfoTrac keyword search, find an article about report writing. Read the article for key points. Prepare a report-writing tip list as a handout, overhead transparency, or computer slide presentation as directed by your instructor. Be prepared to deliver this information to the class.

WebTUTOR *Advantage*

Directions: Access your WebTutor Advantage product. Complete the short-answer portion for Chapter 11, and send the answers to your instructor.

Case Studies

11-1

Communication Situation: Your instructor has authorized you to prepare an *analytical* formal report, which will be shared with future classes. The report will cover employment opportunities within the company that you investigated in Exercise 8-6. Information that you gathered in other Chapter 8 exercises may be helpful as well as the salary information that you gathered for Exercise 9-2. Your report will include:

Company history (background, location, size, and market; stock information if available); description of products and/or services

Description of work environment, if available

Job titles for which you qualify (hiring requirements and job duties for each position)

Possible career path

General salary range

Other helpful job-related information

Include your conclusions and/or recommendations about the company as a potential place of employment.

Part A

Task: Apply the CBO approach to plan and develop this analytical report. Gather the necessary information to make the report complete.

Step 1: Determine the Objective
State the objective of the message.

Step 2: Visualize the Audience
Consider the following criteria, and list information to help you visualize your audience.

- Age:

- Profession:

- Education:

Case Studies

Step 3: List Supporting Information
Gather relevant information.

Step 4: Prepare an Outline
Identify the pattern of organization you will use for this message. In the following space, organize the information in an outline.

Case Studies

Part B

Task: Apply the CBO approach to plan, develop, and prepare this *analytical* formal report. Write the report in formal language. Direct the report to your instructor. Include a *title page*, *transmittal memo*, *table of contents*, and *report body*. Use either the MLA or the APA style for parenthetical citations and include a *works cited* or *references* page. Include an appendix if necessary. Provide a *conclusion* about the company as a potential employer and a *recommendation* about whether students should apply for positions. The final report should reflect the six *C*s of effective messages and acceptable formal report format.

11-2

Communication Situation: Your instructor has authorized you to prepare a formal report based on the articles you read and the URLs you recorded in Exercise 11-8. The report must include at least one visual.

Task: Apply the CBO approach to plan, develop, and prepare this *informational* formal report. Gather additional information from other sources, such as informational interviews, if necessary. Write this report in *formal language,* and direct the report to your instructor. Include a *title page*, *transmittal letter*, *table of contents*, and *report body* with headings. Use either the MLA or the APA style for parenthetical citations and include a *works cited* or *reference* page. An appendix is optional. Because this report is informational, include only a *summary*. The final report should reflect the six *C*s of effective messages and acceptable formal report format.

Case Studies

11-3

Communication Situation: You are responsible for locating a field trip site relevant to a class in which you are enrolled. After investigating a few sites, you are ready to make your recommendation.

Task: Apply the CBO approach to plan, develop, and prepare an *analytical* informal report for your instructor. Write the report in informal language. The memorandum report should include the location; tour hours; key benefits of visiting the site, such as advanced technology, reputation of company; and job availability. Add other details to make this message complete. Gather information by visiting the site, telephoning or e-mailing for information, using the Internet, reading company publications, or using other suitable information-gathering techniques. Provide a *conclusion* about the desirability of the site. The report should reflect the six Cs of effective messages and an acceptable memorandum format.

Case Studies

11-4

Communication Situation: As president of the organization that represents your career area, you are preparing a brief report on the key points of conducting a meeting. This report will be distributed to committee chairs to help them hold productive meetings.

Task: Use both online and print sources to find information about conducting meetings. Plan, develop, and prepare an *informational* memorandum to distribute to the head of each committee. Include key points for conducting successful meetings. You may summarize main points from Robert's Rules of Order and from other sources that provide relevant information. Use headings if appropriate. Your report should reflect the six Cs of effective messages and acceptable message format.

11-5

Communication Situation: Your instructor has assigned an informal research project investigating topics of interest to the general public. After your investigation, you will prepare an informal report in a format assigned by your instructor.

Task: Visit http://www.findlaw.com/. Choose a topic from Public and Consumer Resources. Link to a minimum of four sources for information. Use the information to prepare an *informational* report for your classmates. Arrange information in the indirect pattern. Use headings if appropriate.

Case Studies

11-6

Communication Situation: As the marketing manager for a small business, you believe that your company should purchase cell phones and service for five key employees. Your company is on a tight budget, so cost is a concern. You need to compare the features and prices of three cell phone services.

Task: Apply the CBO approach to plan, develop, and prepare a proposal for the company president and chief financial officer to recommend a cell phone package. Use the direct organizational pattern, informal language, and memorandum format. Sources of information include vendor web sites, consumer reports, store personnel, and interviews with current users.

Features and services that you must investigate are nationwide long distance, text messaging, voice activation, and available free time. Provide details about other features that you believe are important. Comment on the helpfulness of the personnel and/or web site. Include prices for equipment that will accommodate company needs and prices for various packages. Prepare a table to include in the proposal. Arrange the information in the table so the reader can easily compare the package features and phone and price information. Your proposal should reflect the six *C*s of effective messages and acceptable message format.

Case Studies

11-7

Communication Situation: You are responsible for preparing a one- to two-page set of instructions for your classmates. Suggestions include accomplishing a class-related task, registering for classes, traveling to a particular destination, applying for financial aid, or some other relevant task.

Task: Apply the CBO approach to plan your instructions. Include a visual to clarify the instructions, if appropriate. Your final instructions should reflect the six *C*s of effective messages and be prepared in an easy-to-follow format.

Part A   Number Usage

Directions: Rewrite each sentence correcting any number usage errors.

1. Our company now has three managers, twelve associates, and 18 field representatives.

2. 23 employees have chosen early retirement.

3. I believe a 3/4 vote is needed to pass the amendment.

4. I made 3 8-minute presentations at the recent telecommunication conference.

5. He captured 875 thousand votes, which was less than thirty percent of the eligible 3 million voters.

6. Her last-minute effort resulted in more than five thousand dollars in donations.

7. Can you meet on the 14 at two o'clock in the afternoon?

8. The carton weighed at least twenty five pounds and contained ten reams (five hundred sheets in a ream) of various colors.

9. The company's stock opened this morning at $41.13, but the stock closed down 96 cents.

10. Mattie noticed that accounts receivables dropped four to five percent last month.

Part B   Skills Application

Directions: In the following memorandum, underline the errors in spelling, grammar and sentence structure, punctuation, capitalization, and numbers. Write the corrections in the space above the errors. (Ordinarily, memos are single-spaced. In this memo, extra space has been added for you to insert corrections.)

September 12, 20—

TO: April Stevens
FROM: June Campbell
DATE: September 12, 20—
SUBJECT: Your Trip to Paris

You're trip to Paris is coming up quick, so I want to share some of

this Paris facts. The city, located on the banks of the seine river,

about ninety miles from the English channel, have a approximate

population of two million; the metropolitan population is

approximately eleven million.

      Paris is an enchanting city—a cultural and intellectual center

that has fascinated writers poets, and artists for 100s of years. Paris

is sometimes called the city of light, which is a tribute to it's beauty.

      You will be able to move around Paris easy because the

transportation system is extensive and convenint. The Paris metro

which was built in 1,900 and modernized in the nineteen seventies,

has sixteen principle metro lines and a high speed express subway

system servicing the suburbs.

Reference Guide

Effective Communication for Colleges

The Reference Guide supplements the information in the text and in the illustrations of this book. However, the Reference Guide is not a complete guide to grammar, punctuation, mechanics, or source format guidelines. Consult a variety of reference sources when you have questions that are not covered in this guide. The Reference Guide is divided into 13 sections.

PARTS OF SPEECH

Words perform various functions. A complete thought expressed in words is a **sentence**. Words or groups of words in a sentence are called **parts of speech**.

A given word is considered a part of speech based on usage in a sentence. The eight parts of speech are **nouns** and **pronouns** (which name), **verbs** (which assert), **adjectives** and **adverbs** (which qualify), **prepositions** and **conjunctions** (which connect), and **interjections** (which express sudden or strong feeling). A change in the function or use of a word will change the part of speech.

> Will you review the **report** before tomorrow? (noun)
>
> Please **report** to the judges' stand before the race begins. (verb)
>
> Lena inserted the pages into the correct **report** folder. (adjective)

Nouns

A **noun** names or refers to persons, places, objects, ideas, and other things. When a noun names one person, place, object, idea, or thing, the noun is **singular**; when two or more are named, the noun is **plural**.

Singular Nouns	Plural Nouns
bird	birds
thought	thoughts
mouse	mice

Kinds

Nouns are classified as common, proper, concrete, abstract, collective, and verbal. **Common nouns** are general names given to persons, places, and things. Common nouns are not capitalized except at the beginning of a sentence.

director	business
city	holiday

Proper nouns are names of particular persons, places, and things. Proper nouns are always capitalized.

Samuel Boutwell	Gulf Medical Services
Cincinnati	Orange Bowl

Concrete nouns name persons, places, things, and activities that our physical senses can perceive.

rose	printer
stadium	contest

Abstract nouns name ideas, qualities, and conditions beyond physical sensing.

assistance	faith
friendship	cooperation

Collective nouns name a group or a collection of objects or persons.

team	jury
squadron	club

Collective nouns may be singular or plural. When the noun represents the group or unit, the meaning is singular.

> The committee is meeting tomorrow.

When the noun indicates the individuals who make up the unit or group, the meaning is plural.

> The committee have received parking decals.

Verbal nouns are discussed on pages 420–421.

Possessive Case Nouns

Possessive case nouns indicate ownership. To write the possessive form of a noun, first determine whether the noun is singular or plural. Generally, to form the possessive case, add an apostrophe and *s* to singular nouns and to plural nouns that end with any letter other than *s*. Add only the apostrophe to plural nouns that end with *s*.

Singular Nouns	**Add 's for Possessive Case**
reader	reader's
class	class's

Plural Nouns with Non-*s* Endings	**Add 's for Possessive Case**
men	men's
children	children's

Plural Nouns with *s* Endings	**Add ' for Possessive Case**
readers	readers'
owners	owners'

Apply these special rules to form certain possessives:

1. Add ' only to singular nouns of more than one syllable that end in *s* if an additional syllable would make the pronunciation awkward.

> Dr. Torres' diagnosis was documented on the medical chart.
>
> Miss Adams' resignation was accepted.

2. **Add** **'s to the last term in a singular compound noun.**

> Her mother-in-law's car was built at a plant in Tennessee.
>
> The editor-in-chief's document was stored electronically.

3. **Make each name possessive to indicate separate ownership for two people.**

> Julia's and Danielle's computers were designed by Venture, Inc.

4. **Make the last name in the group possessive to indicate joint ownership.**

> Watson and Ford's software was marketed by Unique Designs.

5. **Use the punctuation preferred by an organization to show possessive case.**

> Clean and Green's annual report was printed in the newspaper.
>
> The Schools Advisory Committee elects officers in June.

Pronouns

A **pronoun** is a word used as a substitute for a noun. An **antecedent** is a word for which the pronoun stands.

> The students received certificates that they mounted on the wall. (The pronoun *they* refers to the antecedent *students*.)

Pronoun-Antecedent Agreement

A pronoun must agree with its antecedent in person, number, and gender. (See Section 4, pages 431–432, for additional pronoun-antecedent agreement discussion.)

Person

First-person personal pronouns *(I, me, my, mine, we, us, our, ours)* denote the speaker.

> *I* reviewed the manual before *we* discussed any changes.

Second-person personal pronouns *(you, your, yours)* name the ones spoken to.

> *You* should hike in the Grand Canyon on *your* next vacation.

Third-person personal pronouns *(he, him, his, she, her, hers, they, them, their, theirs, it, its)* designate the ones or objects spoken about.

> *She* received the accounting award at graduation.

Number

A **singular** personal pronoun refers to one person or thing.

> *He* rode a new bicycle in the race.

A **plural** personal pronoun refers to more than one person or thing.

> *They* own four antique cars.

Gender

When reference is made to males, personal pronouns are of **masculine gender**. Personal pronouns that refer to females are of **feminine gender**. A reference to neither males nor females uses **neuter gender**; a reference to either males or females uses **gender-free** terminology.

> *He* operated the forklift in the warehouse. (masculine gender)
>
> *She* served as parliamentarian. (feminine gender)
>
> *It* can be repaired for less than $500. (neuter gender)
>
> *They* attended the ethics seminar. (gender free)

Kinds

Pronouns are classified as personal, relative, interrogative, demonstrative, indefinite, and reflexive. **Personal pronouns** (see the complete list on page 416) rename persons, places, and objects.

> The faculty members donated $700 to *their* fellowship fund.
> *(Their* renames *members*.)

Relative pronouns *(who, whom, whose, which, that)* join an adjective clause to an antecedent.

> The *speaker* (antecedent) *who* (relative pronoun) discussed ethics is from Tampa.

Interrogative pronouns *(who, whom, which, what,* and *whose)* ask a question.

> *Who* will attend the first meeting?
>
> *Which* student won the contest?

Demonstrative pronouns point out persons or things to which they refer. The singular demonstrative pronouns are *this* and *that*; the plural pronouns are *these* and *those*.

> *This* is the newest scanner.
>
> The computers delivered yesterday are *those*.

Indefinite pronouns refer to nonspecific persons or things. Common indefinite pronouns are *any, another, anyone, anybody, some, someone, somebody, none, nobody, many, few,* and *everyone*.

> *Nobody* left work early.
>
> *Everyone* used presentation software during the seminar.

Reflexive pronouns combine some form of the personal pronouns with *self* or *selves*. A reflexive pronoun either reflects the action described by the verb or emphasizes the noun or pronoun.

> Manuel cut *himself* on the broken glass. (reflects action)
>
> The aides *themselves* will help on Monday. (emphasizes noun)

Personal Pronoun Usage

Case	Person	Number	
		Singular	Plural
Nominative or Subjective	1	I	We
	2	You	You
	3	He, She, It	They
Objective	1	Me	Us
	2	You	You
	3	Him, Her, It	Them
Possessive (Modifying Noun)*	1	My	Our
	2	Your	Your
	3	His, Her, Its	Their
Possessive (No Noun)	1	Mine	Ours
	2	Yours	Yours
	3	His, Hers, Its	Theirs
Reflexive	1	Myself	Ourselves
	2	Yourself	Yourselves
	3	Himself, Herself, Itself	Themselves

*The possessive forms of all pronouns are written without apostrophes.

Case Forms

The three case forms of personal pronouns are nominative (subjective), objective, and possessive. **Nominative** or **subjective case pronouns** (*I, you, he, she, it, we, they*) are used as the subject or predicate pronoun of a sentence. A **predicate pronoun** follows a form of the verb *to be* and renames the subject.

> *She* chaired the legislative committee. (subject)
>
> The pharmacy technician is *he.* (predicate pronoun)

Objective case pronouns *(me, you, him, her, it, us, them)* are used as direct objects, indirect objects, or objects of a preposition. A **direct object** receives the action expressed by the verb.

> Luan nominated *me.*

An **indirect object** tells *to* or *for whom* something is done or *to* or *for what* something is done.

> Cynthia bought *us* ice cream.

When a pronoun follows a preposition such as *of, in, for, on, to, with, from,* and *by* and is linked to the sentence, the pronoun is an object of the preposition.

> Alice gave the report to *them.*

Possessive case pronouns *(my, mine, you, your, yours, his, her, hers, its, our, ours, their, theirs)* show ownership. To show ownership of a modified noun, use *my, your, his, her, its, our,* or *their.*

> The HW200 is *our* new scanner.

To show ownership without a modified noun, use *mine, yours, his, hers, its, ours,* or *theirs.*

> The laser printers are *ours.*

Verbs

A **verb** is an assertive word that expresses an action *(run, sing, think)* or state of being *(is, am, are, seem).* Action verbs may express physical actions *(slide, draw, move)* or mental actions *(know, believe, memorize).*

Main and Helping Verbs

When a sentence has only one verb that expresses an action or state of being, the verb is a **main verb**.

> Jolene *stamped* the envelopes.

Sentences may have a combination of two or more verbs in a single unit; these verbs form a **verb phrase**.

> Jolene *had stamped* the envelopes yesterday.

In a verb phrase, the last verb is the main verb. All other verbs in the phrase are helping verbs. Helping verbs indicate whether the action of the main verb will occur in the future (Jo *will see* the show) or has occurred in the past (Jo *had seen* the show). Helping verbs also can show whether the subject receives the action (The show *was seen* by Jo) or performs the action (Jo *has seen* the show).

Classes

The three basic classes of main verbs are transitive, intransitive, and linking. A **transitive verb** requires a direct object to express a complete meaning. (Refer to page 425 for direct objects.)

> The research assistant *completed* the statistical analysis.

A personal pronoun used as a direct object of a transitive verb must be in the objective case.

> Ying Sheng identified *him* as the artist.

An **intransitive verb** does not have a direct object and does not link a modifier to the subject.

> The team assistant *keyboards* rapidly.

Linking verbs connect the subject to a complement (a predicate noun, pronoun, or adjective). Principal linking verbs are forms of to be—*am, is, are, was, were*—and verb phrases ending in *be, been,* or *being.* Other commonly used linking verbs are *seem, appear, taste, feel, smell, hear, sound, remain, grow, look,* and *become.*

> The environmental engineers *are* Mario and Deborah.
>
> The store *remains* open all night.

A personal pronoun used as a complement to the subject must be in the nominative case.

> The judge is *she.*
> Our director is *he.*

Properties

A verb may vary in these five properties: voice, person, number, mood, and tense.

Voice

Voice shows whether the subject performs the action **(active voice)** or receives the action **(passive voice)**.

> Margo *wrote* the lyrics. (active voice)
> The lyrics *were written* by Margo. (passive voice)

Person

Person indicates whether the subject names *who* or *what* speaks (first person), *whom* or *what* is spoken to (second person), or *whom* or *what* is spoken about (third person). Subjects and verbs must agree.

> *I shall attend* the meeting tomorrow. (first person)
> *Will you attend* the meeting with me? (second person)
> *Who will go* with you to the next meeting? (third person)

Number

Number indicates whether the subject means one (singular) or more than one (plural). A singular subject requires a singular verb; a plural subject requires a plural verb. (See Section 3, pages 429–431, for a subject-verb agreement discussion.)

Mood

The purpose of a sentence determines the **mood** of the verb. **Indicative mood** is used to state facts and ask questions.

> Harbour Construction Company *is expanding.*
> *Will* you *participate* in the seminar?

Imperative mood is used to express a request, an instruction, or a command.

> Please *answer* the telephone.
> *Insert* the edge last creased into the envelope.

Subjunctive mood is used to express an idea that is a supposition, a wish, or a thought that is doubtful or uncertain.

> I wish I *were* in the mountains.
> If I *were* in command, you would be promoted.

Tense

Tense indicates the time of action or state of being. Six verb tenses exist in the English language. **Present tense** is used to express an action occurring at the present time or a customary action.

> Hannah *answers* the telephone.
>
> Mo *plays* soccer every Saturday. (customary action)

Past tense is used to express an action that occurred before the statement.

> Hannah *answered* the telephone yesterday.
>
> Mo *played* soccer in his homeland.

Future tense is used to represent an action that will occur in the future.

> Hannah *will answer* the telephone for the next two weeks.
>
> Mo *will play* soccer in a new league next year.

Present perfect tense is used to emphasize that an action was completed at some indefinite time before the statement is made.

> Hannah *has answered* the telephone for several months.
>
> Mo certainly *has played* soccer before now.

Past perfect tense is used to emphasize that an action was completed in the past before some definite past action or event.

> Hannah *had answered* the telephone before she became a permanent employee.
>
> Mo *had played* competitive soccer before he moved to New Jersey.

Future perfect tense is used to emphasize that an action will be completed in the future before some definite future action or event.

> Hannah *will have answered* the telephone for three months by the end of June.
>
> Mo *will have played* soccer for six years by the end of this season.

Principal Parts

All verbs (except linking verbs) have three **principal parts**: present tense, past tense, and past participle. The principal parts are used when forming the tenses of verbs. The past tense and past participle of **regular verbs** are formed by adding *-d* or *-ed* to the present form.

Present Tense	Past Tense	Past Participle
sail	sailed	sailed
trade	traded	traded

However, when a verb ends in *y* preceded by a consonant, the past tense and past participle are formed by changing the *y* to *i* and adding *-ed*.

Present Tense	Past Tense	Past Participle
apply	applied	applied
notify	notified	notified

The past tense and past participle of an **irregular verb** are formed in any other way than by adding *-d* or *-ed* to the present form.

Present Tense	Past Tense	Past Participle
sing	sang	sung
write	wrote	written

Verbals

Verbals are the verb forms that are used as nouns, adjectives, and adverbs. The three kinds of verbals are participles, gerunds, and infinitives. A verbal with complements and modifiers is a **verbal phrase**.

Participles

A **participle** is a verb form used as an adjective. Two kinds of participles are present participles and past participles. **Present participles** are used as modifiers of nouns or pronouns (adjective usage) or as part of a verb phrase. Add *-ing* to the present tense of verbs to form the present participle.

> The *roaring* muffler needs to be replaced. (adjective usage)
>
> Daniel *is riding* his bicycle in the parade. (verb phrase)

A past participle can also be used as an adjective and as part of a verb phrase. Add *-d* or *-ed* to the present tense of regular verbs to form the past participle.

> The computer, *loaded* with new software, was installed this morning. (adjective usage)
>
> The file cabinet *was loaded* onto the moving van. (verb phrase)

The past participles of irregular verbs are formed in various ways.

> The *written* report was duplicated. (adjective usage)
>
> The last report *was written* carelessly. (verb phrase)

Gerunds

A **gerund** (verb form ending in *-ing*) is always used as a noun. A gerund or gerund phrase may have any of the uses of a noun (subject, object of a verb, predicate noun, adverbial noun, appositive, object of preposition).

> *Exercising regularly* helps maintain a healthy heart. (subject)
>
> Pedro enjoys *jogging.* (object of a verb)
>
> My favorite leisure activity is *reading.* (complement after a linking verb—predicate noun)

Is this activity worth *risking your life*? (adverbial noun)

His duty, *monitoring the seismograph,* requires patience and time. (appositive)

Tim cut the grass after *washing* the car. (object of preposition)

A noun or pronoun that modifies a gerund is in the possessive case.

I was pleased at Rick's *completing* the task so quickly.

The teacher appreciated *your* reading to the children.

Infinitives

An **infinitive** is the verb form usually preceded by *to* and used as a noun, an adjective, or an adverb. *To* is sometimes omitted from the infinitive.

She did not help them [to] move the furniture.

The infinitive or infinitive phrase may have any of the uses of a noun.

To secure employment requires a focused search. (subject)

I had hoped *to secure employment* by May 1. (object of a verb)

My primary goal was *to secure employment.* (predicate noun)

I had no desire except *to secure employment.* (object of a preposition)

I had but one desire, *to secure employment.* (appositive)

The infinitive or infinitive phrase may be an adjective or an adverb modifier.

The recycling plant *to be dedicated Thursday* has state-of-the-art equipment. (adjective usage)

Trevor was invited *to attend the ceremony.* (adverb usage)

Bill seemed *to like the work.* (predicate adjective modifying *Bill*)

Adjectives

An **adjective** is a qualifier or modifier that tells *what kind, which one,* or *how many* about nouns or pronouns. The two kinds of adjectives are limiting adjectives and descriptive adjectives. **Limiting adjectives** indicate precisely how many persons, places, things, or concepts are involved. Use the limiting adjective *a* before words that begin with a consonant sound and before *h* when pronounced as in *hot, u* when pronounced with a long sound as in *unit,* and *o* when pronounced with a *w* sound as in *one.* Use the limiting adjective *an* before words that begin with a vowel sound, except the long *u.*

Use A

A mouse pad was on the desk.

A heated debate preceded the vote.

A unique gown was displayed in the museum.

A one-syllable word is not divided between lines of text.

Use *An*

Nancy entered into *an* agreement with the landlord.

Please post *an* enlarged copy.

Mark dropped *an* ice cube into the coffee cup.

The school district employed *an* occupational specialist.

Other limiting adjectives include *all, any, both, every, no, some, that, those, this, these,* and *the.*

Descriptive adjectives describe the characteristics of persons, places, things, and concepts.

> *Forty* people attended the seminars. (tells *how many* people)

> The artist used *vivid* colors. (tells *what kind* of color)

Descriptive adjectives have three degrees of comparison: positive, comparative, and superlative. The **positive degree** names a quality and is the base form of the adjective.

The **comparative degree** compares two people or things. Form the comparative degree by adding *-r* or *-er* to the base form of one- or two-syllable adjectives. If the adjective ends in *y,* change the *y* to *i* before adding *-er.* In other instances, use the comparative helping words *more* or *less* along with the base form of the adjective.

Use the **superlative degree** to compare more than two people or things. Form the superlative degree by adding *-st* or *-est* to the base form of one- or two-syllable adjectives. If the adjective ends in *y,* change the *y* to *i* before adding *-est.* In other instances, use the superlative helping words *most* or *least* along with the base form of the adjective. Some adjectives are irregular and change form.

Positive	Comparative	Superlative
slow	slower	slowest
easy	easier	easiest
beneficial	more beneficial	most beneficial
good	better	best

Adverbs

An **adverb** is a modifier that tells *how, when, where,* or *to what extent* about verbs, adjectives, and other adverbs. Most adverbs are formed by adding *-ly* to an adjective. A few adverbs are not formed from adjectives. Three examples are *just, so,* and *quite.* CAUTION: *Lovely, friendly, ugly,* and *lonely* are adjectives, not adverbs.

> Mikka ran *swiftly* in the last race. (modifies verb)

> An *extremely* hot day may wilt the flowers. (modifies adjective)

> The students listened *quite* intently. (modifies adverb)

Adverbs have three degrees of comparison: positive, comparative, and superlative. The **positive degree** is the base form of the adverb. Form the **comparative degree** of adverbs ending in -*ly* by using the helping words *more* or *less* before the adverb. Some adverbs form the comparative degree by adding -*er* to the base form. Form the **superlative degree** of adverbs ending in -*ly* by using the helping words *most* or *least* before the adverb. Some adverbs form the superlative degree by adding -*est* to the base form. Irregular adverbs change form.

Positive	Comparative	Superlative
rapidly	more rapidly	most rapidly
near	nearer	nearest
well	better	best

Prepositions

A **preposition** is a word that connects a noun or pronoun to some other word in a sentence.

Prepositions may be single words:

about	behind	in	to
above	between	off	under
among	for	on	up
before	from	through	with

Prepositions may also be a group of words:

in spite of	in front of
on account of	because of
in back of	instead of
ahead of	by way of

A **prepositional phrase** is a group of words consisting of a preposition, its object, and the modifiers of the object. Prepositional phrases may be adjectives or adverbs.

> The documents *in the tray* should be filed. (adjective—tells *which* documents)
>
> *During the conference*, he discussed protecting the wetlands. (adverb—tells *when*)

When a pronoun is the object of the preposition, use the objective case of the pronoun.

> Dorothy often acts *like me*. (*Like* is the preposition, and the objective case of the pronoun *me* is the object of the preposition.)
>
> *With whom* did Marsha discuss the report? (*With* is the preposition, and the objective case pronoun *whom* is the object of the preposition.)

Conjunctions

A **conjunction** connects words, phrases (word groups not containing a subject and verb), or clauses (word groups containing a subject and verb) in a sentence. The three general classes of conjunctions are coordinating, subordinating, and correlative conjunctions.

Coordinating conjunctions join words, phrases, or clauses of the same rank: *and, but, or, nor, for.*

Subordinating conjunctions join a subordinate or dependent clause to a main clause. Main clauses have a subject and verb and express a complete thought. Subordinate or dependent clauses do not express a complete thought and depend on the main clause for meaning. (See pages 426–427 for a discussion on clauses.)

after	before	than	until
as	if	that	when
because	since	though	

Correlative conjunctions occur in pairs and join words, phrases, or clauses of the same rank.

both . . . and	not only . . . but also
either . . . or	neither . . . nor
whether . . . or	

Interjections

An **interjection** expresses strong or sudden emotion. Single words or complete statements may function as interjections.

Oh!	Yes!	Wow!
Listen!	Impossible!	Your idea is fantastic!

Section 2: **SENTENCE STRUCTURE**

A **sentence** expresses a complete thought. In a sentence, words may be used individually or as part of a phrase or clause.

Parts

Sentence parts may be classified as essential, modifying, or connecting. **Essential parts** are words or groups of words that contain the basis of the thought in the sentence. The **subject** (that about which something is said), the **verb** (that part that expresses action or being in reference to the subject), and any **complement** (the word or phrase necessary to complete the thought) constitute a basic sentence. **Modifying parts** are words or groups of words that help explain or make more definite any sentence part. **Connecting parts** are words that connect parts of the thought.

The subject words include common and proper nouns, pronouns, gerunds, and infinitives acting as nouns. A complete subject is made up of subject word(s) plus any or all of these elements: modifier(s), conjunction(s), and preposition(s).

The complete verb consists of the main verb, sometimes called the predicate verb, plus any or all of these elements: modifier(s), conjunction(s), preposition(s), and complement(s).

The five types of complements are subject complements, direct objects, indirect objects, objects of prepositions, and objective complements. Two styles of complements are often called subject complements because they refer to a *subject word.* The subject complements are predicate adjectives and predicate nominatives.

Predicate adjectives follow these linking verbs: *be, being, been, am, is, are, was, were, appears, become, seems, looks, hears, smells, tastes, feels, sounds, remain*, and *grows.* The **predicate adjective** is the subjective complement that modifies or describes the subject.

> After a three-hour discussion, the results *remain* **unchanged**.
>
> Vivian *appeared* **calm** after the accident.
>
> James *is* **lonely** since his friend moved to another city.

The **predicate noun** or **pronoun (predicate nominative)** is the subjective complement that names or means the same thing as the subject. Nominative case pronouns are used as subjective complements.

> That house is my *property.* (noun)
>
> The man at the pool is *he.* (pronoun)
>
> The award winners are *he* and *I.* (compound pronouns)
>
> A good policy is *to keep* your promises. (infinitive)
>
> A popular environmental activity is *watching whales.* (gerund)
>
> His proposal is *that we conduct our research on the Internet.* (noun clause)

The **direct object** is the complement that completes the meaning of a transitive verb and names the receiver of the action.

> Katlin drove the *truck.* (noun)
>
> Joshua greeted *us.* (pronoun)
>
> I learned *to play soccer.* (infinitive)
>
> Sandra recalled *having seen him last year.* (gerund)

An **indirect object** is a noun or a pronoun that shows *to whom* or *for whom* the action of the transitive verb is done. Objective case pronouns are used as indirect objects. The indirect object precedes the direct object.

> Mail *Philip* the survey results. (Mail the results to Philip.— noun)
>
> Dorothy, give *me* the survey results. (Give the results to me.— pronoun)

Objects of prepositions are nouns or pronouns that complete the connections that prepositions begin. Objective case pronouns are used as objects of prepositions.

> Bill played basketball *in the gym*. (noun)
> You may go *with him*. (pronoun)
> Ahmed is interested *in recycling glass*. (phrase)
> We learned *about how they recycled tin cans*. (clause)

Phrases

A **phrase** contains words that are grammatically related but does not contain a subject and verb. The six types of phrases are noun, verb, infinitive, participial, prepositional, and gerund.

> The *environmentalist's recommendations* were accepted. (noun)
> Six new computers *will be purchased*. (verb)
> The designers are doing their best *to finish early*. (infinitive)
> *Seeing the danger*, Walter swerved to the right. (participial)
> Pablo met the production manager *at the studio*. (prepositional)
> *Writing effective messages* requires planning. (gerund)

Clauses

A **clause** contains a subject and a verb. A main clause is **independent** and forms a simple sentence.

> Betsy uses ceramic cups.

A **dependent clause** must be combined with a main clause to form a sentence and is usually introduced by a subordinating word such as *who, because,* or *that.*

> Cecilia is the team captain *who met the referees.*

The three kinds of dependent clauses are noun, adjective, and adverb clauses.

Noun Clauses

A **noun clause** is a dependent clause used as the subject of a sentence or more often used as a direct object after verbs such as *say* or *know.* Noun clauses may be introduced by words such as *why, how, whether, if, that, what, whoever,* and *whatever.*

> *How we travel to the meeting* depends upon time and costs. (noun clause used as subject)
> Wesley knows *why the system crashed.* (noun clause used as object of the verb *knows*)

Adjective Clauses

An **adjective clause**, a dependent clause used as an adjective, modifies a noun or a pronoun. Adjective clauses are usually introduced by relative pronouns such as *who, which,* or *that.* Adjective clauses may be restrictive or nonrestrictive.

A **restrictive clause** identifies or limits the meaning of the modified word and is essential to the meaning of the sentence. A restrictive clause is not set off by commas.

> Al only buys toys *that meet child safety standards.* (The adjective clause *that meet child safety standards* tells the particular kind of toys. The clause is essential to the meaning of the sentence.)

A **nonrestrictive clause** adds something of interest and is not essential to the meaning of the sentence. The nonrestrictive clause is set off by commas.

> Dillan's sister, *who is a graduate of Lake University,* edited the magazine. (The adjective clause *who is a graduate of Lake University* gives additional information about Dillan's sister.)

Adverb Clauses

An **adverb clause**, a dependent clause that functions as an adverb in the sentence, modifies a verb, an adjective, or another adverb.

> Erin ran *because she was frightened.* (modifies verb *ran*)
>
> We are pleased *that you have started a recycling program.* (modifies predicate adjective *pleased*)
>
> Jane was so happy *that she clapped her hands.* (modifies the adverb *so*)

Sentence Types

The four types of sentences are declarative, interrogative, imperative, and exclamatory. All types of sentences begin with capital letters; however, the sentences end with various punctuation marks determined by the type and purpose of each sentence.

Declarative Sentences

A **declarative sentence** is a statement of fact, an opinion, or an observation. A declarative sentence ends with a period.

> Maria will return to the office today.

Interrogative Sentences

An **interrogative sentence** asks a question and usually ends with a question mark.

> When will Maria return to the office?

Imperative Sentences

An **imperative sentence** makes a command or gives a direction to an assignment. An imperative sentence ends with a period. The subject of an imperative sentence often is not expressed; *you* is the understood subject.

Return the unused materials to the storage room.

A noun in direct address may be used in imperative sentences to get attention.

Mrs. Palmer, please follow the other members.

Exclamatory Sentences

An **exclamatory sentence** expresses strong or sudden feeling, such as surprise, wonder, enthusiasm, or despair. An exclamatory sentence ends with an exclamation point.

Turn off the fire alarm!

Sentence Styles

The four sentence styles are simple, compound, complex, and compound-complex. A style is determined by the number and kind of clauses in a sentence.

Simple Sentence

A **simple sentence** has one main clause. However, any sentence element in a simple sentence may be compound.

Maria smiled. (single subject and single verb)

Kip and he sell and lease cars. (compound subject and compound verb)

Mrs. Crane bought paper and staples. (compound object)

Compound Sentences

A **compound sentence** contains two or more main clauses of equal importance.

The coach swam, and the students ran.

Armondo bought a new car; however, he kept the old one.

Complex Sentences

A **complex sentence** contains one main clause and one or more dependent clauses. In the following examples, the dependent clauses are italicized.

When Jean completed the report, she telephoned Ashley.

These are the students *who were elected state officers*.

Compound-Complex Sentences

A **compound-complex sentence** contains two or more main clauses and at least one dependent clause.

When your area code changes to 850, remember to update your checks, stationery, and other printed material; remember to make your friends and relatives aware of the change.

Subjects and verbs must agree in number. A singular subject needs a singular verb; a plural subject needs a plural verb. The subject is used to determine the correct number of the verb.

> *One* of the club officers *writes* poetry. (singular subject and verb)

The subject, not a prepositional phrase that modifies the subject, is used to determine the correct verb. In the previous example, *one* is singular, while *officers* is plural. *Officers* is the object of the preposition *of*. The object of the preposition should not be confused with the subject of the sentence.

> The *sprinters* on our team *practice* daily. (plural subject and verb)

In this example, the subject, *sprinters,* is plural and requires a plural verb.

With Singular Words

These indefinite pronouns are singular and require a singular verb: *anybody, anyone, each, either, everyone, neither, one,* and *someone.*

> *Anyone* can join the club.

> *Each* of us is a potential winner.

The nouns *kind, sort,* and *type* are singular and need singular verbs.
> The other *kind* of cartridge is easier to install.

With Singular Units

Weights, measurements, periods of time, and amounts of money usually require singular verbs because they are thought of as one unit.
> *Ten pounds* is considered heavy for a laptop computer.

With Compound Subject Joined by *And*

Compound subjects—singular subjects connected by the coordinating conjunction *and*—must have a plural verb.
> The *notepad and pen* are in the desk drawer.

When a compound subject is joined by *and* and means the same person, place, or thing or is considered to be a unit, the verb becomes singular.
> The *producer and director* is Mr. Hernandez.

> *Fish and chips* is a popular dish in the British Isles.

With Nouns Having Singular Meaning

Some nouns ending in *s* are singular in meaning and are used with singular verbs: *ethics, measles, two-thirds, mathematics, athletics.*
> *Athletics* receives attention from all the media.

With Plural Pronouns

The indefinite pronouns *few, many, both, others,* and *several* are plural. As plurals, they require plural verbs.

> A *few* of the directors are interested in the project.

The indefinite pronouns *all, any, most, more,* and *some* may be singular or plural. They are plural only if they refer to many individual units.

> *Some* of the document was deleted. (singular—part of a whole)
>
> *Some* of the examples were missing. (plural—individual items)

With Collective Nouns

Collective nouns, such as *team, family, flock,* and *class,* require singular verbs when thought of as a unit.

> The *team* travels four months each year.

When the members are thought to be functioning individually, a plural verb is used.

> The *team* are being measured for their new uniforms.

With Plural Noun Forms

Some nouns have only plural forms and are always used with plural verbs: *scissors, trousers, spectacles, shears.*

> The *scissors* have sharp points.

With Parenthetical Phrases

Phrases that include the words *with, along with, together with,* or *as well as* are parenthetical and do not affect the number of the subject.

> Bryna, *as well as* Jess and Lynne, plays soccer on a select team.

With Coordinating Conjunctions

Singular subjects joined by coordinating conjunctions *either . . . or, neither . . . nor,* and *not only . . . but also* are singular and require a singular verb.

> *Neither* the secretary *nor* the office manager schedules appointments for Dr. Yee.

If one of the subjects joined by one of these conjunctions is singular and the other is plural, the verb will agree with the nearer subject.

> *Not only* the manager *but also* the clerks were well trained.

With Adjective Clauses

When relative pronouns, such as *who, what,* and *that,* are the subject in an adjective clause, the antecedent will determine the number.

> She likes a laptop *that* has a trackball.
>
> I like laptops *that* have trackballs.

To make a statement about "the only one" among a larger number, a singular verb is needed in the adjective clause.

Eddy purchased *the only one* of the computers that was on sale.

When the phrase "only one of the" is used in an adjective clause, the clause applies to the entire group.

Only one of the TVs that were on sale was within my price range.

Section 4: PRONOUN-ANTECEDENT AGREEMENT

The antecedent of a pronoun is the word for which the pronoun stands. A pronoun must agree with its antecedent in person, number, and gender.

Sabrina washed her uniform. *(Sabrina* is the antecedent of the pronoun *her*.)

With Singular Antecedents

When two singular antecedents connected by *and* refer to one person, object, or idea, the pronoun will be singular.

The team leader and editor approves the budget. (one person)

When two singular antecedents connected by *and* refer to different persons, objects, or ideas, the pronoun will be plural.

The charge nurse and the lab technician have prepared their reports. (two different people)

When two singular antecedents connected by *and* are preceded by *each, every, many a, many an,* or *no,* the pronoun will be singular.

Every man and boy uses *Mr.* as his title.

Singular antecedents connected by *or* or *nor* require singular pronouns.

Bette or Candace should be ready with her recommendations.

In a sentence with *neither . . . nor* or *either . . . or,* the pronoun will agree with the nearer noun.

Neither the doctor nor the nurses begin their vacations this week.

With Compound Antecedents

When a compound antecedent consists of both a singular and plural noun, the plural noun should come second; thus, the pronoun will agree with the plural noun.

The doctor and the nurses agree with their holiday schedule.

With Collective Nouns

If a collective noun is used as a unit, the personal pronoun will be singular.

> The committee is prepared to give its recommendation.

If a collective noun refers to each person individually, the personal pronoun will be plural.

> The panel identify service projects to receive their contributions.

With Antecedent Referencing Gender

When the gender of the antecedent is unknown, use both the masculine and feminine pronouns to agree with the antecedent.

> Everyone has his or her own ideas about politics.

When two antecedents joined by *or, nor,* or *and* are of different gender, both the male and female pronouns are used.

> Either George or Jane will be hired, but he or she must be interviewed.

To avoid *he* or *she* expressions, consider making singular antecedents plural.

Awkward	Preferred
Each manager should improve his or her communication skills.	All managers should improve their communication skills.
A teacher should not leave his or her students alone in the classroom.	Teachers should not leave their students alone in the classroom.

Section 5: **PUNCTUATION**

Statements may include end punctuation and internal punctuation.

End

Punctuation that marks the end of a sentence is called **end punctuation**. End punctuation includes periods, question marks, and exclamation points.

Period

The period is the most frequently used punctuation mark. Use a period:

1. At the end of declarative and imperative sentences.

> Our office bought new scanners.
>
> Lock the door when you leave.

2. At the end of an interrogative sentence that is really a courteous request.

> Will you please send a reply by e-mail.

3. After most abbreviations and initials.

> Smythe and Mahan Inc.   Lt. John Davidson
>
> Dr. S. F. Kramer   a.m., p.m.

A period is omitted after two-letter state abbreviations, except at the end of a sentence.

> Pensacola, FL, is referred to as the "Cradle of Naval Aviation."
>
> ZIP Code 38753 is assigned to Inverness, MS.

When an organization is known by abbreviations, use capital letters with no spaces and no periods.

> CBE (Council for Basic Education)
>
> AT&T (American Telephone and Telegraph Co.)

4. Between dollars and cents in figures and between whole numbers and decimal fractions.

> $75.35   2.25 meters   1.5 gallons

Question Mark

Use a question mark:

1. After most interrogative sentences.

> Have you used that printer before?

2. After a direct quotation in question form.

> The contractor asked, "Do you want to use an oil-based paint?"

3. After each item in a series requiring an answer.

> What are the arrangements? the date? the time? the location?

Exclamation Point

Use an exclamation point:

1. After an emphatic interjection.

> Stop!   Wait!   Help!

2. After exclamatory sentences.

> "The roof is leaking!" she shouted.

Internal

Punctuation that marks a pause or a break in a thought pattern is called **internal punctuation**. Internal punctuation marks include commas, semicolons, colons, quotation marks, omission marks, parentheses, brackets, underscores, hyphens, dashes, and apostrophes.

Comma

The comma is the most frequently used internal punctuation mark. Use a comma:

1. To separate the elements in a series.

> Cole Co. hired an assistant, a designer, and a receptionist.

2. After introductory words, phrases, or clauses.

> Hopefully, you will be able to read my handwriting.
> For assistance, please call Ms. Warner at 555-0144.
> When the storm alarm sounds, please turn off the computers.

3. Between main clauses joined by a coordinating conjunction.

> Quang graduated in May, and Lenora graduated in August.

4. To set off parenthetical, transitional, and other expressions that are not necessary to the meaning of the sentence.

> Diane Matthews, the head nurse, administered the medication.
> However, the doctor wrote the prescription.
> Pensacola, the home of the Ice Pilots, is in northwest Florida.

5. To separate two adjacent, equal-ranking adjectives. Equal-ranking adjectives can be joined by _and_.

> He wore a tattered, torn sweater.

Omit a comma between modifiers that cannot be joined by _and_.

> She bought him an expensive silver money clip.

6. To set off short direct quotations.

> Andrew said, "Please follow me."

7. To separate the parts of dates and addresses. Omit commas in international datelines and between two-letter state abbreviations and ZIP Codes.

> The conference is scheduled for Tuesday, April 11, 20—, at 8:30 a.m., in the Sequoia Room of the Pacific Hotel, 1100 Canyon Drive, San Jose, CA 95127-0101.

General Business Dateline	**International Dateline**
February 17, 20—	17 February 20—

8. In place of omitted expressions understood from a preceding unit in the sentence.

> Timothy recently moved to San Diego; Betsy, to New York.
> Cheryl operated the computer; Clarence, the printer.

Semicolon

Use a semicolon:

1. **Between the main clauses of a compound sentence when the conjunction is omitted.**

> Add food waste to a compost; use the rich soil in potted plants or in a vegetable or flower garden.

2. **Between the main clauses of a compound sentence when conjunctions such as *therefore*, *however*, and *moreover* are used.**

> First impressions are important; therefore, dress properly for your interview.

3. **To separate a series of phrases or clauses if one or more items contain a comma.**

> The chairman, Mr. Salvoza, announced the winners: Andrea Dublin, accounting; Martha Pulwitz, medical office procedures; David Baggett, carpentry concepts.

4. **Between a main clause and a list of examples introduced by such expressions as *for example, namely, for instance*, or *e.g.***

> Effective communication includes six qualities; namely, courtesy, clarity, conciseness, concreteness, correctness, and completeness.

Colon

Use a colon:

1. **To introduce an enumeration or a listing.**

> These are my favorite vacation cities: Seattle, Paris, and London.

2. **To introduce a question or a long direct quotation.**

> The question is: Will you comply with the regulations?
>
> Rep. Dave Pavlock said: "The Clean Water Act must do a better job of addressing a wider array of water quality problems."

3. **Between hours and minutes expressed in figures.**

> Please submit your report by 4:30 p.m. today.

Quotation Marks

Use quotation marks:

1. **To enclose a direct quotation.**

> Frank said, "If you wash dishes by hand, use a dishpan and do not leave the tap running."

Use single quotation marks to enclose a quotation within another quotation.

> James said, "I practice water conservation and remember your advice: 'When shaving, do not let the water run continuously.'"

2. **To enclose titles of articles and other parts of complete publications, short poems, song titles, television programs, and unpublished works.**

> "Solar Campaign Seeks Converts" (article)
>
> "Walks Along the Coast" (poem)
>
> "Home on the Range" (song)
>
> "Good Morning America" (television program)
>
> "The Need for Wetlands" (unpublished work)

3. **To enclose special words or phrases or coined words that your readers may be unfamiliar with or may consider as inappropriate in a particular message.**

> One of the fastest-growing segments of the travel industry is "ecotourism."
>
> The CPU is considered the "brain" of the computer.

4. **To indicate technical terms that may be unfamiliar to your readers.**

> Lyle's "RAM" is insufficient for his work needs.
>
> The marketing manager wants to include a "tip-in" in the new business psychology book.

Omission Marks (Ellipses)

Use omission marks—three spaced periods (. . .):

1. **To indicate that something has been omitted from a quotation.**

> ". . . was the date we agreed upon."

If the omission comes at the end of a sentence, use the correct end punctuation after the omission marks.

> Mr. Mainella said, "We can be on the cutting edge . . . ."
>
> Edith Collins asked, "Can we promote tourism and protect the wetlands by . . . ?"

2. **To mark or create a momentary delay before presenting a special point.**

> In response to my comment that morale was low, you suggested . . . practice TQM.

Parentheses

Use parentheses:

1. **To set off references, explanatory details, and added information.**

> The average lifespan of litter (see Chart 1) depends on the climate.

2. To enclose identifying letters or figures in lists.

> Develop and maintain these communication skills: (1) listening, (2) reading, (3) speaking, (4) signaling, and (5) writing.

3. To enclose figures following amounts that are spelled.

> Duncan paid the Coburn Law Firm Nine Hundred Fifty and 75/100 Dollars ($950.75).

Brackets

Use brackets:

1. To indicate remarks that you insert in a direct quotation. Brackets mark language that is not part of the quotation.

> The biologist said: "Natural attractions [trails, wildlife sanctuaries, and stretches of rivers for canoeing] are increasing in popularity among tourists."

Brackets may also indicate that an error in a quotation was made by the person quoted; insert *sic* within the brackets immediately after the error.

> One engineer wrote: "Insulate to keep the heat where its [*sic*] needed the most."

2. To enclose parenthetical material in a passage already enclosed in parentheses.

> Mr. Slayton's memorandum (to plan a county career fair [see Mr. Slayton's September 1 memo to Howard Lester]) was discussed with the board before the vote was taken.

Italics

Use italics in the following instances:

1. To indicate titles of complete works, such as books, magazines, and newspapers.

> The *Coastal Traveler* lists and describes economical rental property.

2. To highlight cited words, examples, and words being defined.

> The noun *criteria* is plural; the singular form is *criterion*.
>
> The word *swam* is the past tense of *swim*.

3. To identify proper names of such vehicles as aircraft, spacecraft, ships, boats, and trains.

> Randall included a ride on the *Orient Express* as part of his vacation.

Hyphen

Use a hyphen:

1. To join compound numbers from twenty-one to ninety-nine that are keyed as words.

> twenty-nine over fifty-five

2. To indicate word division when part of a word must be divided from one line to the next.

> plan-ning knowl-edge gradu-ation

3. To show that two or more words are being used as a unit to modify a noun.

> up-to-date information thank-you message

Eliminate the hyphen in such modifiers when they follow the noun unless an up-to-date dictionary shows that the expression is always hyphenated.

> Kay developed a proposal that was *well written*.

Hyphens are not used between compound words that are shown as single words in a current dictionary.

> Four *stockholders* did not vote.

A hyphen is not used if a current dictionary shows an expression as separate words.

> Indianola, the *county seat* in Sunflower County, was named after an Indian maiden.

4. To separate certain prefixes in some words.

> editor-in-chief low-tech attorney-at-law

Check a dictionary for the current status of words.

> supersonic miniseries wetlands

5. To mark between the parts of fractions written as words.

> Mark ran at least *one-half* of the distance between his home and school.

6. To mark words or figures in a series of words or figures that modify the same noun.

> Students may enroll for a *one-*, *two-*, or *three-credit* course in office technology.
>
> In warmer weather, shade *south-* and *west-facing* windows.

7. To spell in writing a word or name.

> r-e-c-o-m-m-e-n-d V-o-l-l-e-r-o

Dash

Use a dash (two unspaced hyphens):

1. To set off parenthetical material with strong emphasis.

> The most obvious—and probably the most obtainable—strategy is the integration of environmental and energy policy.

2. To indicate a change of thought.

> The county must submit an environmental plan by January—but the city is not bound by the recommendation.

3. To introduce the name of an author following a direct quotation.

> "Our goals include printing maps and lists of natural recreation sites."—Collins

4. To introduce an explanation, an example, or a list presented after such expressions as *for example*, *for instance*, *e.g.*, or *namely*. The dash is less formal than a semicolon.

> Technology is changing education—e.g., laser discs, voice synthesizers, color printers, and creative software are changing the way students learn.

5. To indicate an interruption.

> "Dennis, don't open the—." The warning was too late!

Apostrophe

Use an apostrophe:

1. To indicate possession and other relationships when used with an *s*.

> Gillian's car was painted yesterday.

Add the apostrophe before or after an *s* ending, depending on the situation, for the possessive case of nouns.

Singular Possessive	Plural Possessive
child's	children's
secretary's	secretaries'
doctor's	doctors'

Add *'s* for the possessive of indefinite pronouns.

> somebody's   everyone's

Add *'s* to the last element of compounds to indicate joint or common possession.

> Samuel and Arnold's project was completed.

Add *'s* to each noun to show separate possession.

> The author's and editor's reports were submitted on time.

Generally, use an *of* phrase to make inanimate objects (things that do not have life) possessive.

Awkward	Preferred
The track's surface was cracked.	The surface of the track was cracked.

2. **To indicate where one or more letters are omitted in a contraction.**

aren't	can't	don't	you're

3. **To form the plural of letters, symbols, and abbreviations if the apostrophe makes the term clearer.**

m's	t's	12s	$s

Placement of Punctuation Marks

Follow these guidelines when two or more punctuation marks occur adjacent to one another:

1. **A period in an abbreviation precedes any other punctuation mark.**

> Will the meeting begin at 9:30 a.m.?
>
> Lori, who works for Unique Assoc., purchased a camera.

2. **Place the period or the comma inside closing quotation marks.**

> Dr. Perez said, "Set up a home recycling center."
>
> When we wrote "Ethics for Everyone," did you keep a disk copy?

3. **Place a semicolon outside closing quotation marks.**

> You referred to the concept "conflict resolution"; did you mean on our team?

4. **Place a question mark or an exclamation point punctuating a quotation inside a closing quotation mark.**

> The moderator asked, "Are you ready for the question?"
>
> The former editor frequently exclaimed, "Hold the presses!"

5. **When the entire sentence is in the form of a question or an exclamation and includes a quotation, place a question mark or an exclamation point outside the closing quotation mark.**

> Why did he say, "Seek a manufacturer that can verify low levels of toxic emissions and recycled content in its products"?
>
> When the tornado siren sounded, the safety officer shouted, "Go to the basement"!

6. **With a closing parenthesis or bracket, place periods, question marks, and exclamation points inside the parenthesis if the parenthetical material is a separate sentence.**

> Send fewer faxes. (Fax paper is usually not recyclable.)

The environmentalists were ecstatic. (Over 10,000 acres of wetlands were preserved!)

The e-mail message was transmitted. (Has the message been lost in cyberspace?)

7. Place punctuation marks inside a closing parenthesis when the marks apply to parenthetical material within a sentence; otherwise, place the marks outside the closing parenthesis.

Two web sites (http://www.collegenet.com/ and http://www.finaid.org/) offer information on financial aid.

Will home banking be accepted by consumers (many people think so)?

8. Place commas, semicolons, and colons outside a closing parenthesis or bracket.

When you interview prospective financial planners (necessary in the selection process), ask for written payment schedules.

Readers expect written courtesies (e.g., terms like *Thank you* and *Please);* such terms help build goodwill.

Dr. Li stated (on page 2 of *Cable News*): "Computers make up a large part of the technology in every classroom."

Spacing for Punctuation

With the increasing use of microcomputers and word processing software, spacing rules will be adapted to accommodate equipment requirements and to increase uniformity. Many word processing operators space once after a period that ends a sentence when another sentence continues on the same line and once after a period used with itemized numbers or letters.

Traditional rules, however, indicate spacing twice in the following situations:

1. At the end of a sentence after a period, a question mark, or an exclamation point.

Allen will move to Detroit. His sister will live in Charleston.

What Internet sites did you search? I recommended three sites.

Our output has tripled! Computers have made a difference.

2. Immediately after a colon within a sentence, except in time references.

The professor made this assignment: "Search for student newspapers at http://www.yahoo.com/news/newspapers/."

The laboratory is open from 7:30 a.m. until 5:30 p.m.

Space once after other punctuation markings—except for the following. Do not space immediately before or after:

1. A period inside an abbreviation.

Thomas Duncan, Ph.D., will meet us at 4 p.m.

2. A period used as a decimal point.

The increase was 1.5 percent, not 2.5 percent.

3. A hyphen or a dash.

The department will complete a self-study before the review.

Yes, I can—but not with this software.

4. An apostrophe within a word.

Doris Cummings is Michael's agent.

Section 6: CAPITALIZATION

Capitalizing the first letter of a word attaches importance to the word. Follow these guidelines for capitalization. Capitalize:

1. The first word of a sentence.

Every college web site is different.

Please sign in before you take your seat.

2. A proper noun or an adjective derived from a proper noun.

Tallahassee is the capital of Florida.

Keiko learned to prepare Italian cuisine.

3. The names of days of the week and of months.

I leave on Monday, June 23, for my two-week trip to Ireland.

Your doctor's appointment is scheduled for Tuesday, August 7.

4. The names of holidays and special seasons. Names of seasons, such as spring and winter, are not ordinarily capitalized.

The banks were closed on Memorial Day.

Students had a spring vacation during the week after Easter.

5. Titles immediately preceding a name and titles following a name in an address or keyed signature.

Ms. Patricia Hammer	Mrs. Jerri Bell, Mayor
Dr. Thompson	Chan Ying, Director
Commissioner Bruntlett	Robert Marklein, Manager

Titles used after a name in a sentence or in place of a name usually are not capitalized.

The commencement speaker was Matthew Tait, president of E-Z Software Company.

Do you know a phone number for the director of human resources?

6. **The pronoun *I*.**

> When you go to the movie, I will go with you.

7. **Terms of family relationship used with the name of a person or in place of the name of a person.**

> Aunt Opal and Uncle Charles will visit us this winter.
>
> We are visiting Cousin Fran in London next month.

8. **Names of studies made from proper nouns and names of specific courses (usually followed by a number).**

> Aaron enrolled for Spanish in his freshman year.
>
> Did you register for Psychology 102 this term?

9. **The first and all other important words in the titles of written works (documents, books, journals, newspapers, reports, and so on) and their contents (chapters, sections, articles, and so on).**

> Linda writes a daily column in the *Gulf Breeze Gazette.*
>
> Siri read the discussion of ethics in Chapter 6.

Capitalize *a, an, the,* and conjunctions or prepositions only when they are the first or last words in a title or subtitle.

> Have you read *The Clan of the Cave Bear*?
>
> Robbie played "Somewhere in Time" on the flute.

10. **The first word of a direct quotation.**

> Annelle said, "Stretch your minds, and explore new possibilities."

11. **The names of official documents, treaties, wars, important historical events and periods, and departments of government.**

> John Hancock was the first person to sign the Declaration of Independence.
>
> Christopher was injured in World War II.

12. **The words *river, lake, ocean, church, club, society, association, college, corporation, company*, or *building* when used as part of a proper name.**

> The American Association of Dental Assistants will meet at Hagler College.

13. **The names of products.**

> Have you tasted the new Dazzler soda?
>
> Janie Metzger designed Emerald Coast logos for the shirts.

Common nouns used with proper nouns but not actually part of them are not capitalized.

> Pronto and Renew *scanners* were purchased by three departments.
>
> Please order two dozen blank Omega *videotapes*.

14. **The proper names of places, regions, natural features, and their abbreviations.**

> Follow the Beartooth Highway to Cooke City, which is located near the northeastern entrance to Yellowstone National Park.

> The Sahara spans several countries in northern Africa.

Capitalize words designating directions only when they are part of a proper noun or when they refer to a specific region.

> My family will tour the Eastern Seaboard this summer.

> Linda and Jim drove west from New Orleans to Houston.

Capitalize words such as *city*, *state*, and *county* only in official documents or as part of proper nouns.

> The governor stamped the document with the seal of the State of Wyoming.

> Key West is the southernmost city in Florida.

15. **Both letters in two-letter state abbreviations.**

> Her address was 499 Armitage Avenue, Melrose Park, IL 60164-6499.

16. **The first word and all titles and nouns in the salutation of a letter and the first word in the complimentary close.**

> Dear Miss Fitzgerald   Sincerely yours

17. **Words used with a number for identifying a person or an item.**

> Ashley received student ID No. 4206-88-4940.

> The property control number for the VCR is M-7983.

18. **The word *dollars* and each word expressing part of a sum of money in legal statements.**

> Pay Five Hundred Twenty and 35/100 Dollars ($520.35) to Value Motors.

19. **Words referring to the Deity.**

> The words, *the Almighty*, were included in the song.

20. **The names of engineering and artistic works.**

> Alexander Gustave Eiffel designed the Eiffel Tower for the International Exposition of Paris of 1889.

> Many homes in Albania have reproductions of the *Mona Lisa*.

21. **Names and abbreviations of political, religious, business, athletic, and other organizations and their major divisions and departments.**

> The Chamber of Commerce is located at 200 West Garden Street.

> Have you ever been audited by the IRS?

In business documents, numbers are expressed with figures or words. In messages written in paragraph form, numbers are expressed in both figures and words. On business forms, such as invoices, sales tickets, or purchase orders, figures are generally used.

Use Words For:

1. Numbers from one to ten.

> Alice ordered six computers, and Glenda ordered two printers.

2. A number beginning a sentence.

> Three students were inducted into the Hall of Fame.

3. Isolated fractions or indefinite amounts in a sentence.

> Approximately two-thirds of the students graduated within four years.

> About forty guests attended the Glasgow's anniversary party.

4. Names of small-numbered streets and avenues (ten and under) and house or building number One.

> The office supply store is located at 1300 Ninth Avenue.

> Dr. Harbour's address is One Cordova Towers, Wilmington, VT 05363-1001.

5. Dates and times in formal writing or when the month is omitted.

> The wedding reception will begin at four o'clock.

> The celebration is scheduled for the seventh.

Use Figures For:

1. Dates and time.

> My first grandchild was born on November 11, 1982, at 5:15 p.m.

2. A series of fractions.

> Practice keying these fractions: 1/2, 2/3, 3/4, 2/5, 4/6, 5/7, 6/8, and 7/9.

3. Numbers preceded by nouns.

> Correctness was discussed in Chapter 2, Section 4.

4. Measures, weights, dimensions, and distances.

> A No. 10 envelope is 9 1/2" by 4 1/8" and is called a standard business envelope.

5. Definite numbers used with the percent sign (%) on business documents; use *percent* with approximations and in formal writing.

> On the invoice, insert 8 1/2% as the interest rate.
>
> Approximately 60 percent of the high school graduates did not attend college.
>
> In Anne's dissertation, 98 percent of the respondents indicated that communication skills were important for job success.

6. Sums of money. Even sums of money may be keyed without the decimal.

> Sachi paid $379.50 for her new television.
>
> Your change is 37 cents.
>
> Maria's rent is $600 a month.

7. Numbers from one to ten used with numbers above ten.

> The zoo recently acquired 2 antelopes, 8 gibbons, and 12 rare birds.

8. Addresses greater than number One.

> Jacobson Inc. opened a branch office at 8 North Palafox Road.

Use Words and Figures For:

1. Two numbers used together. Express the shorter sounding number in words.

> Robin taught two 45-minute aerobics classes.
>
> Maxum Truck Lines ordered 144 six-ply tires for the vans.

2. Sums of money on legal documents.

> Susan, the court reporter, repeated the judge's order: "Pay Nine Hundred Thirty Dollars ($930) to Whitcomb Enterprises."

Section 8: **SPELLING**

Spelling is a skill that can be improved with practice. As you develop a practice plan, refer to the following basic spelling rules. If you are uncertain about the spelling of any word, consult a current dictionary.

1. When a one-syllable word ends with one consonant preceded by one vowel, double the final consonant when a vowel ending (*-er, -ing, -est*, and so on) is added.

drop	dropped
get	getting
wit	witty
hot	hottest

Exceptions:

busing	gases

Do not double the final consonant when a consonant ending (e.g., *-ness, -ly, -ful*) is added.

glad	gladness
sad	sadly
mourn	mournful

2. **When a two-syllable word ends with one consonant preceded by one vowel and accented on the last syllable, double the final consonant when a vowel ending is added.**

occur	occurred
omit	omitted
confer	conferred

Do not double the final consonant when a consonant ending is added.

equip*	equipment
allot	allotment
incur	incurs

*The letter *u* following *q*, when sounded, has the consonant sound of *w*. Therefore, these words (such as *equip*) have only one sounded vowel before the final consonant.

3. **Drop the final *e* when a vowel ending is added to a root word that ends with *e*.**

accommodate	accommodating
hope	hoping

Retain the final *e* when a consonant ending is added to a word that ends in *e*.

accommodate	accommodates
hope	hopefulness

Exceptions:

abridgment	acknowledgment
argument	awful
wisdom	duly
ninth	truly
wholly	judgment

4. **When a word ends with *-ce* or *-ge* (soft sound), retain the *e* when adding *-able* or *-ous*.**

advantage	advantageous
change	changeable
manage	manageable
enforce	enforceable
service	serviceable
trace	traceable

5. When words end with *y* preceded by a consonant, change *y* to *i* when any ending is added (except *-ing*). Retain the *y* when *-ing* is added.

satisfy	satisfied	satisfying
vary	varies	varying

When a termination *-ing* is added to words that end with *-ie*, change the *-ie* ending to *y*.

die	dying
lie	lying
tie	tying

6. Use *i* before *e* except after *c* or when sounded as *a* as in *neighbor* and *weigh*.

I Before E	E Before I After C*	E Before I After Sound of A	
convenience	conceive	eight	feign
believe	receive	weight	veil
achieve	receipt	neighbor	freight
niece	deceive	vein	heir
piece	perceive	their	reign
relieve		sleigh	
siege			
yield			

*Use *i* before *e* with the sound of "sh" (*efficiency*, *sufficient*).

Exceptions:

height	leisure	protein
either	plebeian	seize
neither	weird	foreign

7. When nouns end with *o* preceded by a vowel, add an *s* for plural forms.

curio	curios
ratio	ratios
folio	folios

When nouns end with *o* preceded by a consonant, add an *es* for plural forms.

potato	potatoes
tomato	tomatoes
hero	heroes

Exceptions:

Eskimos	silos
kimonos	dynamos
mementos	

When nouns end with *o* and refer to music, add an *s* for plural forms.

trio	trios
radio	radios
banjo	banjos
solo	solos
soprano	sopranos
alto	altos

8. Some nouns that end with *f* or *fe* form plurals by adding an *s*.

roof	roofs
chief	chiefs
proof	proofs
safe	safes
tariff	tariffs
plaintiff	plaintiffs

Others, however, change *f* to *v* and add *-es*.

half	halves
leaf	leaves
shelf	shelves
thief	thieves
self	selves

9. Compound nouns form plurals by changing the *principal word* from singular to plural.

Singular Compound	Plural Compound
brother-in-law	brothers-in-law
attorney-at-law	attorneys-at-law
man-of-war	men-of-war
runner-up	runners-up

10. Some nouns change forms for plurals.

Singular	Plural
mouse	mice
ox	oxen
child	children
goose	geese
man	men
foot	feet
woman	women

11. Plurals of commonly used foreign words may be formed in a variety of ways. Consult a current dictionary for foreign words not listed.

Singular	Plural
analysis	analyses
basis	bases
datum	data
crisis	crises
memorandum	memorandums *or* memoranda

12. When words end with the sound of "seed," the spelling varies. Three words are spelled with *-ceed: proceed, exceed, succeed.* (Note this variation: *procedure.*) One word is spelled with *-sede: supersede.* All other words with the "seed" sound are spelled with *-cede.*

Section 9: WORD DIVISION

When a word must be divided at the end of a line, follow the word division guidelines. If you are in doubt about dividing a word, consult a word division manual.

1. Divide words only between syllables.

  con- ve- nience   knowl- edge   thought- ful

Do not divide one-syllable words.

  thought   play   freeze

2. Do not divide words of five or fewer letters even if the words have more than one syllable.

  oboe   owner   agent

3. Retain more than one letter with the first part of a word and more than two letters with the last part of the word.

  identi- cal   ideals   elimi- nate
  guarded   speaker   enor- mously

4. Usually, divide a word between double consonants.

  writ- ten   win- ner   bor- rower

However, when adding a suffix to a word that ends in double letters, divide after the double letters of the root word.

  tell- ing   call- ing   odd- ness

5. When a final consonant is doubled in adding a suffix, divide between the double letters. Maintain the correct spelling for the root word.

  omit- ting   regret- table   begin- ning

6. **Divide after a one-letter syllable within a word.**

origi- nal   sepa- rate   congratu- late

However, when two single-letter syllables occur together, divide between the letters.

gradu- ation   evalu- ation   enunci- ation

7. **When the single-letter syllable *a*, *i*, or *u* is followed by the ending *-ly*, *-ble*, *-bly*, *-cle*, or *-cal*, divide before the single-letter syllable.**

hast- ily   cap- able   chem- ical

Exceptions:

dura- ble   musi- cal   practi- cal

8. **Divide hyphenated words only at the hyphen.**

self- esteem   three- fourths   sister- in- law

9. **Do not divide abbreviations, contractions, or figures.**

WCOA   *not* WC- OA
wouldn't   *not* would- n't
$175,436   *not* $175,- 436

10. **Avoid dividing proper names. Separate titles, initials, or degrees from a surname only when impossible to write otherwise.**

Susan A. Smith   *or* Susan A.
                                    Smith

Ms. Nancy Johnson   *or* Ms. Nancy
                                              Johnson

11. **If dividing the parts of a date is unavoidable, separate the day of the month from the year.**

January 31,
20—

When words sound alike or look alike, you carefully choose the correct word. If you are unsure of the correct word choice, review the words listed in the following table and consult a dictionary. Exercises for choosing correct words among frequently confused words appear on the Student CD, Reference Guide, Confused Words.

Word	Meaning	Example
ad	an advertisement	Please run this ad in the newspaper.
add	to find the sum of; to increase	Susannah will add the numbers to get the total.
advice	opinion given	The lawyer gave good advice to the client.
advise	to counsel	Roy asked the counselor to advise him.
all ready	completely ready	The passengers were all ready to board the next train.
already	before this time	The freight train had already left the station.
basis	a fundamental principle	The basis of his theory was explained in his book.
bases	plural of *basis*	Hard work and honesty are bases of the American work ethic.
capital	chief; first in importance	Lack of communication is a capital reason for business failure.
capitol	a building in which a state legislature meets	The capitol in Jackson is on State Street.
choose	to select or decide	Please choose Times New Roman as the type font.
chose	past tense of *choose*	The coach chose the team members last week.
cite	to quote; to refer to	He cited an Internet source as the basic reference.
site	location	The site of the new theater is the corner of Main and Water Streets.
sight	vision; to see	Freda was excited when she sighted the comet in the night sky.
compliment	a flattering comment	Robert appreciated the manager's compliment.
complement	something that completes or makes perfect	Tech Advanced has a full complement of computer equipment.

Word	Meaning	Example
conscience	a sense of right or wrong about one's conduct or motives	The biologist stated that lack of environmental controls disturbed his conscience.
conscious	fully aware; intentional, deliberate	Tim made a conscious effort to complete the trip on time.
continual	happening at frequent intervals	The employees made continual demands for wage increases.
continuous	going on without stopping	A continuous line appeared on the screen.
correspondence	message writing	Frank received correspondence from a friend in Spain.
correspondents	persons conducting correspondence	Mrs. Black and Mr. Jones were the correspondents on the messages.
council	an assembly for consultation or discussion	Mr. McCorvey was elected to the city council.
counsel	advice	His parents gave him good counsel.
consul	a government official	Mary's uncle was a consul appointed to Mexico.
desert	arid, barren land	We had difficulty finding water as we crossed the desert.
desert	to abandon	Billy asked his friends not to desert him.
dessert	the last course of a meal	Lilly made strawberry shortcake for dessert.
dew	moisture condensed from the atmosphere	The dew provided enough moisture for the growing plants.
do	to perform or execute; to ask a question	Please do this task last. Do you understand?
due	owed or owing	The rent was due.
dues	a regular fee or charge	The membership dues were $15.
eligible	fit to be chosen; legally	Chris was eligible to retire.
illegible	impossible or hard to read, especially because of handwriting	Roberta has been trying to improve her illegible handwriting.
ensure	to make sure or certain	Use a dictionary to ensure correct spelling.
insure	to issue or obtain insurance on or for	Insure the package for $25.

Word	Meaning	Example
farther	at or to a greater distance	Ramona traveled farther than Will.
further	to a greater extent; additional	John, please further revise your manuscript.
formally	in a formal manner	The guests dressed formally for the ball.
formerly	previously	Jane formerly had been employed by Vertex.
last	most recent; after all others	The director was the last person to leave the set.
later	toward the end of the day or night; more recent	The pharmacy was open later than the clinic. Clifford's later poems have a space theme.
latest	occurring after the usual or proper time	The latest corrections were made after the president read the copy.
latter	near to the end; being the second mentioned of two	The disease was in the latter development stage. The director gave two commands; she followed the latter one.
like	agreeable to one's taste; to wish or prefer	The birds like sunflower seeds.
as	to such a degree or extent; for example	The other margins should be as shown on this table.
loose	not fastened; not bound together	The wind blew the loose papers.
lose	to have no longer	Please do not lose your money.
loss	disadvantage from losing	The business suffered a loss of over $2 million.
one	singular in number	Please toss the balls to me one at a time.
won	earned success	The softball team won the state tournament.
past	earlier or former	You may continue working the same hours as you worked in the past.
passed	ended; completed; approved	The House passed the bill after weeks of debate.
patience	calm endurance; self-control	The children demonstrated patience as they waited in the doctor's office.
patient	willing to wait	The students were patient as they waited to register.

Word	Meaning	Example
patients	persons who are being treated by a doctor	How many patients will Dr. Dewey see today?
physical	pertaining to the body	Each employee is given an annual physical examination.
fiscal	relating to financial matters	The fiscal reports were mailed to the stockholders.
precede	to go before; to come before	The Smith Company will precede the Smythe Company in the files.
proceed	to advance	You may proceed without waiting for the other students.
quiet	calm; without noise	A quiet, cool room will lessen the stress.
quit	stop; halt	Please don't quit the team.
quite	almost completely; to a considerable degree	The supervisor was quite pleased with the production rate.
right	correct; true privilege	Circle the right answer. You have the right to remain silent.
rite	ceremony	The captain of the ship performed the marriage rites.
write	to inscribe	Write your name in the blank at the top of the page.
stationary	fixed; not movable	The pilings were 15 feet deep to make the building stationary.
stationery	writing materials	Bond paper was used for the stationery.
their	belonging to others	The teachers earned their degrees from various universities.
there	in or at that place	Please remain there for a few minutes.
they're	contraction of *they are*	They're going to summer camp.
weather	atmospheric conditions	The weather was hot and humid.
whether	if	The director asked whether they should attend the meeting.
who's	contraction of *who is* or *who has*	Who's listed on the new roster?
whose	shows possession	Whose papers are those?

Replace inefficient words and phrases with concise expressions. Exercises for developing concise expressions appear on the Student CD, Reference Guide, Concise Expressions.

Insufficient Words/Phrases	Concise Expressions
advise	say; tell
along the same lines	similarly
as a consequence	therefore
as a result	therefore
attached hereto	attached; enclosed
be of assistance	assist
bring to conclusion	conclude
by means of	by
by reason of the fact that	because
due to the fact that	since; because; as
during the time that	while
every one of the	every
for that reason	because
for the month of March	for March
for the most part	usually
in a satisfactory manner	satisfactorily
in all cases	always
in all circumstances	
inasmuch as	because
in case you	if you
in many cases	frequently; often
in many circumstances	
in order to	to
in regard to	regarding
inside of	inside
in some cases	sometimes
in some circumstances	
in the amount of	for
in the case of	*do not use this phrase*
in the event of	if
in the event that	
in the majority of instances	usually
made out of	made of
make your selection	select
on behalf of	for
on the occasion of	when
take into consideration	consider
to the best of my knowledge	I believe

Insufficient Words/Phrases	Concise Expressions
under date of	*give date of message*
under separate cover	separately
with reference to	
with regard to	about; regarding; concerning
with respect to	

Section 12: CORRECT WORD CHOICE

Select correct words and phrases to help ensure accuracy in your messages. Exercises for making correct word choices appear on the Student CD, Reference Guide, Correct Word Choice.

Word/Phrase	Proper Meanings	Example
almost	nearly; a little short of	Christina added almost two minutes to her speech.
most	much; many	Most of the engineers agreed that the project was worthwhile.
annoy	disturb; make angry	Please do not annoy David.
aggravate	irritate; increase	Loud noises may aggravate headaches.
anyone	person (emphasis on *any*)	Anyone who has keyboarding skill may apply for the job.
any one	individual person or thing	Any one of you may become an officer in this club.
anyway	in any case; use one word when *any* is stressed	You may go anyway.
any way	any method, process, or route	You may travel to Canada any way you choose.
cannot	unable to do	You cannot paste the text until you copy or cut the text.
can not only	used with *only*	Sheldon can not only run 40 miles, he can also swim 200 laps.
everyday	usual; routine	Rising early is an everday occurrence for me.
every day	each day	Every day you should brush and floss your teeth.
everyone	everybody	Everyone will participate in the recycling program.
every one	each one	Every one may choose a different chair height.
into	insertion; inclusion	The spreadsheet software arranges the debits and credits into columns.

Word/Phrase	Proper Meanings	Example
in	location	She participated in the Southern Regional Skating Championships.
maybe	perhaps	Maybe you should leave early.
may be	to indicate a possibility	The snowstorm may be here by tomorrow.
nobody	person	Nobody attended the board meeting.
no body	group composed of people	No body of state officials can raise the necessary funds.
no one	not one person	No one volunteered for the task.
none	not any	None of the work was acceptable.
somebody	person	Somebody rang the doorbell.
some body	group composed of people	Some body of delegates will sit in this area.
sometime	undetermined or inexact time	I will complete the budget report sometime today.
some time	period of time	Preparing the mailing list takes some time.
sometimes	now and then	Sometimes I have an opportunity to sleep after the alarm rings.

Section 13: SOURCE FORMAT GUIDELINES

In business writings, particularly reports, source acknowledgments consist of individual citations and a reference list. **Citations** give credit to those persons and writings from which information, illustrations, and charts are taken. Citations also note the authority for direct quotations.

Three commonly used citation formats are parenthetical (sometimes called internal), footnotes, and endnotes. **Parenthetical citations** provide the author information immediately following the citations. **Footnotes** are numbered consecutively and are listed at the bottom of the page containing the information being acknowledged. **Endnotes** are numbered consecutively and are listed on a separate page.

At the end of the report, a reference list includes the sources (books, encyclopedias, periodicals, and so on) that were cited in the text and may identify other beneficial sources. The reference list is titled **Works Cited** when you follow the Modern Language Association (MLA) handbook. The list is labeled **References** when you follow the American Psychological Association (APA) manual. Sample citations based on both the MLA and APA formats are shown on pages 457–458. The examples are for typical references. Refer to a complete style manual for additional entries.

Source Format Guidelines

Books	Modern Language Association (MLA)	American Psychological Association (APA)
One author	Jones, Alvin R. Writing Understandable Reports. New York: Hero Press, 2003.	Jones, A. R. (2003). *Writing understandable reports.* New York: Hero Press.
Two authors	Charest, Myrtis, and Opal Grant. Successful Report Writing. New York: Hero Press, 2003.	Charest, M., & Grant, O. (2003). *Successful report writing.* New York: Hero Press.
Three authors	Maddox, Patricia, Celeste Reed, and Lesca Black. A Communication Guide. Chicago: Druid Printers, 2002.	Maddox, P., Reed, C., & Black, L. (2003). *A communication guide.* Chicago: Druid Printers.
More than three	Price, Clara, et al. A Layman's Guide to Report Writing. Chicago: Druid Printers, 2003.	
More than six		Link, T., Bozeman, M., Jacobs, D., Davis, E., Jones, B., Brown, J., et al. (2002). *A simple manual to report writing.* New York: Apex Printers.
Editor	Wiltshire, Norene, ed. Report Writing. Boston: Jacobs Publishers, 2003.	Wiltshire, N. (Ed.). (2003). *Report writing.* Boston: Jacob Publishers.
No author	You Can Write. New York: United Press, 2003.	*You can write.* (2003). New York: United Press.

Periodicals		
Newspapers	Mood, Rebecca. "Writing Tips." Today's Communicator. 29 Oct. 2003: 70–71.	Mood, R. (2003, October 29). Writing tips. *Today's Communicator,* pp. A2, A3.
Magazines	Walker, Jose. "Cell Phone Etiquette." Business Outlook 6 May 2003: 94–96.	Walker, J. (2003, May 6). Cell phone etiquette. *Business Outlook, 24,* 94–96.
Scholarly Journal	Dickerson, Eleanor. "Writing Guides for Teachers." Elementary/Secondary Instruction 34.2 (2002): 133–48.	Dickerson, E. (2002). Writing guides for teachers. *Elementary/Secondary Instruction, 34*(2), 133–148.

Encyclopedias	Modern Language Association (MLA)	American Psychological Association (APA)
Author	Borges, Isaac. "Publishing Guidelines." Writers Encyclopedia. 22 vols. New York: Writers Press, 2002.	Borges, I. (2002). Publishing guidelines. In Writers encyclopedia (Vol. 22, pp. 397–400). New York: Writers Press.
No author	"Publishing Guidelines." Writers Encyclopedia. 2002 ed.	Publishing guidelines. (2002). In Writers encyclopedia (Vol. 22, pp. 397–400). New York: Writers Press.

Governmental Publications		
	United States Dept. of Health and Human Services. Improve Your Health. Washington: GPO, 2003.	Health and Human Services. (2003). Improve your health. (DHHS Publication No. ADM 70-1100). Washington, DC: U.S. Government Printing Office.

Note: Although the examples in this text are single-spaced, both the *MLA Handbook for Writers of Research Papers* and the *Publication Manual of the American Psychological Association* indicate that all references should be double-spaced in a report.

Style Guides for Electronically Accessed Sources

Providing accurate citations for information that exists on electronic media requires additional components than those commonly used in citing printed sources. Include information to ensure the reader will be able to identify and locate the electronic document. Since the Internet and electronic information sources are in a constant state of change, citation guidelines are constantly being reviewed and revised. You may locate examples of suggested styles for both printed and electronic referencing at the following sites:

http://www.columbia.edu/cu/cup/cgos/idx_basic.html

http://www.mainland.cc.tx.us/library/internet/intsub/ref_cit.htm

http://owl.english.purdue.edu/handouts/research/r_apa.html

MLA

If no author is given for a web page or an electronic source, begin with and alphabetize by the title of the work; and use a shortened version of the title for parenthetical citations. List the date you access web postings because information available at one date may no longer be available later. Include the complete address for the site. MLA requires the use of angle brackets < > around the electronic address.

If a specific illustration is not covered in this discussion, consult the latest edition of the *MLA Handbook for Writers of Research Papers*.

Online Journal or Magazine

Author(s). "Article Title." *Name of web site*. Date of posting/revision. Name of institution/organization affiliated with the site. Date of access <electronic address>.

Brantley, Clarice, and Michele Miller. "Communication Tidbits and Hotlinks." *The Balance Sheet*. 01 May 2003. South-Western. 21 May 2003 <http://www.swep.com/swepstuff/balancesheet/indextext.html>.

Electronic Mail

The MLA electronic mail (e-mail) format also is used for personal interviews and personal letters. For interviews and letters, no titles are given. Rather than keying *E-mail to Clarice Brantley*, you would key *Personal interview with Clarice Brantley*.

Author/Writer. "Title of the message/subject line (if any)." E-mail to the recipient. Date of the message.

Stone, David. "Insurance Seminar." E-mail to Clarice Brantley. 21 May 2003.

Timely Tip

Since electronic sources vary, you may have to adapt the citation structure to represent the cited information.

APA

If a particular example is not covered in this reference, consult the latest edition of the *Publication Manual of the American Psychological Association*.

Online Journal or Magazine

Since online information is frequently altered, the date of access should indicate the date you last visited the site. Divide the URL only after a single or double slash mark. After the URL is listed, a period is not inserted.

> Author(s). (Date of publication). Title of article. *Title of Periodical*. Volume number (if available), page numbers (when given). Retrieval date, URL.

> Brantley, C., & Miller, M. (2003). Communication tidbits and hotlinks. *The Balance Sheet*. Retrieved May 21, 2003, from http://www.swep.com/swepstuff/balancesheet/indextext.html

Electronic Mail

APA considers electronic mail (e-mail) a personal communication, not easily retrieved by the general public. When you cite an e-mail message in the body of your report, acknowledge the source in your parenthetical citation.

Example: The writer has stated this idea recently (Michele Miller, e-mail to Robert Davis, May 1, 2003).

Format Guide

When you prepare a business document, provide balance by arranging the message in a selected format and by checking the overall appearance. The Format Guide provides basic format guidelines for printed documents. Refer to Chapter 4 for electonic message guidelines.

For additional information about memorandum, letter, and envelope formats, review a current office reference manual or keyboarding/document-processing textbook.

Section 1: MEMORANDUM FORMATS

Even though people within an organization use spoken and electronic messages, written documents also are needed. Written messages, sent from one employee to another, are called memorandums, interoffice memorandums (memos for short), and interdepartmental communications.

Two memorandum formats are standard and simplified. The standard memorandum usually is keyed on a form with printed headings or in a word processing template. Illustration 1 is an example of a standard memorandum.

Drake Petroleum Co.

1411 Main Street   Titusville, PA 16354-4411

814-555-0174

drake@titus.petro.com

TO: All Employees
FROM: Lynn Stafford, Human Resources Director   *LS*
DATE: May 1, 20—
SUBJECT: Summer Work Schedule
                        DS
Beginning June 1, all office personnel will work a four-day week. The hours will be from 7:30 a.m. until 4:30 p.m. with one hour for lunch.
                        DS
If you use the childcare facilities in the Norris building, please discuss this schedule with Brian Jones, childcare supervisor. Mr. Jones must know the number of children who will eat breakfast in the cafeteria.
                        DS
sr

Illustration 1 **Standard Memorandum**

Illustration 1 depicts the **standard memorandum format** with a 1-inch right margin. The TO, FROM, DATE, and SUBJECT lines are spaced to match the preprinted or template headings. The single-spaced paragraphs start at the left margin. A blank line (DS) appears between the paragraphs.

A simplified memorandum may be keyed on either letterhead or plain paper. In the simplified memorandum, omit the headings (*TO*, *FROM*, *DATE*, and *SUBJECT*). Illustration 2 is an example of a simplified memorandum.

Illustration 2 **Simplified Memorandum**

Drake Petroleum Co.

1411 Main Street   Titusville, PA 16354-4411

814-555-0174

drake@titus.petro.com

1 May 20—

QS

All Employees

SUMMER WORK SCHEDULE

DS

Beginning June 1, all office personnel will work a four-day week. The hours will be from 7:30 a.m. until 4:30 p.m. with one hour for lunch.

DS

If you use the childcare facilities in the Norris building, please discuss this schedule with Brian Jones, childcare supervisor. Mr. Jones must know the number of children who will eat breakfast in the cafeteria.

Lynn Stafford

QS

Lynn Stafford, Human Resources Director

DS

sr

Illustration 2 shows the **simplified memorandum format**. Use 1-inch left and right margins, and begin the dateline on line 6 for a half sheet and line 10 for a full sheet, followed by a quadruple space (QS). Key the receiver's name in uppercase and lowercase letters. The subject line (the topic of the message) may be keyed in all capital letters or in capital and lowercase letters. Single-space the message. Double-space (DS) between all other parts of the simplified memorandum with this exception: Quadruple-space between the last paragraph line and the writer's name. Key the business title (optional information) on the same line as the writer's name or on the next line.

The company policy or letter-writing manual, the letterhead layout and design, and your individual preference affect the choice of letter format and punctuation style. Business letters contain basic parts: heading, opening, body, and closing. The parts appear in an order that makes reading and responding easy. You may insert optional parts for clarification. When you prepare a letter, provide balance by arranging the parts in a particular format and by checking the overall appearance.

The two punctuation styles are open and mixed. **Open punctuation** means that no punctuation follows the salutation and complimentary close. **Mixed punctuation** means that a colon follows the salutation and a comma follows the complimentary close.

For letters requiring two or more pages, use plain paper of the same quality as the letterhead and include a second-page heading. Begin the second-page heading on line 6, and follow the heading with a double space. Continue to use the same side margins as used on the first page. As shown in Illustrations 3 and 4, you may use either the blocked or the horizontal form for the second-page heading.

Illustration 3 **Blocked Second-Page Heading**

Begin on line 6.

Info Exchange, Inc.
Page 2
May 11, 20—

DS

DS before the next line of the message.

You certainly created a captive audience with PBL members. A list of questions is enclosed.

Illustration 4 **Horizontal Second-Page Heading**

Begin on line 6.

Info Exchange, Inc.   2   May 11, 20—

DS

DS before the next line of the message.

You certainly created a captive audience with PBL members. A list of questions is enclosed.

The three business letter formats are full block, modified block, and simplified. The three formats are shown in Illustrations 5, 6, and 7 on pages 464–466. Two personal business letter formats are shown in Illustrations 8 and 9 on pages 467–468. Review the message content as well as the marginal notes within each illustration. Also review the boxed information at the bottom of each illustration.

Communication Consultants, Inc.

230 Saratoga NW, Atlanta, GA 30303-3023
Telephone: 404-555-0134
Fax: 404-555-0184
http://www.comm.con/atl/bus.html

Dateline

March 3, 20—

QS

*Letter address
with an attention
line*

Piedmont Environmental Protection Services
Attention Ms. Evelyn Grant
6060 St. Anthony Street
Charlotte, NC 28287-6087

DS

*Salutation with
open punctuation*

Ladies and Gentlemen

DS

Message

The Environmental Protection Institute has asked me to conduct a letter-writing workshop for personnel in the Piedmont area. The workshop is scheduled for March 30 through April 2 at the Belvedere Plaza in Charlotte.

DS

Please send me copies of your letterhead and a statement about your preferred letter format by March 15. The Institute will refund your mailing expenses.

DS

*Complimentary
close with open
punctuation*

Sincerely yours

Allen M. Kelly

QS

*Name of the writer
Business title*

Allen M. Kelly
Marketing Manager

DS

Reference initials

cb

Illustration 5 depicts a **full block format** letter (all lines start at the left margin) with open punctuation (no colon after the salutation and no comma after the complimentary close). Since an attention line is used, an appropriate salutation is *Ladies and Gentlemen*.

Illustration 5 **Full Block Format with Open Punctuation**

Piedmont Environmental Protection Services

Charlotte Branch
6060 St. Anthony Street
Charlotte, NC 28287-6087
Telephone: 704-555-0122
Fax: 704-555-0172
E-mail: pied@environ.char.gov

Dateline at center

March 8, 20—

QS

Letter address

Mr. Allen M. Kelly
Marketing Manager
Communication Consultants, Inc.
230 Saratoga NW
Atlanta, GA 30303-3023

DS

Salutation with mixed punctuation

Dear Mr. Kelly:

Subject line

LETTERHEAD AND PREFERRED LETTER FORMAT

DS

The environmental protection employees in the Piedmont area certainly need your workshop on letter writing. We all have questions about several of our routine letters. From this reply, you can tell that I prefer the modified block format with block paragraphs and mixed punctuation.

DS

Message

Directors in other cities prefer different letter formats. I have discussed your workshop with them and have asked them to send you copies of their letterhead and statements about their preferred letter formats by March 15.

DS

Will you join me for dinner on March 29? Please call me to discuss your plans.

DS

Sincerely,

QS *Evelyn Grant*

Complimentary close with mixed punctuation

Name of the writer at center

Evelyn Grant
Director

Business title at center

DS

Reference initials

ph

Copy notation

c   Mr. Warren Bowers
    Mrs. Joan Exum

Illustration 6 models the **modified block format** with mixed punctuation, a subject line, and a copy notation. The dateline, complimentary close, keyed signature, and title start at the center. All other lines begin at the left margin.

Illustration 6 **Modified Block Format with Mixed Punctuation**

Piedmont Environmental Protection Services

Raleigh Branch
5400 Chapel Hill Road
Raleigh, NC 27601-7540
Telephone: 919.555.0181
Fax: 919.555.0182
E-mail: pied@environ.vale.gov

An international dateline or a standard dateline format may be used.

10 March 20—

DS

Mailing notation

EXPRESS MAIL

DS

The address may be keyed in all caps for a mail merge. A business may elect to omit the comma before Inc.

MR ALLEN M KELLY
MARKETING MANAGER
COMMUNICATION CONSULTANTS INC
230 SARATOGA NW
ATLANTA GA 30303-3023

TS

Subject line

LETTERHEAD AND PREFERRED LETTER FORMAT

TS

Message

For five years, employees at the Raleigh branch have used the simplified block letter format. This form was chosen for the following three reasons:

DS

Enumerated items

1. New employee training time is reduced.
2. Minimum time is spent keying and making decisions since the salutation and complimentary close are omitted.
3. The subject line aids the reader by highlighting the message. Key words in the subject line assist office personnel in coding, sorting, storing, and retrieving documents.

DS

You captured our attention by asking for copies of letterhead and for ideas on letter formats. Four employees from the Raleigh branch will attend your workshop in Charlotte.

DS

Mr. Kelly, you may share this letter with others at the workshop. Please schedule time to answer individual questions on the last day of the workshop.

Complimentary close omitted

Mrs. Joan Exum   QS

Name of the writer
Business title

MRS. JOAN EXUM, DIRECTOR

DS

Reference initials

wp

Illustration 7 shows the **simplified format** (the salutation and complimentary close are omitted) with a mailing notation. Always include a subject line. The addressee's name may be used within the letter to personalize the message.

Illustration 7 **Simplified Letter Format**

736 Ninth Street
Durham, NC 27705-7361
February 17, 20—

QS

Mrs. Kathryn R. Miller
Maxwell and Miller Realty
94 Broad Street
Spartanburg, SC 29301-1001

DS

Dear Mrs. Miller:

DS

Please send me a brochure that describes the Homestyle Campus apartment complex. Also, I need answers to the following questions:

DS

- What is the minimum length for a rental contract?
- How much is the monthly rental fee?
- Are utilities included with the monthly fee?
- What deposit is required?
- How many people may share an apartment?

DS

Since my classes begin on June 1, I would like to move to Spartanburg by May 29. Mrs. Miller, please indicate the date that a Homestyle Campus apartment will be available in May.

DS

Sincerely,

QS *Margarita Perez*

Margarita Perez

Illustration 8 shows the **social or personal business message** in the modified block letter format (the return address is keyed above the dateline). The illustration depicts mixed punctuation. The salutation may be followed by a comma instead of a colon; the typed signature is optional.

Illustration 8 **Social or Personal Business Message/Return Address Above Dateline**

February 17, 20—

QS

Mrs. Kathryn R. Miller
Maxwell and Miller Realty
94 Broad Street
Spartanburg, SC 29301-1001

DS

Dear Mrs. Miller

DS

Please send me a brochure that describes the Homestyle Campus apartment complex.
Also, I need answers to the following questions:

DS

- What is the minimum length for a rental contract?
- How much is the monthly rental fee?
- Are utilities included with the monthly fee?
- What deposit is required?
- How many people may share an apartment?

DS

Since my classes begin on June 1, I would like to move to Spartanburg by May 29.
Mrs. Miller, please indicate the date that a Homestyle Campus apartment will be
available in May.

DS

Sincerely

Margarita Perez   **QS**

Margarita Perez
736 Ninth Street
Durham, NC 27705-7361

Illustration 9 shows the **social or personal business
message** in the full block letter format (the return
address is keyed below the writer's name). The
illustration depicts open punctuation.

Illustration 9 **Social or Personal Business Message/Return Address Below Writer's Name**

The envelope size determines the way you fold a document. When the document has evenly folded sections, the paper thickness is distributed appropriately within the envelope. Thus, the envelope is less likely to become jammed in postal equipment.

Fold the document to make opening easy for the receiver. The creases should highlight the intended receiver's name and address if possible.

Large Envelopes

For large envelopes (No. 10), follow these three steps to fold and insert a document. (See Illustration 10.)

1. With the document face up, fold slightly less than one-third of the sheet from the bottom toward the top. The bottom edge of the page approximately underscores the receiver's name.
2. Fold the top of the document down to within one-half inch of the bottom fold. The exposed portion of the document provides a thumbnail hold for the reader to use when unfolding the document.
3. Insert the document into the envelope with the last crease at the bottom.

Small Envelopes

For small envelopes (No. 6 3/4), follow these four steps to fold and insert a document. (See Illustration 10.)

1. With the document face up, fold the bottom up to one-half inch from the top.
2. Fold the right third toward the left side.
3. Fold the left third to one-half inch from the last crease to provide a thumbnail hold for the reader.
4. Insert the document into the envelope with the last crease at the bottom.

Window Envelopes

Follow these three steps to fold and insert a document into a window envelope. (See Illustration 10.)

1. With the document face down and the top toward you, fold the upper third down.
2. Fold the lower third up so the address is showing. Remember that if the document address begins on line 15, the address location is correct for a window envelope.
3. Insert the document into the envelope with the last crease at the bottom.

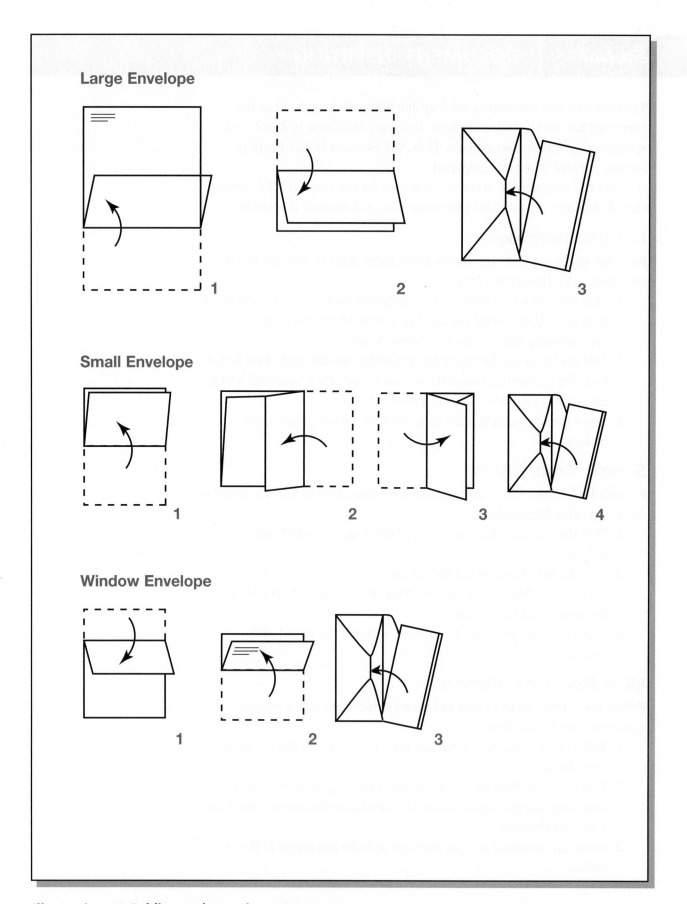

Illustration 10 **Folding and Inserting a Document**

When you key an address in capital letters with no punctuation and correctly position the information on an envelope, the optical character recognition (OCR) equipment in the post office quickly sorts the mail. Businesses often print mailing labels and envelope addresses from – electronically stored data. Remember these points when addressing envelopes:

- For a small envelope, start the address on line 12 about 2 inches from the left margin. On a large envelope, start the address on line 14 about 4 inches from the left margin. Remember 12/2 and 14/4.
- Key the address in block format using single spacing and no punctuation.
- If you use an attention line, key the attention line as the second line of the envelope address.
- Key the city, state abbreviation, and ZIP Code on the last line. The United States Postal Service recommends that you leave one space between the state abbreviation and the ZIP Code.
- Key addressee notations, such as *HOLD FOR ARRIVAL, PLEASE FORWARD,* or *PERSONAL,* a triple space below the return address and three spaces from the left edge of the envelope. Key these notations in capital letters.
- Key mailing notations, such as *SPECIAL DELIVERY* and *REGISTERED,* below the stamp on line 8 or 9. Key these notations in capital letters.
- If the envelope does not contain a printed return address, place your name and return address on the second line from the top edge of the envelope three spaces from the left edge. Envelope addresses are shown in Illustration 11 on page 474.

For international mail, the country name, printed in capital letters, appears as the only information on the bottom line of the address. Key postal zone information on the same line with the city. The following examples show international envelope addresses:

Examples: ***International Envelope Addresses***
Miss Petra Weiffen
Sipla SA
109 r de Molenboek
1020 Bruxelles
BELGIUM

Monsieur Timothy Pierron
Directeur General
Comiot SA
29 rue de Missine
F – 75017 Paris
FRANCE

Mrs. Angela Huchinson
97 Clifton Avenue
Anniston, AL 36201-2097

MRS ROMANA SMYTHE
3099 HIGHLAND COURT
POMPANO BEACH FL 33068-6899

Caughman Enterprises
P.O. Box 335
Williston, VT 05495-4005

REGISTERED

SANSOM AND SANSOM ASSOCIATES
ATTENTION MR REGINALD MABRY
45 WASHBURN AVENUE
PORTLAND ME 04101-1014

Mailing notation below stamp

AC Electric Company
523 Main Street
Racine, WI 53403-5230

HOLD FOR ARRIVAL

LAZARO RAMIREZ
MILFORD HOTEL
800 HIGHWAY 50 W
PUEBLO CO 81008-8800

Addressee notation below return address

Illustration 11 **Envelope Addresses**